CATCHING HELL FROM ALL QUARTERS

CATCHING HELL FROM ALL QUARTERS

Anti-Klan Activists in Interwar Missouri

Sean Rost

UNIVERSITY OF MISSOURI PRESS
Columbia

Copyright © 2025 by
The Curators of the University of Missouri
University of Missouri Press, Columbia, Missouri 65211
Printed and bound in the United States of America
All rights reserved. First printing, 2025.

Library of Congress Cataloging-in-Publication Data

Names: Rost, Sean, 1987- author.
Title: Catching hell from all quarters : anti-Klan activists in interwar
    Missouri / Sean Rost.
Description: Columbia : University of Missouri Press, 2025. | Includes
    bibliographical references and index.
Identifiers: LCCN 2024056854 (print) | LCCN 2024056855 (ebook) | ISBN
    9780826223289 (hardcover) | ISBN 9780826275134 (ebook)
Subjects: LCSH: Ku Klux Klan (1915-). Realm of Missouri--History. |
    Anti-racism--Missouri--History. | Missouri--History--20th century. |
    Missouri--Race relations--History--20th century.
Classification: LCC HS2330.K63 R67 2025 (print) | LCC HS2330.K63 (ebook)
    | DDC 305.8009778--dc23/eng/20250122
LC record available at https://lccn.loc.gov/2024056854
LC ebook record available at https://lccn.loc.gov/2024056855

♾™ This paper meets the requirements of the
American National Standard for Permanence of Paper
for Printed Library Materials, Z39.48, 1984.

Typefaces: Adobe Jenson Pro

To my family

CONTENTS

List of Illustrations	ix
Preface	xi
Acknowledgments	xiii
Introduction	3

CHAPTER ONE
"The Black Clouds of Bigotry"
The Origins of the Ku Klux Klan in Missouri — 19

CHAPTER TWO
"Masked Malcontents"
Violence, Vigilantism, and the Anti-Klan Press — 73

CHAPTER THREE
"We Will Tear Off This Mask of Secrecy"
Building an Anti-Klan Coalition — 109

CHAPTER FOUR
"A Curious and Interested Spectator"
The "Klan Issue" in Missouri Politics — 145

CHAPTER FIVE
"Behind the Mask"
Fraud, Bribery, and Scandal in Missouri's Invisible Empire — 177

CHAPTER SIX
"Kampaigning"
Activism, Lily-Whitism, and the
Political Realignment of Missouri's Black Voters — 209

viii   Contents

CHAPTER SEVEN
"The Spirit of the Klan"
The Fracturing of the Anti-Klan Coalition   241

Epilogue   283

Notes   299

Bibliography   359

Index   377

ILLUSTRATIONS

FIGURE 1.	Map of Missouri	18
FIGURE 2.	A Ku Klux Klan flyer at Dedication Day, 1924	21
FIGURE 3.	Ceremony at the Second Imperial Klonvokation, 1924	27
FIGURE 4.	Lodge of Sorrow at the Second Imperial Klonvokation, 1924	28
FIGURE 5.	Meeting of delegates at the Second Imperial Klonvokation, 1924	29
FIGURE 6.	Joseph E. Mitchell, date unknown	78
FIGURE 7.	Wallace Crossley at the signing of the Federal Suffrage Amendment, 1919	91
FIGURE 8.	Arthur Mastick Hyde, ca. 1920	102
FIGURE 9.	George L. Vaughn standing with members of the March on Washington General Committee, 1942	111
FIGURE 10.	Luke E. Hart, ca. 1920s	117
FIGURE 11.	Perl Decker at Park College, 1927	139
FIGURE 12.	James A. Reed, date unknown	149
FIGURE 13.	Sam A. Baker, date unknown	169
FIGURE 14.	Merchants Bank Building, 1924	191
FIGURE 15.	Doctors of General Hospital No. 2, date unknown	214

x   Illustrations

FIGURE 16.   Jordan Chambers, 1941   222

FIGURE 17.   Harry Hawes, date unknown   227

FIGURE 18.   Editorial cartoon by Daniel Fitzpatrick titled
The Bund-Klan Axis, 1939   257

FIGURE 19.   Ferdinand Isserman, date unknown   261

FIGURE 20.   Leon Birkhead, date unknown   269

FIGURE 21.   Anti-Klan protesters in
Hannibal, Missouri, April 1982   285

PREFACE

In the spring of 2013, I made an interesting discovery while working on a graduate school seminar paper on the 1924 sheriff's campaign in my childhood home of Cole County, Missouri. By that point I had studied the second Klan for more than two years, so the Cole County sheriff's race initially offered me little new information. I quickly saw that, much like in other campaigns, the local Klan tried to ensure victory by running candidates in both the Republican and the Democratic primaries. The gambit worked, as the two winning candidates, L. C. Withaup, a local mechanic, and Fred Hueller, a former police officer and assistant comptroller for the Permanent Seat of Government, both held close ties to the hooded order. Withaup openly admitted his Klan affiliation and, according to the *Jefferson City Democrat-Tribune*, declared that he was "proud of the label."[1]

Faced with the prospect of a Klansman as sheriff, an anti-Klan movement sprouted in Cole County to collect signatures on a petition to place Felix Senevey, who had finished a close second in the Republican primary, on the November ballot as an independent candidate.[2] Born near Bonnots Mill in Osage County in 1861, Senevey came from a prominent Catholic farming family. Moving to Jefferson City around 1904, he found employment as a saloon keeper before Prohibition shuttered his profession, and thereafter he had to find what work he could around town to make ends meet.[3] The petition campaign was successful, with Senevey billed as the anti-Klan candidate. Drawing heavy support from Republicans who had backed his initial primary bid as well as anti-Klan Democrats, Senevey forced the Klan to abandon Fred Hueller and its plan to just let the best man win and secure Withaup's election. Ultimately, Withaup defeated Senevey by a razor-thin margin, but the turmoil of the campaign severely splintered the Cole County Klan.[4]

While going line by line through the seemingly endless list of individuals who contributed their signatures to the Senevey petition, I came across familiar names. My paternal and maternal great-grandparents lived in one of the close-knit German Catholic communities that dot rural Cole County, and they had been around the same age when they signed the petition in the 1920s as I was as I turned its pages nearly a century later. Under headings for Wardsville and the rural routes around Jefferson City, I slowly made out their names, indicating their support for Felix Senevey and their apparent opposition to the Ku Klux Klan. What followed was an in-depth examination to understand not only how they came to sign the petition, whether via door-to-door campaigning, at a parish meeting of the local Catholic church, or when stopping by the local general store for supplies, but also why. Had they known Felix Senevey? Had they voted for him in the Republican primary? Were they opposed to the Klan?

Conversations with surviving descendants of the respective families who had direct knowledge of my paternal and maternal great-grandparents yielded few answers. To the best of everyone's recollection, they never brought it up in casual conversation or at the dinner table. Instead, the quest to discover why my great-grandparents had been among hundreds of local residents who signed the anti-Klan petition propelled my investigation further. What started out as a project about the Ku Klux Klan in Cole County quickly grew from a localized study to one that encapsulated the entire state of Missouri. Now, more than a decade later, I still ponder all the reasons my great-grandparents signed the petition. While I will probably never know the full story, this book serves to explain the complexities of an anti-Klan coalition made up of organizational leaders, newspaper publishers, and politicians, as well as small-town ministers, local organizers, and, yes, petition signers.

ACKNOWLEDGMENTS

Acknowledgments are challenging. Your goal is to thank the countless individuals who helped you, but you also worry that someone will get unintentionally left out. In the end, you stare at the long list of individuals and realize just how many people contributed to the overall project. So, let's begin.

I want to thank the following institutions for their generous support of this project through fellowships and grants: Dissertation Fellowship and William Wilcher Endowment Grant from the Department of History at the University of Missouri–Columbia, James S. Rollins Slavery Atonement Endowment from the Black Studies Department at the University of Missouri–Columbia, Graduate Fellowship in American Political History and Research Grant from the Kinder Institute on Constitutional Democracy, Research Grant from the Cushwa Center for the Study of American Catholicism at the University of Notre Dame, and the John Tracy Ellis Dissertation Award from the American Catholic Historical Association.

Having worked at the State Historical Society of Missouri for several years, I am more aware than ever of the important work that archivists, librarians, and staff do in collecting and processing collections so they can be available to the general public. Even before I started with SHSMO, I spent many days in the research center combing through these important resources. I want to offer my heartfelt thanks to my amazing colleagues at SHSMO who helped this project in innumerable ways from start to finish.

Additionally, I want to thank staff at the University of Notre Dame Archives, Special Collections Research Center at the University of Chicago, Indiana Historical Society, Archives & Special Collections at Ball State University, Library & Research Center of the Missouri

Historical Society, Archdiocese of St. Louis's Office of Archives and Records, David M. Rubenstein Rare Book & Manuscript Library at Duke University, Missouri State Archives, Harry S. Truman Presidential Library & Museum, Pius XII Memorial Library at St. Louis University, Missouri River Regional Library, Ellis Library's Special Collections & Rare Books at the University of Missouri–Columbia, Patrol Records Division of the Missouri State Highway Patrol, Black Archives of Mid-America, Jackson County Historical Society, University of Missouri Archives, Frances Willard House Museum & Archives, Knights of Columbus Supreme Council Archives, and Library of Congress.

I would also be remiss if I didn't acknowledge the scholarly community of faculty, staff, and colleagues who inspired me. Shawn Hull and Steve Hageman at William Woods University introduced a twenty-year-old former engineering major to history. I'm forever grateful. At Lincoln University, Thomas Gubbels, Debra Foster Greene, and Roger Jungmeyer helped steer me through a master's thesis that formed the earliest parts of this project. At the University of Missouri–Columbia, I am forever indebted to the Department of History and the Kinder Institute on Constitutional Democracy for taking a chance on me. A graduate student writing group that featured Craig Forrest, Chris Deutsch, Carey Kelly, and Sam Rogers helped the structure, formatting, argument, and resources of my original dissertation. Additionally, since there was a significant overlap between our projects, Mary Beth Brown provided exceptional guidance on a number of subjects, including research collections to review, scholarly literature to read, and individuals to contact. I also found tremendous scholarly and morale support in the hallowed halls of the now demolished Read Hall from Sarah Lirley, Brandon Flint, Luke Schleif, Caitlin Lawrence, Zach Dowdle, Jonathan Jones, Will Mountz, Josh Nudell, Hunter Hampton, Jonathan Root, Darin Tuck, Jenna Rice, Lawrence Celani, Doug Genens, and Cassie Yacovazzi. My dissertation committee of Keona Ervin, John Wigger, Larry Brown, Jeff Pasley, and Catherine Rymph provided valuable contributions that shifted this project from a small study of a few Missouri counties to a wide-sweeping look at the entire state. They ensured that this project did not come to simple conclusions.

I also need to devote a special section to individuals who ensured this project's completion. Andrew Davidson, David Rosenbaum, and the staff at the University of Missouri Press helped guide this first-time author through the hills and valleys of publishing a manuscript. Their suggestions improved the text tremendously, and they were generous in their patience when it came to deadlines. Gary Kremer has been my boss for more than seven years at the State Historical Society of Missouri, and it has been an honor to have daily thought-provoking conversations with one of the preeminent scholars of Missouri history. You will find his name several times in the citations of this book, but more than that, his recommendations for other material to seek out for this project proved invaluable. My fellow former Read Hall resident and desk mate Danielle Griego deserves special attention because she never allowed me to give up on this project, even when I had serious doubts about its completion. She pushed me to meet goals and deadlines and offered helpful advice on manuscript drafts. But more than that, if you enjoy this book, hers is even better. Finally, Catherine Rymph served as my PhD adviser and one of my most ardent supporters. This book would not have been possible without her guidance and wisdom. I am a better scholar, teacher, and person because of my time as her student. There is not enough space in this acknowledgment to thank her properly.

Last, but certainly not least, I must thank my amazing family. You all were always there for me and never gave up on this dream. You showed support and, at times, even tough love. My parents, David and Pam, offered substantial help at different phases of the project, including my father serving as my research assistant at the Library of Congress. My grandparents, Medard and Dorothy, Bernard and Barbara, and Rich and Dorothy, were a constant source of inspiration. My in-laws, Tim and LaDonne, Paige and Dan, and Kayla and Jordan, as well as my nieces and nephews, were ready and willing to assist when it came to child care and playdates so I could research, write, and teach. With the exception of my daughter Berkeley, my remaining children, Sutton, Copeland, and Kaiser, were all born at some point during this project's evolution. You offered me smiles, laughs, and comfort. Finally, my wife, Adrienne, was essential to this project. I often tell people that I prefer to sleep on any major decision before giving my answer. In reality, I take these decisions to her, and we talk through all scenarios because her wisdom and knowledge far surpass mine. Her love and support put every single word on all these pages.

CATCHING HELL FROM ALL QUARTERS

INTRODUCTION

WITH THE CONGREGATION of St. Louis's Fourth Christian Church entranced by his oration, J. F. Craig fell to his knees in prayer. Strategically removing a miniature American flag from his coat pocket, Craig kissed the object and asked God to "bless everybody, particularly the Ku Klux Klan, for we are catching hell from all quarters." Craig's fiery oration left little doubt about what "quarters" he referred to as he called upon the crowd to stop doing business with Jewish, Greek, and Italian merchants; question the loyalty of Catholics; denounce racial equality; and commit to deporting "all the foreign-born back to the lands whence they came."[1] They surely had trouble—as Craig suggested to residents of the river city—because there was an urgent need to fight back against the enemies of the Klan, who had allegedly spent "millions of dollars in slandering" an organization that was attracting "hundreds of thousands of the flower of American manhood." Returning time and again to the subject of Americanism and patriotism, Craig accented his comments by kneeling in reverence before the miniature flag.[2]

Referred to in the press as an Atlanta-based minister, John Freeman Craig, or J. F., as he was often billed, was as shadowy a figure as the hooded men he claimed to represent. In his retelling of his life, Craig was born in 1864 to a Scotsman father who had served in the Union army during the Civil War and a Native American mother. He claimed to be a member of the Winnebago Tribe raised on a reservation in Manitowoc County, Wisconsin, though he told his St. Louis audience that he was a "half-breed American Indian, with the blood of the Aztecs in my veins." By the early twentieth century, Craig had traveled extensively on the vaudeville and lecture circuit, including a brief period as a member of Barnum & Bailey's Circus and Buffalo Bill's Wild West show. He had also been a "spieler" at the 1904 World's Fair in St. Louis. He told admirers that he

4   Introduction

knew Theodore Roosevelt and Sitting Bull, and, describing himself as an expert on Native American culture and history, Craig was frequently referred to as Chief White Eagle.[3]

Craig stopped in St. Louis in October 1922 on a larger tour of the United States, where he hoped to rally "all 100 percent Americans" under the banner of the revived Ku Klux Klan. To this end, he told the *St. Louis Star* that the hooded order proudly claimed sixty-five thousand members in Missouri, with twenty thousand alone on the other side of the state in Kansas City. Setting up his recruiting operation at the Hotel Claridge—under the name "Dr. John Freeman" because he feared the "minions of the Pope"—Craig had been invited by Rev. C. C. Crawford, a local Klan lecturer and pastor of the Fourth Christian Church, to speak to the congregation about why the city needed the Klan.[4] While those in attendance dabbed their eyes during his eloquent defense of Americanism, Craig told the crowd of the importance of white supremacy: "We're mighty glad we're white. . . . The Lord didn't intend to have colors mixed else he would have mixed them up himself."[5]

Despite the initial round of eye-catching newspaper headlines, Craig received little fanfare or attention in later press coverage.[6] He claimed he would be in St. Louis for three weeks lecturing on the Klan's tenets alongside Henry Brandon, who spoke on the Puritan Daughters, a women's organization similar to the Klan though not a direct auxiliary, but soon after, he drifted across the state to Kansas City to continue his crusade. Once there, he again made headlines when he challenged Kansas governor Henry J. Allen to a public debate on the merits of the Klan. Allen ignored the request, noting that the Klan would eventually have its day in court. Craig instead debated with Dr. Wesley Civert Travis of the Kansas City Scriptural Bible College at Lewis Theater in Independence, Missouri.[7] Taking opposing sides on whether "the Ku Klux Klan is a Menace to American institutions," Travis and Craig tangled for most of the evening on the thorny topic. Travis charged the hooded order with secrecy and lawlessness, while Craig defended the Klan, though he critiqued the leadership of the group's Kansas City delegation. Appointed as moderator for the debate, William "Billy" Parker, a Scottish-born labor organizer turned anti-Catholic publisher of the Missouri-based *New Menace*, arose at the end and devoted his time at the podium to promoting his new organization, the American Clan, and encouraged the audience to attend that group's inaugural meeting in Kansas City, its new headquarters.[8] When a crowd estimated at six hundred assembled the following week to hear more about the American Clan, Craig was nowhere to be found, and Parker discovered the doors to the rented auditorium were locked. The manager of the facility later said, "I knew that Catholicism would be run down, that the Jews would be censured, and that the clan would spare no words to further its own interests. Therefore I didn't think it advisable to permit the meeting to be held."[9]

From the moment that the first cross burned and the Ku Klux Klan revived under William Joseph Simmons as an homage to its Reconstruction-era ancestor, scholars and writers have grappled with this so-called second, or interwar years, Klan and its place in American society. In the Roaring Twenties, authors such as John Moffatt Mecklin, Stanley Frost, and Henry P. Fry, himself a former Klansmen, published prominent books on the organization, with Mecklin arguing that "the Klan draws its members chiefly from the descendants of the old American stock living in the villages and small towns of those sections of the country."[10] Even writer Frederick Lewis Allen, known for his critiques of modernity and culture in the Jazz Age, concluded that the Klan provided a "chance to dress up the village bigot and let him be a Knight of the Invisible Empire."[11] These early interpretations of the Klan dominated societal perspectives on the group through the interwar period.

When the Klan experienced another revival during the postwar civil rights era, a new generation of scholars and writers put their own unique stamp on the Klan. Often credited with revealing the Klan's secrets, though contemporary scholars have disputed his words versus his actions, Stetson Kennedy's *I Rode with the Ku Klux Klan* (later retitled as *The Klan Unmasked*) detailed the writer's infiltration of the Georgia Klan and subsequent efforts to distribute information to law enforcement and journalists, including the scriptwriters of the popular radio program *The Adventures of Superman*, where the man of steel battled with dastardly Klansmen. Alongside Kennedy, columnists Walter Winchell and Drew Pearson frequently targeted the Klan in their syndicated newspaper columns nationwide.[12] While the writings of Kennedy, Pearson, and

Winchell critiqued, and in some cases, lampooned the hooded order, academics like Charles Alexander, David Chalmers, and Kenneth Jackson came to the conclusion in their own research that concerns over a loss of status in a modern and diverse world transformed rural and urban men into moral vigilantes who turned to the Klan to preserve their traditional way of life.[13]

By the latter half of the twentieth century, while scholars critiqued the conclusions on status anxiety, the efforts by Alexander, Chalmers, and Jackson to utilize surviving Klan records continued to dominate the study of the Invisible Empire. This newer generation of scholarship from the likes of Robert Goldberg, Shawn Lay, William Jenkins, Leonard Moore, Kathleen Blee, and Nancy MacLean continued to examine these records while also lifting back the white hood to reveal the social, political, economic, religious, and gendered dynamics of the second Klan and its membership.[14] The most recent iterations of Klan analysis have coincided with the centennial of the 1920s and, in some cases, have served as a response to the reactionary politics of the new millennium. While these works tend to continue the local focus on Klan hot spots, not unlike the scholarship of the last fifty-plus years, they have also offered surveys of larger themes such as the Klan's place within popular culture, gender identity, political movements, and Christianity.[15]

This study inverts the traditional history of the second Ku Klux Klan by examining the efforts of anti-Klan activists who challenged the growth, recruitment, and political ambitions of the Invisible Empire during the 1920s and 1930s through editorial crusades, educational campaigns, public pressure on elected officials, political investigations, and, in some cases, countervigilantism. This activism occurred nationwide during the interwar years, roughly 1918 to 1939, yet the subject itself has largely been overlooked in most scholarship on the second Klan. Scholars such as William Jenkins, David Goldberg, Leonard Moore, Shawn Lay, Lynn Dumenil, Felix Harcourt, Kenneth Barnes, and James H. Madison have devoted small portions of their articles and monographs to anti-Klan activism, but little has been written on the rise and fall of the second Klan from the perspective of those who fought so strongly to dismantle it.[16] Instead, most scholars who have examined the second Klan focus on regions of the United States and local communities where the Klan

Introduction 7

successfully recruited new members, gained political power, and established its own vision of reform. Those who do reference Klan opposition in their works tend to examine it from a bookend approach by focusing on the role of activists in initial opposition to the Klan when the group first arrived in a region or as a contributing force in accelerating the decline of the hooded order in the latter half of the 1920s. Ultimately, few scholars have analyzed areas where the Klan was not as successful in its goals, and little has been written on the role of anti-Klan activists who continually, and at times effectively, challenged the organization throughout its second life span. Examining these locations where the Klan met sizable opposition potentially yields tremendous amounts of new scholarship that analyzes the variations of the Klan at the local level. Such an approach significantly contributes to an understanding of early-twentieth-century activism undertaken by Catholics, Jews, and African Americans. As scholar Lynn Dumenil notes, "Militancy and organization activism in this period suggest that the victims of intolerance were far from passive or helpless."[17]

This study also expands on existing scholarship of the second Klan at the local level by focusing on Missouri, a state that has yet to receive considerable attention. Outside of a collection of secondary literature referencing local activity, Missouri has not garnered a sizable monograph analyzing the Invisible Empire within its borders. The state of Missouri provides an excellent case study for the rise and fall of the second Klan as the organization gained a large membership, spread its message of Americanization, and obtained a notable level of political power in some parts of the state, particularly Jasper and Buchanan Counties. However, these efforts were not universally embraced across Missouri, and the response of Missourians—from farmers and laborers to business leaders and politicians—to distance themselves from the Klan and openly oppose its tenets reduced the Klan to a relatively powerless organization at the state level. Ultimately, despite membership totals comparable to neighboring states, the Missouri Klan was unable to translate its recruiting success into political power due to significant local opposition.

While opposition to the Klan in Missouri is notable, especially in comparison to the second Klan's growth and subsequent anti-Klan activism nationwide, the most important element of this project involves analyzing anti-Klan activism to understand the complexities and limitations that existed in challenging the Invisible Empire. These Missouri anti-Klan activists came from diverse backgrounds and included newspaper editors and publishers; members of organizations such as the National Association for the Advancement of Colored People (NAACP), American Unity League (AUL), Catholic Central Verein (CCV), Knights of Columbus, and B'nai B'rith; and prominent state politicians such as Governor Arthur Hyde, Senator James A. Reed, and Congressmen L. C. Dyer and Harry Hawes. Some groups even took on the "anti-Klan" moniker to signify their singular focus, including the Joplin Anti-Klan Organization, Carthage Anti-Klan Association, and Jasper County Anti-Klan Association. During the interwar period, these various entities and individuals tried to form a unified Klan-fighting force, yet personal quarrels and internal differences over how best to challenge the hooded order splintered any hope of a single coalition.

For all of their efforts to rebuke and reject the organization, anti-Klan activists were unable to fully stop the Klan's spread across Missouri, or the United States. At its height, the Klan claimed roughly four million members in forty-eight states, and the organization was quite successful in expanding the group to include women's and children's auxiliaries. Though activists succeeded at times in coordinating efforts between various groups, grand plans for an interracial, interdenominational, and bipartisan anti-Klan coalition, at both the local and the national levels, never fully materialized. Additionally, while some activists later became noted religious, political, and civil rights leaders, with some even serving in the vanguard of the long Black freedom struggle, others, particularly Senator James A. Reed, did not have racial equality in mind when they openly fought the Klan. Put simply, anti-Klanism did not always equate to antiracism and antibigotry, because, just as anti-Klan activists came from diverse groups, so too did they also have varying reasons for opposing the Invisible Empire. This last point is especially important because at the same time that anti-Klan activists were challenging an organization composed of white supremacists, some of their own members openly embraced and defended key tenets of white supremacy.

Yet despite the fractured nature of Klan opposition nationwide, anti-Klan activists in Missouri did achieve elements of success in their efforts to fight the Klan. Though, similar to other states and scholarly conclusions, Missouri did have its share of anti-Klan activists who appeared long enough to rebuke the organization when it first arrived and championed their cause as the group's membership declined, this study demonstrates that those who fought the Klan did so on a *daily* basis. Furthermore, though the Klan was able to wield considerable control in towns like Joplin and St. Joseph by the mid-1920s, anti-Klan activists were not deterred by these initial setbacks and continued to mobilize to eliminate the hooded order's influence in municipal affairs. An excellent example is the Jasper County Anti-Klan Association, which repeatedly failed to unseat Klan-sympathetic politicians before eventually winning several key elections and ousting the mayor of Joplin. Finally, and most important, the Klan did not translate its recruiting success in Missouri into substantial influence over state affairs because prominent leaders from both major political parties ensured a bipartisan rejection of the Invisible Empire. While anti-Klan activists nationwide largely failed in their efforts to rein in the spread of the Invisible Empire, their Missouri brethren experienced surprising success in using their power in the press, the pulpit, and the polls to stymie the Klan in the Show-Me State.

A considerable portion of Missourians encountered the Ku Klux Klan in some form during the 1920s. For some, it coincided with the depiction of Klansmen as heroic figures in the bright flickering lights of local movie theaters showing D. W. Griffith's *The Birth of a Nation*. This point was not lost on the *St. Louis Star,* which noted that "the mystery in which [the Klan] is veiled stirs a sense of vanity, and there is a strong social element in its makeup, with a romantic glamor over its activities. . . . [T]he Ku Klux movement is quite like a movie stunt . . . [and] the real reason for its revival is doubtless the interest in the old Ku Klux stirred by 'The Birth of a Nation.'"[18] For others, it was by way of endless copies of anti-Semitic, anti-Catholic, and so-called patriotic literature sold by mail order or published in newspapers across the country, including Henry Ford's *Dearborn Independent* and Aurora, Missouri's *Menace, New Menace,* and *Monitor,* as well as their most popular correspondent, a former Lead Belt schoolteacher turned presidential candidate by the name of Gilbert O. Nations. For most, however, it was simply around town, whether through community gossip, in the pages of local newspapers, the donation of supplies to a charitable cause, or a public lecture given under the auspices of the Klan, as was the case with J. F. Craig's stops in St. Louis, Kansas City, and Independence.

Even before the first cross burned or shadowy, white-robed figure paraded through small towns in Missouri, the seeds of anti-Klan activism were planted as local newspapers dispensed with sensational and eye-catching headlines about the Ku Klux Klan. In many cases, this initial coverage bordered on Lost Cause hagiography as Reconstruction-era Klansmen were romanticized reminiscent to their portrayal in *The Birth of a Nation*. Newspaper publishers and editors were also unsure how to describe the supposed fraternal patriotism that the new Klan promised, and many simply reprinted what hooded organizers and recruiters sent them outlining the organization's goals and key tenets. Yet as newspaper pages filled with promises of 100 percent Americanism, they were joined by disturbing stories of brandings, whippings, and tar and featherings. These "masked malcontents," as the *Jefferson City Democrat-Tribune* described them, looked the part of robed Klansmen and allegedly undertook similar vigilante activities as hooded members.[19] By the early to mid-1920s, these stories dominated headlines and slowly shaped public perceptions about the Ku Klux Klan. In response, Klan officials tried to right the ship by cracking down on vigilantism and distributing propaganda, both in print and in person, that cast the organization's membership as the saviors of old-time Protestantism at war against dangerous and un-American elements of modern society. At the same time, however, rumors of vigilantism, combined with the vitriolic rhetoric promoted by Klan members, drew the ire of newspaper publishers eager to assuage worried readers that this brand of 100 percent Americanism was not American at all.

As Klan recruiters and spokesmen, such as J. F. Craig, filtered into Missouri, media coverage quickly took on a sizable role in shaping public opinion regarding the Klan, particularly at the local level. The result was a propaganda battle played out on street corners, church pulpits, courthouse squares, and editorial pages that asked Missourians to identify their true feelings about the Ku Klux Klan and, in turn, convince their friends, neighbors, and community leaders to unite behind the cause they

Introduction 11

felt was right. While J. F. Craig's call to action may have brought a few new recruits—the *St. Louis Globe-Democrat* mentioned at least twelve men immediately signing membership cards at the Fourth Christian Church—his message was also challenged in the burgeoning anti-Klan press. The *St. Louis Post-Dispatch* mocked Craig's use of "theatrical effect," particularly when he frantically searched his coat pockets for the misplaced flag during a dramatic climax, and the newspaper's editorial page soon featured letters from citizens denouncing Craig's comments, including one concerned St. Louisan who called upon the federal government to "take drastic action to dissolve this klan [sic]."[20] At the *St. Louis Star*, Craig's concern about "catching hell from all quarters" was ridiculed by the editorial staff, who advised "Dr. John Freeman" that the "reverend gentleman is unnecessarily alarmed over what might befall him at the hands of law-abiding St. Louisans." Assuring its readers that anyone—within reason—could exercise their right to free speech, the *Star* concluded that "if there are enough ignorant and prejudiced, un-Christian, and small-minded men and women in St. Louis to form a klan [sic] of the variety described by the Rev. Craig, St. Louis should know about it. The bigger the group the greater the indictment of our educational system, and our Protestant sects."[21]

Though some Missouri editors and publishers, particularly in rural counties, defended the Klan's activities amid criticism, newspapers whose readers were the overwhelming targets of Klan rhetoric and vigilantism served as the most prominent voices in the anti-Klan press. Yet they also struggled with how to not only define the Klan threat—varying between publishing negative editorial commentaries and lampooning cartoons to advising readers on letter-writing campaigns and directing public pressure at elected officials—but also convince others interested in an anti-Klan coalition to join the cause. Catholic and Jewish newspapers intensely debated among themselves the Klan's claims of 100 percent Americanism and what, if any, anti-Semitism and anti-Catholicism could be found in the words of men like J. F. Craig, while Missouri's African American press, particularly its two most prominent Black newspapers, the *St. Louis Argus* and the *Kansas City Call*, differed greatly in their approach to an anti-Klan coalition. While the *Argus* implored its readers to lead the charge against the Klan and noted the irony of Klansmen complaining about "catching hell from all quarters" and appealing to Christianity while attacking "Jews, Negroes, Catholics, Greeks and all foreigners generally in a most vile and scurrilous manner," the *Call* argued that there was no cause for concern: "Why should Negroes who are busy making ends meet get excited over a conspiracy which others more powerful than themselves, will advise and correct?"[22] Instead, the *Call* laid out a plan of attack that placed the burden on other groups: "The Klan is doomed. The wider it spreads, the more enemies it will have, and the more exposed to attack it will be. This is the time for Negroes to attend their own business. The Roman Catholics have always been able to stand alone. The Jews are no weaklings assailed, and will cure all the ills the Klan can invent."[23]

The response of newspapers to Klan activities, both alleged and confirmed, produced an almost instantaneous reaction from local, state, and national groups whose membership knew the Klan up close and personal. For fraternal orders like the Masons, Elks, Knights of Pythias, and others, whose members could potentially don white robes and hoods after leaving the lodge hall, there were internal debates about issuing public statements in support or opposition to the Klan.[24] For groups geared toward Catholic, Jewish, and African American members, the question shifted from whether to denounce the Klan or to make a statement accompanied by a targeted campaign to refute Klan propaganda. Throughout the 1920s, several of these organizations, particularly the Catholic Central Verein, Knights of Columbus, American Unity League, National Association for the Advancement of Colored People, and the Anti-Defamation League of B'nai B'rith, worked in and out of public view to challenge the Klan's recruiting tactics and political objectives and called on their members to publicly take action against the Klan, pressure political leaders into investigating alleged hooded activities, and develop plans for a bipartisan, interracial, and interdenominational anti-Klan coalition.

The idea of a broad anti-Klan coalition was ambitious in theory but not sustainable due to infighting and disagreements over leadership. As evidenced by the critiques put forth by the *Argus* and *Call* regarding action against the hooded order, participants in an anti-Klan coalition had to overcome opposing views as well as the assumption that someone

Introduction 13

else would lead the charge. In the pages of both the *Argus* and the *Call*, beyond open debates about challenges to the Klan, ideological battles between the NAACP and Marcus Garvey's Universal Negro Improvement Association (UNIA), a Black nationalist fraternal organization, also received considerable attention, particularly when Garvey met with Klan official E. Y. Clarke and immediately called off any further attack against the group in favor of promoting his support for Pan-Africanism. Around the same time that Garvey's position on the Klan shifted, Knights of Columbus supreme advocate Luke E. Hart called on Missourians and the Catholic press, many of whom had previously worked with the Catholic Central Verein and Knights of Columbus, to collect information and seek legal action against anti-Catholic speakers. He urged them to continue these efforts against an "Invisible Empire" full of "bigoted, narrowminded individuals" because "if this does not show the need for organization, I cannot see why there should ever have been any need for it."[25] Additionally, though the Jewish press and affiliated organizations such as the Anti-Defamation League of B'nai B'rith, American Jewish Committee, American Jewish Congress, and the Jewish Federation agreed that something had to be done to address anti-Semitism and groups like the Klan, they differed greatly in their individual approaches to the issue. Ultimately, while each anti-Klan group expressed a willingness to assist in the fight against the hooded order, much of their editorials and correspondence centered on the hope that Protestant denominations, whose members made up the vast majority of Klan members, would take the lead in any such challenge.

Just as J. F. Craig and other Klan members found little sympathy in the press or among anti-Klan groups, so too did their promotion of 100 percent Americanism encounter hostility on the campaign trail. Klansmen and -women, as well as opposing anti-Klan forces, turned their focus to municipal, county, statewide, and federal elections as the key to extending the hooded order's influence. Even the smallest political gains on the school board, city council, or county offices were interpreted as significant barometers of the organization's strength. For the Klan, these political ambitions were clouded by claims of nonpartisanship where Klansmen and -women were advised to vote their conscience. Within the walls of the klavern, however, officials issued marching orders for members to back preferred candidates, though they were also careful to ensure that no one party was favored over the other, particularly in local chapters where Democrats sat next to Republicans who sat next to men and women whose views spanned the political spectrum. Just as Klan members rubbed shoulders with politically diverse supporters under burning crosses, so too did they also make strange bedfellows in their local party committees where attempts to put sympathetic candidates on the ballot were often met with stiff opposition from those who identified as anti-Klan. The result was not just fractured political gatherings, as was the case with the state and national party conventions when anti-Klan planks produced fiery responses, but also independent and third-party campaigns, such as Gilbert O. Nations's long-shot bid for the White House in 1924, that rallied supporters to their cause when they deemed their traditional political home to be under Klan or anti-Klan control.

Political commentators of the interwar period noted the strong reaction that alleged Klan affiliation had on political candidates and voters and referred to this quandary as the "Klan issue," where those seeking office were advised to deliver statements regarding their sympathies to, or outright opposition of, the hooded order. Newspaper coverage of J. F. Craig's visit to St. Louis's Fourth Christian Church appeared alongside articles and editorials on the Klan issue in that year's hotly contested midterm election. In Missouri's US Senate race, James A. Reed, the Democratic incumbent and a noted opponent of the hooded order, accused his Republican challenger, E. E. Brewster, of being "the beneficiary of the support of the Ku Klux Klan."[26] Upon hearing the accusation, Brewster responded that he knew "nothing of the activities of the Klan except as I have read them in the papers" and charged that Reed raised the specter of the group only to court African American voters.[27] Not to be outdone, when Reed alleged that Republican governor Arthur Hyde would not openly discuss his own stance on the Klan, Hyde issued a public statement not only denouncing the group but noting that his previous anti-Klan comments had been published "more than a year before Senator Reed's desperate political plight developed his position."[28]

While political office seekers could inevitably offer vague remarks promoting their patriotic views of a diverse United States, members of the burgeoning anti-Klan coalition, especially newspaper publishers,

Introduction 15

spent most campaign seasons demanding answers regarding the Invisible Empire. These efforts to get candidates to speak out on the Klan issue turned out to be the greatest success of the anti-Klan coalition, while also proving to be the greatest source of division. When it came time to cast ballots, anti-Klan allegiances were tested by political ties that spanned generations. As the Klan issue threatened to doom familial ties and political campaigns, it ultimately produced a path back to power for Missouri Democrats who found themselves largely shut out of major offices during the 1920s after years of statewide dominance. To this end, Democratic officials slowly developed a decadelong grassroots campaign to convince Black voters, many of whom had aligned with Republicans since the end of the Civil War, to switch political allegiances away from what was perceived as a Klan-backed GOP. Touting Republican "kampaigning," Democrats reaped the benefits of promoting the Klan issue, but also found it a double-edged sword as voters and party members were not always willing to unmask their true sentiments about the Invisible Empire.

At the same time that men like J. F. Craig claimed that the Klan was "catching hell from all quarters" in the press, through organizational grassroots opposition, and on the campaign trail, so too were they, in their own way, contributing to this attack. Not long after it was announced that he would debate Dr. Wesley Civert Travis, Independence Klan No. 27 issued a public statement that Craig was "in no way officially connected with these headquarters, and is wholly without authority to speak for the Knights of the Ku Klux Klan."[29] While it was never entirely clear what prompted Craig's exile from the Klan—or if he ever really was a member—the reasoning for Independence Klan No. 27's prompt response to his lecture was most likely related to an internal split within several local klaverns, particularly Wyandotte Klan No. 5 in neighboring Kansas City, Kansas.[30] One group of former Klansmen attempted to form a new organization called the American Clan, led by William "Billy" Parker, which promised "no imperialism, no hoods, no pussyfooting." Others sought a return to the hooded order first organized by William Simmons, who had led the Klan as imperial wizard since its reestablishment in 1915, which, with the help of the Southern Publicity Association, had increased membership into the millions by the early

16 Introduction

1920s.[31] In 1922, however, around the same time Craig crisscrossed Missouri, a coup led by Texan Hiram Evans ousted Simmons as imperial wizard. Evans quickly banished those he felt challenged his power, and the resulting fallout only deepened the factionalism.[32]

Building upon the racial, religious, and xenophobic fears of many Americans, William Simmons and his successor, Hiram Evans, were able to appeal to white supremacy and establish their "Invisible Empire," yet, for all its recruiting successes and political ambitions, the Ku Klux Klan of the interwar period never dominated American society at the level its founder and early leaders hoped. While the Klan was especially strong in states like Indiana, Colorado, and Oregon, it could not replicate similar successes throughout the United States. Additionally, a series of scandals involving high-ranking officials like Simmons, E. Y. Clarke, John Galen Locke, and D. C. Stephenson, as well as Missouri Klansmen C. C. Crawford, Heber Nations, O. L. Spurgeon, and Pierre Wallace, contributed to the organization's decline in the latter half of the decade. By 1930, the Klan was a shell of its former self, with a population that had dipped to roughly one hundred thousand. As former members spurned the Klan in favor of new groups that appealed to isolationism, anti–New Deal rhetoric, and bigoted ideologies, and potential recruits could not spare a dime—let alone ten dollars—to join, Hiram Evans spent most of the early years of the Great Depression trying to salvage his Invisible Empire. When he stepped down as imperial wizard in the late 1930s, the Klan floundered amid scandals, poor leadership, and questionable ties between itself and groups like the Black Legion, Silver Shirts, and German-American Bund. In the 1940s, the Internal Revenue Service pursued a federal investigation into financial discrepancies and back taxes and soon filed a lien against the Klan. By the end of World War II, however, newspapers around the country boldly declared, as did *Cosmopolitan*, that the "Klan rides again," amid a backdrop of Cold War Red Scare hysteria and renewed efforts to slowly integrate Jim Crow America.[33]

Though many Americans would like to claim that the Ku Klux Klan is and was a fringe organization, the hooded order reached unrivaled influence and membership in the early twentieth century because a significant portion of the country's population embraced its message. This point has been made by scholars such as Kelly J. Baker, Linda Gordon, and Felix Harcourt, who note that the Klan was ultimately successful in making many of its views mainstream in American culture, even as millions of Americans secretly—and not so secretly—fled the organization and hid or burned any evidence of their membership by the end of the 1920s.[34] As such, it should not be surprising that there was a kernel of truth in J. F. Craig's words in 1922. While his membership estimates exceeded what contemporary scholars have set as Missouri's probable Klan population, he nevertheless hinted at a growing movement that would get only bigger as the decade progressed. Additionally, though his comments elicited instant opposition and fueled efforts at anti-Klan coalition building, some of the key tenets of the Klan highlighted in his speech nevertheless found a receptive audience from the pews of the Fourth Christian Church to the far corners of the vast United States, including among those alleging to be anti-Klan. Ultimately, as the reaction to Craig's words demonstrates, the Klan contributed not only to a fracturing of local communities, political parties, and even American society in the 1920s but also to a fracturing of the tenuous anti-Klan coalition organized to destroy it.

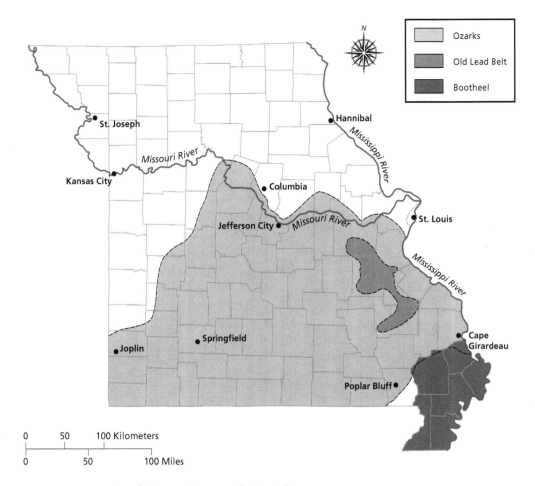

FIGURE 1. Map of Missouri. Courtesy of Chris Robinson.

CHAPTER ONE

"The Black Clouds of Bigotry"

The Origins of the Ku Klux Klan in Missouri

JOHN P. GORDON was noticeably ecstatic when members of the press inquired of him about the upcoming parade and festivities. October 6, 1924, was Dedication Day in Jefferson City. The new state capitol building, which had risen like a mythical phoenix from the charred rubble of its predecessor's fiery demise in 1911, held its ceremonial grand opening. Boosterism intermingled with the usual politicking of an election year in the Jefferson City crowds as organizers and attendees reflected on Missouri's past, present, and future. Drawing prominent dignitaries, including Senator Seldon Spencer, Assistant Secretary of War Dwight F. Davis, and four former governors, the event featured speeches and a parade that circled the city's business district.[1] At the center of it all was Gordon, chairman of the Dedication Day executive committee, who promised attendees that the day would be "one of the greatest historical events of this State."[2]

As dusk fell, a crowd of roughly twenty thousand patiently waited on the capitol grounds for the grand finale. The silence of the October air was shattered as an artillery unit unleashed a twenty-four-gun salute that reverberated through the capital city and crossed the Missouri River into neighboring Callaway County. Next, Forrest C. Donnell, a young attorney who would later serve as a governor and US senator for Missouri, told the crowd of the evening's festivities, including a pageant featuring more than two thousand participants dedicated to "the building of a commonwealth, Missouri, mother of the West." With the close of his introduction, a collection of electric lights was turned on to reveal a large stage temporarily built on the capitol steps. The crowd responded with wonder to the illumination of the stage, and, according to the *St. Louis Post-Dispatch*, the large granite capitol building in the background "seemed to drink it in."[3]

19

Set in four epochs, each presided over by a former first lady, the pageant retold the state's history in theatrical fashion with "moving picture rapidity." The first scenes opened with a re-creation of early explorations of the land and its waterways, including Hernando De Soto's discovery of the Mississippi River and the travels of Jacques Marquette and Louis Joliet. As they departed, Daniel Boone led a group of settlers onto the stage, where they staked their claim to the frontier and soon battled with Native Americans. When it came time to show the Louisiana Purchase, Meriwether Lewis and William Clark looked on, and the crowd cheered as the flags of Spain and France were lowered and replaced with the American flag. As the pageant's history drew closer to the modern day, including portrayals of the Missouri Compromise, Civil War, and the literary works of Mark Twain, dark, ominous clouds appeared on the horizon—uninvited guests. Not long after the third epoch opened with suffragist Edna Gellhorn depicted as America reciting an address from Woodrow Wilson as soldiers and nurses rushed into view, signifying the start of World War I, the rain began. Organizers pleaded with the audience not to disperse as a group of men in overalls performed the "Anvil Chorus" from *Il Trovatore*. The crash of their hammers as they reenacted the capitol's construction was met with equal force from the growing thunderstorm. As the rain intensified and the crowd rushed for cover, the pageant abruptly concluded. From barges on the Missouri River, fireworks shot into the air with "their many colored lights mingling with the flash of lightning in an angry sky."[4]

The festivities in Jefferson City in October 1924 served as a dual celebration. To most attendees, the pomp and circumstance of the event centered on speeches, pageantry, and a parade. Unable to attend, President Calvin Coolidge sent his regards and referred to Missouri as "a mother of states, and a mother of statesmen, always claiming a prominent part in influencing national concerns."[5] Most newspapers praised the grandeur of the new facility and the statewide representation of dignitaries, yet some critics also dwelled on what was left unsaid in the celebration. Though organizers included a theatrical version of the Missouri Compromise and the Civil War, they opted not to acknowledge the state's slaveholding past. Instead, a retelling of the battle of Wilson's Creek ended with "Missouri and her attendants [clasping] the hands of the blue and gray soldiers." This omission was not lost on the *St. Louis Argus*, which denounced the segregated nature of the festivities, including separate seating accommodations, as "an insult to the colored people of the state."[6]

FIGURE 2. A Ku Klux Klan flyer is visible at the Dedication Day ceremonies for the Missouri State Capitol. Courtesy of Dr. Joseph Summers Collection. Missouri State Archives.

Yet to a growing number of Missourians—including John P. Gordon—the festivities also proved to be the high-water mark of power for the state's Ku Klux Klan. Of course, that was unbeknownst to them at the time. The Klan was everywhere in Missouri in 1924, including the state's capital city. Dedication Day attendees would have been well aware of this not-so-invisible empire. For those along the parade route, they would have noticed a food stand operated by the local Klan chapter. Members littered the city with pamphlets and flyers advertising upcoming events, including a Klan rally on the outskirts of town. From photographs taken during the festivities, it is apparent that at least one flyer even made it to the front of the capitol stage. The Dedication Day local executive committee also featured multiple men with ties to the Klan, including R. M.

Talbert, Bert Landmann, and John P. Gordon, whom the *Argus* referred to as the "leading kluxter in Cole County" and who was rumored to be opposed to the inclusion of Catholicism in the festivities, particularly a pageant scene depicting Jacques Marquette's planting of a cross.[7] In an awkward turn of events, Gordon had to introduce Archbishop John J. Glennon for the opening invocation. Given the opportunity to speak, and no doubt aware of the Klansmen and -women mingling among the crowd, Glennon called on God to bless the new capitol building so that corruption might never be found within its walls and "the black clouds of bigotry might never darken its dome."[8]

In many ways, William Joseph Simmons—and his robed subordinates, later turned rivals—could not have found a more opportune time to revive the Ku Klux Klan. In 1915, Simmons spent an eventful three months confined to an Atlanta hospital recovering from an automobile accident, where he occupied most of his time dreaming of an organization that would replicate the Lost Cause lore of the original Ku Klux Klan. A former Methodist circuit rider, Simmons often thought of starting his own fraternal organization while serving as a local organizer for the Woodmen of the World. Developing titles and terminology based on mythology and the Reconstruction Klan, Simmons soon rallied recruits to his cause throughout Atlanta. By the end of 1915, the Ku Klux Klan's rebirth occurred in a cross-burning ceremony on top of Stone Mountain in Georgia.[9] Though the Klan initially became popular in and around Atlanta, historian Shawn Lay has argued that in the early years, "it appeared highly unlikely that the second Klan would ever develop a following in places [far outside the South]."[10] Indeed, at first, the Klan remained relatively obscure. It was a fraternal organization among hundreds of other such organizations.

The Klan's and Simmons's fortunes changed dramatically, however, in 1920 when the organization obtained the services of the Southern Publicity Association. Headed by Edward Young Clarke and Elizabeth Tyler, the Southern Publicity Association had previously worked with the Salvation Army, Red Cross, and the Anti-Saloon League (ASL). Clarke and Tyler helped transform the Klan from an obscure fraternal organization into a hyperpatriotic group concerned about so-called core

American values, including 100 percent Americanism and white supremacy. The concerns of the original Klan, primarily violently resisting the freedom and new rights of formerly enslaved people, now expanded to include immigrants, Catholics, Jews, and key elements of modernity in society. Relying on modern advertising and sales techniques, Clarke and Tyler sent recruiters known as kleagles out to communities across the country to sell Americanism and Klan membership at ten dollars per person with a message tailored to local concerns ranging from law enforcement, declining morality, and fraternal bonding to white supremacy, anti-Catholicism, and anti-Semitism. Kleagles frequently contacted local leaders of fraternal orders as well as clergymen to boost their introduction to the community. The result was instantaneous. By 1921, Klan membership had skyrocketed from a few thousand to around one hundred thousand, and Klan chapters, or klaverns as the organization called them, sprouted up in towns throughout the American South, the Midwest, and the Southwest.[11]

Though the second Klan rose steadily under the leadership of Simmons and his alliance with Clarke and Tyler, growing pains and an internal power struggle plagued the organization by the early 1920s. At its center, this divisiveness originated with hooded leaders who felt they knew better than Simmons about the Invisible Empire's potential. Led by Dallas dentist Hiram Evans and Indiana organizer D. C. Stephenson, a group of power-hungry Klansmen staged a coup against Simmons in 1922, convincing him to take on the new role of emperor. Despite its lofty title, Simmons quickly became a powerless figurehead, as Evans assumed the role of imperial wizard. Now commanding the Invisible Empire, Evans moved quickly to diminish Simmons's influence, including pushing Clarke and Tyler out of positions of power, while at the same time protecting his flank from his own rivals, such as Stephenson.[12]

At the time that Simmons was deposed, the Klan was wrestling with the structure of its membership. Seeking to recruit not only men but family men, hooded leaders debated how best to also keep spouses and children connected to the organization. Klan leaders like Simmons, Evans, and Stephenson heard the claims made by women for their inclusion and pushed for female membership to build their own power within the organization's hierarchy. With Evans in charge of the Klan and hooded officials dragging their feet on the logistics of membership, Stephenson and Simmons saw an opening. Three months before the official organization of the Women of the Ku Klux Klan (WKKK), Simmons established his rival Kamelia. Stephenson followed with the Indiana-based Queens of the Golden Mask.[13] The Women of the Ku Klux Klan was officially chartered on June 10, 1923, with its main headquarters initially located in Little Rock, Arkansas.[14] Membership in the WKKK was open to "white Gentile female native-born citizens over eighteen years of age who owed no allegiance to any foreign government or sect . . . [and] who were not Catholic, Socialist, Communist, or so forth."[15] With annual dues set at ten dollars, the WKKK replicated the Klan in many ways, including an agenda based on nativism, racism, and xenophobia couched as Americanism.[16] Yet as the *Imperial Night-Hawk* clearly laid out, it was to be an organization separate from the Ku Klux Klan "composed entirely of women . . . [and] operated exclusively by women for women."[17]

Headed initially by Arkansas native Lulu Markwell and later Robbie Gill Comer, the WKKK pushed for political and social reforms such as public education, Americanization programs, censorship of public amusements, child-welfare legislation, and effective Prohibition enforcement. The organization also brought in the wives, mothers, sisters, and daughters of Klansmen, as well as women previously unattached to the Klan, to consolidate the number of Protestant women's clubs that preached 100 percent Americanism. The WKKK did this by appealing to the political activism of postsuffrage women while also embracing the tenets of traditional values and home protection that the Klan trumpeted. At its height, the WKKK had a total membership of roughly a quarter- to a half-million spread out over thirty-six states.[18]

Building upon the concerns of women who joined the Invisible Empire, the WKKK slowly spread across Missouri. Noting increased activity in St. Louis, a WKKK advertisement in the *Patriot* declared, "Noble Womanhood Is Answering!"[19] Within the state, the rise of the WKKK was tied to recruitment through traditional Klan avenues as well as the integration of rival women's groups into the organization, though separate clubs like the Protestant Women of Missouri and Kamelia continued to exist.[20] By the mid-1920s, WKKK chapters existed in

"The Black Clouds of Bigotry"   25

several locations throughout the state, including St. Joseph, Kansas City, St. Louis, Jefferson City, Springfield, and Joplin.[21] The Missouri WKKK also grew due to a recruitment campaign undertaken by the state's Klan-affiliated newspapers. Located in Klan-controlled St. Joseph, the *Missouri Valley Independent* was happy to publish the dates, locations, and summaries of WKKK events held in Missouri, particularly in Buchanan County.[22] Across the state in St. Louis, the *Patriot* reported on KKK and WKKK activity throughout the Midwest and Upper South.[23] In addition to articles on the activities of Klanswomen in St. Louis, the *Patriot* also published commentaries from Lulu Markwell and James Comer on women's involvement in the WKKK.[24] By 1924, the newly named *Missouri Kourier* featured its own women's page dedicated to topics of interest for WKKK members, including articles on public education, literature, motherhood, and politics.[25]

While the inclusion of women within the Invisible Empire has been well documented, far less has been written about the hooded order's attempt to develop youth auxiliaries. The Klan frequently held events targeted at the entire family, from meetings and lectures to picnics, games, and plays, but the first youth-centered membership drive did not occur until 1923. A year later, Hiram Evans issued a declaration establishing the Junior Ku Klux Klan as an organization intended for boys aged twelve to eighteen who attended public schools and were born in, or had parents born in, the United States. Additionally, the organization was meant to be a training program that allowed candidates to transition into full membership in the Klan.[26] From these promising origins, the Junior Ku Klux Klan seemingly floundered. Evans's announcement of the group in 1924 also authorized its headquarters in Atlanta and named Paul Poock as the national director. Still, within the year, the headquarters was moved to Kansas City, Missouri. Despite this move to the state, both the *Klan Kourier* and the *Missouri Valley Independent* said little about the activity at the new headquarters outside of reprinting articles from other Klan publications, covering local events, and notifying members that E. A. Kuntzman of St. Louis had been appointed as realm director. Prominent Klansman William M. Campbell felt compelled to remind Klan members of the need to grow the Junior Klan when his November 1926 "Grand Dragon's Bulletin" in the *Missouri Valley Independent* emphasized, "In a few short years, the Klansmen of today will have passed on, and the Klan of tomorrow will depend on our boys."[27]

If little is known about the creation and structure of the Junior Ku Klux Klan, even less coverage has been devoted to the Tri-K Club, an auxiliary organization under the umbrella of the WKKK intended for girls aged twelve to sixteen with "Protestant parentage."[28] Scholar Linda Gordon argues that the Tri-K Club functioned in a similar capacity as the Junior Ku Klux Klan, whereby participants would eventually transition into the adult ranks. As such, Tri-K members were taught morality and piety in preparation to be the mothers of the next generation of 100 percent Americans.[29] In introducing the Tri-K Club in 1925, the *Missouri Valley Independent* asked its readers to "urge their daughters to become members of the Klub and join with the Junior Klan in building a mind among the young men and young women that will result in a nation of patriots possessing a national conscience."[30] Despite promoting these lofty goals, however, the newspaper offered only passing reference to the Tri-K Club for the remainder of its existence, mostly in connection with national KKK and WKKK events.[31]

Not long after outlining plans for both youth auxiliaries, the Ku Klux Klan held its Second Imperial Klonvokation in Kansas City's Convention Hall. Over four days in late September 1924, Klan officials set out "to review the Klan of yesterday, to analyze the Klan of today, to build for the Klan of tomorrow."[32] Hiram Evans, more than a year into his tenure as imperial wizard, also intended to use the Klonvokation to solidify the previous factionalism that emerged from his fight with William Simmons. "The future of America, and of the white race, hangs in the balance," Evans told the assembled Klansmen. "[We] are men who see and deplore the ills of the present, and who likewise have a vision of redemption."[33] He did not mince words with whom or what caused these "ills" that attempted to weaken Americanism. According to Evans, adherents to "Universalism, Sovietism [*sic*], Communism, Socialism, Anarchism, Judaism, and . . . Roman Catholicism . . . [are] assailing the foundation of our civilization." "We should, we will, preserve our race purity," Evans asserted to the crowd. "We must do the work to which we are divinely called."[34]

"The Black Clouds of Bigotry" 27

FIGURE 3. Ceremony at the Second Imperial Klonvokation, 1924. Courtesy of Kansas City Convention Hall Records (K0269). The State Historical Society of Missouri.

FIGURE 4. Lodge of Sorrow at the Second Imperial Klonvokation, 1924. Courtesy of Kansas City Convention Hall Records (K0269). The State Historical Society of Missouri.

"The Black Clouds of Bigotry" 29

FIGURE 5. Meeting of delegates at the Second Imperial Klonvokation, 1924. Courtesy of Kansas City Convention Hall Records (K0269). The State Historical Society of Missouri.

In discussing plans for the future, however, Klan officials also addressed a dark cloud on the horizon: anti-Klan activism. While singling out the "Simmons-Clarke" faction by name, Evans also alluded to anti-Klan organizations and legislation, alleged staged riots across the country, persecution of Klan members, and "attempts in many States to abolish the Klan."[35] Even Kansas City, the host site for the Klonvokation, had been home to similar activities, as local Klansmen explained to their hooded brethren how the city was a "hot-bed of Roman Catholicism" where anti-Klan work was "so vicious that we found it necessary to adopt measures to safeguard . . . the local officers here."[36] Such activism had caused great unease among Klansmen, while leaving "little time for the inculcation of Klan principles and the education of the millions being enrolled in our membership."[37] Yet Evans assured his followers that counteractivism, along with "the guidance of Divine Providence," allowed the Klan to continue to flourish. "We *will* make America a perfect nation," the imperial wizard told those assembled, "[thus] fulfilling the ideals of the great Statesman and Father who laid the foundation upon which to build a civilization better than the world has ever known, wherein free men may live and rear their children in liberty, security and justice— untainted by the blood of alien races and unhampered by mental and spiritual tyranny."[38]

Evans intended for such a statement to boldly inspire Klansmen who worried about the organization's long-term effectiveness, as well as serve as a rejoinder to those who argued that the Invisible Empire was withering under anti-Klan pressure. However, even Klansmen had to admit that the empire was not as vast as Evans and others implied. The "Report of the Imperial Kligrapp" showed that nearly three thousand Klan chapters existed nationwide, yet these numbers were severely skewed. While more than 80 percent of the Klan's membership lived in the Upper Midwest and the modern-day Sunbelt, fewer than 20 percent of Klansmen resided in New England, the mid-Atlantic, and large portions of the West.[39] In many ways, this uneven distribution of Klan membership would ultimately contribute to the organization's inability to mobilize effectively in national politics. Nevertheless, Evans and others trumpeted these statistics, showing millions of men, women, and children who faithfully and devotedly pledged their allegiance to the Invisible Empire.

In its assessment of the festivities surrounding the Second Imperial Klonvokation, the *Kansas City Post* seemed surprised by the makeup of the unmasked individuals who assembled each day at Convention Hall. "The delegates, as they lined up for entrance presented an appearance similar to that of business men at any kind of a club or professional gathering," the newspaper told readers. "Some wore college fraternity pins, many looked the type of prosperous business men, others bore the marks of craftsmen."[40] The scene detailed by the *Post*, as well as countless others depicting Klan members partaking in day-to-day activities, has long drawn the attention of scholars. Who were these Klansmen and -women? Why did they join the hooded order? How did they function within the Invisible Empire? To understand Missouri's hooded population, there must first be an examination of the long-standing social, cultural, and economic issues in the state that would have been familiar to potential members and how the Klan tapped into these themes in its recruiting messaging.

On March 7, 1921, the offices of the *Joplin Globe* received a mysterious package containing literature on the Ku Klux Klan. For the staff of the *Globe*, the materials confirmed suspicions that Klan activity was indeed taking place in the Missouri Ozarks. By the next morning, the newspaper had devoted a sizable portion of its edition to the contents of the package. If the Klan truly did drop off the items with the intent of distribution, the organization was not disappointed. Soon, every newspaper subscriber in the city laid their eyes upon the Klan's plan for 100 percent Americanism. The recruiting pitch that ensued not only led to the eventual creation of Ozarks Klan No. 3 in Joplin but also served as the foundation for the hooded order's spread across Missouri.[41] While some of the mythology and terminology used by the Klan may have sounded unusual to the casual reader, the basis of much of the organization's tenets were all too familiar to—and in many cases embraced by—a sizable population of Missourians. These tenets touched on subjects such as race, religion, and political reform that were important to the personal identities of many.

The recruiting message that echoed from church pulpits, county courthouses, and town theaters was similar in various communities across the United States. In addition to reinvigorating the goals of the order of old, the new group also lumped in so-called dangers of modern society. From secularism and new social norms to political activism, feminism, and civil rights, the organization sought to return the United States to Protestant small-town values. At the same time, though existing within a country that acknowledged itself as a nation of immigrants, the group tried to restrict the cultural and political identity of new immigrant communities. Not surprisingly, much like the plight of formerly enslaved people and their white supporters at the hands of the Reconstruction Klan in the nineteenth century, Jews, Catholics, and various immigrant groups, particularly from southern and eastern Europe, bore the brunt of the reconstituted Klan's fury.

While the tenets of the Klan were simultaneously repeated in various klaverns, the recruiting focus did differ to some degree based upon community. In Missouri, the recruiting message boiled down to four chief subjects: white supremacy, anti-Catholicism, Prohibition enforcement, and political reform. One of the major themes that dominated much of the initial materials sent to the *Joplin Globe* centered on white supremacy. "We avow the distinction between the races of mankind as same has been decreed by the Creator, and shall ever be true in the faithful maintenance of white supremacy and will strenuously oppose any compromise thereof in any and all things."[42] The literature also invited readers to reflect back on the Civil War and Reconstruction and remember how the "great threat of the white race on the horizon would have spread throughout the entire nation had not the white robe of the Ku Klux Klan kept unrevealed those courageous and devoted hearts that were concentrated to the saving of the Anglo-Saxon civilization of our country."[43]

Though its influence was marginal at best during the 1860s and 1870s as compared with other southern states, the Missouri Klan nevertheless reflected back on its Reconstruction ancestor when it came to regulating the rights of African Americans and promoting white supremacy. Established as a slave state in 1821—the very delay between the Missouri Compromise of 1820 and its statehood date of August 10, 1821, being a direct result of disagreement over restrictions on people of color in the state constitution—Missouri's earliest legislation was directly tied to the French Code Noir and American laws aimed at protecting and expanding commerce through enslaved labor. Though the Missouri General

Assembly enacted emancipation in the waning months of the Civil War, the quest for civil rights in its aftermath was a long and difficult road that allowed some mobility for formerly enslaved people while also ensuring that a culture of segregation was enforced.[44]

While political terrorism connected to vigilantism and bushwhacking had existed before, during, and after the Civil War, it did not always fall under the banner of the Ku Klux Klan in Missouri. Though it originated in Pulaski, Tennessee, in 1866, the Klan was largely an unknown entity within Missouri, outside of national coverage in local newspapers, until 1868. According to historian Elaine Frantz Parsons, the original members of the Reconstruction Klan were "elites and intellectuals, above and opposed to the violence of rough men, but also . . . men who felt the stern responsibility to restore their collapsed society," and historian Eric Foner argues that the Klan quickly became a "military force serving the interests of the Democratic Party, the planter class, and all those who desired the restoration of white supremacy."[45] The origin story of the Klan suggests social fraternity, not vigilantism, as the intention of group founders, yet the Klan and its violent night riding would not remain solely in Tennessee. Less than five years after the Civil War, the Klan existed in most of the states of the old Confederacy.[46]

The flames of the original Klan movement in Missouri were fanned by the state's conservative and Democratic press, particularly in the Missouri River valley, that opposed the civil rights pushed by the Radicals and favored a return to the "white man's country" that men like Horatio Seymour and Frank P. Blair Jr. promoted. In the election years of 1868 and 1870, the conservative press, particularly the *Lexington Weekly Caucasian*, played up fears of Black rights while also promoting the mysterious rituals of the "Ku-Klux" or "K.K.K."[47] Far from influencing the 1868 election in Missouri, the Klan's growth in the state was, as Elaine Frantz Parsons has noted in other southern states, sporadic, incomplete, and uneven. It was not until the early 1870s that alleged Klan atrocities became more visible in central and southeastern Missouri. Even then, however, the attacks were infrequent and largely failed to impact political activity.[48] Nevertheless, some of Missouri's political leaders felt that something had to be done to prevent the state from replicating the violence that terrorized the South.

Following the passage of the federal Ku Klux Klan Act in 1871, Governor B. Gratz Brown used it to deal with cases of vigilantism around the state.[49] Though the conservative press denounced the Ku Klux Klan Act, Brown, citing the new law, used the state militia and local law enforcement and deputized private citizens to rein in suspected Klan activity.[50] However, as historian Aaron Astor has noted, government officials and some members of the Radical press were quick to label any violence as Klan activity, even when the evidence was largely nonexistent.[51] Nevertheless, Brown responded in full to citizens' requests for government intervention against the Klan because, as one letter writer informed the governor, these attacks "make us mutch [sic] trouble and give this part of Missouri A [sic] bad name."[52]

When violence flared up in southeast Missouri, Brown and Adjutant General Albert Sigel dispatched Edmund S. Woog to investigate the matter. Traveling through several counties, Woog noted in his correspondence that much of the activity was tied to the Ku-Klux, or the "Dead Men," as residents of Stoddard County called the group. Woog noted that the organization was "nothing less than a band of robbers, murderers & horse thieves."[53] Though quick to attack the Klan for its alleged role in the atrocities, Woog also criticized local residents for their complicity in the events because "instead of manfully shouldering a gun to hunt down this band . . . and bring them to justice, [they] sign a petition, humbly asking these cut throats [sic] to please stop, and not rob, whip and murder any more."[54] While Woog and Brown supported the idea of deputizing private citizens to stop rumored Klan attacks and arrest those responsible, some Missouri residents complained that these county militias allowed Ku-Klux members to infiltrate local law enforcement and intimidate their enemies under the cover of a badge.[55] Additionally, the conservative press was quick to attack the governor and state officials when atrocities allegedly committed by the Klan turned out to be more myth than reality upon closer review, as was the case in Saline County in 1872.[56]

Despite several key setbacks, including limited enforcement capabilities, complications in obtaining criminal evidence, strong defense from accused individuals, and problems surrounding witness intimidation, the Ku Klux Klan Act strengthened the fight by state and federal authorities against the group. The act brought forth hundreds of indictments against alleged vigilantes. Additionally, it helped restore order to portions of the South and allowed African Americans to exert greater citizenship rights. While the protection of these rights proved to be short-lived due to the emergence of southern redeemer governments and the implementation of Jim Crow by the end of the nineteenth century, the Ku Klux Klan Act served as an effective tool in combating the nation's terrorist epidemic immediately following the Civil War.[57] Yet, though it proved successful in curtailing some of the violence, the Ku Klux Klan Act met with stiff opposition from Democrats who referred to it as the Force Act and expressed concerns over the loss of local control and individual freedom. Senator Carl Schurz of Missouri proved to be one of the staunchest opponents of the Enforcement Acts because he considered the Ku Klux Klan Act to be an excessive example of federal control.[58]

Though it was roughly fifty years since the Klan's last ride through the state, the reorganized hooded order nevertheless tapped into the memory of the organization that still resided in the minds of many Missourians. In the 1920s, however, a recruiting message promoting white supremacy and keeping African Americans in their place took on a more nuanced approach. After all, while Jim Crow existed in the state, African Americans held more political rights than their brethren in other southern states. For example, once enfranchised during Reconstruction, Black voting rights were curtailed at times but never fully revoked. Also, with a robust two-party system in the state, Republicans and Democrats both appealed to Black voters during political campaigns. While Republicans traditionally held stronger support from Black voters through the end of the nineteenth century, efforts from urban Democrats to prevent the enactment of more rigid Jim Crow legislation proposed by rural Democratic political leaders were not forgotten.[59]

No doubt aware of the obvious connections that could be made between the revitalized Klan and its Reconstruction predecessor, the organization sought to clarify what its modern branding of white supremacy meant. "We are not a negro-whipping organization," Klan documents assured readers, "but we do believe in white supremacy, and when we say we believe in white supremacy we can say we believe in it and do no man an injustice."[60] Though the actions of its members did not always match

36   Chapter One

its words, the Klan typically walked a fine line on the issue of vigilantism and lynching. Missouri was far from immune from such violence, including the extermination and removal of Native Americans and Mormons before the Civil War; the vigilantism of Bushwhackers, Reconstruction Klansmen, and Baldknobbers in the mid- to late nineteenth century; and the expulsion of Black residents through racial pogroms at the turn of the twentieth century.[61] Between 1889 and 1918, Missouri recorded eighty-one lynchings of which fifty-one of those killed were African Americans. Within the same span, five counties, Pike, Mississippi, Greene, Lawrence, and Howard, experienced at least three lynchings each. Governors typically called up the National Guard or enlisted local law enforcement to quell the violence. Still, even these actions were critiqued for rarely stopping lynch mobs before they claimed their victims.[62]

With this history in mind, the Klan often cited its stance on law enforcement and the prevention of vigilantism among its tenets. The Klansman's Creed proclaimed: "I do not believe in mob violence, but I do believe that laws should be enacted to prevent the causes of mob violence."[63] However, the organization did little to move the needle on the status quo, whether it was advocating for civil rights or attempting to suppress lynch mobs. When Hiram Evans visited St. Louis in 1923, he openly appealed to residents to consider how the Great Migration impacted their own community versus the Jim Crow South: "I cannot help but sympathize with St. Louis and other Northern cities after reading about the so-called race problem. . . . [T]he South has dealt successfully with the problem for years . . . regardless of what black agitators, vote snaring politicians or the newspapers have to say." Acknowledging that mob violence did happen in the South, though not necessarily condemning it, Evans reminded those assembled that "we have a lynching down there occasionally, I'll admit, but if I remember correctly, it was not so many months ago when you had one right here in Missouri."[64] While promoting the tenets of white supremacy, Klan officials also made sure to reference the organization's benevolent endeavors toward African Americans, including financial contributions to Black churches and charitable causes. Trying to emphasize that the organization did not have antipathy toward people of color, Evans reminded supporters

"The Black Clouds of Bigotry"   37

that African Americans could have "his automobile, farm or whatever he wants, except social equality."[65]

At the same time, the othering of who was considered white and thus deserved the full rights of citizenship in a white man's country did not begin and end with African Americans. "We shall fearlessly proclaim to the foreign element in this country, to those who are here as our invited guests, that the white man built this country," Klan materials in the *Joplin Globe* declared.[66] William Simmons echoed this sentiment by warning Missourians that granting citizenship to all immigrants would only lead to a dangerous future for the United States.[67] Yet for many Missourians, Simmons's and the Klan's claims that there was a need for limitations on foreign immigration and foreign influence were far from new. Though some Missourians may have asserted that legal and extralegal measures were needed to regulate the activities of enslaved and formerly enslaved people, they also expressed concern about the state's increasing immigrant population, including Germans, Irish, Greeks, Italians, and Jews, throughout the nineteenth and early twentieth centuries. No doubt influenced by prejudice against ethnic and racial groups deemed inferior, these Missourians initially detested the arriving settlers for their opposition to slavery, particularly Germans who flocked to the state by the thousands between 1820 and 1850, establishing communities along the Missouri River valley. They were soon joined by immigrants from the old country attempting to escape revolutions, political upheaval, economic depressions, and famine. By 1920, Missouri's foreign-born and second-generation immigrant population totaled more than 20 percent of the state's total population. From their positions of power within the state, nativist Missourians increasingly worried that a day might come when the foreign-born population would outvote them and their interests.[68]

In addition to fearing increased foreign-born immigration to the state, some Missourians also expressed contempt for the non-Protestant faiths practiced by many of these new arrivals. Though the group's largest period of immigration into the state occurred in the latter half of the nineteenth century, Jews had lived in Missouri since the colonial period. In his seminal work on St. Louis Judaism, scholar Walter Ehrlich found a small but notable Jewish population in the city dating back to the late eighteenth century. Having by far the largest percentage of Jewish residents in Missouri, St. Louis served as an early hub of community and religious activity. Even into the early twentieth century, Jews in neighboring counties reported traveling into the city for services and other events. Slowly but surely, however, Jews made their way into every major region of the state by the late nineteenth century, establishing businesses, synagogues, and other community structures. Scholar Mara Cohen Ioannides notes that by the 1920s, Missouri's Jewish population stood at more than fifty thousand.[69]

Beyond a small Jewish population, Catholicism was by far one of the largest religious denominations in the state. During French and Spanish colonialism, Missouri was a predominately Catholic territory and banned Protestant worship for a time. However, with the Louisiana Purchase, the region's rigid Catholic boundaries disappeared in favor of open religious toleration. Communities like St. Louis and Ste. Genevieve held large Catholic populations, and, as the nineteenth century wore on, more and more Catholic immigrants arrived and set up communities throughout the state, particularly along the Missouri River between Jefferson City and St. Louis.[70] Their arrival coincided with a wave of nativist sentiments across the United States that led to the distribution of anti-Catholic pamphlets, especially the alleged convent narratives of women like Maria Monk; several anti-immigrant riots in prominent American cities, including St. Louis; the brief formation of a political movement dubbed the American Party that achieved varying levels of success prior to the Civil War, particularly in St. Louis municipal elections; and the rise and fall of numerous nativist and anti-Catholic groups, including the Order of Americans, United American Mechanics, American Patriotic League, National Order of the Videttes, and, most notably, Order of the Star Spangled Banner (also known as the Know-Nothings) and American Protective Association (APA).[71]

With the continued growth of Catholicism in the United States, including the arrival of Archbishop Francesco Satolli as part of Pope Leo XIII's apostolic delegation to the United States, as well as the four-hundredth-anniversary celebration of Christopher Columbus's discovery of the Americas at the World's Columbian Exposition in Chicago, the APA and other nativist groups saw a surge in membership in the 1890s

"The Black Clouds of Bigotry" 39

as some Americans feared a Catholic takeover of the country.[72] The so-called patriotic press, including APA-affiliated newspapers, fanned these flames by printing and circulating fake documents purportedly written by Catholic officials discussing plans to overthrow the government and destroy Protestant churches.[73] By the close of the nineteenth century, the APA had expanded across several regions of the United States, though the organization never gained a foothold in the South. After St. Louis was selected as the host site for the APA's national convention in 1892, Missouri experienced a brief surge of support for the group. Webster Davis was elected mayor of Kansas City in 1895 with APA backing, three nativist newspapers were published in the state, and even the St. Louis Catholic newspaper *Western Watchman* had to admit that the "A.P.A.'s were never as strong in this city as they are at present. . . . [E] very bum politician of both parties has been converted to it."[74]

Despite its sudden ascendency, the APA proved short-lived due to internal factionalism and the fact that anti-Catholicism never became a prominent political issue in the 1890s.[75] While the group faded from existence by the early twentieth century, with only a handful of chapters sprinkled across the Midwest up to World War I, the hysteria that had given rise to it remained entrenched in American society. Several anti-Catholic publications continued after the APA with the goal of promoting patriotism and Americanism. One of this period's largest and arguably most successful anti-Catholic newspapers was the *Menace*. Published in tiny Aurora, Missouri, the *Menace* set out from the beginning to inform readers that American values and institutions, such as the public school system, were "the antidote for papal poison."[76] The newspaper began in 1911 under the ownership of W. F. Phelps and Thomas Earl McClure. Though it struggled at first to corner the market on anti-Catholic publications, the weekly newspaper grew quickly and soon alleged that it had more than a million subscribers.[77] The *Menace* grew so successful that the railroad lines and post office in Aurora had to expand to accommodate the increasing demands for both the newspaper as well as anti-Catholic books and pamphlets put out by the Menace Publishing Company.[78]

With a lengthy list of subscribers and the glowing endorsement of Tom Watson, the populist politician turned white supremacist provocateur, the *Menace* soon claimed in its slogan that it had turned Aurora into the "World's Headquarters for Anti-Papal Literature."[79] After several years in the business, W. F. Phelps opted to retire from the *Menace*, and his associates turned to William "Billy" Parker to continue the publication. Born in Scotland in 1872, Parker immigrated to the United States as an adult at the end of the nineteenth century. He worked initially as a grocer in Boston, but his interest in organizing soon brought him to Pennsylvania, where he was employed as a labor organizer in the coalfields. It was in this harsh terrain that Parker, by his own accounts, first laid eyes on a copy of the *Menace*. The publication spoke to him, and soon enough he was speaking to others about the dangers of Catholicism around the globe.[80] By 1914, Parker's name appeared in the *Menace* as one of the countless lecturers picking up where groups like the APA had let off. Not merely satisfied with the lecture circuit, Parker soon helped organize the anti-Catholic Free Press Defense League. Though headquartered in Fort Scott, Kansas, the league held close ties to the *Menace*, even offering legal defense for the newspaper when its publishers found themselves in federal court. From that fateful alliance, and for the remainder of the 1910s, Parker and the league's activities received significant coverage in the *Menace*.[81]

It was through the *Menace* and the nativist lecture circuit that Billy Parker became familiar with a former Missouri Lead Belt schoolteacher named Gilbert O. Nations. Born in Ste. Genevieve, Missouri, at the end of the Civil War, Nations spent his early life in the schoolhouse before trying his hand in law and politics. His time in the classroom, church pulpit, and courtroom transformed him into a mesmerizing speaker, and he soon caught the eye of local political kingmakers. Despite repeatedly failing to win election as school commissioner, Nations soon shocked the relatively small political world of St. Francois County when he was elected probate judge and became the first Republican to hold county-level office in twenty-five years.[82] While his victory made him a favorable candidate for higher office among St. Francois County Republicans, opposition from local political bosses against Nations during his campaign for Missouri's thirteenth congressional district altered the course of the judge's life.[83] Realizing that political opponents within his own party favored a thriving saloon business in the Lead Belt's mining towns,

Nations became a vocal supporter of the growing temperance movement and crisscrossed Missouri on behalf of the Anti-Saloon League and Woman's Christian Temperance Union (WCTU), lobbying unsuccessfully for a state constitutional Prohibition amendment.[84] Around the same time as his campaigning for temperance, Nations went public with his commentaries and opinions on the Catholic Church. Between 1911 and 1920, Nations published multiple books on what he saw as the dangers of Catholicism in the United States. He also became a frequent and popular contributor to the *Menace*, which allowed him to address a large audience about what he saw as fearful changes in American society.[85]

Having found a home among the more than one million subscribers of the *Menace*, Nations soon found a partner in Billy Parker, and the pair toured the country as part of a speakers bureau organized by the Free Press Defense League with the *Menace* touting them as "the gatling gun of the patriotic movement."[86] Soon, the duo also rose to the top of the Free Speech Defense League, with Nations serving as president and Parker as secretary-treasurer. After Phelps retired from the *Menace*, the league took over the newspaper's management and reorganized the Menace Publishing Company with Marvin Brown as president, Nations as vice president, and Parker as secretary-treasurer.[87] Parker moved to Aurora to help manage the company's day-to-day affairs, but his presence in the newspaper offices had a negative effect. As the world emerged out of World War I, the *Menace* suffered due to a significant drop in subscribers. Additionally, Parker was seemingly in over his head and grossly mismanaged the publication. When a mysterious fire destroyed the offices and press of the *Menace* in 1919, Parker launched a halfhearted effort to resurrect the newspaper, first as the *Menace* and later as the *New Menace*.[88]

While the *New Menace* could not recapture the success of its predecessor, ceasing publication in the early 1930s, Parker and Nations used their decadelong tenure as speakers and publishers to transition into the orbit of the Klan easily. Parker toured the country touting anti-Catholicism, the *New Menace*, and the hooded order, while Nations's writings were reprinted in several Klan-affiliated newspapers. He later served as editor and publisher of *Fellowship Forum* and the *Protestant*, two newspapers frequently cited in the Klan press.[89] The duo even shared the stage at Klan rallies, including a series of appearances at Kansas City's Convention Hall.[90] During the 1920s, Nations remained in the Klan's good graces, including when he ran for president in 1924 as a candidate for the newly formed American Party, fully acknowledging that he welcomed hooded support. Parker continued as a prolific speaker and publisher. However, his attempts to lead a rival group called the American Clan cost him what little influence he still had within the Invisible Empire.[91]

Building from Parker and Nations's potent brand of anti-Catholicism that appeared in the pages of the *Menace*, Klan recruiters wedded warnings about papal control with threats that vice and Prohibition violations could be directly tied back to foreign-born influence in many communities. The result was an immensely effective membership pitch that stirred up anti-immigrant and antiurban sentiments from the bitter Prohibition battles that had taken place only a decade prior. Even in towns that lacked sizable immigrant populations, organizers could still paint a picture of wet politicians cavorting in the smoky rooms of local ward meetings or at the state capitol or bootleggers flooding Main Street with big-city booze, such as what was rumored to be produced at the St. Louis–based Anheuser-Busch. Speakers also frequently critiqued wide-open towns full of bars, brothels, and gambling dens, as well as prosecutors and judges who seemingly let law violators off the hook. It is not surprising then that Klan officials promised to support local, state, and federal agents in their enforcement of the law.[92]

The Klan was aided in this effort, both directly and indirectly, by the work of groups like the Anti-Saloon League and the Woman's Christian Temperance Union, which had already established entrenched foundations in many local communities. Founded in Ohio in the late nineteenth century, the ASL and WCTU grew into notable temperance organizations that wielded tremendous political influence. Both organizations entered Missouri by the end of the nineteenth century and quickly got to work on local option campaigns to restrict the menace that threatened to drown many towns and their residents—the saloon. Though the ASL and WCTU were successful in their bids at local option laws in a vast majority of the state's counties, Missouri's urban centers and immigrant communities, especially the political pull of Anheuser-Busch, arguably one of the largest breweries in the United States, were able to fight off larger attempts at statewide Prohibition, including a particularly contentious 1910 referendum campaign. When Prohibition was enacted in 1919, and the Volstead Act became the law of the land at the dawn of the 1920s, the ASL and WCTU continued to wield considerable strength and influence in the state.[93]

With a shared sense of responsibility in eradicating alcohol and its consumers and purveyors, the Klan, ASL, and WCTU frequently found themselves in close proximity. Interestingly, the Southern Publicity Association, the same advertising agency that helped William Simmons turn the Klan into a household name, also offered its promotional services to the ASL.[94] However, the ASL, like many nationwide organizations, had mixed feelings about the Invisible Empire. In many cases, prominent leaders stayed silent on the hooded order and offered few words of encouragement or denouncement. Scholars note that ASL attorney and advocate Wayne Wheeler was well aware of the criticism directed at the organization regarding the Klan, even as he advised confidants to root out hooded influence within certain local and state branches.[95] When William H. Anderson, a prominent ASL official, was asked about the organization's stance on the Klan, he defiantly declared that neither he nor, to his knowledge, any member of the ASL was part of the hooded order. Yet in its coverage of Anderson's comments, the Klan-affiliated *Missouri Valley Independent* expressed the sentiment that Anderson "spoke in [the Klan's] defense in the friendliest manner conceivable."[96]

Much like its close alignment with the ASL, the KKK, and in many cases the WKKK, attempted to draw members and support from the WCTU, though the relationship was a tenuous one. Historians Ruth Bordin and Ian Tyrrell have documented examples of nativism, bigotry, and racism within the WCTU, particularly in the push by some members for stricter immigration laws, de jure segregation, a prohibition on office holding for non-Protestants, and mandatory English-language education in public schools, yet scholars have also noted how the organization's "Do Everything" policy embraced diversity, ecumenism, and interracial cooperation. While some of its members did become Klanswomen, particularly Imperial Commander Lulu Markwell, WCTU officials gave little indication about the group's feelings about the Klan. There is a notable silence from national WCTU officials expressing outward support or condemnation for members joining the WKKK. During the 1920s, *Union Signal*, the WCTU's official publication, discussed the only Klan once. The same could be said for the Missouri WCTU. The *Missouri Counselor*, the state organization's publication, never mentioned the Klan in its pages and made only a vague reference to "One Hundred Percent Americanism."[97]

In surveying the actions and claims of both the ASL and the WCTU, it appears that any alliances between the organizations and the Klan were created at the local level. Yet the apparent silence of major leaders in both groups regarding the Klan should be noted. The *St. Louis Star* alluded to as much when it alleged, "It has escaped the attention of many political observers that a number of the chief leaders in the Klan have been at one time or another active in the Anti-Saloon League."[98] The Missouri Klan and the state's ASL and WCTU also found themselves in similar company by way of Nations's family. At the same time that Gilbert O. Nations campaigned on behalf of the ASL and WCTU for a state constitutional Prohibition amendment, his sons, Gus and Heber, were actively involved in the WCTU's Young People's Branch. Though Gus later denied joining the Klan, he was perhaps the most well-known state Prohibition enforcement official and dry raider, while Heber served as the exalted cyclops of the Jefferson City Klan. When Heber was charged with accepting bribes from a St. Louis brewer, ASL and WCTU members rallied to his defense.[99]

Beyond promoting goals that strove to keep people of color and foreign-born individuals marginalized as well as saloons shuttered, the Klan also promised potential recruits that the organization would protect "woman's honor and the sanctity of the home," not only from so-called dangerous elements, but also from criminality and lax law enforcement connected with corrupt government.[100] To this end, while its speakers continuously reiterated a nonpartisan approach to politics at the local, state, and federal levels, it soon became obvious that the quickest path to political relevance was to unite behind the party in power. In Missouri, it was difficult to maintain nonpartisanship, given the state's unique political divisions. While the 1920s witnessed a decade of strength for Republicans in the White House and the governor's mansion, rural Democrats still held considerable sway within the Missouri

General Assembly.[101] As such, it was not uncommon for Klan recruiters to play to both sides when speaking of the need to clean house politically. More often than not, state Klan leaders distributed a list of candidates from both parties they found palatable for support. Nevertheless, some community members still attempted to use the organization to settle old scores and disrupt the fine line of bipartisan nonpartisanship.

Despite the concerns over nonpartisanship, there was one political heavyweight with which to contend in Missouri. Holding court in Kansas City, the political machine of Tom Pendergast not just controlled city matters but also wielded considerable influence within the state Democratic Party. For the Klan, it was not just simply Pendergast's ties to organized crime and vice that garnered opposition, but also the fact that the elder power broker was Catholic. Born in St. Joseph, Missouri, in 1872, Tom Pendergast first came to Kansas City in 1894 to help his brother, James Pendergast, in his business ventures. By the time Tom arrived in Kansas City, James had already spent several years working at an iron foundry before accruing enough capital to own a saloon. Tom quickly went to work managing the Pendergast Brothers Saloon in the West Bottoms, an industrial neighborhood near the Missouri River, while James used the saloon business to gain power in Kansas City's First Ward, which eventually earned him election as an alderman.[102]

The Pendergasts quickly developed a working-class coalition composed of African Americans as well as first- and second-generation immigrants who worked in the city's factories and stockyards. Tom himself soon won election as First Ward deputy constable, then deputy marshal and superintendent of streets. In 1910, Tom was elected to James's alderman seat after the elder Pendergast developed poor health. A year later, when James died, Tom became the head of the Pendergast's political coalition called the Goats. In 1915, Tom stepped down as an alderman and began a lengthy tenure as the leader of the Jackson Democratic Club, ensuring him unelected power over municipal affairs. In addition to his ability to select candidates for office and thus hold significant sway over their policies, Pendergast also owned sizable stakes in several Kansas City businesses. Not surprisingly, he made a hefty fortune as these businesses not only provided the goods and services needed for the growing Kansas City metropolis but also secured lucrative contracts for municipal government projects. During the heyday of Prohibition, Pendergast ensured that booze, bawdy houses, and vice flowed unchecked in Kansas City, or, as it was soon dubbed, "Tom's Town."[103]

While Pendergast's Goat coalition and business empire soon expanded beyond the working-class neighborhoods of the West Bottoms, his control over the Democratic Party did not go unchallenged. Kansas City had several political fiefdoms, many built on tenuous relationships. Pendergast's chief rival was Joseph B. Shannon, an Irish American political boss who controlled most of Kansas City's Northside. Though he made a name for himself as a Kansas City boss, Shannon was actually from St. Louis. Born in 1867, he was the child of Irish immigrants who later moved to Kansas City after his father's death. The Shannons quickly became connected to the Kansas City Democratic Party, and this relationship enabled Joseph to land a patronage job in municipal government in the 1890s. At the end of the nineteenth century, Shannon realized he would find little quarter in the Republican Party or Pendergast's Goat faction. As a result, he built up his own political machine dubbed the Rabbits and vied for control of Kansas City Democratic politics. He served as a delegate to the Democratic National Convention on multiple occasions and later chaired the Missouri Democratic State Committee.[104]

Realizing that Democratic candidates would lose if the party split votes or sat out elections, Shannon and Pendergast agreed to a fifty-fifty share of patronage and candidates to ensure victory. While ideal on paper, the plan often led to suspicion, hostility, and a breakdown of the agreement. Realizing the animosity between the two sides that brewed under the surface of the arrangement, the Klan launched a campaign to unseat Pendergast-affiliated Goats from political office, as well as orchestrate a hooded recruitment effort under the guise of antibossism. While the plan sought to challenge Pendergast's and Shannon's respective power structures, the Klan also worked to fracture both groups by working with some Shannonites when the political temperature was right. Such was the case in 1924 when Shannon, fearing the growing influence of Pendergast in Kansas City municipal affairs and the state Democratic Party, instructed his Rabbits to back Republican candidates against the Goats. With the Klan also backing the party in that election cycle, the result was a sizable Republican victory. Frustrated with Shannon's preference for power over party, key lieutenants, including Casimir Welch and William J. Thompkins, defected from the Rabbit ranks and joined Pendergast's Goats.[105]

Though it had backed Republicans in 1924 to defeat Pendergast's interests in Kansas City, the Missouri Republican Party was far from a welcome home for the hooded order. This was initially largely due to the influence wielded by Governor Arthur Hyde. Originally from Princeton, Missouri, near the Iowa border, Hyde came from a politically connected family. His father, Ira B. Hyde, served one term in Congress before returning home in 1875. His younger brother, Laurence Mastick Hyde, would later serve on the Missouri Supreme Court but initially paired with Arthur and their father at the family law firm in Princeton. Though he came from a Republican family, Hyde briefly flirted with the Progressive Party during Theodore Roosevelt's Bull Moose years in an unsuccessful bid for attorney general of Missouri. Nevertheless, Hyde built a name for himself, first as mayor of Trenton, Missouri, then as an automobile dealer and speaker for Republican candidates. In 1920, Missourians elected him governor. Residing in the governor's mansion, Hyde quickly gained sizable control of the state Republican Party while promoting efforts to reorganize state government. Despite claims by Democrats, including US senator and Pendergast ally James A. Reed, that Hyde had "remained conspicuously silent [and] not lifted a finger in opposition to the klan's [sic] tactics and purposes," the governor had voiced his opinion on the organization multiple times during his years in office. Though he could do little to convince the Missouri General Assembly to pass anti-Klan legislation, he privately confided to a friend that "I am opposed to the Klan and have been ever since it came from the South in the post-war days."[106]

When Hyde left office in 1925, his successor, Sam A. Baker, continued many of his policies, including opposition to the Klan. Born in Wayne County in 1874, Baker was the son of a Civil War veteran who died before his birth. Struggling financially in rural Missouri, Baker worked to help his family and attended school when he could, eventually earning degrees from Missouri Wesleyan College and the Normal School at Cape Girardeau (now Southeast Missouri State University). Pursuing a career in education, Baker served as a teacher, principal, and administrator in districts across Missouri, including Joplin and Jefferson City, before winning election as state superintendent of public schools. He received credit for expanding the state's educational system but lost reelection in 1922. During his gubernatorial campaign in 1924, Baker reminded voters of his work to improve Missouri schools and promised good roads and better relations between business interests and his administration. Targeting the Klan by name, Baker repeatedly attacked his challenger, A. W. Nelson, as being closely aligned with the hooded order and denounced the group whenever possible. He also reached out to Black voters by emphasizing the need to improve segregated schools and promising "No Kluxters on the Republican Ticket."[107]

Though both Hyde and Baker openly denounced the Klan, they could do little as governor to stop the spread of the Invisible Empire across the state, acknowledging in many cases that they were powerless against the organization until it or its members broke the law. Additionally, just as there were notable anti-Klan leaders among Republicans, so too did the state's grand old party receive support and votes from hooded leaders. While the Missouri Klan reiterated time and again that, in the words of Hiram Evans, "the Organization known as the Knights of the Ku Klux Klan is not in politics, neither is it a political party. . . . We will permit no political party and no group of politicians to annex, own, disown, or disavow us," prominent officials such as Heber Nations and William M. Campbell voted overwhelmingly Republican.[108] This is not to say that Klansmen weren't also among Democratic ranks, including John P. Gordon. However, the Republican Party's shift toward lily-whitism over the 1920s no doubt affected members' political leanings.

With a deep well from which to draw and a sizable portion of the citizenry ready to drink up its call to action, the Ku Klux Klan entered the Show-Me State with plans to add another realm to its growing Invisible Empire. As discussed, the road of recruitment built by the Klan nationwide was replicated in many ways in Missouri. Just as the organization spread beyond the South in 1921, some of the first forays into the state can be found in major cities like St. Louis and Kansas City as early as the spring of that year. As the grand goblin of the Domain of the Mississippi Valley, Frank Crippen of New Orleans was dispatched to Missouri in the spring of 1921 to set up shop in St. Louis and begin an active recruiting campaign that would cover the entire state. Asked what the Klan offered to potential members, Crippen applauded the vision of William Simmons to "use the organization as a foe to everything un-American" and promised that the group stood for the "purification and protection of American ideals and aspirations."[109]

Not long after Crippen began his recruiting efforts in St. Louis, William Simmons, anxious to establish a strong foothold in the United States' sixth-largest metropolis, targeted the city in September 1921. First, the imperial wizard issued an open letter to residents imploring them to disregard the negative publicity they had previously heard about the Ku Klux Klan. Soon after, Simmons blew into St. Louis on an unexpected visit, not unlike the thunderstorm that shook the city during his planned speech. Few people in the area had been tipped off about Simmons's plans, and the local Klan struggled to obtain proper finances to stage the event. However, the organization still managed to fill a venue with an audience estimated at one thousand. Onstage, as the *St. Louis Star* ran the image on its front page, Simmons was backed by a group of seated Klansmen in full hooded attire. A fellow Klansman introduced him as a "great American apostle of what George Washington and [Thomas] Jefferson and [Benjamin] Franklin taught." As a band played "The Star-Spangled Banner," Simmons rose from his seat and gazed out over the large crowd, including three hundred local Klansmen. During his time onstage, Simmons defended his beloved Klan. He denounced the violence taking place in parts of the United States and questioned those who tried to link the Klan to such acts. To him, the Klan was just like any other fraternal organization. His message to the possible recruits in the audience was one of patriotism, morality, and 100 percent Americanism.[110]

While Simmons, Crippen, and countless local Klansmen initially organized recruitment efforts across the city, by 1923, two local ministers, C. C. Crawford and Charles McGehee, took over as the lead spokesmen. Born and raised in Illinois, Cecil C. Crawford, or C. C., as he referred to himself, was interested in teaching and ministry at a young age. Soon, he was pastoring a Christian church in Albia in southern Iowa, where he developed an interest in publishing and briefly edited a religious

50   Chapter One

newspaper. By his own account, his ministry and editorial skills gained wide attention, and the *Christian Standard* hired him as a contributor. Owing to his popularity, the *Christian Standard* brought him on staff, which merited a move to Cincinnati. In 1922, Crawford yearned for a return to the pulpit and arrived in St. Louis to take over Fourth Christian Church. Quickly, the youthful Crawford gained a sizable following among his congregation.[111]

Like his pastoral popularity, Crawford also found that St. Louis members of the Invisible Empire were receptive to his oratory and editorial skills. Less than a year after accepting the position at Fourth Christian Church, Crawford invited a Klan speaker to address the congregation. In a show of support for Crawford's advocation of the hooded order, Klansmen presented him with an automobile as a Christmas present. Not long after, Crawford took his vocal support for the Klan beyond the pulpit of his church. In the process, his profile within the Invisible Empire rose dramatically. In addition to speaking engagements in St. Louis, including giving the main address at a Klan event in Creve Couer that drew ten thousand, Crawford embarked on a lecture circuit through Missouri and Illinois on behalf of the Klan. When Hiram Evans came to St. Louis in the summer of 1923, Crawford was allowed to speak to the crowd.[112]

However, Crawford's ascension within the ranks of the Klan did not sit well with some St. Louisans. Crawford issued statements defending his involvement in the Klan. Still, by the latter half of 1923, an opportunity to split his time between the pulpit, the lecture circuit, and a Klan-affiliated publication called the *Patriot* proved too lucrative to pass up.[113] Begun in 1923, the *Patriot* had a short but tumultuous life span in St. Louis. From its beginning, the newspaper openly waged war against the enemies of the Klan and rallied Missourians, as well as Klansmen in neighboring states, to defend the Invisible Empire. At the *Patriot*, Crawford was paired with Frederick Barkhurst, an Iowa newspaperman nearly twenty years his senior who had previously worked for several newspapers across Missouri, including the *St. Louis Evening Times*. From their respective perches on the *Patriot's* editorial page, Crawford and Barkhurst could speak directly to national topics, anti-Klan individuals and organizations, and key tenets of the Invisible Empire. Crawford also dedicated another section of the newspaper to personal vendettas. Labeled "Kutting Kracks at Ku Klux Kritics by Krawford," the minister turned editor focused squarely on anti-Klan forces. In his first edition, he called out the *St. Louis Star* for what he saw as explicitly anti-Klan articles. Soon after, his targets ranged from politicians like anti-Klan Oklahoma governor Jack Walton to letters sent to his home and office denouncing his stance on the hooded order. One of the central themes that appeared not only in Crawford's critique section but pervasively throughout the pages of the *Patriot* was rabid anti-Catholicism.[114]

Within the first year of its existence, however, the *Patriot* and Crawford ran into issues over the management—or mismanagement— of finances. By 1924, Crawford's influence over the newspaper diminished greatly, and the name was changed from *Missouri Fiery Cross* to *Klan Kourier* to *Missouri Kourier*. With this change came an alteration in the newspaper's layout. Gone were Crawford's "Kutting Kracks" and other openly vitriolic and localized attacks. Instead, with a redesign authorized by Klan officials in Atlanta, the newspaper morphed into a more generic version of many other state Klan newspapers and designated the official organ of the Realm of Missouri and Nebraska. Not long after the redesign, Crawford was removed from the newspaper staff and soon exiled from the Invisible Empire for his involvement in alleged mail fraud.[115]

Like C. C. Crawford, Charles McGehee also found his way into the Invisible Empire through his ties to Protestantism. Born in Mississippi, McGehee spent much of his life in the Mississippi River valley. After briefly relocating with his family to Louisiana in the early twentieth century, McGehee eventually found his calling in the ministry of the Methodist Episcopal Church. He served as minister for churches in Mississippi around World War I before eventually being assigned to the pastorate at St. Louis's Haven Street Methodist Episcopal Church, South, around 1921. Almost immediately after arriving in St. Louis, McGehee became involved with the local Klan and utilized his pulpit position as a recruiting mechanism for the organization. Soon after, he began to travel throughout Missouri and Illinois, giving lectures for the Klan.[116] The fact that he wore Klan robes over his minister's robes did not bother many in St. Louis, but when he began to discuss the hooded order in his sermons, officials of the Methodist Episcopal Church, South, started to object. McGehee's support for the Invisible Empire resulted in frequent clashes with Bishop W. F. McMurry, who felt that the Klan should not be "the theme of a sermon within the walls of the Methodist Episcopal Church."[117] After receiving a warning from Bishop McMurry for "cutting loose" in a sermon attacking the Catholic Church, McGehee arranged to switch pulpits with Crawford for a Sunday service. While Crawford denounced the opponents of the Klan at Haven Street Methodist Church, McGehee told those in the pews at Fourth Christian Church of an "invisible empire of righteousness warring against an invisible empire of evil."[118]

When McGehee took to the local press to defend the actions of the Ku Klux Klan, Bishop McMurry had had enough. He called McGehee into a meeting where a heated altercation occurred. McGehee later claimed that McMurry called him a liar before repeatedly striking him in the face. McMurry denied the charges and informed the press that the pulpit and the Klan should not be mixed.[119] "The klan [sic] does not suit me," he told reporters. "I could not join because I am not anti-foreigner, anti-Jew, or anti-negro."[120] Since the confrontation involved the bishop, officials from the Methodist Episcopal Church, South, decided to hold hearings over the matter.[121] Seeking vindication, McGehee went to work lobbying fellow ministers, including some allegedly affiliated with the Klan, to take up an official inquiry against McMurry.[122] As rumors of an investigation swirled, McMurry attacked McGehee's connections to the Klan by pointing out that "I never told Mr. McGehee that I objected to his membership in the Klan. . . . If he wants to parade at night in a mask, that's his business, but I don't believe it will help his work as a minister." McMurry also took the Bible—the very document used by the Klan to defend its existence—and turned it against the Invisible Empire: "Jesus didn't wear a mask, neither did Paul."[123]

As McGehee pushed for an inquiry, Bishop McMurry chose not to reappoint the minister to the Haven Street Church. When McMurry's decision was announced, Crawford invited McGehee and his congregation to the Fourth Christian Church for a special service in honor of the soon-to-be-exiled pastor. At the evening's ceremonies, McGehee made an even more stunning announcement. Citing the altercation with the bishop,

McGehee told the crowd that he would not seek a new appointment and would instead become a full-time lecturer for the Klan. Crawford then presented him with $750 as a first paycheck from the Klan. With emotions running high in the tightly packed church, McGehee declared, to a roar of applause, that "if it comes to a choice between the Methodist Church and the klan [sic], I shall choose the klan [sic]."[124] In 1924, the Methodist Episcopal Church, South, officially relinquished McGehee's membership and expelled him from the ministry.[125] This mattered little to the now great titan of Province No. 1, Realm of Illinois. From his office in East St. Louis, McGehee boasted that his current position afforded him a salary equal to those of "two or three of the best-paid ministers of the Methodist Church in St. Louis."[126]

While Crawford's and McGehee's paths diverged within the ranks of the Missouri Klan, across the state in Kansas City, recruiters quietly crisscrossed the Missouri-Kansas border, slowly building up a bistate presence. Though Frank Crippen received attention in the press for his work in St. Louis, much of the credit for the Klan's growth in western Missouri can be attributed to George C. McCarron. However, a level of mystique surrounds his origins, and perhaps for good reason. At the height of his power within the Klan, he battled allegations that he was secretly Catholic. McCarron was born in Michigan and spent much of his young adult life on the move. At first, his movements mirrored those of the United States Army, serving in the Spanish-American War and later being stationed throughout the West and Southwest. Not long after the conclusion of World War I, McCarron moved from Texas to Oklahoma to help with Klan recruitment. It is not known when he officially joined the Invisible Empire, but he rose quickly through the ranks. By 1920, Oklahoma newspapers referred to him as the king kleagle, or supervisor of recruitment, for the state. Within a year, Klan chapters sprouted up at Tulsa and Muskogee, both within one hundred miles of the Missouri border.[127] Unfortunately, due to the secrecy of Klan activities, records do not indicate when McCarron authorized recruiters to head northeast into Missouri. Press coverage at the time implied that his recruiting territory soon included Oklahoma, Kansas, Nebraska, and western Missouri. By 1923, McCarron moved to Kansas City, set up a regional headquarters, and donned the title of imperial representative.[128]

54   Chapter One

Though different regions of the state could claim their own significance within Missouri's hooded order, Kansas City was arguably one of the most crucial locations within the Klan's nationwide Invisible Empire. There was a reason George C. McCarron shifted from Texas and Oklahoma to Kansas City as he rose through the Klan ranks. Strategically located in the center of the United States, Kansas City was an impressive metropolis by the 1920s, a far cry from the rough-and-tumble cattle town it had been only a few generations prior. As such, Klan leaders saw value in Kansas City as a strong midwestern city with ties to nearly every major region in the United States. But beyond just simply serving as a meeting place for recruiters and leaders, it can be argued that Kansas City, in many ways, became a second imperial headquarters. Not surprisingly, the Klan moved McCarron there to set up a regional office overseeing Missouri, Kansas, Nebraska, and Oklahoma. Prominent lecturers like Dr. C. A. Stewart and Z. A. Harris soon followed with newspapers around the country, billing them as being Klan speakers from Kansas City.[129] Additionally, with George C. McCarron running Klan affairs in the borderlands between the Ozarks and Great Plains, it's unsurprising that his wife, Frances McCarron, soon rose to prominence as a key WKKK official covering the same geographic territory.[130] Likewise, to bring the entire family under the banner of the Klan, Hiram Evans placed the headquarters for the Junior Ku Klux Klan in Kansas City soon after its founding.[131] Finally, the city hosted the Second Imperial Klonvokation in 1924.[132]

In surveying the Invisible Empire in Kansas City, scholar Timothy Rives notes that much more is known about the inner workings of the organization on the Kansas side rather than in Missouri because opposition and court cases from Sunflower State political officials "left a paper trail that makes it easier to follow the tale of the hooded order." Of these Kansas Klansmen, Rives found that most were small-business owners, clerks, or railroad employees who populated local klaverns, including Wyandotte Klan No. 5, originally organized as the Sunflower Club.[133] At the same time, they frequently crossed the state line to coordinate events with their fellow members from Missouri, and the activities were numerous enough for the *Missouri Valley Independent* to declare that "Kansas City is in the best shape ever. . . . Meetings are all well attended, life, energy and good-fellowship characterize every session, and initiations are being made by the score."[134] It should be noted, however, that the newspaper's assessment of activity in the city took place after a schism over violence within the organization in Wyandotte No. 5, that led to several hundred members leaving and attempting to reorganize under a new name.[135]

Like their fellow Kansas Klansmen, the Kansas City, Missouri, Klan also experienced uneasy growing pains. When the organization first arrived in the city, local law enforcement balked at early recruiting efforts and warned residents against participating in hooded activities.[136] With George C. McCarron garnering the lion's share of the headlines, John R. Jones, listed as an imperial ambassador and organizer, quietly worked to establish klaverns throughout the city. He appeared at several notable local events, including large rallies at Convention Hall. By 1923, however, Jones's influence within local Klan circles waned. When deposed former imperial wizard William Simmons visited Kansas City to tell his side of the notorious coup, Jones served as host, while McCarron publicly warned Klansmen not to attend. For his actions, Jones was later banished from the Klan.[137] He was joined in exile by Glen Bruner, an attorney and political candidate, who had shared the podium with Jones at Klan events and shocked the Kansas City political world when he collected more than sixteen thousand votes in a failed bid to be a judge on the Jackson County Circuit Court. Still, he quit the organization over fallout from his defense of an alleged former nun and anti-Catholic speaker.[138] Around the same time, a local branch called Albert Pike Klan No. 45 severed ties with Atlanta officials and joined the National Associated Klans, a secessionist group of former Klansmen.[139]

As John R. Jones and Glen Bruner were on their way out of the Invisible Empire, Harvey C. "Harry" Hoffman emerged as a new face of the Kansas City Klan. Born in Illinois, Hoffman's family came to Missouri in the 1880s. In interviews later in life, Hoffman alleged that Jesse James had lived in the same neighborhood as his family and he spent a brief period in his youth befriending Jesse James Jr. Hoffman also claimed that it was not simply Jesse James that he was familiar with, but also other members of the James Gang, particularly Cole Younger. Hoffman was fond of Younger and bestowed the outlaw's name on his son. Hoffman was considered such an expert on the James Gang that he authored his own article, "The Younger Boys' Last Stand"; served as a consultant for Homer Croy's 1949 book, *Jesse James Was My Neighbor*"; appeared alongside Jesse James Jr. in *Under the Black Flag*, a 1921 silent film about the James Gang; and was called upon several times to debunk theories that Jesse James had lived well into the twentieth century. Though he initially worked as a lineman for the Central Union Telephone Company, Hoffman eventually developed an interest in law enforcement. For more than a decade, between 1909 and 1921, he served in the Jackson County marshal's office, first as a deputy and then as county marshal from 1917 to 1921. His position in the county marshal's office was closely affiliated with his ties to the Pendergast Machine in Kansas City. While that relationship had its benefits at first, Hoffman eventually had a falling-out with the group.[140]

Around the time that he split off from Pendergast, Hoffman aligned himself with the growing Klan presence in the city. He eagerly told the press that twenty thousand people had crowded a Convention Hall Klan rally to denounce Tom Pendergast and James A. Reed. A few years later, when the state's Democratic and Republican Conventions debated the inclusion of anti-Klan planks in their respective party platforms, Hoffman was in attendance and issued a signal of support for the watered-down planks. Soon after, he attempted to rally Democrats in the city to break off from Pendergast and join an independent party movement to reform city government. Pendergast allies alleged that Hoffman's attempts were part of a Klan-backed political apparatus. In perhaps his most famous act as a member of the Klan, Hoffman later claimed that he had officially initiated Harry S. Truman into the organization in the early 1920s, a rumor that the future president disputed and denied for the remainder of his life.[141]

Despite internal factionalism, hooded recruiters spread out from Kansas City on the Missouri side and eventually set up klaverns in Cass, Clay, Platte, Ray, Lafayette, Johnson, and Pettis Counties. In Henry County, Klinton Klan No. 109 established its klavern headquarters in a large brick building on the courthouse square.[142] In Independence, not far from the home of Harry S. Truman, a Klan event drew an estimated twenty thousand people who were mesmerized by an airplane flying overhead with an electric cross affixed to its undercarriage as well as a "snow-white stallion robed completely in the trappings of the Klan bearing a Klansman in full regalia carrying a fiery cross [that] rode swiftly across the horizon and stood as a tabaleaux [sic] on the crest of the hill."[143] When Hiram Evans visited Kansas City in 1923, the *Missouri Valley Independent* told readers that "the great lobby of the Union Station [was] filled to overflowing with thousands of Klansmen and their friends who greeted him with thundering cheers."[144]

From his administrative offices in Oklahoma City and later Kansas City, George C. McCarron directed the operations of the Klan across four states and stood in to represent the organization's interests when needed. McCarron's influence within the Missouri Klan is evident by his repeated statements in the press regarding hooded activities in the state. From defending Klan leaders to outlining the group's political stances, McCarron served as the official spokesman of the Missouri Klan. He also dispatched out-of-state recruiters across Missouri to survey the larger rural regions and ascertain what lucrative areas might exist.[145] This rural growth was desperately needed because, according to the *Missouri Valley Independent*, "Klansmen of Missouri will need to get up and hustle as Kansas is forging to the front so fast Missouri is going to be second for some time not withstanding [sic] the wonderful Klans in St. Joseph, St. Louis, Joplin, and Kansas City, Mo.... Come on Missouri Kluxers."[146]

Zach Harris was one of the most prominent and well-traveled Klan speakers in Missouri. Born near Burlington Junction in 1872, Harris spent most of his youth in northwest Missouri. In the 1890s, he enrolled at Hiram College in Ohio and, after graduating, moved to Fort Wayne, Indiana, to accept a ministerial position. A few years later, after his marriage and the birth of his son, Harris followed his parents to the newly christened state of Oklahoma. Settling in Blackwell, Harris continued as a preacher while pursuing other business and civic interests. Beginning in 1914, he mounted the first of several unsuccessful bids for Congress. When politics did not pan out, Harris turned his attention toward the Klan, rising quickly within the hooded ranks to become a national lecturer by the early 1920s.[147]

Almost immediately, Harris was dispatched to the far corners of Missouri to speak on the Klan's behalf. He did so under various names and monikers, some of his own creation and some, no doubt, created through misinterpretation. At times, he was Senator Harris or Colonel

58   Chapter One

Harris, while in some communities he was simply Z. A. Harris, Z. T. Harris, or Zach Harris. Despite the confusion on names, Harris's message was the same in every community: the United States had devolved into a moral quagmire, and it was up to the Ku Klux Klan to return the country to its proper Christian origins. Within two years of returning to Missouri on behalf of the Klan, Harris estimated that he spoke to three hundred thousand Missourians.[148] Surveying Harris's trips through Kansas, Iowa, Nebraska, and Missouri, the *Missouri Valley Independent* bragged, "Does that look like Klanism was dying out, as the enemy tries to make herself believe?"[149]

In addition to coordinated efforts to distribute Klan information via speakers and promoters, McCarron and state Klan officials also relied on influential local members to increase the Klan population. It is impossible to know the names of every kludd, klaliff, kligrapp, klokard, night hawk, and exalted cyclops in various communities. However, certain individuals' names did emerge in public spaces and thus allowed for a better understanding of the leadership and recruitment pursued by the Missouri Klan. While efforts to "klux" Missouri's urban centers began in earnest in 1921 and 1922, slow but substantial progress was made in nearly every major region of the state. When Governor Hyde issued a proclamation for a "Law and Order Sunday" in January 1923, his office was flooded with letters from statewide klaverns supporting his call to action and promising to "go on record at this time as against mob violence and unconstitutional methods of procedure by any individual, set of individuals, organization or organizations." Combing through his mail, Hyde would have seen correspondence from klaverns in Joplin, Neosho, Aurora, Springfield, Marshfield, Washburn, Granby, Diamond, Willow Springs, Koshkonong, Naylor, Malden, Adrian, Odessa, Higginsville, Holden, Pleasant Hill, St. Joseph, Wallace, Trenton, Fairfax, Agency, Gower, Holt County, and "1205 of Jackson Counties best men" in Independence.[150]

One of the first significant out-state regions to experience sizable Klan growth was in southwestern Missouri when recruiters arrived in the spring of 1921. After distributing the previously mentioned recruiting materials in the pages of the *Joplin Globe*, the organization conducted an informational meeting for business- and professional men at the rooftop garden of the Connor Hotel. More than two hundred men crowded the

"The Black Clouds of Bigotry"   59

meeting to hear a lecturer discuss the key reasons Joplin needed a Klan chapter, including the lack of a Protestant hospital, a large number of immoral businesses, and allegations that local white women had been seen in Black-owned facilities. Soon after the meeting, an advertisement in the *Globe* announced that "the Ku Klux Klan Is an Established Fact in Joplin.... [I]t already numbers among its membership scores of the best citizens" and warned those who opposed the hooded order:

> Do not fool yourself nor be misled nor deceived by the blasphemous talk you hear concerning this institution by those who do it from ignorance or by those who are lawless and corrupt. The Klan knows all about this talk. The man sitting by you on the street car may be a Klansman; the clerk who waits on you; the man who hands out your money at the bank; the man who sits by you at the ball game. They are everywhere. Their ears are open and they find out why you are talking thus.[151]

Calling itself Ozark Klan No. 3, the Joplin klavern, under the watchful eye of Exalted Cyclops Pierre Wallace, quickly established itself as one of the region's first significant hubs of hooded activity. Wallace had spent nearly his entire life in Webb City, Missouri, just north of Joplin. As such, his connections ran deep within the community, and they grew only stronger when he married Flora Rackerby in 1907. While Pierre slowly rose through the ranks of the Joplin Tobacco Company, first as a book-keeper and later as manager, Flora became a central figure in the Joplin, Carthage, and Webb City social scene as she joined several fraternal and community-betterment societies. By the 1920s, she served as the local and district director for the Parent-Teacher Association (PTA). While Flora maintained a very public presence, Pierre Wallace maneuvered in and out of the public eye. On the one hand, he was ever present at social gatherings organized by his wife. On the other hand, his organizational activities were invisible to some.[152]

Though it is difficult to track Pierre Wallace's more shadowy activities, most accounts link him to the origins of Ozarks Klan No. 3 in Joplin. A recounting of his death in 1929 attributes the origins to 1920, though more likely it was the spring of 1921. Under the direction of Wallace, Ozark Klan No. 3 undertook philanthropic ventures for the "benefit of

60   Chapter One

the poor" and declared to those who suggested that the hooded order was violent, "We, as Klansmen, do not condone murder or any other criminal act. . . . We believe we are better citizens for being Klansmen."[153] It also rapidly built up membership in the state's four-corners region and developed a network of organizers and speakers to spread the news of Klankraft throughout southern Missouri. Within a few years, lecturers visited and organized klaverns in multiple neighboring communities, including Webb City, Carthage, Monett, Neosho, Granby, Diamond, Sarcoxie, and Greenfield.[154]

Not long after Joplin joined the Invisible Empire, Klan recruiters moved on to the larger nearby city of Springfield, a major railroad hub linking the Ozarks to Kansas City and St. Louis. There, organizers warned residents that the hooded order was needed locally because "the trouble with Springfield today and the entire nation, insofar as the so-called 'crime wave' is concerned, is not lack of sufficient authority to enforce the law. . . . The trouble lies with the public . . . [who] pays too little attention to the affairs of his city, his state and his national government, how and by whom these affairs are administered."[155] At the same time, sensing local resistance that hadn't yet formed in Joplin, a hooded official told the press that the organization's goals were to promote patriotism, benevolence, and the sanctity of the home. To assuage concerns about nativism and religious intolerance, the official added, "We know that some of our most loyal citizens are foreign born, but in an effort to make the Klan thoroughly American, loyal to the flag, they draw a sharp line that no one—no matter who he is—shall become a member of the Klan unless born on American soil."[156]

Within a year, Springfield Klan No. 12 grew to an estimated three thousand members, and local officials bragged that they were recruiting thirty men a day to join the organization. Hoping to expand the local order to five thousand members by the end of 1922, the group took out sizable advertisements in city newspapers to address its key tenets and warn against vigilantism allegedly undertaken by the KKK.[157] Soon after, it bought a 116-acre plot of land north of town that included Percy's Cave (now known as Fantastic Caverns), a former recreational cavern, for $40,000 with plans to turn it into "a place for the law-abiding public to play and learn in and also making it a fitting meeting place for the members of the Missouri realm of the Ku Klux Klan." Hooded officials estimated they could fit roughly five thousand visitors in the main cavern space for events, with a clubhouse, campsites, lake, and an amphitheater seating six thousand adjacent to the cave. Klansmen soon boasted that the facility would be a "mecca for tourists throughout the continent . . . [that] will do much towards giving all who are not members of the Knights of the Ku Klux Klan a true appreciation of some of the principles upon which the latter stand."[158]

Aboveground, the Klan continued its eastward push through the Ozarks and along the Arkansas state line. By 1923, according to newspaper reports and letters sent to Governor Hyde, klaverns had popped up in Marshfield, Willow Springs, West Plains, Koshkonong, Naylor, and Malden.[159] When recruiting in southeastern Missouri, including the Lead Belt and Bootheel sections of the state, Klan officials initially turned to H. S. Ahrens and C. D. Unsell to survey the region and slowly build up local support. Originally from Oklahoma, both men served as organizers for the Klan and had shifted their territory into Missouri around the same time that McCarron moved his office to Kansas City. Within their first year in southeast Missouri, Unsell and Ahrens claimed they had established Klan chapters in Poplar Bluff, Neelyville, Harviell, Doniphan, Piedmont, Williamsville, Puxico, Dexter, Bernie, Bloomfield, Illmo, Fornfelt, Chaffee, Sikeston, Morley, Charleston, Morehouse, Parma, New Madrid, Lilbourn, Marston, Portageville, Gideon, Caruthersville, Hayti, Steele, Campbell, Kennett, and Senath, with an estimated hooded population in the region of more than six thousand.[160]

If Ahrens and Unsell were credited with expanding the Invisible Empire into southeastern Missouri, O. L. Spurgeon soon laid claim to strengthening its hold on the region. Born in Iowa, Otis L. Spurgeon, or O. L. as he was later billed, knew from an early age that he was interested in ministry. Though he called Iowa home, he enrolled at the Kansas City Theological Seminary in the early 1900s to become a Baptist minister. While still a student, he found work in churches around the Kansas City area, and when he graduated, he headed to Colorado for a brief tenure at a church in Denver. He soon returned to Iowa, first in Boone and later at Nashua. In 1921, after a successful revival in Poplar Bluff, Missouri, Spurgeon was called upon to serve as the new pastor of the Poplar Bluff

First Baptist Church. He stayed in that role until 1923, when a higher calling influenced his resignation.[161]

That higher calling was the Ku Klux Klan, but his fateful decision to resign his pastorate in 1923 was far from his first foray into the Invisible Empire. Spurgeon had already been preaching a message of Americanism and Protestantism years before the Klan's rebirth. As early as 1911, Spurgeon began publicly warning about the dangers of Catholicism. At first, he kept his comments strictly to his pulpit and the pages of the *Word and Way* newspaper. But by the mid-1910s, Spurgeon had become a traveling lecturer on anti-Catholicism.[162] In 1914, Spurgeon had a fateful encounter with a Denver group who challenged his anti-Catholic claims and later physically assaulted him. The attack and Spurgeon's defense of his comments earned him space in newspapers nationwide and gave the *Menace* a Protestant hero to glorify in its pages. Spurgeon's ordeal and the eventual arrests of those involved provided the *Menace* with nearly a month's worth of content.[163]

When he returned to Iowa, Spurgeon led an unassuming life in the pulpit but secretly amassed considerable influence within the expanding Invisible Empire. According to Spurgeon's recollections, he had seen a magazine article about the resurrected Klan and immediately requested more information. Soon after, he became one of the first Klansmen in Iowa. Not satisfied to simply be a member of the hooded order—and given his history within the anti-Catholic speakers circuit a decade earlier—Spurgeon quickly went to work recruiting for the Klan in Iowa and Minnesota. He was assigned as King Kleagle of Minnesota and, in his own words, became an influential Klansman in the Upper Midwest. It was not to last, however, and by 1921, just as the *New York World's* exposé on the inner workings of the Klan hit newsstands, Spurgeon publicly denounced his ouster as king kleagle. He was careful in his criticism, though, as he preferred to attack the men who he felt had done him wrong instead of the organization as a whole.[164]

Nevertheless, soon after arriving in Poplar Bluff, Spurgeon found himself a new home in Missouri's Invisible Empire. Initially, he kept his support for the Klan confined to his Sunday sermons. Yet as the Klan's membership numbers in southeast Missouri grew, Spurgeon went out on the recruiting trail as a speaker. Typically, his circuit contained most of the eastern Ozarks and the Bootheel, but by the mid-1920s, he made stops in Arkansas and Tennessee. Given his previous recruiting skills in Iowa and Minnesota, it is not surprising that Spurgeon was elected exalted cyclops of Poplar Bluff Klan No. 48 and quickly went to work establishing a new klavern building near what was being called Klandale.[165] Spurgeon's time on the road and his involvement in the Klan soon proved problematic for his pastorate, and in late 1923 he announced his resignation from First Baptist Church. The ink was barely dry on his ministerial resignation when Spurgeon announced his resignation as exalted cyclops.[166]

Spurgeon had grown too big for Poplar Bluff. Though he still maintained a presence in the community, he slowly transitioned into a role as a national lecturer, which took him to Memphis. From his new home outside of Memphis, Spurgeon could better travel through Tennessee and help his daughter, Velma, as she embarked on a career as a lady kleagle for the WKKK in the state. Despite his new position, he still found time to cross the Mississippi River back into Missouri on behalf of the Klan, including to dedicate the new klavern in Poplar Bluff in 1924.[167] Yet even with his growing influence within the Mississippi River valley Klan networks, he soon faced a problem similar to what he had encountered years prior in Iowa and Minnesota. As before, Spurgeon denounced mismanagement within the Tennessee Klan and expressed displeasure at the shakeup in leadership. When Klan officials came to Memphis in the fall of 1924 to reorganize the local chapter, a fight ensued—both literally and figuratively. When the dust settled, several local Klansmen, including O. L. Spurgeon, were banished from the Invisible Empire.[168]

After Spurgeon departed southeast Missouri for Memphis, the Klan remained active in the region. In his diary accounts from New Madrid County, businessman Charles Merlin Barnes documented several Klan events near his home in Marston, a town named for his mother's family located a short distance from a massive bend in the Mississippi River. According to his diary entries from the mid-1920s, Barnes took note of KKK and WKKK activity in Marston, Lilbourn, and Malden and attended these gatherings as often as possible. He spoke little of the violence in the region often pinned on the local Klan and instead offered positive reflections on the public lectures given by Klan speakers, including a minister from nearby Portageville who gave, in Barnes's opinion, "a real good talk" in the winter of 1926.[169]

Visiting southern Missouri in 1923, Dr. William M. Campbell found the region to be an ideal location. In fact, after touring several towns, he admitted that all he encountered were "cheerful and enthusiastic, with no clouds on the horizon."[170] Recruiting efforts locally suggested that there was some truth to his words. Nevertheless, while he touted the growth of klaverns across southern Missouri, Campbell also alleged that his hometown was all anyone wanted to talk about during his travels: "Everywhere people were talking about St. Joseph—what we have done here and what we are doing."[171] St. Joseph was on everyone's mind because of the hooded juggernaut that Campbell had helped establish in the town best known for its ties to the Pony Express along the banks of the Missouri River.

Though the Ozarks and later the Bootheel became two of the first regions of the state to embrace the Invisible Empire, St. Joseph Klan No. 4 soon rivaled other klaverns as Missouri's unofficial Klan headquarters due to the leadership of Dr. William M. Campbell. Born in Kansas, Campbell grew up not far from the city that would witness his rise to the top of Missouri's Invisible Empire. His father was a Protestant minister, but instead of following in his footsteps, Campbell opted to enter the medical profession. This pursuit of medicine brought Campbell to St. Joseph, where he graduated from Northwestern Medical College in 1893. He returned to Kansas to practice medicine but eventually returned to St. Joseph after spending time at Jefferson Medical College in Pennsylvania. By the early twentieth century, Campbell was a well-respected doctor in St. Joseph and a member of several fraternal organizations, including the Masons and Odd Fellows.[172] His time in St. Joseph was not without controversy, however, as he was investigated, tried, and found not guilty of manslaughter following the death of a woman from a surgical procedure, or a "criminal operation," as it was referred to in newspapers, he performed on her in 1910.[173] While it is hard to pinpoint exactly when Campbell joined the Klan in accepting his reelection as exalted cyclops of St. Joseph Klan No. 4 in 1924, he noted the work completed under his leadership since 1922.[174]

With Campbell at the helm, St. Joseph Klan No. 4 overcame sizable opposition from municipal officials, including Mayor Elliot Marshall, who told the *St. Joseph Gazette* that he was "so damnably strong against the Ku Klux Klan . . . that I will do all in my power as mayor and personally to stop it."[175] After initially meeting at the Klan Temple at Third and Edmond Streets, the organization later bought the twenty-five-hundred-seat Crystal Theater and turned it into the new klavern headquarters.[176] The local order also frequently utilized Lake Contrary, a recreational park southwest of town, for many of its larger events, including a parade and picnic in August 1923 where Klansmen were asked to "Bring Your Robe! Bring Your Families! Bring Your Protestant Friends" to "Help Make St. Joseph the 'Klan City.'"[177] By the end of 1924, local members could attend meetings of the Klavaliers and Kamelia Kourt No. 1 on Tuesdays, St. Joseph Klan No. 4 on Thursdays, and WKKK on Fridays.[178] Beyond the traditional gatherings, speakers, and philanthropy, St. Joseph Klan No. 4 also received notable attention for its campaign to reform law enforcement in Buchanan County following the death of Nellie Hale in 1922. Finally, the organization held close ties to the *Missouri Valley Independent*, a locally produced newspaper with a readership throughout Missouri, Iowa, Nebraska, and Kansas.

Though it did not publicly carry his name on the editorial banner, the *Missouri Valley Independent* was closely connected to St. Joseph Klan No. 4 and Exalted Cyclops William M. Campbell. Not long after its founding, the publication quickly established itself as the purveyor of Klan news in the Missouri River valley. In addition to filling its pages with news from neighboring klaverns, the newspaper also provided its readers with commentaries on pressing issues in St. Joseph and a steady dose of anti-Catholicism. If its readers weren't already subscribers to anti-Catholic newspapers like the *New Menace*, the *Protestant*, and *Fellowship Forum*, the *Missouri Valley Independent* was more than happy to reprint national articles. While toeing the line of Klan edicts and policies issued from Imperial Headquarters in Atlanta, the publishers also circulated articles expressing support for women's involvement in the Klan, including sharing up-to-the-minute information about the formation of a women's auxiliary and advertisements for meetings of various Protestant study clubs. These study clubs, particularly the Independent Protestant Woman's Association and Grand League of Protestant Women of America, became important feeder groups for membership in the WKKK.[179]

Chapter One

When the *Missouri Valley Independent* first started, it was led by the father-and-son team of Alfred Fleming and C. M. Fleming. Born in Palmyra, Missouri, in 1851, Alfred Fleming, or Ajax as he was also called, had a long career in the publishing industry. After earning valuable experience at a newspaper in his hometown, he moved quickly around the Midwest as a publisher and editor, including stops in Omaha, Nebraska; St. Paul, Minnesota; Quincy, Illinois; and Louisville, Kentucky. In Missouri, his newspaper career took him to St. Louis, Braymer, Richmond, Ash Grove, Springfield, and St. Joseph. When not engaged with newspapers, Fleming spent a portion of his career around the turn of the twentieth century in the United States Consular Service. Though he was frequently on the move, St. Joseph was his home for much of his life. Earlier in life, he helped with the *Herald* and *Gazette* in the city. Still, the *Missouri Valley Independent* earned him a strong reputation for his editorial commentaries in the 1920s.[180] While his father served as editor, C. M. Fleming was the manager. Like his father, C. M. was no stranger to the newspaper business, though his experience was accrued later in life. Born in Davenport, Iowa, C. M. moved with his father from newspaper job to newspaper job in the late nineteenth century, though he spent most of his youth in Missouri. After attending Western Normal College in Nebraska, he initially sought work as a railroad telegraph operator and engineer. By the start of the 1920s, he was back in St. Joseph and working with his father to establish what would become the *Missouri Valley Independent*.[181]

When not covering the daily activities of St. Joseph Klan No. 4, the *Missouri Valley Independent* kept readers updated on the hooded order's spread across the region. In the northwest corner of the state, these recruiting efforts were largely directed by the St. Joseph Klan, particularly Campbell and J. E. Baker, a Methodist minister and lecturer. Having lived in St. Joseph since 1914, Baker was familiar with the revival circuit in northern Missouri and frequently left his pastorate at Spruce Street Methodist Church to give addresses on the tenets of the Klan in towns such as Gower, Union Star, Holt, Hardin, Weston, and Rochester.[182] Baker was joined on the road by other Klan recruiters who slowly established klaverns in places like Fairfax, Maryville, Maysville, Bethany, Trenton, and Chillicothe.[183] In Kirksville, historian Jason McDonald found that the local Klan's "ranks and public presence exploded" by the mid-1920s.[184] Within a short period, the organization and its recruiters had swept across Missouri's entire northern prairie and soon converged on Mark Twain's hometown of Hannibal. Not long after the group's arrival, Zach Harris gave a lecture to an estimated crowd of two thousand, and the Mississippi Valley Knights of the Ku Klux Klan organized a patriotic pageant in Robel Park that featured more than two hundred Klansmen.[185]

While the organization had made successful recruiting strides in Missouri's urban centers, through the Ozarks and the Bootheel, and across the northern prairie, it found difficulty in what is known today as the "German Heritage Corridor." Dotted primarily by German immigrant communities dating back to the early to mid-nineteenth century, the residents of the corridor mounted sizable opposition to the Klan just as strongly as they had opposed earlier attempts at Prohibition. Not surprisingly, progress was slow for the Klan as recruiters met fierce resistance in many communities. It was not until the summer of 1923 that any significant Klan presence was felt between Jefferson City and St. Louis on both banks of the Missouri River. Being the state's capital, Jefferson City stood as a key prize for the Invisible Empire. As such, the organization hoped that the local klavern would hold significant sway over not only civic affairs, but also the centers of the state's political power. It's not surprising then that John P. Gordon and Heber Nations quickly emerged as key liaisons between the capitol and the Klan.

Born on a farm near Corder, Missouri, in 1866, John P. Gordon was the son of Major George P. Gordon, who had ridden with General Joseph Shelby and the Confederate States of America during the Civil War. Making his home in Lexington, Gordon served as postmaster and deputy county clerk for Lafayette County and sat on the Board of Managers of the Missouri School for the Deaf in Fulton. By the turn of the twentieth century, Gordon was a well-respected traveling salesman and made major inroads into the state Democratic Party. In 1908, he was elected state auditor and served in that role until 1916. Described as a "militant Democrat," Gordon never shied away from his ties to both the Democratic Party and his family's southern roots. While it is not known when Gordon joined the Invisible Empire, his name was connected to

68 Chapter One

the hooded order as early as 1924 in relation to the Dedication Day controversy. Gordon acknowledged his ties to the Jefferson City Klan later in life.[186]

If Gordon represented the Democratic side of the Klan in Jefferson City, Heber Nations sat across the political aisle and next to Gordon in the local klavern. Born in Ste. Genevieve, Missouri, in 1888, Heber Nations was the son of Gilbert O. Nations, the editorial firebrand whose commentaries appeared in publications like the *Menace*, the *New Menace*, *Fellowship Forum*, and the *Protestant*. Like his father, Nations spent his youth in the state's Lead Belt region and entered the journalism profession by purchasing the *Bonne Terre News* after graduating from college in Cape Girardeau. In 1914, he moved to Jefferson City to work as a newspaper correspondent and eventually accrued enough capital and clout to buy a controlling interest in the *Jefferson City Daily Post*. His military experience along the US-Mexico border in the campaign against Pancho Villa earned him an appointment as adjutant general of the Missouri National Guard. Finally, Nations's marriage to Alma Conrath in 1918 boosted his status in Jefferson City society and secured a prominent place in the statewide Republican Party. In 1923, Governor Arthur Hyde appointed Nations as commissioner of labor.[187]

With both Nations and Gordon in the fold by 1923, the Klan quickly established a presence in Jefferson City and set up a klavern in the Merchants Bank Building, strategically located across the street from the new state capitol building. The *Patriot* proudly announced that Jefferson City was "swarming with citizen-Klansmen."[188] A few weeks later, fiery crosses were lit at several locations cited for illegal activities, including a roadhouse and a local brothel. In response to the Klan's intimidation, unknown assailants targeted homes and businesses allegedly owned by local Klansmen with gunshots, including the large plateglass window at the office of Heber Nation's *Jefferson City Daily Post*.[189] Not to be outdone, the *Patriot* called upon hooded supporters in Jefferson City to respond to the anti-Klan policies of Mayor C. W. Thomas and Joseph Goldman, editor of the *Daily Democrat-Tribune*.[190]

With its proximity to the local klavern headquarters, the Jefferson City Klan held meetings in the state capitol building on multiple occasions. In February 1924, several hundred guests packed the chamber of the Missouri House of Representatives to hear what was originally described as a "lecture on a patriotic subject by a speaker of national importance." The vague description duped those who regulated who could rent the space because when the festivities began, Z. A. Harris arose and spoke on "Americanism and the Ku Klux Klan." Yet critics of the program alleged that flyers for the lecture were distributed throughout town, including the front door of the nearby St. Peter's Catholic Church, and featured Klan insignia. As letters flooded into the city demanding to know where the governor stood on the matter, Heber Nations confessed that he helped secure the chamber for the local Klan after a speaker representing the Knights of Columbus was allowed access to the same space a few weeks prior: "I deemed it highly probable that local people would be interested in the official attitude of the klan [sic], as given by one of its authorized lecturers."[191] In the aftermath, the *St. Louis Star* editorialized the decision to allow the hooded order within the Missouri House of Representatives chamber by featuring a cartoon of the capitol dome topped by a cross and whip-wielding Klansman instead of the actual statue of the Roman goddess Ceres.[192]

Not to be deterred, the Jefferson City Klan returned to the capitol building in the summer of 1924 to conduct a secret membership meeting discussing potential political candidates the organization would back in that year's primary and general elections. Upon learning not only that the Klan was meeting again in the legislative chambers for the Klonvokation but that hooded officials had locked the doors to prevent unwanted visitors, Hyde ordered the organizers to either open the chamber doors to curious citizens or leave the capitol building. The Klan complied with Hyde's request, but before reporters could properly situate themselves in the upper gallery to observe the festivities, Klan officials moved the meeting across the street to the Merchants Bank Building.[193] While Hyde received his fair share of accolades for his heavy-handed approach to the second Klan gathering, some people were less than pleased that the governor refused to support 100 percent Americanism, as one Missourian advised: "You may yet reach the place where you will be proud of the Klan in Missouri."[194]

At the end of 1924, through orchestrated efforts from the Jefferson City klavern that now numbered an estimated one thousand members,

70   Chapter One

Klan activity was reported in several neighboring counties, including Callaway, Moniteau, Cooper, Gasconade, Maries, and Phelps.[195] In Montgomery County, a Jonesburg resident confided to Governor Hyde that the Klan was "pretty thick here and I know most of them."[196] Over in Boone County, home of the University of Missouri, local newspapers reported that "several [people] have dug down for the ten dollar initiation fee" in Centralia, but the "burning cross had not burned; the white hooded figures had not appeared, and Columbia was still without the Klan."[197] Despite its sizable population of ten thousand—not including students at the town's three colleges—Columbia was one of the last Missouri communities to organize a klavern.

While the Missouri Klan may have felt it was on an upward trajectory membership-wise by the time the Jefferson City klavern held a large rally on the outskirts of town soon after Dedication Day, by 1925 cracks had formed in the supposedly sturdy foundation of the Invisible Empire. When tens of thousands of Klansmen and -women from across the United States paraded through the streets of Washington, DC, in August 1925, many observers viewed the white-robed procession as a show of strength for the hooded order. Back in Jefferson City, some former Klansmen were a little more skeptical. John P. Gordon was noticeably upset when members of the press inquired of him about the upcoming parade and festivities. Unlike Dedication Day—a mere ten months earlier—Gordon had no interest in what was going on under the shadow of the capitol building. Despite rumors that he would be one of Jefferson City's delegates to Washington, DC, Gordon told reporters that he had "not the remotest idea of attending the Washington conference." When pressed for further comment on why he refused to attend Hiram Evans's grandiose Klan parade down Pennsylvania Avenue, Gordon was blunt: "I do not intend to attend any other meeting of the Ku Klux Klan. . . . I see no need for further existence of the klan [sic] as now operated."[198]

Since the Klan had first arrived in Jefferson City, Gordon had never shied away from admitting his membership in the hooded order. Now, however, he joined a growing list of Missourians discarding their robes and distancing themselves from the organization. The *Jefferson City Tribune* congratulated Gordon and declared that "the Klan is doomed

"The Black Clouds of Bigotry"   71

in Jefferson City because it has been found out." Not one to turn down a fight with the secret organization, the *Tribune* used Gordon's exodus to remind readers that "the men who organized it wanted $10, and they were willing to throw a whole community into the throes of religious hatred and strife to enrich themselves. . . . [A] thing like the klan [*sic*] couldn't live long in free America."[199] When asked to explain why he severed his ties to the Klan, Gordon gave a frank portrayal of life in the Invisible Empire:

> Like thousands of others, I was led into the Klan by misrepresenta-
> tion of its policies and purposes. Until I discovered its evil tenden-
> cies, I made no concealment of my membership in the organization.
> Now since I have become convinced that its practices are opposed
> to good citizenship and good government, I shall, with equal frank-
> ness announce that I am no longer affiliated with the Ku Klux Klan.
> Misrepresentation and misguided zeal have brought thousands of
> good men and women into the organization but I am constrained to
> believe that they will abandon it when they realize its evil trend. . . .
> I will say that the klan [*sic*] was claimed to be founded upon the
> splendid principle of assisting, in a lawful way, the enforcement of
> the law and making communities better places in which to live and
> raise our families. This exalted principle has been lost sight of and
> the efforts of the organization turned to arousing strife and hatred,
> to the end that good men and women may be drawn into the or-
> ganization. Assisting in law enforcement has dwindled into a mere
> side line, and the main efforts are devoted to playing small poltiies
> [*sic*] and dividing communities into warring factions.[200]

Hasty exits from the Invisible Empire, much like John P. Gordon's, are an oft-told story in historical literature on the second Klan. By the mid- to late 1920s, a sizable portion of the Klan's membership had quietly renounced their past ties to the organization. Within a few more years, numbers dipped so low that Imperial Wizard Hiram Evans embarked on a cross-country scramble to find a solution to bring individuals back into the fold. His efforts met with little success, as many former mem- bers had put away their robes, hoods, and ephemera into dark corners of their homes and attics. Others outright burned the evidence, which was never to be seen again. It was a curious situation. Men and women were eager and proud to attend the events of a group that promised to remake America into the nation of their remembered and, at times, misremembered youth. Yet, at the same time, it was a group so plagued by scandal and infamy that these same individuals wanted few to know they had ever been part of it. Nevertheless, while few publicized their exit as Gordon did, many former members still held the same views and prejudices that ultimately led them to join the group in the first place.

It is easy to see why scholars have argued that the Klan and its ideology never really disappeared from American life, beyond even the reemergence of its next generation during the civil rights movement after World War II. The tenets promoted by the Klan, including Protestantism, Prohibition enforcement, political reform, and protecting the racial status quo, had deep roots in Missouri. Thus, recruiters found a receptive home and a groundswell of support for the hooded order when the organization arrived within the state's boundaries and promised to abide by such principles. Throughout the early to mid-1920s, the Klan slowly built up a sizable membership base and drew sympathetic support from countless Missourians who never officially joined. Yet the dreams of an army of white Protestant Missourians numbering in the hundreds of thousands as part of a larger Invisible Empire of millions of their fellow Americans never came to fruition. While it is correct to assume that the state membership numbered in the tens of thousands, estimates from Klansmen and -women about their strength during the interwar years were greatly overstated.

CHAPTER TWO

"Masked Malcontents"
Violence, Vigilantism, and the Anti-Klan Press

ON A SUMMER evening in June 1921, Frank Cummel and Sam Malloy awoke to unexpected visitors outside their homes in Fair Play, Missouri. They didn't know what the group wanted, nor could they identify the masked individuals, but before they could ask, the ghostly figures loaded Cummel and Malloy into waiting automobiles and hurried out of town. The vehicles sped through Polk County toward neighboring Cedar County when the caravan stopped at a bridge along a lonely stretch of road. Hustled to the side of the road, Cummel and Malloy were stripped of their clothes and severely beaten with leather straps and other objects. As they prepared to depart for parts unknown, the masked assailants warned the men to leave Polk County as soon as possible. Both men struggled to their feet as the automobiles disappeared into the darkness and walked—bruised and bloodied—back to Fair Play.[1]

In the light of the next morning, Cummel and Malloy displayed their wounds to town officials and recounted the alleged events of the previous night. Word of the incident didn't stay in Fair Play long. The front page of the *Republican* in nearby Springfield recapped the attack for its readers the next day, and by the end of the week, the kidnapping story spread through the Ozarks and across the country. From there, the mystery only deepened. When pressed by authorities and reporters to explain what happened that night, Fair Play residents provided few leads. "Ask the White Caps" was a common response. As to whom the White Caps were, residents didn't provide a clear answer to this question either. While most rural residents confirmed that some type of vigilante group existed, no one knew exactly how many members lived in the area, with numbers ranging from 150 to more than 500. Additionally, some residents explained it as a recent phenomenon, while others claimed that such activities had occurred for several years.[2]

73

74 Chapter Two

Despite the initial inconclusive information, the incident deeply concerned residents of southwest Missouri. The *Fair Play Advocate* warned the masked vigilantes that "such action is never justifiable . . . [because] there is grave danger that it in time will degenerate into an instrument for the avenging of fancied private wrongs."[3] A few days later, a large contingent of residents presented a petition to Polk County officials asking for suppression of the violence and an investigation into threatening letters reportedly left at several homes. With the situation quickly escalating, Prosecuting Attorney G. C. Burnside announced an investigation into the matter.[4] By early July, law enforcement in both Polk and Cedar Counties felt confident that they had identified the individuals involved in the attack, but with little evidence to tie these men to the scene, they were released.[5]

Though there was an anonymous nature to the white-capping activities, the similarities between night riding and mask wearing drew immediate comparisons to recent alleged attacks by the Ku Klux Klan in neighboring states. This connection was not lost on local officials and newspaper reporters, who noted that the attackers supposedly wore masks like the Klan. As stories of the vigilante incident continued to circulate throughout the Ozarks, William Simmons, imperial wizard of the Ku Klux Klan, issued a public statement denouncing the attack and offered a $100 reward for the capture of those involved. Seeking to keep recruitment going in the region and fearing further negative publicity, Simmons assured the public that the Klan did not participate in violent acts and likened the incident to a family quarrel. He also claimed that no Klan chapter existed—yet— in Fair Play; thus, it was doubtful that Klansmen were involved. Finally, Simmons took direct aim at the hooded order's opponents who, in his words, "seek to put the blame for these affairs upon the Ku Klux Klan [and] seek to slander this organization deliberately."[6]

As the Ku Klux Klan slowly grew from its Atlanta roots, newspapers took note of the organization's recruiting efforts as it spread across the country. Since Klan recruiters usually paid for advertisements in local newspapers regarding upcoming events in the hope of attracting both a large crowd and a positive follow-up story afterward, the press tended to merely serve as the reporter of hooded activity in the early years. The press obliged by accepting the organization's money and running short

"Masked Malcontents" 75

articles on these events with little praise or denouncement, sometimes even printing Klan-crafted reviews of events verbatim. Yet out of this regular news coverage emerged a group of editors and publishers who were quite vocal in their criticism and opposition to the Klan. Whether publishing articles on alleged Klan atrocities in their pages or prominently placing editorials that denounced the rhetoric and recruitment of Klansmen, these newspapers undertook the most influential element of early anti-Klan activism and proved to be a thorn in the side of the hooded order.

At the same time, the press's intervention regarding the Klan successfully pushed politicians, community leaders, and private citizens to speak out and investigate the hooded order. With each new rally and fiery cross, newspapers such as the *St. Louis Post-Dispatch*, *St. Louis Argus*, *Kansas City Catholic Register*, *Kansas City Call*, *Poplar Bluff Republican*, *Vienna Home-Adviser*, and *Warrensburg Star-Journal* called on readers to vocalize their opposition to the Klan and demand local and state politicians act accordingly. Klan leaders criticized this call to action, yet it proved quite effective as key state politicians, such as Governor Arthur Hyde, Congressman Leonidas Dyer, and St. Louis mayor Henry Kiel, soon denounced the Klan and signaled their support for a congressional investigation into the violence allegedly perpetrated by Klan members.

Finally, as opposition mounted in the pages of the state's newspapers, the Klan worked quickly to distance itself from and openly condemn vigilantism and violence in Missouri. Two major instances of the Klan objecting to violence and working to stop vigilantism will be covered in this chapter. These grassroots efforts include the fallout from the murder of Nellie Hale in St. Joseph in 1922 and the sharecropper violence that plagued southeast Missouri in the first half of the 1920s. Taken together, these two instances offered a valuable opportunity for the Klan, as well as anti-Klan forces, to make their case that lawlessness needed to be addressed and that they, not their opponents, were the best individuals to stop it. Nevertheless, Missourians continued to associate violence with the ever-expanding presence of the Invisible Empire.

Even before the arrival of the Klan in the state, Missourians kept a close eye on the growth and development of the order throughout the United States because newspapers regularly published information about alleged

Klan activity. Many articles initially focused on the modern Klan and its relationship to its Reconstruction predecessor. The *Columbia Evening Missourian* noted that "the Klan had a purpose during the reconstruction period, and when just government was restored to the South that purpose was accomplished," while the *Kansas City Star* declared that the revived Klan was a "Memorial to the Night Riders of the Reconstruction Days."[7] As much as these early stories appeared to celebrate the Klan, the subject of vigilantism soon became a recurring theme in many newspapers. Several atrocities allegedly tied to the Klan in Texas, particularly the whipping of an African American man and the branding of "K.K.K." upon his face, became feature stories throughout Missouri.[8] A little more than two months after its glorified history lesson of the hooded order, the *Kansas City Star* concluded that the "Lone Star State may take arms against the seas of troubles its modern 'Ku Klux' has stirred up."[9]

As violent acts supposedly committed by the hooded order increased nationwide in the summer of 1921—including the attack of Frank Cummel and Sam Malloy near Fair Play—newspaper editors began to question the motives of the revived Klan.[10] In St. Louis, the *Church Progress* argued that the Klan's role in vigilantism needed to be cleaned up and cleaned out.[11] The *Jewish Voice* advised its readers that if the Klan was successfully broken up, the masks should be removed from its leaders' faces and their regalia "consigned for all times to the bon fire of oblivion."[12] In encouraging similar steps, the *St. Louis Post-Dispatch* connected the Klan to lawlessness and terrorism and demanded that the organization disband.[13] The *Modern View* proclaimed that the group's "strength and numbers . . . are much exaggerated and that its life is destined to be brief."[14] The *St. Louis Star* warned residents of the dangers posed by "mysterious masked men" when they were allowed to become lawless and mete out punishment against rivals and enemies outside of law enforcement and the court system.[15] The only major St. Louis newspaper to initially avoid the subject was the *Globe-Democrat*, which offered reprinted articles about vigilantism in Texas and other parts of the country but brought up the Klan only to suggest that perhaps the hooded order could be utilized to stem the tide of violence, particularly when it came to lynching.[16]

"Masked Malcontents"   77

While the St. Louis press generally expressed anti-Klan sentiments, no local newspaper targeted the hooded order more than the *Argus*. As early as January 1921, roughly four months before Klan recruiters even stepped foot in the city, the *Argus* felt it necessary to issue a strong warning against the organization. There was "no room for the Ku Klux Klan," the newspaper argued, and if the order continued to grow, "the Negroes of today will meet the white robed wizards of the night with a different spirit to what their fathers met it fifty years ago."[17] When it was rumored that William Simmons might visit St. Louis on a grand tour of the United States, the *Argus* suggested that the African American community "fight fire with fire . . . a coat of tar and a coat of feathers will be too good for him."[18]

The *Argus*'s role as the city's chief Klan fighter was rooted in the beliefs of its publisher, J. E. Mitchell. Born in Reconstruction-era Alabama, Mitchell spent much of his early life in the South. After serving in the Spanish-American War and the later Philippines War, he moved to St. Louis in 1904, where his brother William soon joined him. After a brief period of work in the service industry, the Mitchell brothers entered the insurance business, with J. E. becoming the general manager of the Western Union Relief Association (WURA). The *Argus* originally began as a newspaper affiliated with the organization. Still, when the WURA went out of business after only a few short years, the Mitchell brothers turned what would become the *Argus* into a weekly newspaper serving the city's Black population. As historian Debra Foster Greene notes, the *Argus*'s slogan that it was "published in the Interest of Colored People" allowed it to connect with its St. Louis readership and quickly become the city's most prominent African American newspaper.[19]

Due to his prior work in the Western Union Relief Association, J. E. Mitchell held a notable place within St. Louis's African American population. From this perch, Mitchell used the *Argus* to spread his views on the need for uplift in the city. He preached a gospel that adhered to that of Booker T. Washington but also expressed some support for W. E. B. Du Bois. In politics, however, he refused to stray far from the Republican Party, and the *Argus* was a Republican newspaper and stayed that way until the 1930s. The *Argus* kept close tabs on the actions of

FIGURE 6. Joseph E. Mitchell, date unknown. Courtesy of University of Missouri, St. Louis Black History Project Collection (S0201). The State Historical Society of Missouri.

local politicians within the party and frequently criticized city officials for kowtowing to discriminatory and segregationist policies. A common target was Mayor Henry Kiel, who, despite promises to do so during his campaigns for office, had not appointed African Americans to key positions in city government.[20]

In addition to holding Republicans accountable, the *Argus* also closely monitored the activities of the Klan in St. Louis. Historian Debra Foster Greene argues that the *Argus* "spearheaded the African American community's struggle for lawful protection against the activities and actions of the Ku Klux Klan."[21] When local Klan officials claimed that members of city hall and the police department had joined the hooded order, the *Argus* demanded answers from city leaders, citing that those on the city payroll, especially police officers, could not serve two masters—municipal government and the Ku Klux Klan. In pointing to the ouster of Klansmen from law enforcement positions in other cities, the newspaper called on the police department, particularly police commissioner Victor Miller, to fire any officer who admitted to being in the Klan.[22] While waiting for an answer regarding the status of police officers, the *Argus* also demanded that Kiel make a statement on the Klan. Though acknowledging that an outright condemnation was unnecessary, the *Argus* noted that "as Mayor of a City like St. Louis, with its many different nationalities and religious beliefs, we could not but think that Mayor Kiel would have spoken on the subject."[23] Such a statement was important to the *Argus*:

> From Maine to California, the Ku-Klux-Klan has for the past six months been the subject of much discussion. Men from the highest in public affairs to the man in the gutter have passed judgment on this organization, which has caused so much agitation and newspaper comment. We have watched with considerable interest, the conduct of public officials toward the Klan, not only in St. Louis, but in other cities in different section of the country. This observation was made necessary by the announced policy of the Klan to "first get public officials" as members. Following this announcement policy, the mayors of many cities and other public officials denounced the Ku-Klux-Klan and pledged the assistance of their good offices in suppression such an organization.... But to date, we have not heard a word from Mayor Kiel with regard to the activities of the Klan in St. Louis, nor his attitude toward the same. . . . Surely it would be the manly thing for the Mayor, as chief executive of the city, to speak on the subject—"Silence gives consent."[24]

City officials, especially Mayor Kiel, may have been silent on the Klan issue, but this was not the case for the *Argus* and its readers. Drawing on the negative press aimed at the Invisible Empire, the local NAACP focused its attention on the Klan as well as recent showings of *The Birth of a Nation* and declared both to be "a menace to peaceful government." Initially issuing a resolution asking the mayor to stop showings of the film, a committee composed of NAACP members decided to take the matter directly to Kiel. In a short meeting, the committee visited the mayor in his office and addressed concerns they had regarding the film, the Klan, and racial intolerance. Kiel listened to the complaints and then dismissed the group without immediate action. In response to Kiel's seeming indifference, the *Argus* pointed out that the mayor had not changed his opinion of the film since he had previously supported the showing of *The Birth of a Nation* when it first appeared in St. Louis. The *Argus* juxtaposed this reaction by pointing out how quickly the mayor

80   Chapter Two

had acted when Jews protested the selling of Henry Ford's *Dearborn Independent* and its anti-Semitic articles on St. Louis street corners. Finally, the *Argus* called on Victor Miller to do what Kiel would not do: inform the citizens of St. Louis about where the police department stood on the Klan.[25]

Not satisfied with the delay in the mayor's response to the *Argus*'s inquiry, the Missouri Negro Republican League Club and Central Civic League soon organized a mass meeting at the Tabernacle Baptist Church where a large crowd of roughly fifteen hundred occupied every available space both inside and outside of the church. For those in attendance, including J. E. Mitchell and Alderman Luke E. Hart, there was only one subject on the agenda: the Ku Klux Klan. Many of the speakers criticized Mayor Kiel for his inaction, including Rev. T. J. Moppins, who had denounced the Klan in his previous Sunday sermon by claiming that "the wonder that Christian America has such a spirit dominating it at this time, is what give pain to all liberty-loving citizens of the christian [*sic*] world."[26] In drafting another resolution demanding that the mayor take action and denounce the Klan, it is likely that those at the meeting expected Kiel to continue to ignore and dismiss their request. The mayor, however, was more receptive to this new resolution and immediately issued an official denouncement of the Klan.[27]

Despite Kiel's statement against the Klan, the *Argus* continued to push city officials for further action against the hooded order. It called for the mayor to ban all Klan-related activities in the city and for Victor Miller to bring forth an investigation of Klan membership in the police department. The *Argus* also asked Luke E. Hart, who had previously worked with the Knights of Columbus to combat anti-Catholicism, to present an anti-Klan resolution to the St. Louis Board of Aldermen.[28] As the *Argus* had hoped, public pressure over the Klan issue forced the Board of Aldermen to take up just such a resolution at its October 1921 meeting, declaring that "the Board of Aldermen of the City of St. Louis is unalterably opposed to this un-American organization and hereby calls upon the Governor of the State to do all within his power to lawfully suppress the Ku-Klux-Klan within the State of Missouri."[29] After being read, the resolution was brought to a vote and immediately went down in defeat as several aldermen abstained from voting, citing a lack of clear information regarding the Klan's activities.[30] Responding to the resolution's defeat, the *Argus* lambasted the board's abstention, noting that "the public official who does not know anything about the Klan in this enlightened day, may be properly styled a 'pin-head.'"[31] The *Argus* then warned its readers to "remember [that] the men who voted to defeat the resolution are among those whom you voted for along with the 'Straight Republican Ticket.' . . . [T]hey are those who have betrayed your trust and confidence."[32] When the Board of Aldermen took up the anti-Klan resolution again a few weeks later, rumors swirled that local Klansmen tried to pressure aldermen into another no-vote.[33] On its second vote, the anti-Klan resolution tallied more support but was defeated again after falling one vote short.[34]

Though early efforts to oppose the Klan and pressure local politicians into action met with mixed results in St. Louis, the wave of editorial activity soon spread across the state. Just as they had in St. Louis, stories of alleged Klan atrocities filled the pages of Kansas City newspapers. Labeling the Klan a "dangerous organization" during its extensive coverage of violence committed by masked mobs in Texas, the *Kansas City Catholic Register* declared that "the secret methods of the organization make it even more cowardly than those who would lynch suspected black men."[35] The *Catholic Register* also encouraged the work of various anti-Klan groups in battling the "unchristian and un-American" activities of the Invisible Empire of Texas.[36] The *Kansas City Journal* argued that "Ku Kluxism cannot be tolerated by right-thinking Americans."[37] The *Kansas City Call* felt a great unease with the arrival of the hooded order in the "land of John Brown."[38] Yet the *Call* assured its readers that "Kansas may not always think right, but it always thinks out loud and in plain sight where all men can see . . . the supremest [sic] folly the Klan has yet committed is to attempt to plant its exotic, miasmic growth in the sunny vales and plains of Kansas."[39] Nevertheless, the *Call* continued to warn all that would listen that "Lucifer has entered the holy of holies."[40]

The *Call* may have seen a folly in the spread of the Invisible Empire into Missouri and Kansas, but Harry H. Mayer, rabbi of B'nai Jehudah Temple and contributing editor of the *Kansas City Jewish Chronicle*, viewed it differently. In the aftermath of World War I, many in the Jewish community felt the full brunt of a wave of anti-Semitism and

82   Chapter Two

antiforeignism that swept the United States.[41] From its beginning in 1920, the *Jewish Chronicle* served as an important voice for "Jews in the non-Jewish community" by promoting local interests and offering news stories on the experiences of Jews around the world.[42] It was influenced by Mayer in its early years and asserted that "every movement, every enterprise, every undertaking which will help Jews" would get support from the newspaper, while "every movement that is antagonistic to the good name of the Jew, every statement that is defamatory to him, will be vigorously opposed."[43]

For many Jews in Kansas City, it seemed that their neighbors had contracted a disease that Mayer labeled as "Ku Klux Klanitis," an "insidious poison" and a "pernicious germ of class hatred and class tyranny" whose chief symptoms included "defying constituted authority, clashing with state and city officials, invading homes, and violating there the right of the individual to regard his home as his castle." Noting that this contagion had previously been found in places like Texas and California, Mayer now warned that it had slowly begun to infect Kansas Citians, particularly at Wyandotte Klan No. 5, which had recently solicited members and attempted to curry favor with local citizens through a series of church donations.[44] Mayer's concerns drew the attention of Kansas City, Kansas, mayor Harry Burton, who denounced the Klan as "a mistake . . . [that] should have no place among us" and ordered all city employees affiliated with it to resign their positions.[45] While the mayor stood his ground on the issue and even initially agreed to debate a Klan lecturer at the London Heights Methodist Church in 1922, Burton's anti-Klan stance could not stem the tide of Klan support in Kansas City.[46] Yet despite more and more Kansas City residents seemingly contracting "Ku Klux Klanitis," the *Jewish Chronicle* felt confident that the "American people will certainly not tamely submit" to the Invisible Empire.[47]

While newspapers like the *Call* and the *Jewish Chronicle* may have acknowledged the necessity of cooperation in fighting the Klan, they also questioned who should take the lead in challenging the Invisible Empire. For its editor, C. A. Franklin, there were valid reasons that the *Call* would challenge the Klan. Like the Mitchell brothers of the *Argus*, C. A. Franklin was also a southern transplant, who found himself in Missouri. Born in Texas in 1880, Franklin's family had a long history in the newspaper business. After moving to Omaha, Nebraska, in 1887, his father operated the local *Enterprise*. The family stayed in Omaha for a decade, and C. A. enrolled for two years at the nearby University of Nebraska, but his father's failing health soon forced them to move to Denver, where the family managed a newspaper called the *Star*. Upon his father's death, he took over as publisher and editor before eventually moving to Kansas City in 1913.[48]

Despite arriving in Kansas City hoping to improve his newspaper prospects, C. A. Franklin did not publish his first issue of the *Call* until 1919. However, once he began regular publication, the *Call* took off as the preferred African American newspaper of the city. In addition to printing attention-grabbing headlines to draw in prospective readers, the *Call* also devoted extensive space in its pages to stories on African American achievements. Critics, however, sometimes accused the newspaper of avoiding controversial subjects like discrimination and segregation. Historian Thomas Wilson acknowledges this preference for positive stories but also notes that Franklin was a proponent of civil rights activism. When it came to civil rights, Franklin, like J. E. Mitchell of the *Argus*, was an ardent supporter of Booker T. Washington. He printed information related to Du Bois's NAACP and Marcus Garvey's Universal Negro Improvement Association but was not an open supporter of either organization. As a Republican, Franklin was also quite critical of Kansas City's Democratic political machines led by Joseph Shannon and Tom Pendergast. His support for the Republican Party waned as time passed, but for most of the 1920s, he was solidly in the Republican camp.[49]

Perhaps one of the most important decisions made by Franklin during his time in charge of the *Call* was to hire a young editor from Minnesota named Roy Wilkins. Originally from St. Louis, Wilkins moved to St. Paul, Minnesota, following the death of his mother, graduated from the University of Minnesota, and became involved in the St. Paul chapter of the NAACP. Wilkins met Franklin in Kansas City for the NAACP's annual convention in 1923. On the lookout for a new editor, Franklin offered Wilkins a chance to cover the convention for the *Call*. The onetime appointment soon became a job, and Wilkins became the newspaper's city editor.[50] In his new post, Wilkins soon filled the pages of the *Call* with critiques of Kansas City society, including residential segregation, home bombings, local politics, state funding for predominantly African

American institutions, and activities of the Klan.[51] Later in life, after ascending to become the NAACP's executive director, Wilkins referred to Kansas City as a "Jim Crow town that nearly ate my heart out as the years went by."[52]

Before and after Wilkins's arrival, the *Call* monitored the Klan nationwide.[53] In addition to warning about the group's kluxing along the border, the *Call* also denounced the Klan's attempts to sway local politics and public opinion through philanthropy and intimidation.[54] The newspaper was particularly disturbed after the Klan sent letters and donations to several African American churches in Kansas City calling upon the congregations to stand "shoulder to shoulder with your white brethren" against "foreign religious political domination."[55] In appealing to a shared Protestantism, local Klan chapters sought to downplay the notion that the organization was racially intolerant by suggesting that "[w]e have no quarrel with the colored man [because] he is American and as such has the support of American Citizens and we are ever ready to assist him in his lawful pursuit of happiness."[56]

Though it kept a close eye on hooded activity in and around Kansas City, the *Call* confessed that there were much more pressing issues in the African American community than the Klan, and, perhaps, Catholic and Jewish leaders should lead the charge against the hooded order.[57] Such sentiments were not shared by the *Jewish Chronicle*, which expressed concern about why Catholics or Jews should solely shoulder the burden of fighting the Klan. Citing comments by the former US ambassador to Germany James W. Gerard, the *Jewish Chronicle* posited that Jews and Catholics should abstain from fighting the Klan in favor of "right-minded Protestants [who] would exterminate the Klan in a short time . . . [and] slay the dragon." Agreeing with Gerard, Harry H. Mayer assured the readers of the *Jewish Chronicle* that "we can well afford to wait until decent Protestants are aroused by the seriousness of the vicious propaganda and the lawlessness which the 'Invisible Empire' has incited."[58] By late 1924, a survey of prominent Jewish leaders conducted by the Jewish Telegraphic Agency found that most favored a campaign against the Klan organized and carried out by Protestant denominations.[59]

Though local Jews may have been somewhat eager to let Protestants lead the charge against the Invisible Empire, some in the Catholic community, particularly the *Kansas City Catholic Register*, were not ready to give up the fight. With rumors swirling about Klan activity along the Missouri-Kansas border, the *Catholic Register* assured its readers that "the Catholic people of Kansas City, while they are ready to fight the Klan at every step, are not laying awake nights worrying about it."[60] Yet despite strong confidence in local parishioners, the *Catholic Register* still launched an investigative campaign to unmask those affiliated with the group by turning over the newspaper to nonstop Klan coverage during the latter half of 1922. From national stories to local Klan "sidelights," the *Catholic Register* made sure Kansas City residents knew the Klan's every move.[61] In splashing the names of suspected Klansmen on the front page, the *Catholic Register* always offered space in its next edition for explanations and rebuttals from those identified.[62]

By September 1922, the *Catholic Register* took its exposé journalism further. In addition to publishing the identities of those attending, and in some cases parked outside of Klan events, as well as recycling anti-Klan commentaries from other newspapers, the *Catholic Register* found itself in possession of a unique prize: a directory purportedly distributed by the local Klan of affiliated and sympathetic businesses.[63] Wasting little time, the *Catholic Register* reprinted the entire directory in its September 28 edition. From this list, Kansas City Catholics found out whether their barber, dentist, grocer, or insurance agent expressed sympathy with the Invisible Empire.[64] Justin Casey, managing editor of the *Catholic Register*, flatly denied accusations of launching a boycott campaign against Klan-affiliated businesses. Nevertheless, the newspaper continued to publish the names of those closely aligned with the Invisible Empire.[65] This ever-growing list included local ministers who had accepted donations from the Klan as well as participants in an alleged Klan-backed boycott in neighboring Lee's Summit.[66] If anyone had a problem with their name appearing in the *Catholic Register* under such circumstances, the newspaper advised that "the courts are the places for him."[67] Few, if any, challenged the *Catholic Register* through the court system.

While the state's metropolitan newspapers dominated most of the early anti-Klan coverage, outstate editors also made their feelings clear. Surveying the violence throughout the South, the *St. Joseph News-Press*

86 Chapter Two

suggested that the Klan's "Unofficial Constabulary" would cease if there were "a few first class funerals in the ranks of the 'klux.'"[68] In Sikeston, on the northern edge of the Missouri Bootheel, the *Standard* publicly declared its opposition to the Klan and agreed with the neighboring *Southeast Missourian* in Cape Girardeau that the organization was "a growing menace."[69] Down in the Ozarks, the *Springfield Leader* admonished the hooded order for the many outrages laid at the organization's feet and promised that few Americans would join such a group no matter how many members it claimed.[70] At the state capital, the *Jefferson City Democrat-Tribune* warned of "masked malcontents" in the community, and Mayor C. W. Thomas called on residents to "join together, Protestant, Catholic and Jew . . . [and] know no creed or no color but work for the common good of the community."[71] Beneath the hallowed columns of the University of Missouri, students read a sharp rebuke from the *Columbia Daily Tribune* that Boone County would be "an arid field indeed for the slimy, filthy head of the 'invisible empire.'"[72]

Perhaps no rural Missouri editors launched more notable and, at times, aggressive campaigns against the Klan than J. H. Wolpers of the *Poplar Bluff Republican*, John Fugel of the *Vienna Home-Adviser*, and Walter Crossley of the *Warrensburg Star-Journal*. John Henry Wolpers, or J. H., as he was often referred to, was born in Bollinger County in 1880. Raised on a farm near Zalma, Wolpers attended local rural schools, but tragedy struck when both of his parents died in his childhood. While still a young man, he served in the US Army and was sent to Manila during the Philippines War that followed the Spanish-American War. There, he was part of a military police unit that guarded the residence of future president William Howard Taft, who was serving as governor-general of the Philippines. Returning to Missouri, Wolpers enrolled at the local normal school, or teaching college, in Cape Girardeau. After graduating, he taught at a rural school in Dunklin County, took graduate course work at the University of Missouri, married Hattie Kinder, and eventually became principal of the high school in Bonne Terre.[73]

While in Bonne Terre, Wolpers began to reevaluate his career aspirations. He had devoted his early life to education—a subject that would remain important to him for the rest of his life—but he began to develop an interest in the newspaper industry. In 1911, he purchased the *Bonne Terre Register*. A few years later, he moved back to the borderland between the Ozarks and the Bootheel when he purchased the *Poplar Bluff Republican*. Poplar Bluff was home for the rest of his life, and Wolpers quickly became well connected to civic affairs. His obituary noted that Wolpers was involved with the State Bank of Poplar Bluff, the Poplar Bluff Loan and Building Association, Kiwanis, Masons, and the local Methodist church. Additionally, as the good-roads movement swept across Missouri, Wolpers took a keen interest in ensuring Poplar Bluff's place not only as a highway town but as a regional crossroads that connected the town of roughly eight thousand to destinations nationwide. Wolpers's dream was realized when Highway 67, connecting northern Illinois to St. Louis, Little Rock, and Dallas, and Highway 60, linking California to Virginia via eight states, bisected in Poplar Bluff.[74]

Though he was ever ready to promote and boost his new hometown and its citizens, by the 1920s, Wolpers grew weary of criminal elements in Poplar Bluff. In an editorial on local dives and the questionable characters that hung around such places, Wolpers wondered if law enforcement would be able to clean up the town lest it "be appropriate for the organization of a vigilance committee or the Ku Klux Klan to deal with such criminal menaces."[75] While the *Poplar Bluff Republican* later reprinted a short article on Mayor Henry Kiel's statements against the Klan in St. Louis, the newspaper largely ignored the hooded order and its alleged activities for most of 1921 and 1922.[76] When Roy E. Davis, a national lecturer for the Klan, appeared in Poplar Bluff in 1922 as part of a coordinated effort to recruit for the organization in the Bootheel, Wolpers's decision to avoid focusing on the Klan was swiftly reversed.[77] Reporting on Klan activity in neighboring towns, Wolpers warned Poplar Bluff residents that "little good and much harm come out of an organization functioning as is proposed by the Ku Klux Klan."[78]

From the moment that the Klan showed up in Poplar Bluff, Wolpers decided that he had to do all in his power, particularly in the pages of the *Republican*, to stop the spread of the Invisible Empire nationwide. He first went to work disputing the claims by Klansmen such as Roy E. Davis about the situation in communities like Poplar Bluff. To charges that immigrants were overrunning the country and taking control of the government, Wolpers assured readers that "foreign immigration is not injuring this country at the present time."[79] After the local klavern made statewide newspapers claiming that its membership topped five

88   Chapter Two

hundred, Wolpers suggested that such publicity was "a good way to keep prospective investors away from Poplar Bluff."[80] As hooded officials tried to refute and downplay allegations of vigilantism, the *Republican* repeatedly published editorials and reprinted articles related to purported Klan violence nationwide.[81] Finally, when not challenging the claims put forth by the Klan, Wolpers used P. T. Barnum's alleged theory that a sucker is born every minute to ridicule the organization and suggested that the number of individuals willing to pay ten dollars to wear white sheets was a "veritable shower."[82]

Wolpers's efforts to convince residents of Poplar Bluff, as well as the Ozarks and Bootheel, to reject the hooded order certainly met with some levels of success. However, the local Klan's claim that its membership numbered in the hundreds also suggests that the group did have a strong presence in the region. Yet Wolpers's editorial assault did not waver through the mid-1920s. When Poplar Bluff Klan No. 48 built a new klavern called Klandale north of town in 1924, Wolpers referred to it as a "monument to prejudice."[83] At the same time, as local Klansman O. L. Spurgeon defended the Klan's activities "behind the mask" as patriotic and 100 percent American, the *Republican* ran articles and editorials alleging that the hooded order played a questionable role in law enforcement raids on bootleggers.[84] He also warned residents that the group had slowly maneuvered into both political parties by enlisting candidates for county office and the local school board. To this end, Wolpers proclaimed victory when he was elected to the school board through a bipartisan coalition that defeated the Klan's influence in the 1924 municipal election.[85]

While Wolpers turned most of his ire toward the Klan itself, he also directed editorial critiques at fellow newspaper publishers he felt were nonresponsive or openly sympathetic to the hooded order. After newspapers in neighboring Puxico and Dexter printed Klan-affiliated content in their pages, Wolpers accused them of trying to sugarcoat the group's activities and warned, "The community that becomes the victim of a dominating Klan organization has given hostages to ill feelings, suspicion, hate and intolerance."[86] Fellow Bootheel newspapers were one thing, but when rumors circulated that his crosstown rival, Dwight H. Brown, publisher of the *Interstate-American*, was familiar with the inner workings of the local Klan, Wolpers went on the attack. At first, he asked the *Interstate-American* to explain its editorial policy on the Klan. When his questions went unanswered, Wolpers not so subtly published a reprinted article on a large Klan rally in Dunklin County where Brown gave a speech alongside C. C. Crawford and Charles McGehee. A year later, when Brown ran for the state senate, Wolpers used his rival's campaign as an opportunity to praise Republican candidate Oscar V. Seed's denouncement of the Klan while also noting that in Brown's newspaper, "there never has been a word of criticism unfavorable to the Klan published."[87]

As Wolpers rallied southeast Missouri residents to the need to challenge the Klan, John Fugel took up his editorial pen to do the same in central Missouri. Fugel had called Vienna and Maries County home since his pastoral appointment to Visitation of the Blessed Virgin Mary Catholic Church in 1896. Within a decade of his arrival in town, Fugel called for parishioners to raise the necessary funds to construct a new and larger church near the courthouse square. While it is difficult to ascertain when Fugel privately turned his attention toward the Klan, his editorial pen in the pages of the *Home-Adviser* came alive not long after the hooded order and its recruiters canvassed central Missouri in the fall of 1923. Once his editorials began, however, it was easy to decipher where he stood in relation to the Invisible Empire. "Masked Klanism cannot be good Americanism," Fugel's editorial on the front page of the *Home-Adviser* bellowed in January 1924.[88]

In the months leading up to his first anti-Klan editorial, Fugel focused more on the impending confluence of the Rock Island Railroad and a proposed federal highway (now called Highway 63) in tiny Vienna. He also waged war against government corruption, particularly the involvement of a rival newspaper in a minor scandal that saw the legislature refund taxpayer money given under presumed preferential treatment to certain publishers assigned government printing contracts. Fugel's concerns about the printing payments would last for several years in the 1920s and ultimately be resolved in a lawsuit filed against Secretary of State Charles Becker. When he did turn his attention toward the hooded order, it began a years-long campaign that dominated the front page of the *Home-Advisor* and drew the attention of Maries County residents as well as Klan and anti-Klan supporters statewide. It started simply with a reprint of a story from Montana where a Catholic bishop denounced a speech by Klan official Hiram Evans. Adjoining the article, Fugel offered a short editorial explaining his reason for publishing the piece to warn against the "rabid, radical hatred that can only tear down rather than build up."[89] After the article, the *Home-Adviser* returned to its usual coverage of agricultural news, highway prospects, and the usual dose of county boosterism. That would change, however, when the calendar turned to 1924.

The escalation of the anti-Klan campaign by the *Home-Adviser* was rooted in two issues that drew the biggest editorial responses from John Fugel's pen. First, much like his other anti-Klan newspaper brethren, Fugel objected to the alleged vigilantism and mob violence connected with the group. "The hundreds of mask-mob disorders the country over may not all have been executed by official Klan orders," Fugel declared in March 1924, "but there is no gainsaying the present mask-mob inspiration is a Klux hatching."[90] To this end, the *Home-Adviser* ran a series of ads for *The Unveiling of the Ku Klux Klan* and *The Reign of Terror in Oklahoma*, two books that told "a true history of the actions and practices of the 'Invisible Empire.'"[91] To counter claims that the Klan's actions were connected to ridding communities of bootlegging, Fugel repeatedly made clear that he supported Prohibition enforcement and would "join hands in this work with Presbyterian, Unitarian, Methodist, Baptist, Congregationalist, Jew, Negro, Gentile and any other decent element in American citizenry."[92]

Additionally, Fugel, as an ordained priest, took exception to the anti-Catholicism the Klan and its supporters promoted throughout Missouri and the United States. "We advise our Non-Catholic friends to study the Catholic system at close range and first hand, before seriously thinking of joining an organization that may sooner or later issue an order to do violence to a fellow-man."[93] Citing the Klan's circulation of the so-called bogus oath, a notorious piece of propaganda whose adherents claimed was drafted by Catholics and authorized a bloody war against Protestants, the *Home-Adviser* reprinted an offer from the Knights of Columbus for a $25,000 reward for anyone who could prove its validity.[94] He also published rebuttals from local Catholics and non-Catholics who objected to various claims put forth by the Klan and its supporters. "We are native-born citizens," wrote a group of World War I veterans, "[but] because we are of the Catholic Faith your leaders maintain we cannot be full-fledged American citizens."[95] Finally, he took direct aim in his editorials at newspapers that promoted anti-Catholicism, including the *Menace*, the *Patriot*, and the *Klan Kourier*.

John Fugel's anti-Klan activism was not just confined to his editorials in the pages of the *Home-Adviser*. He also participated in a series of public lectures in neighboring communities designed to defend Catholicism and challenge the Klan, such as his presentation in Gasconade County titled "Klan's Influence Not for the Better in America."[96] Two months later, he promoted presentations by Rev. Joseph Hoelting in Belle and Vichy that promised to give attendees correct information about the Catholic Church.[97] He also offered $500 to any Klansmen or hooded supporter who would publicly debate him and convince a group of non-Catholic Vienna residents that allegations against the Klan were not true, including that "Klanism is not responsible for a substantial part of the mask mob violence."[98]

FIGURE 7. Governor Frederick Gardner (*seated center*) signing the Federal Suffrage Amendment, July 3, 1919. Wallace Crossley (*seated second from left*) was lieutenant governor at the time. Courtesy of Women of the Mansion Photograph Collection (P0536). The State Historical Society of Missouri.

92 Chapter Two

Around the same time that Fugel's anti-Klan crusade kicked into high gear, Wallace Crossley's *Warrensburg Star-Journal* began to evaluate the growing influence of the Klan in western Missouri. Born in Cooper County in 1874, Crossley grew up in the region of the state later known as "Little Dixie" due to its sizable population of transplanted southerners and the descendants of the formerly enslaved people they once owned. His mother came from Kentucky, while his father, a Virginian, had fought with General Stonewall Jackson during the Civil War. After earning degrees at William Jewell College and the University of Missouri, Crossley held teaching positions in Mexico, Missouri, and Pilot Grove, Missouri, before moving to Warrensburg in 1900 to serve as a professor of literature at what was then known as Warrensburg Teachers College. His start in the newspaper business began in 1903 when he bought a part-ownership in the *Warrensburg Star*, which later merged with another newspaper to form the *Star-Journal*. Just as quickly as he entered the newspaper field, Crossley involved himself in local Democratic politics and won election to the Missouri House of Representatives in 1904. He was reelected twice to that chamber and later served for one term in the Missouri State Senate before he was elected lieutenant governor in 1916.[99]

When his term ended in 1921, Crossley returned to Warrensburg eager to manage the *Star-Journal* and lend his editorial opinion to issues he felt important to Johnson County residents. In many cases, these editorials critiqued local and state Republicans. When the Klan arrived in Missouri, the *Star-Journal* initially showed little interest in the organization. While Crossley did reprint a notably anti-Klan editorial from the *St. Louis Star*, what coverage he did provide of the hooded order in 1922 and 1923 amounted to short articles on local activities.[100] Crossley's editorials in the early stages of the 1924 election cycle proved to be more pro-Klan than anti-. When Democrats James A. Reed and Harry Hawes openly promoted their anti-Klan positions on the campaign trail, Crossley implored his fellow party members to drop the issue: "We have never believed that the Ku Klux Klan would serve a good purpose, but we recognize the fact that many of the best people in Missouri either belong to the Klan or are in sympathy with it."[101]

From his early stance on the organization, Crossley saw the potential benefits that Klan support could lend to Democratic candidates. This was especially critical in the gubernatorial race where A. W. Nelson faced intense allegations of Klan ties. For his part, Crossley played down Nelson's alleged Klan ties and accused Republican Klansmen of influencing public perceptions about the candidate to doom his bid for the governor's mansion. "That the conspiracy was hatched in the office of Gov. Hyde there is no doubt," Crossley told readers in October 1924.[102] Though he had critiqued Reed's earlier anti-Klan stance, Crossley eventually rallied around the senator when he came to Nelson's defense in the waning days of the campaign.[103]

While he initially held strong convictions that the Klan was not the issue in Missouri politics, Crossley quickly changed his tune by the end of 1924. Almost immediately after the general election, Crossley began to fill the pages of the *Star-Journal* with allegations that the Warrensburg Klan was deeply connected to the local Republican Party and had forced Democratic Klansmen to forgo their preferred candidates in favor of ones approved by the hooded order. In addition to reprinted correspondence and letters to the editor from former Klansmen agreeing with these rumors, the *Star-Journal* also ran a series from an unknown contributor named "TRUTH" called "The Ways of 100% Americans," which, among other subjects, accused the local Equality Club of being a front for the WKKK. Despite his increasingly anti-Klan tone in the *Star-Journal*, however, Crossley still refused to denounce the Klan outright. Instead, he passed over the organization's members in favor of attacking what he saw as political interference and corruption by Klan leaders.[104]

Having criticized the Warrensburg Klan for destroying straight ticket politics, where voters supported a particular political party from the president all the way down to local officials, Crossley himself abandoned the same policy by the municipal election of 1925. When it became obvious that the Klan would wield considerable influence over several key races, Crossley joined an anti-Klan coalition of community leaders who sought to run their own preferred candidates. Yet, again, he did not completely denounce the hooded order. Called to speak before a meeting of anti-Klan supporters, Crossley told the audience that "there were many good men and women in the Klan, [and] that its published creed was in line with the ideals of good citizenship, but that the secret oath which bound the members was devilish, and a menace to society."[105] In the end,

94   Chapter Two

Lesle F. Hutchens was elected mayor of Warrensburg, and the anti-Klan slate of candidates achieved modest success.[106]

Despite the anti-Klan coalition's success in the municipal election, Crossley continued his attacks on the Klan through the mid-1920s on two editorial fronts. First, his political commentaries targeted the Republican Party for the activities of the Klan. When former state labor commissioner Heber Nations was embroiled in a graft scandal, Crossley pointed out his ties to the Klan and Governor Hyde. Noting Sam Baker's anti-Klan campaign for governor in 1924, Crossley questioned why the newly elected chief executive did little to combat the hooded order. After Hiram Evans announced a parade of Klansmen and -women down Pennsylvania Avenue in Washington, DC, Crossley wondered aloud if Calvin Coolidge would welcome the marchers to the nation's capital considering their alleged role in his victory in 1924.[107] Additionally, he used examples of alleged and confirmed Klan violence to warn Johnson County residents of what might befall their community if the Invisible Empire was allowed to spread. Yet as Warrensburg's Klan started to wane in Johnson County, so too did Crossley's editorial attacks on the organization.

To counter claims put forth by editors like Wolpers, Fugel, and Crossley in the state and national press that acts of violence and vigilantism were undertaken solely by those donning the mask of the Klan, Imperial Wizard William Simmons frequently issued public statements dismissing the charges and offering rewards for the capture of those who misused the Klan's identity to commit crimes. No doubt aware that incidents like the alleged assault in Fair Play would negatively impact recruiting, Simmons took out a full-page call to action in the St. Louis Globe-Democrat to "All Lovers of Law, Order, Peace and Justice, and to All the People of the United States." Simmons did not deny that rogue members of the Klan could be responsible for a small portion of the violence, but he asserted that such acts violated the Klansmen code of conduct. As such, he assured readers that those not associated with the order were involved in most of the violence. In Simmons's mind, the Klan's role in American society was to protect their fellow citizens from vigilantism and lawlessness, not inflict it upon others.[108] Finally, Simmons left the ultimate judgment to the American people:

"Masked Malcontents" 95

If we are all that our enemies charge or even one-fourth as wicked as claimed, America has nothing to fear from this Organization, for it will perish. On the other hand, if we are lied about by those who are unworthy and who are not pure Americans at heart . . . the time will come when all their falsehoods and slanderous statements will react on them, and the Knights of the Ku Klux Klan will come into its own and take its place in the hearts of real Americans, where its founders intended it should, as the one greatest force in America to guarantee to all men that this country shall forever be what its founders intended, THE LAND OF THE FREE AND THE HOME OF THE BRAVE, wherein all men, regardless of race, color or creed, can live in peace and happiness, enjoying the greatest amount of liberty and justice in any country in the world.[109]

Simmons's efforts to deflect and challenge charges of vigilantism within the hooded ranks came at a critical time for the expanding Invisible Empire. In September 1921, the *New York World* commenced a lengthy exposé on the organization. Reprinted in newspapers throughout the United States, the exposé focused on sensational information about the Klan, its finances, recruiting tactics, and rituals. While outlining the basic tenets of the Klan, the *World* also focused on the violence associated with the order in Texas and parts of the South. Finally, the exposé included denouncements of the Klan by government officials, religious leaders, and former Klansmen.[110] Most prominently, Henry P. Fry, a former kleagle who later authored a book about his experiences in the Klan called *The Modern Ku Klux Klan*, labeled the organization anti-Catholic and anti-Semitic and explained that such intolerance influenced his decision to leave the Invisible Empire.[111] One of the main goals of the *World* exposé was to bring the secrets and outrages of the Klan to a national audience. The hope was, as the *St. Louis Post-Dispatch* noted:

Publicity would wither it as a cavernous weed is withered by the midday sun. . . . How any sensible man, after reading the highfalutin flubdub [*sic*] of its sacred Kloran, the burlesque of its ritual and the list of its officers, from Imperial Wizard through the Klakard and the Kludd, the Kleagle and the Klarago, can hold his membership is beyond the range of sane judgement. . . . The danger of the organization lies in its playing upon the prejudices and passions of the ignorant and thoughtless and thus inciting violence, but even the ignorant, in light of the exposure of the flubdubbery [*sic*] and spoils of the "Invisible Empire," ought to see the folly of membership. The mystery which is an alluring appeal to the "joiners" has vanished, the mask is off and the grotesque devil is visible.[112]

The *St. Louis Post-Dispatch*'s reprinting of the *World* exposé brought it acclaim from city residents opposed to the Invisible Empire. After publishing the names and addresses of Missouri Klan officers, several groups, including the Knights of Columbus, publicly thanked the editors of the *Post-Dispatch* for the exposé series.[113] Sharing the sentiment, one resident declared in a letter to the editor that "the Post-Dispatch is earning the thanks and good will of true-blue American citizens by its expose of Ku Klux Klan Inc. . . . Knocking 'em cold is a P-D habit."[114] Though the *Post-Dispatch* reaped the benefits of reprinting the exposé, other newspapers soon began to emulate the *World*'s tactics against the Klan, including the *Jewish Voice*, which advised its readers that "the time has come when Fordism, Ku Klux Klanism and every individual or organization that stands for hate and prejudice must be eliminated from American life, otherwise we shall never have AMERICANISM and all that it stands for in this country."[115] With momentum building for federal action thanks in large part to the reaction to the *World* exposé, St. Louis congressman Leonidas Dyer called on the federal government to investigate the hooded order, arguing that "everything possible should be done to suppress and destroy the Ku Klux Klan."[116]

Owing to outside pressure and Dyer's call to action, Congress finally opened an investigation into the Klan in October 1921. Led by the House Rules Committee, a series of public hearings lasted a week and included testimony ranging from firsthand accounts of alleged Klan violence to comments on the Invisible Empire by former and current Klansmen. Among those testifying on the first day of the hearings were Rowland Thomas, an investigator for the *World*; C. Anderson Wright, a former Klansmen from New York; William J. Burns, director of the Department of Justice's Bureau of Investigation; and congressmen from

New York, Massachusetts, and Missouri.[117] Appearing before the committee, Leonidas Dyer argued in favor of a federal investigation into the Klan because "my attention to this matter has been called by the people whom I have the honor to represent in the Congress, the people of the city of St. Louis, and for that reason I have been led to ask for an investigation. . . . Of course, what affects the people of my city largely affects those of the entire country."[118] As he read letters from constituents on alleged Klan violence, Dyer noted that secret clubs did exist in society, but he felt that the organization in question was an extralegal force in many states that was up to no good.[119]

On the second day of the hearings, the imperial wizard arrived to defend his Invisible Empire. Fighting what he claimed was a lengthy spell of tonsillitis and bronchitis, William Simmons underwent a barrage of questions from the committee in the hopes of clearing the Klan's name. During his testimony, Simmons claimed that rival groups were behind the vigilantism. He even announced that the Klan would disband if such charges of violence turned out to be true. Instead, he repeatedly argued that the Klan had loftier ambitions and goals.[120] The back-and-forth between the Imperial Wizard and the committee reached a climax on the hearing's third day when Simmons declared:

> I want to say to my persecutors and the persecutors of this organization in all honesty and sincerity, no matter to what creed or race you may belong in your persecutions, through the medium of the press or otherwise, that you do not know what you are doing. You are ignorant of the principles as were those who were ignorant of the character and work of the Christ. I can not better express myself than by saying to you who are persecutors of the klan [sic] and myself, "Father, forgive you, for you know not what you do," and "Father, forgive them, for they know not what they do."[121]

After uttering these words, Simmons collapsed as the assembled crowd gasped. The committee immediately adjourned for the day.[122] The lack of sufficient evidence, combined with Simmons's performance in front of the committee, produced little support for further investigation or wide-sweeping anti-Klan legislation. Instead, congressional attempts to discredit the Klan only made it stronger. As has been noted by several historians of the 1920s Klan, the publicity given to the Klan during the hearings brought even more recruits into the Invisible Empire.[123]

Within a year of Simmons's fateful testimony before Congress, the Klan underwent a period of profound transition. Having wrested control of the organization away from Simmons during a coup d'état at the 1922 Klan Klonvokation, the newly appointed imperial wizard, Hiram Evans, had big plans for the organization.[124] First, Evans and other Klan officials examined the recruiting possibilities connected to opening membership to white women. In offering the robe and hood to women, the Invisible Empire grew in membership, but such a decision increased tensions between Klan leaders, local klaverns, and newly formed auxiliary organizations. Second, Evans intended to mobilize local klaverns into politically active groups. While Klansmen and newly incorporated Klanswomen realized that the organization lacked the power to be a prominent third party, hooded officials felt confident they could build strong alliances with influential political entities in certain localities. Finally, Evans, though a onetime member of the Dallas Klan's terror squad, hoped that the organization's involvement in more respectable venues like politics and women's recruitment would separate the hooded order from claims of vigilantism and violence.

Though the Klan attempted to cut ties with its night-riding past, old habits died hard in the Invisible Empire, and the hooded order took the blame in prominent cases of vigilantism. Added to this, the general perception—largely cultivated by the anti-Klan press—that the organization was violent hurt recruitment. This was especially true in Missouri. As the state Klan spread out into new recruiting territory beyond its established klaverns, Missouri underwent a series of violent events that deeply concerned state residents. Writing to Governor Arthur Hyde, NAACP executive secretary James Weldon Johnson warned that the "eyes of the nation are upon Missouri."[125] Hyde understood this point well, as he spent substantial time during his administration trying to investigate multiple lynchings, deploy National Guard detachments to prevent anti-Black violence, and address a series of home bombings in the state's urban centers. Yet just as Hyde was attempting to quell these concerns, so too did the Missouri Klan fight to shed the image that it was responsible for these acts of violence. Ultimately, though some within the state's hooded order were successful in building a reputation as law-and-order reformers, the Missouri Klan as a whole experienced difficulty in growing the organization due to its inability to counter claims put forth by the anti-Klan press and separate itself from allegations of violence and vigilantism.

Though it drew its fair share of criticism toward the Klan for the group's seeming boosterism in the face of a tragic situation, perhaps no incident offered a better recruiting opportunity for the hooded order in Missouri than the killing of St. Joseph teenager Nellie Hale. "It all happened so quickly that it seemed only a minute before it was all over," an eyewitness told the *St. Joseph News-Press* of the young girl's death.[126] Hale, who had been out for an automobile ride with her brothers, was accidentally shot by police on the outskirts of St. Joseph in October 1922. The police department initially denied their involvement in her death, arguing instead that the bullet removed from Nellie's body came from a suspected bootlegger. The Hale family, however, felt that reckless shooting by the police during a car chase had inflicted the mortal wound.[127] This assumption was soon verified when witness testimony, physical evidence, and the identities of those in the suspected bootlegger car were revealed in the days after Hale's death.[128]

With evidence mounting against the police department, the three-member police commission concluded that officers had falsely assumed that the vehicle they pursued contained bootleggers and that they fired in the direction of the automobile with no provocation. Instead of hitting its intended, if incorrect, target, the bullet struck Nellie Hale, "an entirely innocent person."[129] Acknowledging public outrage over the killing and concerns voiced by citizens over recent, questionable activity tied to the police force, the commission moved quickly to hold those responsible accountable. Two of the three officers involved in the shooting were immediately dismissed from the police department.[130] Another officer who was under investigation following the shooting death of another St. Joseph resident a few weeks earlier also resigned.[131] However, commissioners voiced caution in the face of public pressure regarding chief of police

Clay McDonald because they felt that any quick decision on his status might be interpreted as bowing to external forces, particularly the local Klan, though commissioner Walter Fulkerson did admit that "Catholics, Protestants, Jews and negroes—all classes are against the chief."[132]

In the aftermath of Nellie Hale's death, St. Joseph Klan No. 4 moved quickly to cloak itself in robes of respectability, reform, and nonviolence. The organization announced its intention to participate in Hale's funeral and scheduled a public forum at Smith Park to discuss law enforcement and public safety. With McDonald's head on the chopping block and members of the police force resigning, the Klan used its Smith Park meeting to pressure the police commission. Speakers, including Exalted Cyclops William M. Campbell, called on the commissioners to hold the police department accountable—or to resign themselves. If commissioners did not meet this request, the Klan was prepared to circulate a petition asking Governor Hyde to remove them. Reminding those in attendance of the death of little Nellie Hale at the hands of an ineffective and oppressive police force, the speakers painted a bleak picture of life in St. Joseph: "It is getting to be so bad in St. Joseph that we are afraid to go out riding in our automobiles with our women and children in the country, or even go to our parks or out in our front yards for fear of being struck by a stray bullet fired by a member of the police department."[133]

While evidence indicates that local police, including Chief McDonald, attempted to pressure the coroner's office into corroborating their version of the bootlegger story, the Klan's involvement in the controversy transcended the issue of corruption.[134] Clay McDonald, the focal point in the investigation, was well known to the local Klan, as only a year earlier, he had shut down a series of recruitment meetings organized by local Klansmen. McDonald's anti-Klan stance had initially received support from many local officials, but now the roles were reversed.[135] McDonald was denounced, and the Klan appeared as the hero—ever ready to pressure the governor into disbanding the police commission in the name of law and order. As the *St. Joseph Observer* noted, "[The police department's] punishment which will follow will be brought about principally by the good work of the local Ku Klux Klan which through a monster mass meeting and law enforcement promptings forced the officials to adopt prompt and vigorous measures to punish the law breakers."[136]

In addition to its public comments during the Smith Park rally, the Klan also used Nellie Hale's funeral as a grand show of hooded power in St. Joseph. Despite a rainstorm, an estimated twenty-five thousand people crowded the streets near Hale's home to witness the funeral procession to Mount Mora Cemetery, which included roughly three hundred Klansmen, many choosing to lift their masks to reveal their identities. Klansmen also flanked automobiles carrying floral arrangements, the casket, and the Hale family. Reinforcing Exalted Cyclops William M. Campbell's claim that "we do not need any police here to keep order . . . we can maintain law and order ourselves," members of the Klan, not the police department, directed traffic along the funeral route. As the procession reached the cemetery, the rain stopped, and the sun made a brief appearance in the afternoon sky. When the graveside services concluded, the Klansmen left the cemetery and solemnly marched to their nearby klavern.[137]

With Hale's funeral concluded and the city's police commission still intact, St. Joseph Klan No. 4 went forward with its plan to pursue a petition drive to convince Governor Hyde to remove the commissioners. This campaign was aided on two fronts. First, Hale's death became a national story in newspapers throughout the United States.[138] In its coverage of events, the *St. Louis Post-Dispatch* devoted multiple pages in an article titled "How Police Autocracy Aroused St. Joseph to Rebel against Lawless Enforcement."[139] The national press also brought attention to the multiple police killings that had recently taken place in St. Joseph. Between May and October 1922, police officers killed Nellie Hale, two white men, one African American man, and a fellow officer.[140] According to the press, the governor had to intervene in some form. A review of his correspondence from late 1922 reveals that Governor Hyde saw a dramatic increase in the amount of mail coming to his office advising him to monitor both police and Klan activity in St. Joseph.[141] Hyde eventually convened a series of meetings in the city in November 1922, but he quickly announced that he would take no action against the police commission.[142]

Hyde's hesitancy to disband or remove police commissioners in St. Joseph was a political decision, but it also contained undertones about his own feelings regarding the Klan. When a delegation of Klansmen

Figure 8. Arthur Mastick Hyde, ca. 1920. Courtesy of Strauss Studio Photographs (P0879). The State Historical Society of Missouri.

and Hale family members visited Jefferson City to lobby for public safety reform in St. Joseph, Hyde was conspicuously absent. In the months leading up to Nellie Hale's death, Hyde had issued multiple condemnations of the Invisible Empire. His comments not only strengthened the claims of the Klan's opponents but also set the stage for bigger battles with the group in the coming years. Hyde first denounced the Klan at a speech in Joplin and followed that up with a well-publicized address at a meeting of the Grand Lodge of Missouri Ancient Free and Accepted Masons.[143] Soon after, Hyde received national recognition for his stance on the Invisible Empire from prominent former Klansman C. Anderson Wright as well as Herbert Bayard Swope of the *New York World*.[144]

Hyde's denouncements carried significant weight, but it is obvious that they were the result of political pressure regarding the Klan. As early as April 1921, Hyde received letters from concerned Missourians

"Masked Malcontents" 103

requesting action against the Klan. In noting the arrival of the Klan in Springfield, a local resident asked Hyde if he would "permit this poison to flow unchecked."[145] The Inter-Racial Committee of the Citizens' League of Kansas City and Jackson County advised the governor, along with Kansas City's mayor and chief of police, to discourage the formation of the Klan in Missouri.[146] The Negro Women's National Republican League reminded Hyde that the "Ku Klux Klan is unamerican [sic] and lawless in spirit, anti-Catholic, anti-Jewish as well as anti-Negro and should be excluded from all American Cities desiring order and amicable relations between the races."[147]

While it had been relatively easy for the St. Joseph Klan and its supporters to portray themselves as the defender of white womanhood and public safety in the wake of Nellie Hale's murder, the organization as a whole did not experience similar success as it continued to face accusations of violence and vigilantism. The argument from hooded officials that the organization disapproved of and even distanced itself from night riding took a major hit when a group of vocal anti-Klan activists in Morehouse Parish, Louisiana, were beaten and kidnapped by men in black masks.[148] Mer Rouge became a national story and was, as historian Charles Alexander argues, "the most famous instance of Klan terrorism, and one of the best-known murder cases of the 1920s."[149] A little more than a year after Mer Rouge, the coal-mining communities around Herrin, Illinois, roughly thirty miles from the Missouri border, erupted in Klan and anti-Klan violence that lasted through the middle of the decade.[150] When the mystery of Mer Rouge reached a fever pitch in the national press, and news broke about rioting in Herrin, the Klan found itself once again in controversy.

With news of Mer Rouge still splashed across the pages of Missouri newspapers, H. S. Ahrens frantically traveled throughout southeast Missouri in the spring of 1923. What had once seemed like a prime location for a membership sales pitch had recently turned into a war zone. The thaw of winter brought anticipation of an agricultural boom year, but it also led to an outbreak of violence. Reports of shots fired at African American homes and warnings to leave the area caused panic throughout the region. Railroad officials and local residents estimated that more than two hundred African Americans, many of them agricultural

104   Chapter Two

laborers, had already fled the area. Not wanting residents to assume that his organization, the Ku Klux Klan, was responsible for the increased vigilantism, Ahrens traveled through most of Missouri's Bootheel denouncing the violence. He felt it necessary to make the trek because some of the intimidating letters sent to local Black residents had been signed "K.K.K." In Pemiscot County, Ahrens distributed more than one thousand handbills offering a hefty reward for information about the guilty parties. He also told the press that "with the better class of citizens in the county, members of the Klan recognized that negroes were necessary to cultivate and pick cotton crops." As such, the Klan was "not participating in anything to disturb the peace of mind of the negroes."[151] When told of concerns regarding recent Klan activity, particularly his own recruitment in the region, Ahrens expressed hope that the organization's actions in stemming the violence would "allay the fear."[152]

Despite predictions of a large crop and confidence from the *Cape Girardeau Southeast Missourian* that cotton would ensure that the region was "destined to become the richest agricultural district of the United States," Klan recruiters found uneasiness throughout the region. Tensions between white and Black agricultural laborers lingered after African American voters had been warned to stay away from the polls during the prior election, and pamphlets bearing skulls and crossbones and signed "K-K-K" were distributed in Pemiscot County.[153] The threat of violence was not new for the region, as six Black men had been lynched in the region since 1902. Additionally, when wealthy landowners attempted to bring in African Americans for agricultural work before 1920, white tenant farmers responded with vigilantism to drive out the competing laborers. Missouri's entire southern border experienced an intense period of racial violence between 1890 and 1920, punctuated by two triple lynchings in Lawrence County and Greene County.[154]

At the start of the 1920s, Missouri's Bootheel was known more for its wheat and corn than its cotton. Large-scale agricultural production in the region was relatively new following the successful draining of swampland in the early twentieth century.[155] What little cotton that was produced struggled on the open market after the nation's economy experienced a depression following World War I, and an intense boll-weevil infestation in the American South left many to wonder if cotton was still a premier crop. By 1922, however, cotton became *the* crop of southeast Missouri

"Masked Malcontents" 105

and emerged as the savior of the region thanks to its hardy nature in the reclaimed swampland. The state's cotton would never rival its sister crop farther south, but the Bootheel's agricultural potential increased interest in the region.[156]

As the cotton crop moved north, so did thousands of African Americans. Seeking a way out of economic limitations, racial violence, and the hardening of Jim Crow, most African Americans relocated to urban locations in the North and West.[157] Some, however, kept their agricultural roots and moved to farming communities on the outskirts of the South.[158] Despite its place along the lower half of the Mississippi River valley, Missouri's Bootheel did not completely replicate the South. Reflecting on his life in southeast Missouri, wealthy planter Thad Snow noted that "the people of the Delta thought and behaved like people of the North rather than like people of the Cotton South."[159] However, though the state lacked an official system of de jure Jim Crow segregation, Snow acknowledged an "overlordship that was mildly intoxicating" when it came to relations between white planters and Black laborers.[160]

While cultural segregation, discriminatory practices, and overt racism were still quite evident, Missouri differed from other cotton-producing states in that African Americans had voting rights and held positions of power in state politics.[161] The promise of a better life and better opportunities brought roughly fifteen thousand African Americans into the Missouri cotton-producing counties of Butler, Scott, Stoddard, Pemiscot, Mississippi, Dunklin, and New Madrid between 1910 and 1930.[162] They quickly found landowners ready to employ them, organizations like the UNIA and NAACP ready to aid them, but also resistance among the large class of white tenant farmers. Black and white laborers shared a lot in common in the cotton fields. Still, as the increasing African American population began to compete for jobs and landowners expressed a preference for Black workers over white workers, violence escalated.[163]

After additional reports of Black intimidation in southeast Missouri, including notes allegedly tacked onto homes proclaiming, "Get out . . . this is a white man's country," filtered into his Jefferson City office, Governor Hyde demanded answers.[164] He wired the sheriffs of Pemiscot, Dunklin, Mississippi, and Scott Counties to inquire about the validity of such claims. He reminded them that it was their duty to maintain order and protect the citizens of their counties.[165] Hyde also forwarded information, including a copy of one of the "K-K-K" election flyers, to US attorney general Harry Daugherty and the Department of Justice.[166] Hyde felt pressure to act on the threats after the US District Attorney's Office in St. Louis went public with numerous complaints of assaults and intimidation it had received from Black tenant farmers and white landowners in Dunklin and Pemiscot Counties.[167] At first, Hyde's inquiries were met with hostility from local residents who disputed the charges. The Caruthersville Chamber of Commerce and Kennett Lions Club, along with several local newspapers, objected to accusations of African American intimidation published in the St. Louis press.[168] Most of the sheriffs told Hyde that the stories of supposed violence were greatly exaggerated and that "peace and quiet prevails here."[169]

Considering the reports received by the Justice Department and concerns about the response from county sheriffs, Hyde sent additional messages to allies in southeast Missouri inquiring about the facts of the situation.[170] Some correspondents corroborated law enforcement accounts and found that "peace and quiet prevails."[171] C. F. Bloker of Caruthersville, however, offered a different opinion. Bloker acknowledged the intimidation of African Americans in the region and admitted that many people had left Pemiscot County, especially after shootings at several local cabins. "The foundation of the trouble is politics," Bloker told Hyde, "and the situation was created in the last election by getting out KKK notices notifying the negroes that they would not be permitted to vote." It was the "trifling white land tenants," Bloker asserted, that were the driving force behind the violence.[172] Bloker's claims were supported by Pemiscot County prosecuting attorney Shelley Stiles, who told the *St. Louis Post-Dispatch* that white laborers in several communities had threatened and assaulted newly arriving African American workers.[173]

Despite assurances from Stiles that southeast Missouri would not descend into chaos, attacks against African American laborers escalated to the point that Hyde sent members of the state national guard to New Madrid and Stoddard Counties, where they found that conditions "warrant temporary protection of a colony of negroes."[174] Tensions were especially high in the towns of Bernie and Parma after Tom Keaton, a local Black laborer, was shot to death while asleep in bed. As the National Guard patrolled county roads to dissuade further intimidation and assaults, Herbert Bleese, a former Stoddard County justice of the peace, as well as two other men were arrested in connection with Keaton's death.[175] In a speedy trial, all three were acquitted, and the courtroom crowd erupted in cheers when the verdict was read.[176]

As the search for guilty parties continued during the violence, an alleged sighting of men in black hoods near the site of one of the attacks turned attention toward the Klan. Such accusations were justified considering the earlier "K-K-K" flyers and the recent events at Mer Rouge, but the organization, which was just starting to make inroads in the Bootheel, denied any involvement. The Klan tried to stop the intimidation in the region because it feared such events would hurt the local economy if Black laborers were driven out and that accusations of violence would be tied back to the hooded order. To separate the organization from the violence, Klansmen from several towns warned possible intimidators that "if baiting continues . . . the klan [sic] will throw back of the law's enforcement the full power of its secret service and extend itself to bring the guilty to justice."[177] With an estimated population in southeast Missouri in the thousands, Klansmen felt they could influence local residents and stem the tide of violence.[178] After all, the local press tended to publish favorable stories about the Klan's philanthropic activities.[179] Yet despite agreeing with the Klan that intimidation had to stop, the local press, particularly the *Charleston Enterprise-Courier* and *Hayti Missouri Herald*, also felt that a close eye needed to be kept on the ever-growing Black population.

By all accounts, the violence that plagued southeast Missouri in the spring of 1923 subsided by the summer. While tensions continued, large-scale violence did not return during the fall harvest or the start of the 1924 planting season. For a time, it seemed that peace and quiet would truly prevail in the region. Still, political activism and the upcoming 1924 general election soon brought many issues back to the surface, with fear centering on the idea of "negro supremacy," a term bandied about by the local press suggesting that the large influx of African Americans into the region would challenge the Democratic Party's stranglehold on the region. While continually questioning the intelligence and mental capacities of the Black population, the newspapers stopped short of calling for their disenfranchisement. Nevertheless, the press repeatedly warned white residents of attempts by Republican politicians, federal investigators, and Black activists with the UNIA and NAACP to court African American voters and push for social equality. Such incendiary articles and editorials no doubt played a contributing factor in the lynching of Roosevelt Grigsby in Charleston in December 1924.[180]

After months of anti-Klan coverage in Missouri newspapers, constant accusations of extralegal violence, and a series of denouncements from some of the state's key political leaders, the *Kansas City Catholic Register* predicted an impending demise for the Ku Klux Klan: "Whether the Klan is dead in Kansas City remains to be seen. Undoubtably [*sic*] it is very, very sick. We shall maintain our men, however, in their organization, until such time as we feel that the Klan is through as a menace to the peace and tranquility of the people of Kansas City."[181] The assertion was premature, as only two years later, the *Catholic Register* reported on the Second Imperial Klonvokation held at Kansas City's Convention Hall. Nevertheless, newspapers like the *Catholic Register* served as the first major contributors to a growing movement against the Klan that would only strengthen as more and more Missourians joined the ranks of a developing anti-Klan coalition that objected to the racist rhetoric, religious intolerance, political manipulation, and vigilantism of the hooded order.

Yet as newspaper coverage of the indecisiveness over which organizations and denominations would lead the charge against the Klan demonstrates, this coalition was tenuous at best and built upon personal grievances and individual prejudices. Without action, the denouncements and political pressures of newspaper editorials were just words on a page. In the future, the opening barrage of the anti-Klan press would need the coordinated grassroots efforts of state and county-level groups as well as national organizations such as the Catholic Central Verein, Knights of Columbus, American Unity League, B'nai B'rith, United Negro Improvement Association, and the National Association for the Advancement of Colored People. Together, this anti-Klan coalition would exert maximum pressure upon Klan leaders and members. Still, it also experienced uncertainty as the rallying cry for action did as much to divide as it did to unite those opposed to the Invisible Empire.

CHAPTER THREE

"We Will Tear Off This Mask of Secrecy"

Building an Anti-Klan Coalition

IN MAY 1921, two members of the St. Louis chapter of the National Association for the Advancement of Colored People, George L. Vaughn and Cora J. Carter, wrote letters to the organization's headquarters in New York outlining recent activities of the local branch. Noting efforts by the group to pressure Governor Arthur Hyde into conducting a thorough investigation into the recent lynching of Roy Hammonds in nearby Bowling Green, Missouri, Vaughn proudly told national leadership that the "St. Louis Branch of the N.A.A.C.P. is quite active these days."[1] A prominent St. Louis attorney in his forties, George L. Vaughn had come to the city in the early twentieth century following his upbringing in Kentucky and education at Lane College and Walden University in Tennessee. Politically active, Vaughn was a founding member of the St. Louis Negro Bar Association (now known as the Mound City Bar Association) as well as the Citizens Liberty League, an organization responsible for promoting Black political candidates, including Charles Turpin, who became the first Black man to win public office in Missouri when he was elected St. Louis constable in 1910. Returning from his military service in World War I, Vaughn rose quickly within the St. Louis chapter of the NAACP, becoming chairman of the executive committee and first vice president. He later received critical acclaim for his eyewitness report of the lynching of James T. Scott in Columbia in 1923, as well as his role in the restrictive covenant case of *Shelley v. Kraemer*.[2]

Among the numerous issues undertaken by the St. Louis NAACP branch in the 1920s, local members had turned their attention to the recent arrival of the Ku Klux Klan in the city. Vaughn indicated as much in his letter when he shared that "besides conducting the drive for Membership, which is succeeding, the Branch is fighting the efforts to organize the Ku Klux Klan in Missouri."[3] However, Vaughn was not the

109

only St. Louis NAACP member concerned about the hooded order, as Cora Carter's letter had preceded his to the national office a few days prior. Also in her forties, Carter was born in New Jersey and later moved to St. Louis, where she worked in domestic labor and as a hairdresser. Well connected in various clubs and organizations, including the Ancient United Knights and Daughters of Africa and the Heroines of Templar Crusades, Carter eventually became a lead organizer for the NAACP's membership campaigns in the city. By the mid-1920s, after serving on the NAACP Resolutions Committee, Carter was elected president of the local branch in Pasadena, California.[4]

In her letter to executive secretary James Weldon Johnson, Carter expressed concern regarding recent Klan recruitment but also inquired about how other NAACP branches dealt with the hooded order.[5] Responding immediately, assistant secretary Walter White advised Carter and her fellow St. Louis members to pressure the mayor, police department, governor, and various city and state officials into stating their position on the Klan. In a tactic frequently used by anti-Klan activists, White wanted prominent officials to be on the record regarding their opinion of the Invisible Empire. No doubt aware of the burgeoning anti-Klan press, White also recommended that NAACP members contact local newspapers to convince them to run exposés and damning editorials about the Klan, thus significantly impacting local recruitment.[6] Finally, White called on NAACP members to launch an interracial and inter-denominational coalition that would effectively challenge the growth of the Klan: "May I strongly urge that you get in touch with organizations like the Knights of Columbus and other Irish-Catholic groups; the B'nai Brith and other Jewish organizations; the local labor groups such as the American Federation of Labor emphasizing upon all of these that the Ku Klux Klan is not only Anti-Negro but Anti-Catholic, Anti-Semitic, and Anti-Labor. We also suggest that you enlist the active opposition to the Klan of church and civic organizations."[7]

Upon receiving a packet of anti-Klan pamphlets from NAACP head-quarters, Vaughn and Carter distributed the information to "others that are interested in the suppression of this tyrannical organization" and expressed hope that "our Branch shall be equally as successful [as New York] in the end."[8] A few weeks after their correspondence, Walter White

"We Will Tear Off This Mask of Secrecy"   111

FIGURE 9. George L. Vaughn (*second from right in the back row*) standing with members of the March on Washington General Committee, 1942. Courtesy of Benny G. Rodgers Photograph Collection (S0629). The State Historical Society of Missouri.

personally followed up with the St. Louis branch when he stopped in the city for a public lecture at Metropolitan AME Zion Church. Before a crowd of more than seven hundred, White listened as local NAACP members outlined their anti-Klan activities and advised the audience on the best way to combat lynching as well as the hooded order. Given his turn at the podium, White recounted the horrific details of the recent race riot in Tulsa, Oklahoma.[9] At the end of June, Vaughn and Carter brought news of the St. Louis branch's activities to the national NAACP conference in Detroit and listened intently as James Weldon Johnson outlined the organization's plan of action over the next year, including federal antilynching legislation, an end to public segregation, protection of voting rights, and "defeat by 'every legal means' of the Ku Klux Klan, both north and south."[10]

While newspapers had primarily led the charge against the Klan during the group's first forays into the state, organizations focused on civil rights, social justice, and religious toleration also turned their attention toward the Invisible Empire. Though they saw the Klan as a common enemy that could be fought in the press, in the courts, at the ballot box, and through educational campaigns, these groups had difficulty uniting in their fight against the hooded order. Ultimately, the groups formed a tenuous bond when confronting the Klan, particularly in the lead-up to local elections, but internal and external disagreements prevented a unified front. Deep concerns centering on racism, anti-Catholicism, anti-Semitism, and politics bubbled under the surface. They offered not only an opening for a splintering attack via Klan supporters but also opportunities for coalition members to question the commitment of others to the cause. Nevertheless, despite the failure to form a bipartisan, interracial, and interdenominational alliance, there was a surprising level of success among the groups rallying their fellow Missourians to challenge the growth of the Klan.

Though several entities in the United States investigated and fought the Klan during the 1920s, the six predominant organizations are the Catholic Central Verein, Knights of Columbus, American Unity League, National Association for the Advancement of Colored People, Universal Negro Improvement Association, and B'nai B'rith—and their affiliated chapters in the state—as well as two local groups, the Joplin Anti-Klan Organization and Carthage Anti-Klan Association, based in southwestern Missouri. Individually, these groups traditionally catered to their members' needs on various issues. The Central Verein, Knights of Columbus, and American Unity League had ties to Catholicism. B'nai B'rith supported Jewish causes. The Universal Negro Improvement Association focused on anticolonialism and Black Nationalism, while the interracial NAACP turned its attention to the plight of people of color in the United States. The Joplin Anti-Klan Organization and Carthage Anti-Klan Association objected to the political influence wielded by the Klan in southwestern Missouri, particularly within Jasper County. Together, at times, they fought the Invisible Empire.

In his assessment of anti-Klan activism during the 1920s, historian David J. Goldberg argues that Oregon's Compulsory Education Act, a law requiring that all students between the ages of eight and sixteen attend a public school in the state, served as the primary rallying cry for

"We Will Tear Off This Mask of Secrecy"   113

Catholics to mobilize against the Invisible Empire.[11] On its surface, the act would seem to have little impact on anyone living outside of Oregon. Indeed, its supporters, particularly the Oregon Klan, intended for the law to shut down parochial schools and private academies, many of which were primarily administered by Catholic institutions, in the state.[12] Yet Klan leaders and members across the country saw great power in the new law and, with enough support from defenders of public school education, felt confident that similar legislation could be passed nationwide, maybe even enshrined through federal policy.

By the time that the *Missouri Valley Independent* reprinted an article in 1924 titled "Klan's Work Needed in Every Community," which spoke of the goals of the organization across the country, including advocacy of a national compulsory public school attendance law, Catholic groups, particularly the Knights of Columbus, were hard at work challenging the Compulsory Education Act.[13] This resistance was bolstered by the fact that the law would not go into effect until 1926. Though the Knights of Columbus, outside of Oregon councils, initially paid little attention to the popular referendum that led to the 1922 law, the organization, under the leadership of Missourian and Supreme Advocate Luke E. Hart, soon joined together with other groups to oppose the law and pursued legal options to challenge similar legislation in other states. In 1925, only one year before the law was supposed to take effect, the US Supreme Court ruled it unconstitutional in *Pierce v. Society of Sisters*.[14]

In reviewing materials from Catholic organizations, particularly the Catholic Central Verein and Knights of Columbus, Goldberg's assertion that the Compulsory Education Act played a significant role in Catholic activism against the Klan is legitimate. However, earlier activism against anti-Catholic groups in the nineteenth and early twentieth centuries cannot be overlooked. The experience gained by Catholic leaders in confronting groups like the American Protective Association and publications such as the *Menace* served them well in their later work against the Klan. So, while organizations may have overwhelmingly confronted the Klan after passage of the Oregon school law, it should also be noted that some Catholics in Missouri, especially those affiliated with newspapers like the *Kansas City Catholic Register*, *St. Joseph Catholic Tribune*, *Vienna*

114   Chapter Three

Home-Advisor, St. Louis Catholic Herald, Church Progress, and *Western Watchman,* closely monitored the hooded order's growth and mobilized against it prior to the law's enactment in 1922.

Founded in 1855, the German Roman Catholic Central Verein was organized as a national federation of benevolent societies and quickly emerged as one of the preeminent organizations committed to German Catholics in the United States.[15] By the early twentieth century, the CCV claimed a membership of roughly 125,000 members scattered throughout the United States, with particular strength in New York, Pennsylvania, Illinois, Minnesota, Wisconsin, and Missouri. Concerning itself primarily with theology, social reform, labor issues, and countering the spread of socialism in the United States, the CCV also took a strong stance against religious intolerance. In 1908, the CCV established a Central Bureau in St. Louis headed by Frederick P. Kenkel. Born in Chicago in 1863, Kenkel was raised Catholic before distancing himself from the church as he entered adulthood. He returned to the faith following the death of his first wife in 1889 and soon became a significant figure in American Catholicism. By the time of his appointment as director, Kenkel was a member of the CCV's Committee for Heranbildung (Education) and editor of one of the most influential German Catholic newspapers in the United States, St. Louis's *Die Amerika.*[16]

Around the time Kenkel received his promotion to the Central Bureau, the CCV established a bilingual magazine called the *Central-Blatt and Social Justice.* Printed in English and German, the magazine featured articles from leading Catholics on social questions, morality, and Christianity. The magazine also was a critical component in the Central Bureau's effort to combat anti-Catholicism, particularly to counter controversial lecture circuits undertaken by provocative speakers who claimed to be former priests and escaped nuns. While this focus on anti-Catholicism largely centered on the *Menace* and similar anti-Catholic newspapers prior to World War I, by the 1920s, the Klan gained the full attention of the magazine.[17] Kenkel used the *Central-Blatt and Social Justice* to keep readers abreast of the anti-Klan work pursued by Catholics in the United States, particularly in the Klan hotbed of Indiana.[18] In his writings on "the anti-Catholic campaign," J. Elliot Ross of Texas advised Catholics to "act more wisely and energetically than we have in the past" to ensure that the religious bigotry associated with the "multi-K'd bamboozlers" did not reach the levels of the APA or Know-Nothings of the nineteenth century. However, Ross was also quick to warn against "fight[ing] fire with fire" because "practically nothing can be done" in the midst of mass hysteria. Instead, Catholics should "keep passion down as much as possible." To Ross, the best way to defeat religious intolerance was to educate non-Catholics about the church to offset the venom dispensed by anti-Catholic lecturers.[19]

Ross's position on the need for a robust educational campaign to counter Protestant suspicions of the church was not new among American Catholics. A sizable portion of Catholics no doubt agreed with Ross's assessment that "fifteen minutes, or ten minutes, or even five minutes a day [of studying the Catholic faith] will accomplish wonders."[20] Yet while some church leaders, including Saint Louis University's Rev. Alphonse M. Schwitalla, SJ, who argued that parochial schools successfully repelled elements of "Knownothingism and A.P.Aism," disputed claims that Catholics were lethargic in their educational efforts, it did concern others like Henry Seyfried of Indiana.[21] In a speech at the annual convention of the Catholic Union of Missouri, Seyfried told the audience, including Kenkel, who was in attendance, that "bigotry will never die out so long as the devil lives.... It is our duty not only to be on the defensive but on the offensive or the aggressive." He called upon those in the crowd to not be passive but to "carry high the banner of Catholicity among Americans."[22]

Together, the Central Bureau and the *Central-Blatt and Social Justice* kept a close watch over the activities of anti-Catholic groups, particularly the Klan, throughout the 1920s. With Kenkel at the helm, the Central Bureau advised supporters to mail in inquiries about anti-Catholic lecturers or libelous charges against religious institutions. In a letter to Rev. G. E. Sommerhauser of St. Louis, bureau workers warned the priest that associates with a lecturer named "Mrs. Neva Miller" had connections with the hooded order.[23] After potential libelous information was printed in the Klan publication *Fiery Cross*, a member of the Convent of the Good Shepard in Fort Thomas, Kentucky, wrote to the bureau to explain the circumstances surrounding rumors that the facility prevented children from seeing their relatives.[24] Writing to Father John Keyes about an alleged fake priest in Kansas City, Kenkel reminded him that "we collect

116 Chapter Three

such material, and even seemingly meagre bits of information, properly pieced together, may prove of value."[25] During the first half of the twentieth century, the Central Bureau collected data on numerous alleged anti-Catholic lecturers across the United States, dispensed the information to concerned parishes, and pursued legal recourse when necessary.[26]

While the CCV appealed primarily to German Catholics, the Knights of Columbus had a much larger nationwide apparatus from which to draw support and counteract religious bigotry. Formed in 1881, the Knights of Columbus began, much like the CCV, as a fraternal organization and mutual-benefit society. From its humble beginnings in New Haven, Connecticut, under the tutelage of Father Michael J. McGivney, the Knights of Columbus grew into a formidable organization that served Catholics in the United States and throughout the world.[27] In addition to its fraternal work, the Knights were also deeply concerned with the image of Catholicism. With the rise of the APA in the 1890s and the subsequent publication of several anti-Catholic newspapers in the United States, the Knights of Columbus increasingly turned its attention to religious intolerance by the early twentieth century. In these years, the Knights of Columbus's Commission on Religious Prejudices began an extensive campaign to stamp out anti-Catholic lectures, pamphlets, and newspapers, but with the dawn of World War I, this work was halted due to the global crisis.[28] At the close of the war, to combat intolerance directed at Catholics and so-called hyphenated Americans, the Knights of Columbus launched a historical commission to educate Americans, particularly schoolchildren, about the contributions made by marginalized groups. The commission's actions resulted in a literature series that highlighted the work of the United States' diverse population, including W. E. B. Du Bois's *The Gift of Black Folk*, George Cohen's *The Jews in the Making of America*, and Frederick F. Schrader's *The Germans in the Making of America*.[29]

Around the same time, the Knights of Columbus renewed its efforts to stamp out the bogus oath. In addition to *The Protocols of the Elders of Zion*, the bogus oath came to be one of the most widely circulated documents distributed by anti-Catholic lecturers and Klan supporters during the 1910s and 1920s. During Joseph Pelletier's tenure as the Knights of Columbus's supreme advocate, the organization took the stance that litigation against the distributors of the bogus oath would achieve limited success and prove extremely costly. Instead, Pelletier advised state councils to prosecute the matter locally.[30] When Luke E. Hart was elected supreme advocate in 1922, however, this policy shifted to a more united effort to combat the literature.[31] Born in Iowa in 1880, Hart was no stranger to anti-Catholicism. He had vocally opposed the hooded order when it arrived in his adopted hometown of St. Louis in 1921 and, in addition to speaking at anti-Klan meetings, took the matter before the Board of Aldermen, though that body took no action.[32] While serving on the Board of Aldermen, Hart emerged as a prominent official within the Knights of Columbus. Starting as a knight in 1908, he served as state deputy and supreme director before he was elected supreme advocate.[33]

FIGURE 10. Luke E. Hart, ca. 1920s. Courtesy of Knights of Columbus Supreme Council Archives.

118   Chapter Three

As Hart rose through the organization's ranks, Missouri Catholics were well acquainted with his policies and positions on key issues due to his "State Deputy's Letter" that appeared on the front page of the *Mariner*, the official publication of the state's Knights of Columbus. Since its start in 1918, Hart and his immediate successor, T. E. Purcell, frequently utilized the editorial section of the *Mariner* to address topics relevant to Catholicism in the state, including reminders that the "enlightenment of our non-Catholic neighbors on the things that the Church teaches is an important work" as well as warnings about those "who have unceasingly devoted their energies in an endeavor to tear down, to create dissatisfaction, and . . . obstruct the work of the State Council."[34] Additionally, the *Mariner* updated fellow knights on the activities of statewide councils. Sprinkled among news about meetings, ceremonies, and financial information, the *Mariner* also allowed councils to share their efforts to combat anti-Catholicism. Not long after the death of Nellie Hale in Buchanan County in 1922, St. Joseph 571 announced the creation of a committee on public information to "fight the propaganda the Klan is creating" and advised fellow knights that "the surest way to thwart [the Klan's] purposes is to turn the searchlight of publicity on them. Make them show their faces. Make them admit membership in the organization or make them publicly repudiate the Klan."[35] A month later, Argyle 2047 of Osage County objected to comments made by Kansas governor Henry J. Allen that the Knights of Columbus and the Klan were similar by declaring, "In times of storm and stress, when Catholic, Jew, and negro were good enough to shed their blood, no Ku Kluxer 'patriot' was in sight, but the K. of C. were on the job and helped the boys here and across the seas in every possible way."[36]

When Luke E. Hart entered the office of supreme advocate, he faced several pressing concerns, but one of the biggest issues was the Klan's involvement in the continued circulation of the bogus oath. Hart answered letters and inquiries on the bogus oath from around the country, especially as they related to materials distributed by the KKK and the *New Menace*, the successor of the *Menace*. Hart wrote to newspapers, including the *New Menace*, asking them to cease publication of the bogus oath. Such efforts, he confessed, had mixed results. He later admitted that little could be done directly to stop newspapers like the *New Menace* from circulating the document due to the newspaper's victory in federal court regarding obscenity in 1916.[37] Hart could collect leads on the publishers of the bogus oath but initially could offer few resolutions other than investigating each report. Not surprisingly, as the hooded order spread into the state, Hart's mailbox overflowed with letters from concerned Missourians seeking his advice on the Klan's use of the bogus oath and offering tips on local hooded activity.[38] After St. Louis residents complained about copies of the Klan-affiliated *Colonel Mayfield's Weekly* stuffed into pages of the *St. Louis Globe-Democrat*, Hart launched an investigation and discovered that the publication was inserted after the *Globe-Democrat* was delivered to select locations.[39] Some writers also inquired about Knights of Columbus materials that could be circulated to counter Klan publications, including a resident in Ripley County who asked for "Anti Klan Booklets and Pamphlets" so they could "put them to good use."[40]

In addition to consulting Catholic Missourians on the best ways to confront religious intolerance, Hart wrote to T. E. Purcell and John Fugel, among others, and advised them on how to address the bogus oath in newspapers sympathetic to the plight of Catholics.[41] While these newspapers prepared an editorial barrage on the bogus oath and its purveyors, Hart worked behind the scenes to expand a legal campaign against publishers of the notorious document. "The order is not only thus challenging its vilifiers, but as Supreme Advocate, acting by direction of the Supreme Knight, it is my duty to initiate prosecution of persons against whom evidence has been secured that they are circulators of the bogus oath," Hart was quoted in the *St. Joseph Catholic Tribune*. "We do not hesitate to call upon every member of the order, upon every Catholic and upon every broadminded fellow-citizen no matter what his denomination, to aid us in running down the circulators of this malign libel."[42] To secure full support, Hart informed Supreme Knight James Flaherty about the circulation of the bogus oath in Missouri and noted that "there has been a great wave of bigotry."[43] Flaherty signed off on the legal campaign immediately.[44] Hart also consulted with and wrote extensively to allies to inquire about the best way to fight the Klan. In a letter to Archbishop John J. Glennon, he admitted, "There can be no doubt that the Ku Klux Klan represents the same element in our population

120 Chapter Three

[anti-Catholicism], but I have no fear of it and I am sure it will never become a factor in our country."[45] Glennon responded immediately and hinted at differing interpretations of addressing the Klan. "Though when our Jewish brethren are attacked they take an entirely different view of it. Perhaps they are too sensitive, and perhaps on the other hand, we are to [sic] callous."[46]

While the CCV and Knights of Columbus's efforts to combat anti-Catholicism were deeply rooted by the 1920s, the American Unity League emerged as a relatively new Klan-fighting organization hoping to mobilize Americans, particularly Catholics, against the growing threat of the hooded order. Founded in Chicago in 1922, the AUL aimed to establish an "all nations" anti-Klan coalition while also seeking to remove the mask of Klansmen by any means necessary—including breaking into the homes, businesses, and headquarters of Klan officials and stealing the records of local klaverns. The organization also worked with ex-Klansmen to collect and distribute damning evidence. Once it secured this information, the AUL published the incriminating materials in its newspaper, *Tolerance*. While this method of identifying Klansmen did have some success, it was not without controversy. Put simply, members committed crimes by obtaining the records under unlawful circumstances. Additionally, with the mass publication of records, Klan chapters began to produce fake membership lists in case of a raid. Not knowing about these fake lists, the AUL quickly found itself in court. Most famously, gum manufacturer William Wrigley Jr. sued the AUL for libel after his name appeared in *Tolerance* as a Klansman. Similar cases led to financial troubles for the AUL and weakened the organization to the point of shutting down.[47]

Despite being headquartered in neighboring Illinois, the AUL struggled to gain a strong foothold in Missouri. Its extralegal attempts to gain Klan records met with some controversy in St. Louis when the Klan-affiliated *Patriot* accused the AUL and *Tolerance* of repeating names of alleged Missouri Klansmen in its published lists to make them seem longer as well as mistakenly including Catholics and members of the Knights of Columbus.[48] Additionally, the *St. Louis Star* warned the group that it should avoid fighting fire with fire when it came to the

Klan and instead opt for an educational campaign about the dangers of the hooded order.[49] Finally, the AUL had hoped to gain the support of Governor Hyde, but he politely refused an appointment to the organization's national committee. Though an outspoken opponent of the Klan, Hyde claimed that organizations created solely to fight the KKK would hurt the overall anti-Klan cause by giving publicity and advertising to the Invisible Empire.[50]

Though newspapers carried articles on AUL activities throughout the United States, few records exist to show how active the organization was in Missouri.[51] Outside of a well-publicized speech before several Irish American groups in Kansas City by P. H. O'Donnell, president of the AUL, and the publication of alleged St. Louis Klansmen's names in *Tolerance*, St. Joseph appears to be the only community to experience any sort of growth of the organization.[52] The AUL's arrival helped shore up anti-Klan strength in St. Joseph during a period of substantial growth in the city's hooded population. The *St. Joseph News-Press* and *St. Joseph Catholic Tribune* declared that "St. Joseph has an anti-Ku-Klux Klan to combat the Ku-Klux Klan." Hinting at the group's diversity, both newspapers announced that the local AUL chapter numbered twelve hundred members and that the "president and vice-president are Protestants, the secretary is Catholic and the treasurer is a Jew."[53] The *Catholic Tribune* also warned Klan members that "our city and county officials . . . are fulfilling their duties and need no prodding from the trouble-brewing 'exalted cyclops' to do so."[54]

The AUL worked quickly in St. Joseph to educate residents on the dangers of intolerance while also setting its sights on the Klan and its fiery rhetoric. After Rev. Victor K. Aubrey of Third Street Presbyterian Church spoke out favorably regarding the Klan, the AUL held a rally called "True Principles of Americanism" featuring several speakers, including state senator T. J. Lysaght. Continuing the theme of Americanism, the St. Joseph AUL held a second rally a few weeks later featuring Mayor Henry Burton of Kansas City, Kansas, who was well known for his opposition to the Klan. Instead of targeting individual Klansmen, the St. Joseph AUL and its speakers promoted political and religious liberty while denouncing the rhetoric of the Invisible Empire. "It shall be the aim and objective of this association," a local AUL advertisement read, "to draw attention to these principles and to combat by open and frank discussion all efforts to discriminate against race, faith or sect."[55]

Despite being one of the most visible anti-Klan groups in the United States, the American Unity League faltered by the mid-1920s. While the organization was able to secure prominent endorsements, such as Thomas Dixon, the author of *The Clansmen*, which inspired D. W. Griffith's *The Birth of a Nation*, its legal trouble over securing and publishing the names of alleged Klan members proved too costly.[56] Newspapers continued to report on P. H. O'Donnell's plans for a national anti-Klan coalition, but the movement soon sputtered. The *Missouri Valley Independent* gleefully reported on William Wrigley's libel suit against *Tolerance*, noting that the AUL was "a great helper to our cause."[57] By 1924, references to AUL activities in Missouri newspapers slowed to a trickle as the organization slowly faded into obscurity.

While it may have taken most Catholics until the enactment of Oregon's Compulsory Education Act to mobilize into a Klan fighting force, African American groups had a long history of opposition to the hooded order that dated back to its Reconstruction-era ancestor. By the early twentieth century, several prominent organizations emerged to assist African Americans, challenge Jim Crow, and promote Black identity. Among these organizations, the National Association for the Advancement of Colored People and Universal Negro Improvement Association stand out not only for their work to facilitate these goals but also for the way they approached the rise of the second Klan. Initially voicing opposition to the hooded order, particularly through their organizational publications, each group took a different path in addressing the Klan as the 1920s progressed. The NAACP eventually emerged as the most vocal and potent Klan fighter, yet the UNIA is also important to study to understand the larger concerns of African Americans during the 1920s.

The momentum that eventually led to the establishment of the NAACP grew out of the oppressive conditions of Black life during the nineteenth century. Amid lynch mobs and the hardening of Jim Crow, a growing dissatisfaction emerged toward the accommodationist policies of Booker T. Washington. With the death of Frederick Douglass in 1895,

Washington emerged as the de facto leader of the United States' African American population; however, Black activists such as Ida B. Wells and W. E. B. Du Bois critiqued his public image as a philanthropist and educator who seemingly kowtowed to white society and refused to critique the ever-increasing epidemic of racial violence. Additionally, prominent white progressives, who had originally backed Washington, turned against him by the early twentieth century. These critics, particularly Oswald Garrison Villard, Mary White Ovington, Henry Moskowitz, Moorfield Storey, and key members of Du Bois's Niagara Movement, eventually aligned to form the NAACP in 1909.[58] By the 1920s, the organization claimed more than three hundred branches nationwide with an estimated membership of nearly one hundred thousand, including seven branches in Missouri.[59]

Since its creation was a reaction to segregation, discrimination, lynching, and the failures of local, state, and national leaders to address these issues, it is not surprising that these topics became the core of the NAACP's mission. The NAACP was very active in combating the threat of lynching and the inactivity of local officials to bring mobs to justice, both in Missouri and nationwide. However, as the 1920s dawned, the NAACP also became increasingly concerned with the growth of the Klan throughout the United States. While never overtaking the organization's main push for litigation and legislation aimed at protecting the constitutional rights of American citizens, the group's anti-Klan crusade still proved quite effective in mobilizing people to challenge the Invisible Empire, even as the NAACP experienced limited growth during the 1920s.[60]

In Missouri, this anti-Klan mobilization occurred simultaneously with the arrival of the hooded order in St. Louis in 1921. Soon after Grand Goblin Frank Crippen notified the press of his plans for recruitment in Missouri, the St. Louis NAACP issued a statement declaring that it intended to actively fight the growth of the Klan in the city.[61] While the St. Louis NAACP took the lead in fighting the Klan, similar activities occurred throughout the state. In Kansas City, the local branch closely monitored the movement of the Klan along the Missouri-Kansas border and advised the national branch that it should write an op-ed response to a *Kansas City Star* article about the growth of the hooded

124   Chapter Three

order under William Simmons.[62] The Klan's recruitment in Missouri also brought a reaction from residents of Cape Girardeau, who set up a meeting to discuss the organization and the lynching of Roy Hammonds in Bowling Green, Missouri. Cape Girardeau's NAACP members then issued a resolution calling on Governor Hyde to prevent "such a shameful, disgraceful and lawless organization from being legalized to operate its nefarious plans in the State of Missouri."[63] Later, when Cape Girardeau mayor James A. Barks asked a Klan recruiter to leave town, local branch member H. N. Jones wrote to NAACP headquarters that city officials "acted so quickly that we were not given time to even call a meeting before the speaker was hurridly [sic] ejected from the city and warned never to return."[64] In southwest Missouri, a threatening letter from Springfield Klan No. 12 to Dr. James B. Clark brought an inquiry from the NAACP. Clark, whose wife, Pearl, was involved in the local NAACP, was warned that "white girls and colored Doctors should stay apart" after it was rumored that he performed secret abortions. Walter White called upon the chief inspector of the Postal Service to investigate the letter, but mail officials advised White and Clark to handle the matter with local law enforcement.[65]

The NAACP also worked to get political support for its campaign against the Klan. In the lead-up to the congressional investigation in the fall of 1921, the NAACP sent out questionnaires to members of Congress regarding their stance on the KKK.[66] Among those polled were Missouri congressmen Roscoe C. Patterson, T. W. Hukriede, and I. V. McPherson. In response, Patterson declared that he was "unreservedly opposed to any secret organization that finds it necessary for its members to hide their faces and forms behind a mask."[67] Hukriede informed the NAACP that "I consider . . . un-American any organization which is founded on race hatred or religious hatred . . . and as the Ku Klux Klan falls in this category, I am unalterably opposed to this organization."[68] McPherson concluded that organizations that "excite riots and usurp the power of government deserve the condemnation of all law abiding citizens."[69]

Perhaps the most significant achievement by the NAACP in its efforts to organize political support against the Klan was the successful recruitment of Governor Hyde. Since Hyde's gubernatorial election in 1920, the NAACP had repeatedly called upon him to take up the cause of African Americans in the state. This pressure intensified in the wake of the Roy Hammonds lynching in 1921 and as the Dyer Anti-Lynching Bill languished in Congress in early 1922.[70] It was in the midst of direct correspondence between Hyde and James Weldon Johnson on these issues that Cora J. Carter, herself quite involved in the anti-Klan campaign, asked the governor if he would be interested in joining the NAACP.[71] Hyde accepted the offer, though it did not get much attention in the press at the time. With the governor enrolled as a "contributing member," NAACP officials no doubt felt certain that Hyde would be more likely to approach racial issues, particularly those surrounding the Klan, with the same goals as the organization.[72]

Despite its success in mobilizing against the Klan, the NAACP found itself in a period of decline during the 1920s due to efforts by some states to suppress the group.[73] Additionally, a new organization, the Universal Negro Improvement Association, threatened to siphon members from the NAACP. Founded a few years after the NAACP, the UNIA was the creation of Marcus Garvey. Born in Jamaica in 1887, Garvey traveled the world at a young age and became a strong advocate for Black Nationalism. While fighting for causes similar to the NAACP in the United States, the UNIA under Garvey also promoted self-reliance, racial uplift, and a "back to Africa" movement that encouraged decolonization and nationhood.[74] By the 1920s, divisions of the UNIA existed throughout the United States, particularly along the East Coast and the Deep South, with its central headquarters located in Harlem, New York. In addition to its members in the United States, the UNIA also claimed widespread support among people of African ancestry around the globe, and its leading publication, *Negro World*, distributed roughly a half-million copies each week to its international audience.[75]

While it mainly focused its organizational attention on Black Nationalism and racial uplift, the UNIA also kept an eye on the growth of the Klan in the United States. When it was rumored that the Klan planned to recruit members in New York, Garvey publicly warned the group that the state's Black population would fight against such actions.[76] The *Negro World*, with Garvey at the helm, also informed its readers about the growth of the Klan throughout the United States, particularly when anti-Klan groups sought to challenge the Invisible

126   Chapter Three

Empire.[77] In February 1921, the *Negro World* advertised an anti-Klan mass meeting in New York City featuring prominent labor activists such as A. Philip Randolph, Chandler Owen, Elizabeth Gurley Flynn, and Paul Robeson.[78] After reprinting a series of articles from the *New York World*'s expose on the group, the *Negro World* editorialized that "if . . . the present Ku Klux Klan is a patriotic, law-abiding and peace-loving organization, why does it take the name and don the mask of the infamous organization of 1868?"[79]

Despite the UNIA's tough talk against the Klan in the early 1920s, Garvey soon moved in a different direction regarding the Invisible Empire. In June 1922, he held a secret meeting with E. Y. Clarke, Klan imperial wizard William Simmons's second in command.[80] An accurate depiction of the meeting is hard to come by, as Garvey was the only one to acknowledge the gathering publicly. Simmons remained silent on the subject and ultimately faced internal pressure from other Klan officials because of the Garvey meeting.[81] In his front-page editorial in the July 22 edition of the *Negro World*, Garvey defended the meeting as an attempt to gain "first-hand information about the Klan's attitude toward the race I represent."[82] However, in the time between his meeting with Clarke and the defensive editorial of July 22, Garvey and the *Negro World* repeatedly offered no resistance to the actions of the Klan across the country. On July 1, after discussing a letter allegedly sent to an Omaha, Nebraska, Black newspaper by the local Klan, Garvey argued that "the bitterest enemy of the Negro is not the white man [or] Ku Klux Klan, but the Negro himself."[83] The theme that the United States was a "white man's country" came up often in Garvey's defense of the Klan, and he was quick to remind his followers that groups actively fighting the Invisible Empire, particularly the NAACP, were out of touch with the wishes of African Americans.[84] "Our Du Boises [*sic*], Johnsons et al. are living in the air," the *Negro World* proclaimed. "They are as far from understanding the Negro problem of America and the western world as a monkey in understanding how far Mars is from Jupiter."[85] Instead, Garvey advised the nation's Black population "not to 'antagonize' [the Klan], not to petition Congress about it, not to obstruct its activities, but to organize, to organize in our own behalf!"[86]

In reviewing the circumstances surrounding the meeting between Garvey and Clarke, scholars have speculated about the reasoning behind both men's agreement to talk in Atlanta. Scholar Judith Stein argues that Garvey wanted to expand the UNIA farther into the South during the early 1920s so he "accommodated to regional ways" and "publicly praised Jim Crow."[87] According to Stein, Garvey's compliance with Jim Crow caught the attention of Clarke who agreed to a meeting in the hopes that it would reinforce the Klan's preferred image of patriotic reformers instead of moral and racist vigilantes.[88] Agreeing in part with Stein's assessment, scholar Mary G. Rolinson notes that Garvey and Clarke both shared an opposition to miscegenation and felt that something needed to be done to stop interracial rape.[89] Garvey's position on the subject gained him support among some white southerners, and the UNIA experienced less harassment while organizing in the region then its chief rival, the NAACP, due to his stance on racial issues.[90] However, one cannot overlook that around the time of his meeting with Clarke, Garvey was preparing for the UNIA's third annual convention in Harlem.[91] As Colin Grant points out, troubles endured by the UNIA during the early 1920s, particularly those centering on his arrest for mail fraud, may have pushed Garvey into a new path to stabilize the organization.[92] When this is considered, Garvey probably knew that the controversy around the meeting would impact recruitment and turn public attention toward the UNIA's "back to Africa" movement as it met for the convention.

Whatever his reason for the meeting, Garvey was condemned by several prominent Black leaders. Influenced by the NAACP, a major "Garvey Must Go" campaign soon followed his meeting with Clarke. Though the discussion with Clarke was not the only reason behind the campaign, Garvey's peculiar support and embrace of the Klan fanned the flames of a fire that had started when opposition leaders like A. Philip Randolph and Chandler Owen felt that he was ignoring racial issues in the United States in favor of his support for Pan-Africanism. Garvey also publicly challenged the NAACP and threatened to siphon members when the organization was entering a rough patch in recruiting. It is unsurprising then that the NAACP took part in the "Garvey Must Go" campaign considering the tumultuous relationship between it and the UNIA, but that William Pickens, one of his key allies, took part and caught Garvey off guard.[93]

William Pickens, despite his role as a field organizer for the NAACP, was a supporter of Marcus Garvey. Before joining the NAACP in an official capacity, he had even contemplated joining the UNIA.[94] However, his support for Garvey was tested following the June 1922 meeting. When Garvey offered a special invitation to an upcoming UNIA ceremony, Pickens declined, citing, "I gather from your recent plain utterances you are now endorsing the Ku Klux Klan."[95] In grilling Garvey over his supposed support for the Klan, Pickens noted that the rank-and-file members of the UNIA's many divisions would not stand for such an alliance with the Invisible Empire. As he closed his letter, Pickens offered an outright rejection of any honorary title that the UNIA or Garvey might bestow upon him in the future and argued that he "would rather be a plain black American fighting in the ranks AGAINST the Klan and all its brood than to be the Imperial wizard of the Ku Klux of the allied Imperial Blizzard of the U.N.I.A."[96]

William Pickens's comments, combined with information on the larger "Garvey Must Go" movement, received considerable coverage in Missouri newspapers, particularly in communities with UNIA divisions. Both the St. Louis Post-Dispatch and the St. Louis Star relayed the allegations put forth by Garvey's critics to their readers.[97] The St. Louis Argus reprinted Pickens's letter to Garvey, in which he criticized the UNIA leader for his sentiments on the Klan.[98] However, despite the attention paid to the "Garvey Must Go" campaign, it is hard to know how Garveyites in Missouri responded to their leader's comments on the Klan. While Garvey's earlier denunciations of the Klan no doubt inspired his followers to join in anti-Klan protests, the continued support for the UNIA in St. Louis, Kansas City, and southeast Missouri following the 1922 meeting suggests that members did not overwhelmingly flee the organization over the Klan issue.[99]

The decision of Missouri UNIA members to continue to align with the organization despite the growing opposition to Garvey's activities is significant, considering the anti-Klan sentiment within the state and the growth of the Invisible Empire in communities with UNIA divisions. Members remained loyal in southeast Missouri even after Garvey responded to violent threats made against Black laborers in the region by advising them that "this is a white man's country" and that they should focus their attention on "the building up of a country of their own."[100] Despite the continued success of the UNIA in the midst of the "Garvey

Must Go" campaign, its central figure struggled with internal and external issues for the rest of the 1920s. Following his conviction for mail fraud, members of the "Garvey Must Go" campaign got their wish when Marcus Garvey was deported from the United States in 1927.[101] The central offices of the UNIA moved from Harlem to Jamaica and eventually to London following his deportation, but the organization struggled to maintain its recruiting success as the decade wore on.[102]

Just as African American organizations experienced division over how to address the growth of the Klan, so too were American Jews unsure about the best way to mobilize against the Invisible Empire. However, one group, the Independent Order of B'nai B'rith, emerged as the most vocal proponent of battling anti-Semitism. Founded earlier than other anti-Klan organizations, the Independent Order of B'nai B'rith was established in New York City by German Jews in 1843.[103] Like other organizations of that era, B'nai B'rith began as a fraternal group with community improvement as its main goal. Additionally, the group offered key benefits for those who held membership. Throughout the first fifty years of its existence, B'nai B'rith built a strong foundation around protecting Jewish rights in the United States and worldwide.[104] At the dawn of the twentieth century, B'nai B'rith turned its attention toward growing anti-Semitic sentiment nationwide. One of the biggest incidents to garner the organization's attention was the trial of Atlanta Jewish businessman Leo Frank, who experienced extreme anti-Semitism for his alleged role in the murder of Mary Phagan. After Georgia's governor commuted Frank's guilty sentence to life imprisonment, a mob kidnapped Frank and lynched him in nearby Marietta.[105]

Though formed before the lynching of Leo Frank, B'nai B'rith established the Anti-Defamation League as an auxiliary of the main organization to combat such examples of anti-Semitism.[106] The circumstances surrounding Frank's death became the central focus of the ADL in its early years, though this was not its sole campaign. "The evidence of prejudice and discrimination has been abundant, both in social and in business circles, as well as in public life," declared Adolf Kraus, president of B'nai B'rith, in 1913.[107] The ADL also focused particular attention on an article series published in Henry Ford's *Dearborn Independent* titled

"The International Jew." Inspired by *The Protocol of the Elders of Zion* and Werner Sombart's *The Jews and Modern Capitalism*, and crafted by Ford associates Ernest G. Liepold and William J. Cameron, "The International Jew" examined an alleged conspiracy undertaken by Jewish leaders to influence and dominate global affairs.[108] In response to "The International Jew," B'nai B'rith and the ADL launched a series of pamphlets objecting to the articles' blatant anti-Semitism and calling on prominent Americans to denounce Henry Ford. This campaign met with moderate success, though Ford did not immediately remove the content from his *Dearborn Independent*.[109]

By the 1920s, at the same time that the ADL waged war against Henry Ford, the organization confronted a new threat in the Klan. With the rise of the Klan out of the South, the ADL became more politically active to prevent anti-Semitic legislation. In a twelve-month period between 1920 and 1921, the *Modern View* announced that the ADL had "distributed among educators, public officials, clergymen, publicists, and public libraries nearly 300,000 pieces of literature in which the nefarious activities of anti-Semitic agencies in this country has been exposed and the charges which they have made, conclusively answered."[110] Yet, despite its activism, historian Deborah Dash Moore has noted that the ADL was relatively weak in the 1920s compared to the Klan. The organization found some minor success in its campaign against the Klan, but overall, the ADL and B'nai B'rith could do little to stop the spread of the Invisible Empire.[111]

While American Jews mustered only limited success against the Klan nationwide, their brethren in Missouri still actively worked against anti-Semitism and the hooded order. Jews had lived in Missouri prior to statehood, but it was not until 1855 that St. Louis established the first B'nai B'rith lodge.[112] Kansas City soon followed with its own lodge in 1868, and by the early twentieth century, Jews could be found throughout the state, though most tended to live in urban communities.[113] In 1921, the St. Louis Board of Aldermen considered a bill pushed by prominent local Jews, including Missouri ADL chairman Abraham Rosenthal, to levy a fine on publications, specifically the *Dearborn Independent* and the anti-Catholic *New Menace*, that attacked any race or religion.[114] City policemen soon began arresting anyone selling the *Dearborn Independent*, but the local press heavily criticized the policy.[115] Inspired by the efforts to remove objectionable newspapers from St. Louis streets, Ebn Ezra Lodge No. 47 started a recurring speakers series highlighting the ADL's work against anti-Semitism. At the same time, Missouri Lodge No. 22 launched a fund-raising campaign to fight back against "a definite movement in our country against all Jews and Judaism, directed by men who devote their entire time to the sowing of the seeds of hatred."[116]

While the *Jewish Voice* supported the arrests of those connected to the *Dearborn Independent*, it was unsure how to address St. Louis's growing Klan population that likely read the targeted newspapers.[117] When an alleged Klan document emerged suggesting that members fire Jewish employees and boycott Jewish businesses, the newspaper asked Imperial Wizard William Simmons to "give us the official attitude of the Klan towards the Jews."[118] After receiving a reply from Klan leaders in two states, the *Jewish Voice* assured its readers that the organization's official literature was not antagonistic to Jews.[119] The *Kansas City Jewish Chronicle* disagreed with the newspaper's conclusion. It argued that the Klan's "anarchistic policy . . . in addition to their outrages in defiance of the courts and the Constitution of America . . . is sufficient to condemn them." Still, the *Modern View* initially sided with the *Jewish Voice* in its stance that the Klan was not anti-Jewish.[120]

Abraham Rosenthal, Missouri ADL chairman and editor of the *Modern View*, initially expressed the belief that the Klan did not have "real or radical ill-will toward any self-respecting, law-abiding Jew" and added that "alleged organized Jewish opposition [to the Klan] is not justified nor necessary. It is inadvisable and injudicious. If opposition is imperative, it should not be by sects but by ALL citizens united, independent of creed. If the Klan opposes Catholics because of an alleged, prior, superior, allegiance to Papal authority, that misconception and error should be cleared up by Catholics themselves. Nor need the industrious negro fear, in our opinion, as long as he does right and as long as the government firmly stands true to the Constitution and the flag, in Washington."[121] Reprinting Imperial Wizard Hiram Evans's comments that the Klan was not antagonistic to Jews, the *Modern View* left it "to the judgment of our readers."[122] The newspaper soon changed its opinion, however, after comments emerged, allegedly from Klan officials,

132   Chapter Three

claiming that Jews were unblendable and un-American. This "vile libel," according to the *Modern View*, showed "malice and ignorance" toward Jews. "While its antagonism and narrow, bigoted opposition to the Jewish people had long been no secret to anyone who followed the un-American tactics of the masked mob," the Klan was now "unmasked" and all of its prejudice revealed.[123]

As is indicated by the shift in opinion about hooded activities among Missouri Jews, anti-Klan groups were bolstered by the investigative work and editorial commentaries of the press. Still, they also differed on how to address the Invisible Empire. Rosenthal's comments about Catholics and African Americans needing to speak out about concerns within their own communities highlight this problem. Additionally, the *St. Louis Argus*, while championing the NAACP campaign, including the anti-Klan efforts of sympathetic city leaders like Luke E. Hart, was quick also to ponder if he was "sincere in his denunciation of the Klan."[124] Such charges and pressure likely stung Hart, especially considering his appearance at an anti-Klan rally organized by the NAACP in 1921. However, he was also aware that the Knights of Columbus and the Catholic Church were still largely segregated institutions. Catholic schools in St. Louis and statewide would soon integrate, and Hart was involved in the eventual desegregation of the Knights of Columbus, but both did not occur until the 1940s.[125] Perhaps the biggest issue that divided the anti-Klan coalition was politics. It was one thing to support the anti-Klan activism of private organizations, but to dissolve the long-standing tradition of straight-party politics in favor of rallying around candidates of varying ideologies because they opposed the hooded order was another matter entirely.

While these national organizations and their state-level branches communicated their sentiments about the Klan and worked to address the differences that prevented a united coalition, a small but significant grassroots movement was under way in southwest Missouri. To this end, the mayoral race in Joplin in 1922, won by businessman Taylor Snapp, served as a barometer of hooded strength in the region and became a rallying cry for anti-Klan supporters to band together against the Invisible Empire.[126] Though Snapp did not actively solicit Klan support during his mayoral campaign, critics later claimed that his victory over Charles Patterson in 1922 ushered in a period of close alliance between city hall and the local klavern.[127] With few KKK documents surviving from the county, it is hard to prove that a victory for Snapp was a victory for the Klan. However, when given the opportunity, Snapp did not distance himself from the Klan. It was Snapp who approved plans for a Klan parade through Joplin to honor visiting Imperial Wizard Hiram Evans.[128] Snapp was also in attendance at Joplin's First Congregational Church when Klansmen arrived to give a donation.[129] Finally, and perhaps most damning, Snapp was reportedly seen meeting in secret with local Exalted Cyclops Pierre Wallace on at least one occasion.[130]

He may have won the mayor's race without overt hooded support, but Taylor Snapp's victory stirred strong anti-Klan feelings in Jasper County. In a letter to Missouri secretary of state Charles Becker, a Jasper County resident warned that "sentiment [regarding the Klan] seems to be equally devided [sic] and some Citizens and [sic] arming themselves as a defense of their homes and property, if relief is not furnished in time a clash is inevitable resulting in much bloodshed."[131] Such forebodings worried Governor Hyde, and he wrote to express hope that legislation in the upcoming year would give more power to state and local authorities to deal with issues involving the Klan.[132] The prediction of an inevitable clash in Jasper County over the Klan eventually came true, but it was more a war of words than of bloodshed.

In Jasper County, a fight over the Ku Klux Klan had been growing behind the scenes for most of 1921 and 1922. The Klan had reached considerable size in Joplin, Carthage, Webb City, and Cartersville by the start of 1923, but opposition, which had been largely nonexistent initially, began to mount. This anti-Klan sentiment came alive at a retirement banquet for Judge J. D. Perkins when one of the principal speakers, Frank Forlow, a Webb City resident and president of the Jasper County Bar Association, used his time at the podium to call out the Klan as unconstitutional.[133] While Forlow's words may have seemed out of place at a banquet honoring a retiring civic official, others in Jasper County shared his feelings on the Klan. Less than a week later, the Jasper County Bar Association announced that it would hold a meeting to gauge the general opinion of its members toward the Klan.[134] This decision was likely influenced by Forlow's words but also by the actions of the nearby Springfield Bar Association, which announced plans to ban all members associated with the Klan.[135]

The Jasper County Bar Association ultimately decided on a course of action that included issuing a public denouncement of the Klan as a "menace to government," pursuing action to remove Klan members, and calling on the Missouri General Assembly to pass laws that would outlaw the Invisible Empire. The Bar Association's denouncement angered the Invisible Empire of Jasper County. Ozark Klan No. 3 soon published lengthy responses in the *Joplin Globe* detailing the Klan's record in favor of patriotism and efficient law enforcement.[136] It also suggested that some of the men who signed the anti-Klan resolution got their civic positions through party loyalty instead of public record:

[We] sought no fight in this community which is ours, as well as yours. The KU KLUX KLAN is founded on principles of Right and Justice, which principles are the foundation of civilized government and existed long before the bar of justice was graced by your presence, and which principles will endure long after the disgruntled, and dissatisfied, and hard-to-die politicians, and intolerant squealers of intolerance among you have dropped by the wayside. While the best things your Association has ever been known to do is to pass resolutions and make speeches, the KU KLUX KLAN in Jasper County is, and has been since its organization, unceasing in its work for the betterment and advancement of the interests of ALL CITIZENS, and while your members seem very anxious that we "come out in the open," we assure you that no one, whose conscience is clear and whose conduct is above reproach, need have any fear of our "invisibility."[137]

After the Klan's scathing comments in the *Joplin Globe*, the Jasper County Bar Association reconvened to discuss the hooded order again. This time, the anti-Klan sentiment was not unanimous, as several attorneys voiced their opposition to the original resolution. Claiming they were not Klansmen, opponents of the original resolution cited that the information collected on the local Klan was based on hearsay and, thus, not reliable. The nearly four-hour meeting was also muddied by a list that was circulated containing the names of suspected local Klansmen, including the names of some Bar Association members who had spoken out against the Klan. One who did not question his name being on the list was Jasper County sheriff Harry Mead, who admitted that he had joined the Klan at one time but had left near the end of 1922.[138]

While the Jasper County Bar Association had somewhat succeeded in denouncing the Klan in 1923, local sentiment still leaned favorably toward the Invisible Empire. With the municipal election approaching in the spring of 1924, Jasper County's anti-Klan supporters felt it necessary to alert the voting public to the dangers of hooded rule. Under the guidance of local attorney George Grayston, who had been active in the efforts to denounce the Klan in the Jasper County Bar Association, the Joplin Anti-Klan Organization quickly formed with the intent of supporting candidates in the municipal election, particularly for public property and public utilities commissioner, health and sanitation commissioner, and local school boards.[139] Though members of JAKO did not specify why they targeted these commissioner positions, their reasoning is quite clear as both incumbents, J. M. Lane and Dr. M. B. Harutun, were rumored to be Klansmen because of their prior comments supporting the organization's reform goals.[140] If it could not get either man to admit their Klan ties, JAKO hoped to at least pressure other municipal and county candidates into making statements regarding the Invisible Empire.

The chief concern of the Joplin Anti-Klan Organization was that voters were unknowingly casting ballots for candidates who were sympathetic to the Klan. By making these ties visible, the organization hoped local voters would repudiate the Invisible Empire. JAKO soon launched an advertising campaign in the *Joplin Globe* and *Joplin News-Herald* to make local residents aware of the secrecy of the Klan and implore them to register to vote. The group reminded voters that the "Anti-Klan Organization wants not only good men to govern our city but wants free men, men who will counsel with all good citizens irrespective of race, creed or color . . . [and] whose course will not be determined by the prejudiced edict . . . of some secret organization, who meet in the dark hours of the night and who attempt to hide their identity during the day."[141] In its other ads, JAKO discussed "atrocities," "criminal Klan

136 Chapter Three

leaders," and how the "cross of Jesus Christ is not a fiery cross."[142] In placing before potential voters a long list of accusations against the Klan, the goal was simple, as one JAKO member defined it: "We will tear off this mask of secrecy and make candidates come out in the open and state their stand."[143]

With municipal primaries fast approaching, George Grayston, with the support of JAKO, publicly released a list of preferred candidates. To counter J. M. Lane as commissioner of public property and public utilities, JAKO backed L. L. Travis and R. P. Brown. In the race for commissioner of health and sanitation, Dr. W. H. Lanyon and W. E. Pierson received JAKO support.[144] JAKO's backing of two candidates for each commissioner position was an interesting choice, though it is likely that the relatively new group did not want to alienate potential supporters. Grayston indicated as much when he argued that JAKO did not center votes on a particularly anti-Klan candidate because "it would have been unfair to have discriminated between good men who had the courage ... to challenge the klan's [sic] control of the city."[145] Yet it seems evident that JAKO hoped that one of its candidates would have a strong enough showing to earn a place on the April ballot. With a heavier than usual vote expected, there was much to be won by the up-and-coming JAKO.

As the primary results came in for both parties, it quickly became apparent that Lane and Harutun had sizable leads in their respective races. However, JAKO still claimed victory after Travis and Lanyon finished second in their races, guaranteeing them a spot on the final ballot. Interestingly, in a public statement after the election, Grayston indicated that JAKO would back Travis for commissioner of public property and public utilities over Lane, but the organization had no preference between Harutun and Lanyon. Despite allegations of Klan ties with Harutun, JAKO felt confident that he was not a Klansman.[146] As for the race between J. M. Lane and L. L. Travis, Grayston did not mince words:

An analysis of the vote gives every reason for encouragement to those opposed to secret government. Three out of the four men nominated are positively not Klansmen. Mr. Lane got the klan [sic] vote. . . . As to Mr. Travis, he makes no concealment of the fact that he is not a member of the Ku Klux Klan. For this reason, in the coming election, Mr. Travis will receive the almost unanimous support of Joplin citizens actively opposed to the klan [sic]. Not only will he receive strong support because he is not a member of the klan [sic], but also because he is a strong man of high character, a resident of Joplin for twenty-nine years and well-fitted to fill the office of commissioner of public property and public utilities. . . . Many citizens believe that his election will do much to abolish secret government in our city and tend to remove the distrust and bitterness that the klan [sic] movement has engendered in our churches, our schools, our lodges and our civic organizations and even our business life. A vote for Mr. Travis means a vote for harmony among our citizens; a vote for him means lighted streets all night; a vote for him means a vote for city government conducted in the open light of the council chambers and not in a klavern.[147]

Joplin was not the only southwest Missouri community engulfed in a Klan/anti-Klan war. In nearby Carthage, Klan support from both Democrats and Republicans led anti-Klan backers to hastily consider forming a third-party group. Led by Judge Howard Gray, Allen McReynolds, and former Klansman Harry Mead—men like Grayston, with ties to the Jasper County Bar Association—the Carthage Anti-Klan Association (CAKA) formed soon after JAKO. Though both groups were not directly connected, they did share a common concern: if Klansmen or their sympathizers are on the ballot, they must be defeated. Due to its late formation, CAKA was unable to place candidates on the ballot for the municipal election. Instead, the organization endorsed an unofficial ticket of candidates from both parties. The most prominent name on the list was Charles Drake, Carthage's Democratic mayor.[148]

Having started separately, the anti-Klan groups in Joplin and Carthage quickly moved toward becoming a countywide organization. Only days before the municipal elections in both towns, the organizations decided to hold mass rallies in each community. To build toward both events, JAKO and CAKA inundated the *Joplin Globe*, *Joplin News-Herald*, and *Carthage Evening Press* with daily reminders of the threat posed by a Klan government.[149] "We charge that our liberties are endangered, our institutions are threatened, our citizens are intimidated," JAKO warned potential voters. "There is no longer an open and free discussion of the affairs of our City Government or of the conduct of the administration of our public schools."[150] If residents were concerned about these issues, JAKO advised them to attend an upcoming meeting at the Joplin Theater, which was opened to all residents to ensure "that there may be an intelligent decision by the voters of this city in the coming city election as to whether you prefer to have your city governed from the city hall or from the cave (Klavern) in Belleville."[151]

When the night of the big anti-Klan rally arrived, a large overflow crowd filled the theater. "I thank you for coming here, members of Ozark Klan No. 3," Perl Decker told the occupants of the front row as he opened his JAKO speech. "I much prefer to address you here than at your cave at Belleville."[152] Decker and the other speakers knew that the Klan had not so secretly infiltrated the meeting, but they cared little as each man took his turn denouncing the Klan and ridiculing those that wore "sheets over their bodies and pillowslips over their heads."[153] Though the list of speakers featured prominent men from throughout Jasper County, the main draw was Perl Decker. Decker, an ardent Prohibitionist and former US representative from Missouri, had lived most of his life in Joplin and watched as the city slowly became part of the Invisible Empire. He was aware of the activities of JAKO, and his personal correspondence indicates that he worked behind the scenes for the organization.[154] Now onstage in front of eighteen hundred Jasper County residents, Decker tore the Klan apart.

The central theme of Decker's speech was the role of the American citizen in denouncing religious intolerance, but, time and again, Decker returned to the subject of secrecy. "Secret lobbies, secret organizations, secret influences have always been the cause of debauchery and corruption in American politics," Decker told the audience. "If [the Klan] had their way the real course of our national congress and our state legislature and our school managers would be guided by the prejudiced edict of the head of their secret organization."[155] He presented dark scenarios to his listeners where Joplin's affairs were discussed and decided upon not in city hall but at the Klan's cave at Belleville—an example not too far off from reality in Jasper County. "Why should high-minded citizens of Joplin . . . appear before our city commission or before our school board,"

"We Will Tear Off This Mask of Secrecy" 139

Decker pondered, "if the course has already been shaped and determined by the meeting of a secret organization."[156]

After warning the crowd about the dangers of hooded politics, Decker next discussed the hooded order's violent legacy and laid out examples of moral vigilantism tied to the Klan. Perhaps, Decker argued, Klansmen had not undertaken these actions, but with such secrecy surrounding the organization, there was no way to know. Finally, Decker gave the audience and the Klansmen in attendance a history lesson. He told his listeners of the American presidents who had denounced religious intolerance. He spoke of the Catholic and Jewish soldiers of long-forgotten wars who defended their country despite bigotry against them. He closed with a

FIGURE 11. Perl Decker at Park College, 1927. Courtesy of Perl D. Decker Papers (C0092). The State Historical Society of Missouri.

140   Chapter Three

reminder about the price paid by all Americans to ensure liberty and freedom for their fellow citizens:

> If these boys, Jew and gentile and Protestant and Catholic could fight and die in time of war for that flag we love, can not we who are Protestants stand up like men, even at the risk of losing a little business, even at the risk of losing a little popularity, can we not stand up to fight to see that these Jewish boys and these Catholic boys and their fathers and their mothers, and their sisters and their brothers have the full enjoyment of the blessings and privileges emblemized by that flag for which they fought and died?[157]

With the meeting concluded, the message was as clear as the banners hanging in the Joplin Theater: "Vote for Visible Government." While the residents of Joplin considered JAKO's warning regarding the role of the Invisible Empire in their civic affairs, CAKA held its own rally in nearby Carthage. Smaller than the one in Joplin, the Carthage meeting, featuring Allen McReynolds and Howard Gray as the main speakers, filled every available space in the city's circuit court with the crowd crammed into adjacent hallways. McReynolds, a native of Carthage, denounced recent attempts by the Klan to donate Bibles to area public schools. Speaking on religious intolerance, he reminded the audience of the anti-Catholicism of past generations where "I was taught to believe the basement of every Catholic church in this country was filled with guns and ammunition and that at the word of the pope the Catholics would take up arms against this country."[158] The theme of past intolerance continued with Howard Gray, who told the audience that the Klan reminded him of the American Protective Association. He assured those in attendance that the Klan would meet a similar fate as the APA because it was "organized for personal gain" with a membership composed of people "duped into believing it an organization of Americans."[159]

After nearly two weeks of charges and attacks directed at it, Ozark Klan No. 3 took out ads in the *Joplin Globe* and *Joplin News-Herald* to defend the Invisible Empire. "Be Not Deceived," the local order warned voters. "Any statement to the effect that the Ku Klux Klan controls or dominates the Joplin city administration, or that it is attempting to do so, is an absolute lie!"[160] To charges that it met in darkness and secrecy, the Klan pointed out that the Knights of Columbus, B'nai B'rith, Odd Fellows, Masons, and even the city's own Anti-Klan Organization held similar secret meetings. According to the Klan, the real question surrounding the election was simple: "Do you want clean, efficient government by clean officials, qualified by ability to perform their duties to all the people, or a government by officials put forward through swapping of political favors and pre-election promises, or by those whose qualifications are that they need the money?"[161]

The growing tension between Klan/anti-Klan factions was not lost on the editors of the *Carthage Evening Press* and the *Joplin Globe*, who feared that party allegiance and straight-ticket politics would dissolve in the fray. The *Evening Press*, though an ardent opponent of the Klan, felt that "there are bigger things than the Ku Klux Klan . . . [and] the Republican party is one of them." Warning its readers against joining any third party organized by anti-Klan supporters, the *Evening Press* instead advised Republicans to support the party's candidates based on their merits "regardless of their Klan or anti-Klan affiliations."[162] Though not as partisan in its response as the *Evening Press*, the *Globe* hoped for a positive outcome in the election. Amid ads for both the Ku Klux Klan and JAKO in its March 30 edition, the *Globe* posited that "if the fight for and against the Ku Klux Klan in Joplin results in getting a good vote out at the annual city election day after tomorrow it will at least have accomplished some good."[163]

April 1, Election Day, saw a heavy turnout throughout Jasper County. Though it had existed for only a short time, JAKO was confident in its campaign and felt sure that voters would prefer visible government to the Invisible Empire. Yet when the returns came in, it soon became clear that the Klan still controlled large portions of Jasper County. In Joplin, Klan-backed candidates swept the municipal election. Up in Carthage, the preferred candidates of CAKA were defeated as well.[164] Though they had championed a message of liberty, tolerance, and uncorrupted government, the failure of both anti-Klan groups lay in their organization. While their membership included individuals who supported the actions of the Jasper County Bar Association meeting, there was no clear attempt to build upon this sentiment and establish an official anti-Klan

142   Chapter Three

organization until several months later. By the time JAKO and CAKA went public, there was less than a month until Election Day, insufficient time to mount a serious challenge to a well-entrenched Klan operation.

The need for continued activism from Jasper County anti-Klan supporters after the municipal election was not lost on Howard Gray. As president of the Carthage Anti-Klan Association, Gray had been one of the first Jasper County residents to denounce the Klan publicly. Working alongside Allen McReynolds, George Grayston, and Perl Decker, Gray served as one of the chief opponents of the Invisible Empire in Jasper County. But more than anyone else, the municipal election campaigns of JAKO and CAKA took a personal toll on Gray. During one of his public speeches, his wife received two anonymous phone calls at the family's home warning of an attack on her husband at a meeting. Frightened by the revelation, Mrs. Gray headed to the meeting with a few family members, where they found Howard Gray unharmed and unaware of the threats. Upon leaving the venue, Gray received a police escort back to his residence. The ordeal sent Mrs. Gray into a state of shock, and she spent several days recovering.[165] Nevertheless, Jasper County's anti-Klan supporters continued despite the threats. Only days after the municipal elections, George Grayston renewed the call to action: "The leaders of the anti-klan [sic] movement were not discouraged over the showing made by the new organization, which accomplished a great deal in its brief two weeks preceding the primary and election. It is the intention to perfect and enlarge our organization. . . . [W]e will carry on the battle for free government in city, state and nation as provided for in the constitution of the United States."[166]

Building upon the editorial activism of anti-Klan newspapers—and no doubt pressured into action by readers, publishers, and members alike—national organizations such as the Catholic Central Verein, Knights of Columbus, American Unity League, National Association for the Advancement of Colored People, Universal Negro Improvement Association, and B'nai B'rith, as well as local groups like the Joplin Anti-Klan Organization and the Carthage Anti-Klan Association, committed themselves to challenging the Invisible Empire. For some, like the CCV, Knights of Columbus, and NAACP, the fight against religious intolerance and racism was personal and served as one facet of larger organizational goals. Others, like the AUL, JAKO, and CAKA, came into existence as a direct result of hooded activity. At times, these organizations linked arms as part of an interracial, interdenominational, and bipartisan coalition. Yet just as often, these same groups were at odds with one another on a variety of policies and grievances, including how to structure and lead the years-long campaign against the Klan.

Going forward, these alliances would be further strained by the inclusion of politics into the relationship. Though these various groups could, at times, put their differences aside to focus on a common goal of stopping the spread of the Klan and challenging its key tenets, the addition of the "Klan issue" in political matters, particularly forcing candidates to state their feelings on the hooded order, threatened to rip the fragile coalition further apart. While anti-Klan activists were eager to channel their opposition to the hooded order into the platforms of their respective political parties, they soon found resistance from Klan supporters under the same tent, as well as political leaders more concerned with victory at all costs. Indeed, politics made strange bedfellows.

CHAPTER FOUR

"A Curious and Interested Spectator"
The "Klan Issue" in Missouri Politics

AS THE BURNS family prepared for bed at their farmhouse just outside Syracuse—a tiny dot on the map between Jefferson City and Kansas City on the Missouri Pacific Railroad—a gunshot rang out. C. S. Burns, a forty-year-old tenant farmer and the family patriarch, fell dead. In his retelling of the events of that evening, twenty-year-old Raymond Burns claimed that he had loaded the family's double-barrel shotgun at the request of his father, who wanted the firearm ready at a moment's notice should the family be awoken in the middle of the night. Instead, before the weapon could begin its nocturnal vigilance, Raymond's act of loading the gun led to its accidental discharge. Within seconds, its contents had ricocheted off a nearby heating stove and imbedded in C. S. Burns's chest.[1] Within days, newspapers around the United States covered Burns's death, with the *Baltimore Sun* reporting an article titled "Fear of Political Revenge Cost Missourian His Life."[2]

The Burns's nighttime routine of loading their double-barrel shotgun and placing it precariously within arm's reach each night was born out of the threatening letters that had come to the family's doorstep in Morgan County over the preceding weeks. C. S. Burns had been an unassuming farmer. Due to the agricultural depression that plagued Missouri after World War I, Burns struggled to pay off his mortgage, and the local bank threatened to take away his furniture and farming implements.

C. S. Burns was a wanted man. It wasn't the bank that wanted him, however, or his creditors. The board of directors at the bank in nearby Boonville had treated Burns leniently regarding the mortgage. Instead, countless Missourians were angry over the recent outcome of the state's gubernatorial campaign. Burns, a man who had never run for political office, had swung the election in 1924 simply by recounting the tale—in front of a notary public—of his meeting with Democratic candidate

146 Chapter Four

Arthur W. Nelson in Moniteau County. When the story hit the front page of the state's newspapers in October 1924, Nelson's bid to be the state's next governor was doomed.[3]

"I met and shook hands with and talked to Dr. A. W. Nelson of Cooper County," Burns recalled when asked about his meeting with the gubernatorial hopeful. The two had crossed paths in California, the county seat of Moniteau County, in June 1923. When asked why he was in California, Burns confessed that he was "at a meeting of the Ku Klux Klan . . . and was a member of said organization at the time." In explaining how this related to Nelson, the Democratic candidate for governor, Burns announced that he "saw him initiated into this order at said meeting." With that, Burns concluded his testimony and signed the affidavit in front of notary public W. H. Olney. The statement ended up in the hands of W. F. Phares, chairman of the Republican State Committee.[4] Two weeks before Election Day in October 1924, Phares went public with Burns's affidavit, as well as a second affidavit, signed by B. L. Morris and F. A. Collins, claiming that Nelson's name appeared in a Klan record book in Tipton, Missouri. In laying the affidavits before the eyes of Missouri voters, Phares sent shockwaves through the state. As he sprang an October surprise, Phares reminded voters that only months prior, "both the Republican and Democratic state convention[s] of Missouri . . . incorporated in their platform a declaration denouncing the Ku Klux Klan as un-American, unpatriotic, and opposed to the constitution."[5] Yet, Nelson, according to Phares, had bucked this bipartisan objection to the Klan by concealing his secret membership in the hooded order.

With his gubernatorial campaign thrown into shambles, A. W. Nelson and his advisers quickly crafted a rebuttal to Phares's claims. While on a campaign stop, Nelson issued a statement denying affiliation with the Klan. The affidavits, Nelson asserted, were the culmination of a whispering campaign aimed at discrediting him. "I know that I have never received any communication from the klan [sic], never have joined it, never made application to join it and never paid any initiation fee, dues or anything of the kind," Nelson told the press. Yet, to defend himself, Nelson revealed information that doomed his campaign and prevented his election a few weeks later. While brushing aside the comment that his name appeared in the Tipton Klan book, Nelson did admit meeting

Burns in California in 1923. However, he felt that the farmer was "honestly mistaken or is maliciously making a misstatement" in his affidavit. According to the candidate, he had only signed a card to gain admittance to the Klan event and left the rally before any official ceremonies. He had been "a curious and interested spectator."[6]

The "Klan issue" was the most important element in Missouri politics in the mid-1920s. No other issue dominated the attention of politicians, the press, and voters like the fiery crosses and white robes of the secret society. Despite attempts by political candidates and some newspaper editors to shift the focus to subjects like taxation, corruption, agriculture, and the various missteps of political rivals, the Klan issue always returned to the forefront. This issue centered on political candidates and their relationship or affiliation with the Invisible Empire. For some, being a preferred candidate of the Klan was enough to boost a campaign at the local level. For others, even the smallest rumors of Klan support had to be squelched through public denunciations of the organization. Still others gave only passing reference to the hooded order in the hopes that both Klan and anti-Klan voters would carry them through on Election Day. With the Klan publicly announcing the candidates it supported and the anti-Klan press ratcheting up its attention on the hooded sentiments of select politicians, candidates from the municipal to the federal levels quickly realized that their campaigns needed to address the subject of the Invisible Empire.

This so-called Klan issue, a rallying cry to potential voters about whether they favored the tenets and policies of the Klan or anti-Klan side, came to a head in three notable political campaigns in the first half of the 1920s. In 1922, as incumbent James A. Reed sought reelection to the US Senate, he utilized the Klan issue to assemble an urban white ethnic and anti-Klan voting bloc on his behalf against a growing list of opposition, including Republicans, Woodrow Wilson–aligned Democrats, and the hooded order. Two years later, as the Klan reached the zenith of its power and the anti-Klan coalition developed into a more effective fighting force, the races for president and governor highlighted the controversial and problematic nature of the Klan issue. Though not the dominant policy matter of the 1924 presidential campaign, the Klan issue was featured in

148   Chapter Four

debates from the state and national party conventions through Election Day as Calvin Coolidge, true to his nickname, Silent Cal, spoke little about the group, while his main challengers, John Davis and Robert La Follette, filled newspaper pages with their denunciations. At the same time, Gilbert O. Nations, a long-shot candidate from Missouri, openly endorsed the activities of the Klan and called upon members of the Invisible Empire to spearhead his takeover of the White House. In the midst of the presidential campaign, Missouri's gubernatorial race evolved from a broad primary field of candidates vying for Klan and anti-Klan support to a head-to-head challenge between A. W. Nelson and Sam A. Baker with the Klan issue at its center.

Analyzing the Klan issue in Missouri politics in the mid-1920s, political campaigns served as a key point of fracture within the hooded order. While the Klan would not decline nationwide until the latter half of the 1920s, this deterioration developed from the organization's results at the ballot box in 1922 and 1924. As scholars such as Thomas Pegram, Rory McVeigh, David Chalmers, and Nancy MacLean argue, the Klan's electoral failures, particularly in 1924, combined with its lackluster handling of governmental affairs in the communities it already controlled, produced resentment among frustrated members.[7] These failures also contributed to a growing resurgence of anti-Klan strength, particularly in southwest Missouri communities like Joplin and Carthage, where the Klan had grown especially robust by the mid-1920s. Missouri Klan members grew increasingly dissatisfied with their electoral performance during and immediately after the 1924 election. Not only was the state Klan unable to convince voters that the organization's ideologies and reform goals were essential for the management of local government, but its heavy-handed approach in recommending that members back specific candidates brought resentment from Klansmen and -women who felt a loss of individual autonomy within an increasingly politically active Invisible Empire.

Perhaps more than any other Missouri legislator in the 1920s, Senator James A. Reed was a polarizing figure, despised nearly as much within his own Democratic Party as in the Republican Party. His 1922 campaign for reelection to the Senate was arduous and led to a temporary rift within the state's Democratic Party. However, Reed's place as the most vocal political leader within Missouri's anti-Klan coalition earned him just as many supporters as detractors. To this end, Reed found eager support from Catholics, Jews, and members of the Kansas City Pendergast Machine, but steep opposition from Republicans, Prohibition-supporting Democrats, prominent women's groups, Klan members; and African Americans, many of whom critiqued his stances on immigration, civil rights, and lynching. Ultimately, while Reed successfully held enough of the anti-Klan coalition together to offset those eager to "Rid-Us-of-Reed," the volatile nature of his campaign demonstrates just how tenuous the anti-Klan coalition was, particularly when it came to party affiliation, local control, and political identity.

FIGURE 12. James A. Reed, date unknown. Courtesy of Missouri Legislators Portraits (P1084). The State Historical Society of Missouri.

Born in Ohio in 1861, James A. Reed spent his life in the Midwest. At a young age, his family moved to Iowa, where he eventually attended Parsons Seminary. After earning his legal credentials, Reed practiced law in Iowa before relocating to Kansas City in 1887. Within a decade, he had already climbed through the city's Democratic apparatus. He served as a county counselor and Jackson County prosecutor before being

150   Chapter Four

elected mayor in 1900. He served two terms as mayor and briefly flirted with a gubernatorial campaign in 1904 but ultimately decided to return to his legal practice. In 1910, he won his first election to the US Senate, with a subsequent reelection victory in 1916.[8]

While Reed's early congressional career was marked by a successful tenure on the Senate Banking Committee, including the placement of Federal Reserve Banks in St. Louis and Kansas City, his reelection bid in 1922 faced sizable opposition on two fronts. First, fellow Kansas Citian and attorney R. R. Brewster survived a contentious Republican primary and stood ready to battle Reed in the general election.[9] Second, Reed's opposition to the League of Nations and disregard for the policies of former President Woodrow Wilson made him a pariah among Democrats. With Wilson openly suggesting that a more qualified candidate deserved Reed's seat in Congress, state Democratic leaders enlisted Breckinridge Long, former assistant secretary of state, to enter the Democratic primary. Reed leaned heavily on his alliances in Kansas City's political machines for supporters among white ethnic urban voters and then outflanked his primary opponent by pitching himself as a friend of the farmer and shaking enough hands to secure the votes to neutralize Long's rural base. The tactic worked. Reed won the primary by a slim margin of six thousand votes. However, historian Franklin D. Mitchell has argued that Republican voters may have had a hand in the senator's victory since the state did not effectively enforce its closed primary.[10]

Though it was Prohibition, not the Invisible Empire, which initially emerged as the major issue in the state's 1922 election cycle, the specter of Klan political mobilization nationwide left many to wonder if the hooded order would court candidates before November. Like their earlier efforts in 1921, anti-Klan newspapers kept readers abreast of the movements of the Klan around the country in 1922. They continued to pressure politicians and local officials to speak out in condemnation of the Invisible Empire, particularly as rumors of Klan infiltration into politics swirled. The *Argus* overwhelmingly favored transparency among political candidates and looked forward to "determined efforts on the part of some state officials to stamp out the activities of the Klan."[11] However, the *Argus* also worried that the press's calls to action had fallen on "deaf ears" and warned that "Local, State, or National constituted

"A Curious and Interested Spectator" 151

authorities . . . should not for one moment relax their efforts to swat the Ku Klux Klan wherever that monstrous organization shows its head."[12] Noting the electoral success of the Klan in Oregon, the *St. Louis Post-Dispatch* declared that "when an organization chartered on intolerance and mob violence . . . can obtain possession of the government by offering public spoils to this interest and that, to this class and that, the days of American democracy are numbered."[13] Agreeing with the *Post-Dispatch*, the *Jewish Voice* lamented that "this nation cannot encourage hatred and prejudice and elect public officials on such a platform if it is to retain its respect. . . . [T]he deadliest blow that has been struck against the forces of Liberty in this country is the victory of the Ku Klux Klan."[14]

While the US Senate race was a statewide campaign, most of the animosity surrounding it centered on Reed and Brewster's hometown of Kansas City. As late summer turned to fall, tension and uneasiness fell over the city. The publication of a Klan business directory left many merchants wondering if the disclosure would affect their bottom line. Added to this, ministers who received donations from the Klan felt pressure from their congregants to identify their sentiments regarding the Invisible Empire. In one particular example, Rev. William Hovie of the Grand Avenue Temple was warned that if alleged hooded meetings continued within the walls of his church, it would be bombed.[15] Not long after this threat, the National Business Men's Protective Association, a professional sounding title for the local Klan, planned a massive event at the Convention Hall in downtown Kansas City that drew a substantial crowd.[16]

The headliners of the Klan's rally at Convention Hall were a who's who of Kansas City hate peddlers. John R. Jones, a national organizer for the Klan who was currently in a tug-of-war with a few local Klansmen over control of Kansas City, was the main speaker. Joining him on stage was Rev. E. L. Thompson of the Jackson Avenue Church; Rev. J. W. Darby of the Central Christian Church; Glen Bruner, an independent candidate for Circuit Court Judge; and Billy Parker, editor of the *New Menace*.[17] While each man generally kept to key Klan talking points such as patriotism and Americanism, Thompson used his time at the podium to launch into a heated tirade directed at the *Kansas City Catholic Register*. To counter the recent publication of the Klan directory by the

Chapter Four

Catholic Register, Thompson called on his audience to consider boycotting Catholic establishments as a show of hooded strength.[18]

In addition to the religious overtones of the Klan's activities in 1922, observers also noted the political nature of events like the Convention Hall rally that foreshadowed possible Klan involvement in the November election.[19] The *Kansas City Star* editorialized that the Klan had sound ideas about the need for government reform but felt that this did not, and should not, include religious intolerance. Rumors also circulated that the Klan had aligned with the Republican Party in Kansas City to fight the congressional campaign of Reed as well as the political machines of Tom Pendergast and Joe Shannon.[20] In addition to plans to topple the Democratic machines, those who attended Klan rallies in Kansas City heard the speakers attack local issues. Glen Bruner, whom the *Catholic Register* referred to as "a plain week-kneed [sic] opportunist who is trying to ride the waves of anything that will bring him notoriety," used his time at Convention Hall to give a stump speech on behalf of his electoral campaign.[21] "I believe in the sovereignty of our state rights—in the separation of church and state—in freedom of speech and press, and the maintenance of our free public schools," Bruner told potential voters. "I would give up my life, if need be, to uphold these principles for which I stand." Billy Parker, no doubt trying to increase subscriptions to the *New Menace*, appealed to patriotism by reminding the crowd that the Klan "will step down into the valley of the shadow of death and lift Liberty from the muck and mire—placing it on the pedestal where it was mounted by the forefathers of our country."[22]

As the battle for the hearts, minds, and allegiances of local Klansmen raged in Kansas City, the Invisible Empire held another large rally at Convention Hall closer to Election Day. In addition to the collection of speakers from the earlier event, this meeting also featured Gilbert O. Nations. The late-October Convention Hall meeting was to be political in nature and anti-Catholic in rhetoric. "The speakers were under orders to 'give Casey hell,'" the *Catholic Register* said of the Klan's attack on its editor Justin Casey, "and all the venom of many years of hate surged through the mind of Parker and Nations ... to sell [their] anti-Catholic medicine to the audience." At one point, while accusing the Knights of Columbus and students of Rockhurst College, a local Jesuit school, of

"A Curious and Interested Spectator" 153

hiding among the spectators, *New Menace* publisher Billy Parker offered a $500 check to anyone who could convince local Catholic officials to debate him.[23] Turning to politics, Parker called on the women in attendance to make their voices heard at the ballot box: "I know the men made a dirty mess of politics. . . . [I]t is up to you . . . to clean it up . . . [in] city hall, the school board, and the public schools of the city."[24] Targeting Shannon, Pendergast, and Reed by name, Klansmen called on the audience of nearly fourteen thousand to sing an alternate version of "Goodby Mule with the Old Hee Haw":

> Goodby Tom and Goodby Joe
> You and Reed will have to go
> You may not know what it's all about
> But you bet, by gosh, you'll soon find out;
> The town is full of K.K.K.
> The only thing that they will say,
> Is goodby Tom and goodby Joe,
> The crooked gang has got to go[25]

Less than a week after the Klan meeting, and only days before Election Day, Reed took to the Convention Hall stage to defend his campaign, criticize the policies of "mamma's darling boy" Arthur Hyde, and defeat the Klan. "He gave [the Klan] both barrels at the opening," the *Catholic Register* gleefully told its readers, "and when he was through, the hide of the Klan was hanging on a fence, thoroughly cured and scientifically tanned." Reed told the crowd that Klansmen had arrived at the rally solely to disrupt his speech with a mass walkout. When he dared those who "meet behind pillow cases and who wrap themselves in sheets" to start the exodus, no one left.[26] As Reed worked over the Klan, an audience member urged him on, shouting, "Beat it now, Kluxer, while the going is good."[27]

Reed's decision to make attacking the Invisible Empire a cornerstone of his 1922 congressional campaign was intentional, as he hoped to unite the growing anti-Klan coalition behind him. However, the political ploy aimed at appealing to his usual white ethnic urban constituents while also garnering favor with those opposed to the hooded order, particularly

Catholics, Jews, and African Americans who tended to vote Republican, strained the already tenuous coalition. When he spoke out against intolerance, voter suppression, and masked hatred, Reed presented himself as a defender of Missourians from the threats of those who hide behind "pillow sheets."[28] For his supporters within the anti-Klan coalition, such comments only made it easier to back Reed. The *Catholic Register* acknowledged that Reed had always given Catholics a fair deal, even if he was not one of them.[29] The *Jewish Chronicle* identified him as "an old friend of the Jewish people."[30] When the Young Men's Hebrew Association invited him to give a Constitution Day lecture at Temple Shaare Emeth in St. Louis, Reed used the platform to champion the positive impact of Jews in American history while reminding his audience that "any society or group which preaches the doctrines of religious intolerance and race hatreds in the United States is an enemy of constitutional government and should be driven from the country."[31]

While Reed's political stances may have garnered him support from segments of the Catholic and Jewish population, his public comments and voting record alienated white female reformers and African American voters. Reed publicly denounced the Nineteenth Amendment and the Sheppard-Towner Act, and his "wet" stance on the issue of Prohibition made him enemies with the League of Women Voters and the Woman's Christian Temperance Union.[32] In the eyes of many African Americans, Reed was comparable to Ben Tillman and James Vardaman, two of the nation's most vitriolic white-supremacist politicians. The *Kansas City Call* argued that his "record of hate" showed that "no man in public life outside the black belt of the South . . . has gone as far as he to prove his unvarying opposition to the race."[33] Most objectionable was his opposition to the Dyer Anti-Lynching Bill. Reed claimed that he was not against legislation aimed at holding lynch mobs accountable for their actions but preferred state laws on such matters over federal policy.[34] Despite a meeting with members of the NAACP and pressure from the African American press, Reed refused to budge from his position.[35] As for the Invisible Empire, the *Call* questioned Reed's motivation for fighting the Klan. "He wants us to believe that only one devil can exist at one time, and if it is the Klan, then it is not Reed," the *Call* warned its readers. "He forgets that we remember his past."[36]

"A Curious and Interested Spectator"   155

Reed's anti-Klan stance also allowed him the opportunity to suggest that Republicans, particularly R. R. Brewster and Governor Hyde, were secretly tied to the Invisible Empire.[37] Though Hyde had come out with an anti-Klan statement in 1921, Reed repeatedly called on the governor to make his true feelings on the Klan known. Having little to conceal, Hyde openly reminded voters that he was anti-Klan.[38] Turning to his congressional opponent, Reed called potential voters to support him in counterbalancing the Klan mobilization supposedly backing Brewster.[39] In response, Brewster reiterated his anti-Klan stance on the campaign trail, reminding those in the audience that the Klan "is not for me and I'm not for them."[40] At Lexington, Brewster hit back at Reed's accusations by suggesting that the senator would have probably joined the Klan if he were not a politician because he had done little in office to help African Americans.[41] Despite Brewster's appeal to anti-Klan voters, such tactics had little impact on the Reed campaign. The hooded order opposed Reed and favored Brewster, even with his anti-Klan sentiments, as the lesser of two evils.[42] Reed won reelection in 1922 largely based upon his popularity among Missouri voters, both urban and rural, regarding his opposition to Prohibition.[43] However, his anti-Klan stance, though not as strong of a political factor as it would be in 1924, was also key to Reed's victory.

As the votes were tallied, it soon became apparent that rallies, donations, and intimidation had done little to sway the voters of Missouri to the Invisible Empire. In Kansas City, the Democratic Party reaped the benefit of accusations of Klan/Republican ties, as many voters rejected the hooded order at the ballot box. In the end, the Klan had been repudiated. However, the *Catholic Register* still noted the large number of votes cast in defeat for candidates like Glen Bruner that left "an odor arising from the name of our fair city that makes the stench of a polecat as the famous attar of roses." The *Catholic Register* did not stop there with its postelection critique of Bruner:

Glen Bruner has no ability, no character, nothing in his entire make-up that would appeal to any one. On the contrary he is an egotist of the first order, the type of fellow who really believes that his good looks are deadly to the female of the species and that it is his bounden duty to see that the said females do not lack the beneficent sunshine of his vamping disposition. He was begat from a sire and dam who were bred in the bone bigots and he was reared in that same atmosphere of intolerance and selfishness. He could not be fair to even his children in spite of the fact that he loves them better than his own life, he would take from them the God-given care of their own mother if he could. Glen Bruner is everything that a good citizen shouldn't be.[44]

There may have been "twenty thousand other Glen Bruners in Kansas City," but the *Catholic Register* felt that the Klan had been wounded by the outcome of the election, particularly as rumors circulated that the Klan canceled a planned victory parade in the city.[45] To celebrate the demise of the Klan in the election and conclude its campaign against the Invisible Empire, the *Catholic Register* mocked the hooded order with "An Ode to Jones, DeNise & Co.":

> Goodbye Tom, Goodbye Joe
> Me and the Klan will have to go,
> You beat us so bad we've got to get out.
> And believe me b'gosh [*sic*] it was an awful clout
> The town seemed full of K. K. K.
> But the darned old votes didn't count that
> So it's goodbye Tom, and goodbye Joe
> Us crooked guys has got to go[46]

While Reed had secured a third term in the Senate, his eyes were on a bigger prize. Almost immediately, he began to craft a presidential bid for 1924. To do so, however, he had to gain the support of the deeply fractured state Democratic Party. Still splintered over Reed's feud with Woodrow Wilson, a sizable portion of the state party turned to the former president's family for a more palatable alternative to the outspoken Kansas Citian. Through the latter half of 1923 and the spring of 1924, anti-Reed Democrats rallied around William McAdoo, son-in-law of Woodrow Wilson and former US secretary of the treasury. To counter these efforts, Reed called out McAdoo for his alleged ties to E. L.

Doheny, an oil tycoon known for his role in the Teapot Dome scandal. The accusations damaged McAdoo among Missourians but did little to bolster Reed's campaign. Ultimately, Reed saw that there was no clear path for him to the White House at the national convention, let alone the state convention, in 1924 and quietly dropped his bid in the hopes of reorganizing for 1928.[47]

While scandals and past policy positions dominated the campaign for delegates on the Democratic side, Republican harmony easily pushed their delegates to back Calvin Coolidge for a full term in office. Nevertheless, the state conventions in April 1924 presented turmoil for both Republicans and Democrats as divisive battles for control between Klan and anti-Klan factions threatened to tear the respective parties apart. The Democrats met first in Springfield, and their convention quickly devolved into factionalism as rural delegates made it clear that they had no intention of approving an anti-Klan plank for fear of reprisal from the Klan on Election Day.[48] Despite rural pushback, urban delegates expressed confidence that a vote on such a measure would eventually reach the convention floor. To assuage both sides, the writers of the possible anti-Klan plank used vague language advocating for religious liberty and strict law enforcement. The document still emphasized anti-Klan sentiments, but it was crafted with the hope of not alienating possible Klan-leaning delegates. In addition to addressing an anti-Klan plank, state Democrats arrived at the convention to attack Republicans on the trade and tax policies of the Hyde administration, which were seen as detrimental to Missouri's agricultural interests.[49] Democrats also planned to hit Republicans on scandals surrounding state officials, including state pure food and drug commissioner Charles Prather and state labor commissioner Heber Nations.[50] Finally, the convention paid homage to Woodrow Wilson, who passed away in February.[51]

Foreseeing that the Democrats were trying to avoid the Klan issue with a noncommittal plank on intolerance, the *St. Louis Post-Dispatch* claimed that the party was "expected to yield to the persuasion that it is better to be successful than to be right."[52] After all, the *Post-Dispatch* continued, wouldn't Democrats be in a stronger position on the Klan issue if they denounced the Invisible Empire and Republicans did not? Likewise, the newspaper posited that if both parties denounced the Klan

158   Chapter Four

and actively fought against its influence, there would be no need to worry about any repercussions from promoting an anti-Klan plank. By pushing such an "innocuous platform," the *Post-Dispatch* condemned state Democrats for the "offering of pacifiers to offend nobody."[53] Sensing that anti-Klan Democrats' efforts to pursue a more expansive denouncement of the hooded order had been halted, the *Patriot* declared that "the St. Louis Irish Catholic coalition . . . met its Waterloo."[54]

At the convention's opening, state Democrats tried to stave off internal dissension by avoiding extensive discussion of the possible anti-Klan plank. However, urban delegates had had enough by the middle of the relatively harmonious convention. They wanted the anti-Klan plank brought to the floor of the convention for a vote after the Resolutions Committee opted to seemingly bypass the issue by rejecting a resolution declaring that "we denounce any organization whose purposes, whatever they may be, are based upon race hatreds or religious prejudices" by a two-to-one margin. Committee members, including some who admitted to opposing the Klan, then issued a consensus opinion that the party should not pick a fight with the Invisible Empire.[55]

As the announcement of the Resolutions Committee's decision circulated through the convention floor, pandemonium ensued when urban delegates pushed for a roll call on their anti-Klan resolution. The aisles of the convention hall filled with Klan and anti-Klan supporters who pushed their way to the front podium to plead their respective cases. The repeated demands for a roll call on the anti-Klan resolution were met with a swift rebuke from the chairman's platform. Given a chance to speak, anti-Klan delegates asked their fellow convention attendees if they were going to allow the party to evade the issue. John Taylor of Keytesville wondered aloud if the United States Capitol would remain in Washington, DC, or move to the Klan's headquarters in Atlanta. As the convention teetered on all-out war, David A. Ball, from the northeastern Missouri town of Louisiana, rose to speak.[56] "You are trying to lug in here things that don't belong here," he told anti-Klan delegates. Turning to the convention crowd, Ball offered a vigorous defense of the Invisible Empire. "They are good sincere citizens," he advised the crowd. As a round of hisses sounded from portions of the convention floor, Ball argued that "if you had continued Ku Klux Klans [*sic*] in St. Louis with masks on you'd have fewer bootleggers than you've got. . . . The best men in Missouri advocate what I'm talking about here."[57]

To counter Ball's claims, George M. Coombs Jr., assistant prosecuting attorney of Jackson County, offered the anti-Klan response. Outraged over Ball's comments, Coombs directed his words at the Klan sympathizers in the crowd. "Two years ago the Democratic Party declared against the Klan," he reminded the crowd. "But now out of the mists of yesterday rides a white and ghastly specter. Faster and faster thud the hoofbeats of horses that you ride in the dary [*sic*] system of hatred. Before you lie the bodies of persons unborn into which crash the hoofs of your narrow fanaticism. You are robed in cowardice and you bear upon your breasts fiery crosses symbolical of brutality, intolerance and cruelty."[58] At the end of Coombs's attack, and as the grumbling of opposition reverberated in the hall, delegates from Kansas City, including those aligned with Joe Shannon and Tom Pendergast, descended upon the chairman's table. After several heated discussions, the delegates agreed upon a plank promoting civil and religious liberty and freedom of the press against "assaults from any source." State Democrats finally passed an anti-Klan plank, which was vague and weak.[59] The *Kansas City Post* summed up the convention with this title: "Klan War Ends State Conclave."[60]

With Springfield still simmering from the Klan/anti-Klan fight that enveloped the Democratic convention, state Republicans met in the Ozarks town a few weeks later to hash out several electoral issues—including the Invisible Empire. However, since Democrats refused to denounce the Klan overtly, indications pointed to Republicans reaching a similar decision. This point was not lost on the *St. Louis Argus*, which expressed surprise at the Democrats' failure to pass their own anti-Klan plank and prodded state Republicans to "swat" the organization when the chance presented itself.[61] At least one unnamed delegate assured his fellow Republicans that Missouri Klansmen would overwhelmingly favor the party because of the Catholic ties of the Democratically aligned Pendergast Machine. There was also a feeling that urban Republicans would not be as strongly anti-Klan as their Democratic counterparts, particularly since the Klan had allegedly aided the Republican Party in Kansas City.[62] All the convention delegates had to do was pass a plank similar to the Democrats and ensure that the issue did not engulf the

160 Chapter Four

convention in controversy. Yet as delegates arrived, many wondered if the St. Louis contingent would wage a solo war against the Invisible Empire.

If Republicans assumed that they could avoid the Klan issue and still retain a high level of voter support from African Americans, they were mistaken. Already uneasy over the party's lack of motivation to denounce the Klan, Black Republicans worried that party officials were not keeping their promises on issues like civil rights and patronage, particularly delegate appointments. Many hoped that Walthall Moore, the first African American member of the Missouri General Assembly, would be a serious contender for a delegate spot at the national party convention, but when Moore was stricken from consideration by backers of Governor Hyde, resentment bellowed from the African American press. This objection was somewhat tempered when Moore and W. L. McKee of Poplar Bluff were eventually made alternate delegates, but concerns continued to bubble under the surface.[63] For 1924, at least, Republicans put the issue of African American support to rest by strengthening the bite of the proposed anti-Klan plank. Adopted over few objections, much like the rest of the planks of the Hyde-dominated convention, the anti-Klan resolution stated that the Republican Party had "no sympathy with any movement that fosters religious or racial hatreds," and "we . . . express our unalterable opposition to any organization or movement which proscribes any class of citizen because of birth, religion, race or color."[64]

The Republicans' anti-Klan resolution, as the Democrats before them, made no specific reference to the Klan. While Republicans felt comfortable with the relative safety of their so-called stronger plank, the Ku Klux Klan overwhelmingly supported it. In a statement issued by Imperial Representative George C. McCarron and sent from the hotel room of Jefferson City exalted cyclops Heber Nations, the Klan expressed its agreement with the resolution because it was "in harmony with all of the fundamental principles of the Ku Klux Klan."[65] Despite the sudden hooded approval of an allegedly anti-Klan plank, delegates did not feel it necessary to amend the wording. This did not sit well with the editors of the St. Louis Post-Dispatch, who, despite agreeing that the Republicans' position was stronger than the Democrats, criticized the party for not mentioning the Klan by name. Since both parties had seemingly avoided the issue, the Post-Dispatch notified voters that it was their responsibility to "take the matter in hand and reject the candidates of any party who do not clearly and specifically condemn and repudiate the klan [*sic*] organization."[66]

While the Republican's anti-Klan plank faced criticism in the press, Louis Aloe, a prominent Jewish businessman from St. Louis, supported it. Aloe, who had dealt with anti-Semitism and the Klan as a member of the city's Board of Aldermen, felt it necessary to speak out on the Invisible Empire and called out those who were not making a "real man's fight" against the Klan, particularly Louis Marshall of the American Jewish Committee. Marshall, one of the most prominent Jews in the United States, publicly denounced attempts by various state conventions to adopt anti-Klan planks, arguing that "if left alone, the Klan will die a natural death." In response, Aloe expressed concerns that Marshall was "not familiar with the situation of the Klan in the Middle West, in the South, or in the Southwest."[67] In a letter to J. A. Harzfield of Kansas City, reprinted in the *Modern View*, Aloe made it clear that he was not "lacking in backbone, courage, and real manhood." "Decent men hate a coward, and I shall raise my voice in 'political denunciation' of the Klan whenever the occasion is appropriate," he told Harzfield, because "the quickest way to destroy the Klan is to demonstrate to the Klan merchant and Klan politician that the anti-Klan is stronger than the Klan."[68]

Louis Aloe's fiery rhetoric may not have been shared by all anti-Klan politicians in Missouri. Still, many hoped that delegates to the national party conventions would adopt the tactics of some at the state level and attach resolutions denouncing the Invisible Empire to the party platforms. At the Republican National Convention in June 1924, however, little progress was made to denounce the Klan by name during the festivities of what historian Bruce Schulman referred to as a "stage-managed coronation of the incumbent" in Cleveland.[69] Having succeeded in forestalling major repudiation within Republican ranks—with the exception of Calvin Coolidge not selecting the Klan-backed James A. Watson as his running mate—Imperial Wizard Hiram Evans moved his political operations east to New York City in anticipation of the Democratic National Convention. When the Democrats held their convention a few weeks later at New York's Madison Square Garden, turmoil quickly ensued in a political tug-of-war later dubbed the "Klanbake."[70] Missouri's delegation was not immune from this dissension, as a tussle requiring police intervention broke out between delegates when an attempt was made to

162   Chapter Four

include Missouri's placard pole in an anti-Klan parade on the convention floor.[71] In the end, much like the plank passed at the Republican National Convention, Democrats did not have the votes to denounce the Klan by name. Instead, they warred for 103 ballots over a presidential candidate, ultimately compromising on former solicitor general of the United States and ambassador to Great Britain John W. Davis.[72]

When the respective conventions concluded, anti-Klan activists left for their home states disappointed. Though prominent state party leaders, including Senator James A. Reed, former governor Herbert Hadley, and current governor Arthur Hyde, all expressed support for an anti-Klan plank if it were presented, the Democrats and Republicans offered only vague rebukes of the Invisible Empire at the state and national levels.[73] After trumpeting the need for delegates to denounce the Klan by name throughout their respective conventions, the *St. Louis Argus* felt that both parties had given in to weakness and cowardice.[74] "With the two major parties afraid to point a finger at the klan [*sic*], why should not brighter dreams enthrall Emperors and Dragons and Kleagles and inspire them to new aggressions and larger conquests," the *St. Louis Post-Dispatch* lamented.[75]

If larger conquests were the dreams of the Invisible Empire, Washington, DC, and the White House were ideal locations. While the Klan pledged to be nonpartisan and allow members to support their preferred candidates, the order's hierarchy could not help but wade into the political swamp, as was the case with Hiram Evans openly campaigning for Coolidge to pick James E. Watson as his running mate. For Missouri Klansmen and -women, their marching orders came from their local klavern and from prominent state Klan official William M. Campbell. Seeking to unify Missouri Klan members behind a select group of candidates for state and federal office, the organization held a Klonvokation in the house chamber of the state capitol building in Jefferson City in mid-July. Upon learning of the Klan meeting, Governor Hyde ordered the group to allow curious citizens and reporters into the chamber or leave the capitol grounds. The Klan complied with Hyde's request, but before onlookers could observe the festivities, the meeting was moved to the nearby Merchants Bank Building, the headquarters of the Jefferson City Klan.[76]

In the aftermath of the state Klonvokation, rumors swirled about which candidates had earned hooded support. While this gossip had major implications in state-level races, there was little mystery about the preferred presidential candidate. As was common practice for the Klan, the organization hitched itself to candidates that supported some key elements of its tenets and had a viable chance to win on Election Day. As such, the Klan eschewed lesser-known candidates more closely aligned with the organization in favor of major party leaders. In the 1924 presidential campaign, this list was especially short. Only a few weeks after his nomination, Democratic challenger John W. Davis publicly denounced the Klan. Not to be outdone, Robert La Follette, mounting a notable third-party run under the Progressive Party banner, told the press that he would "campaign vigorously against the Ku Klux Klan."[77] Coolidge, however, demurred on the issue and allowed his running mate, Charles Dawes, to offer a soft critique of the hooded order. From then on, while Davis and La Follette made Klan condemnation a feature of their public appearances, neither Coolidge nor Dawes broached the subject again.[78]

Whether it was fallout from the contentious major party conventions, divided sentiments over the influence of the Invisible Empire, allegations of Republican corruption, or "Coolidge or Chaos," as the president's campaign team dubbed the other contenders, a sizable portion of American voters turned toward alternative candidates, ranging from progressives and socialists to prohibitionists and nativists, in the race for the White House. Gilbert O. Nations was one such candidate who found his name splashed across the pages of major US newspapers when his supporters selected him as their candidate for president of the United States. Not bad for a onetime rural teacher who couldn't even win election as a county school commissioner in his first foray into politics. Nations's campaign for president was ambitious and unrealistic. He openly admitted at times that he had no shot of winning. Running as the candidate of the newly formed American Party, Nations was undoubtedly aware of the long odds of reaching the White House. In addition, he was a seemingly unknown figure in national politics.

To the typical Republican, Democratic, or even Progressive voter, Gilbert O. Nations had achieved few accolades in the political arena in his fifty-seven years of life. He failed to get past the Republican primary in Missouri's thirteenth congressional district, and his highest political office was probate judge in St. Francois County. Yet, to the more than one million subscribers of the *Menace*, one of the United States' largest anti-Catholic newspapers, Nations was well known and well regarded due to his frequent publications and fiery oratory on the specter of Catholic power within the United States. After earning a PhD from American University, Nations moved to Washington, DC, and kept a close watch on the political affairs of the nation's capital while serving as a professor at his alma mater, specializing in Roman and canon law. While there, he issued regular reports on Congress to various newspapers, including the *Missouri Valley Independent* and the *Klan Kourier*, typically under the headline "Washington Dispatch."[79] He soon followed his dispatches up with the *Protestant*, a magazine billed as "a concise monthly digest of FACTS about patriotic issues, Protestant affairs, and papal intrigues."[80] As the 1924 political campaigns began, Nations published a booklet titled *Who's Who in Congress*, which laid out his assessment of the stances of Congress members on moral and religious issues.[81] Nations bragged about the "tremendous stir created among politicians and the press by this little booklet," while the *St. Louis Post-Dispatch* viewed the publication as confirmation that he was the "head of the Ku Klux Klan lobby in Washington."[82]

As Nations's power within the patriotic movement reached his zenith, he was selected by the newly formed American Party to be its presidential candidate in 1924. Nations certainly realized the long-shot nature of his candidacy. He had a hard time getting his name on many state ballots, including his home state of Missouri, and his original vice presidential candidate on the ticket quit less than two months into the campaign to focus on his own congressional run.[83] Nevertheless, Nations used his time on the campaign trail to embrace the Americans who had backed him since his days with the *Menace* and to court new supporters eager to consider an alternative to two-party politics. To interested voters, Nations promised an administration that would promote public education, restrict immigration, enforce Prohibition, and keep the United States out of the World Court and League of Nations. In reviewing the party's platform, the *Missouri Valley Independent* advised its readers, "One hundred percent Americanism, or, as it will, from this time on,

"A Curious and Interested Spectator" 165

be known, the American Party, headed by Judge Gilbert O. Nations, for President, IS FOR religious and Civic Freedom and unalterably opposed to the GREATEST ENEMY religious and civic freedom ever knew, this same Roman Catholic Political Hierarchy, called the Roman Catholic church."[84]

Not long after he received the nomination, however, it quickly became clear that the American Party had become the Klan Party. American Party leaders dismissed this claim, but when Nations gave a speech in Pennsylvania in July 1924, the sight of parents intently listening to a speech that embraced the KKK while their children ran around in miniature Klan costumes was hard to overlook.[85] Additionally, Nations and the American Party organized most of their campaign events in Pennsylvania, Ohio, and Indiana, strongholds of Klan power at that time. Klansmen donned their white robes at these rallies, and Nations criticized Catholic and Jewish power in the United States, especially on the US Supreme Court, all the while claiming that bigotry and racial prejudice could not be found within the Invisible Empire.[86] Turning to his major presidential opponents, Nations decried the alleged indifference of Coolidge and Davis, and their respective parties, to the issue of Prohibition and their denouncements of the Klan and referred to La Follette as being "as wet as Lake Michigan."[87] While a rift did emerge between some American Party officials who felt that Klan leaders were steering members toward Coolidge and the Republicans, Nations continued to defend the hooded order as a "splendid body of men."[88]

As the presidential campaign came into the home stretch, Nations had little to worry about the injection of the Klan issue into the race. After all, as an open defender of the hooded order, there was little debate regarding where he stood about the group. Additionally, considering his long-shot odds, the anti-Klan press largely ignored his candidacy outside of reprinted articles on his nomination and the St. Louis Post-Dispatch's assessment that the American Party's platform "embraces practically all the intolerances and bigotries that are festering in the dark recesses of the fanatical mind."[89] Nevertheless, the fact that Nations's embrace of the Klan was largely dismissed by the hooded order in favor of other candidates must have stung the presidential aspirant. Even the Missouri Valley Independent and the Missouri Kourier, Klan-affiliated state newspapers

166   Chapter Four

that frequently promoted Nations's commentaries on the issues of the day, offered little support for his White House bid. Instead, the *Missouri Valley Independent* advised readers that an alternative party and candidate might be better sought in 1928: "If Nations is living he will be the man. If not another will have arisen to carry Old Glory to victory."[90] In the end, Nations finished a distant seventh, while Coolidge easily defeated all challengers, including John W. Davis and Robert La Follette.[91]

Casting a careful eye over the Klan issue in local, state, and federal campaigns, the *Kansas City Jewish Chronicle* warned that 1924 would "prove a barometer of the strength that can be mustered in a typically American community of average intelligence by the forces of darkness, malevolence, and class hatred."[92] While some people were relieved that the so-called anti-Klan planks of the state and national parties had been benign enough to placate both Klan and anti-Klan supporters, others realized that the latter half of 1924 was going to be a bloody battleground with the hooded order at the center. With the Klan undertaking a recruiting campaign aimed at increasing membership and electing sympathetic candidates for public office in many communities, anti-Klan activists understood that weakness against white-robed forces showed complacency, or, worse, quasi support. Noting the Klan's political influence in Indiana, Georgia, and Texas, the *St. Louis Post-Dispatch* advised its readers that "the only safety for the opponents of secret invisible government through a masked organization is to make the issue open to defeat the klan's [sic] plans to control nominations and to condemn the organization unequivocally by name."[93]

As it had done earlier in the 1920s, the press used this influence to pressure candidates into making public statements regarding their stance on the Klan during both the primaries and the general election. Newspapers like the *St. Louis Argus* and *Kansas City Call* worked alongside the NAACP to distribute questionnaires to prospective candidates inquiring about their position on key issues important to the African American community, including the Dyer Anti-Lynching Bill, enforcement provisions within the Fourteenth and Fifteenth Amendments, residential segregation, equal educational opportunities, and the Ku Klux Klan. Not surprisingly, the *Call* found that several candidates were "unsatisfactory," while many more failed to respond to the questionnaire. However, a few Republicans running for state office gained a favorable "recommended" status for their answers.[94]

While this direct questioning was aimed at candidates at all levels of government, the most highly publicized discussion of the Klan issue took place in the state's gubernatorial campaign. Though the list of major party candidates running for governor was eventually whittled down to two, Sam A. Baker and Arthur W. Nelson, the campaign to reach their respective party's nomination was far from easy. On the Republican side, Baker competed against Lieutenant Governor Hiram Lloyd and former St. Louis police commissioner Victor Miller. For the Democrats, it was a four-way race between Nelson, St. Louis lawyer George Moore, Jackson County public administrator Floyd Jacobs, and former federal judge Henry Priest. Though each man preferred to stick with key issues like agriculture, law enforcement, and taxation as the main talking points of the primary, the Klan soon took a central role. Nelson, who portrayed himself as a simple "dirt farmer" despite being one of the largest land-owners in Cooper County, faced accusations from George Moore that he was secretly a member of the Klan. Nelson quickly dismissed this claim, but his vague remarks in defense of his record left the door open for further attacks from Democrats and Republicans.[95]

A. W. Nelson, however, was not the only candidate mired in Klan rumors. Citing a whispering campaign aimed at tarnishing his own record, Victor Miller felt compelled to compose a public letter explaining that he had never joined the Klan.[96] When rumors of his alleged Klan affiliation continued, Miller decided to include the denouncement in his public addresses.[97] For George Moore, there was no denying where he stood on the Klan. While leveling an attack on Floyd Jacobs for alleged Klan ties, Moore also denounced the candidacy of Henry Priest because the former judge was stealing some of his anti-Klan supporters. The *Post-Dispatch* agreed that too many anti-Klan candidates on the Democratic side would be detrimental in the primary, but it nevertheless felt that Priest had a right to campaign.[98] Priest, however, had his own problems. Along with Moore, he was a regular target of the Klan press. To make matters worse, at a campaign stop in Hannibal, Klansmen infiltrated his audience and staged a mass walkout when he denounced the Invisible Empire.[99]

168 Chapter Four

The two candidates who avoided most of the Klan charges were Hiram Lloyd and Sam Baker. In his research on the 1924 gubernatorial campaign, scholar John J. Large argues that Lloyd and his supporters may have been responsible for the Klan allegations directed at Victor Miller. As for Baker, he brushed aside rumors that he was a member of the Jefferson City Klan by pointing out his record on issues of intolerance while serving as the state superintendent of public schools. However, Baker did have some questions to answer when his name appeared on the list of preferred candidates released by the Klan. Since the sample ballots listed candidates supported by the Klan for each party, Baker shared the governor's spot with Nelson. The rest of the preferred candidates for various state-level positions split between both parties.[100]

When the primary votes were tallied, Nelson and Baker, both preferred candidates of the Klan, had won their respective party's nomination. As for other preferred candidates for state office, the Klan had some positive results as Republicans Phil A. Bennett, L. D. Thompson, Frank Atwood, as well as Democrats Kate Morrow, George Middlekamp, John H. Stone, and James T. Blair, were all victorious. However, William O. Stacy and Gus O. Nations were defeated.[101] Nations, the son of Gilbert O. Nations and brother of Klansman Heber Nations, had the support of the Missouri Klan, but his political advertisements throughout the campaign stressed that he held no ties to the Invisible Empire.[102] Surveying the carnage at the end of a bloody primary season, the *Post-Dispatch* felt that "a liberal bolt against the domination of the Anti-Saloon League, the hooded terrorism of the Ku Klux Klan and the official lawlessness embodied in both those organizations is due in Missouri and in the nation."[103]

With the Klan issue saturating election campaigns from municipal contests to the presidential race, it is not surprising that it was the focal point of the gubernatorial campaign in the final push toward Election Day. As seen above, the campaign for governor was muddied during the primaries as each candidate faced accusations and rumors surrounding their possible Klan affiliation. Out of this quarrel emerged Sam Baker and Arthur Nelson. They were bloodied by the campaign, but they soon emerged as the leaders of their respective state parties. Yet if either man assumed that the Klan issue would go away after the primaries, they were wrong. Instead, both faced accusations of having joined Klan chapters in their home counties (Nelson in Cooper County, Baker in Cole County).

More than anything else, the Missouri governor's race felt the impact of a series of affidavits released by the state Republican Party that detailed Nelson's alleged close relationship with the Invisible Empire. "We do not believe that the people of Missouri desire their chief executive to be Janus-like," Republican State Committee chairman W. F. Phares told the press upon releasing the documents.[104] The timing of the affidavits, combined with Phares's moral outrage over the allegations, was intended to smear Nelson's campaign with little opportunity for an effective rebuttal before Election Day. In many ways, this tactic worked. Though rumors of Nelson's Klan affiliation had emerged during the previous summer, the new affidavits and Nelson's admittance that he had been to at least two Klan events undermined the Democrat's gubernatorial campaign.[105]

W. F. Phares's decision to release the affidavits attesting to A. W. Nelson's Klan status only two weeks before Election Day sent the state's Democratic Party scrambling to counter the charges. Nelson initially

FIGURE 13. Sam A. Baker, date unknown. Courtesy of Ruth Rust Studio Photographs (P0860). The State Historical Society of Missouri.

170   Chapter Four

brushed the accusations aside, as he had done in the primaries. Soon after, Democratic State Committee chairman Joshua Barbee issued a statement denouncing Phares and the Republicans. "This is a desperate attempt of the Republicans to save what they recognize as a losing fight," Barbee told the press as he publicly questioned the validity of the claims.[106] When challenged by Nelson and Barbee, Phares defended the three men who had signed the affidavits: F. A. Collins, B. L. Morris, and C. S. Burns. Citing their membership in the Klan, Phares declared that Collins and Morris had access to the order's membership book in Tipton. Turning to Burns, Phares admitted the Morgan County resident was a former Klansman but argued that he was a reputable farmer. Phares also claimed that a prominent Klansman told him that to gain access to the California rally, Nelson would have had to have been either a Klansman or an applicant for admission. Finally, pointing out similar accusations made during the primary, Phares reminded voters that this was not the first time that Nelson and the Klan were linked.[107]

Only two days after the initial release of the affidavits, A. W. Nelson declared the Klan issue closed, but his supporters and the press kept the issue very much alive. Leo Felton, Dr. L. M. Gray, and Ed Patterson all signed affidavits claiming that they saw Nelson leave the grounds before the Klan initiation ceremony in California. Felton added that as a member of the Knights of Columbus, he had observed many Klan gatherings around Cooper County but had never seen Nelson. Additionally, Dan Chapman, the exalted cyclops of the Tipton Klan, issued a statement denying that F. A. Collins and B. L. Morris were Klansmen. According to Chapman, C. S. Burns had been a member but was dropped by the group for lack of participation. Though he claimed that Nelson was not a member of the Tipton Klan and that he had not seen him at the California rally, Chapman certainly did not help Nelson's case by implying that if Nelson had been initiated in California, he would be in that chapter's membership book, not Tipton's book.[108]

With affidavits and claims appearing right and left, the press and the respective political parties began to craft stories about the controversy to influence voters with only days remaining in the campaign. The Democrats portrayed the allegations against Nelson as part of a larger conspiracy. Labeled the Hyde-Phares Conspiracy in honor of Republican Governor Arthur Hyde and Republican State Committee chairman W. F. Phares, this alleged conspiracy was a top-down plot aimed at destroying Nelson and the Democrats on the eve of the election. To aid the conspiracy theory, the press quoted C. P. Anderson, a state grain inspector, who claimed he was given paid leave by the Republican State Committee to scour Cooper County looking for people to sign affidavits against Nelson. This charge earned some merit, as C. S. Burns, a lifelong Republican, signed one of the key affidavits.[109] In addition to the theory of a top-down conspiracy, Democrats alleged that Joseph Thompson, Governor Hyde's personal secretary, and Sam Baker, the Republican candidate for governor, had both tried secretly to become Klansmen.[110]

When not attacking the Republican hierarchy, Democrats reminded voters of Nelson's rural background and generous demeanor. Largely avoiding the urban areas of St. Louis and Kansas City for most of his campaign, Nelson devoted considerable attention to rural Missouri and played up his "dirt farmer" image. This agricultural appeal to rural Missourians won over many farmers concerned about land values, taxation, and farm relief. Still, it also drew the ire of Republicans who ridiculed Nelson's common-man branding. To add to this man-of-the-people persona, a story circulated soon after the initial affidavits alleging that Nelson had no hard feelings toward C. S. Burns and recommended that the Boonville National Bank extend Burns's mortgage as a sign of goodwill because he was in danger of foreclosure.[111]

To the conspiratorial allegations put forth by Democrats, the Republicans responded in full. Rumors began to spread that Nelson, in addition to seeing the Klan at the Southwest Missouri Fair, had secretly met with Imperial Wizard Hiram Evans while in Carthage.[112] Another allegation stated that the headquarters of the Kansas City Klan prominently displayed a portrait of Nelson.[113] Additionally, when pressed by Democrats about the secretive nature under which the original affidavits were obtained, Republicans questioned the validity of Leo Felton's affidavit by pointing out that he had not been a member of the Knights of Columbus since 1913.[114] They also assured voters that numerous residents of Cooper County stood at the ready to attest to Nelson's

172   Chapter Four

Klan affiliation.[115] Finally, as he toured the state on behalf of Republican candidates, Governor Hyde repeatedly referred to Nelson by his alleged Klan membership number, 111.[116]

With a little more than a week remaining until the Election, Democrats desperately tried to shift the gubernatorial campaign back to its original focus: land values, taxation, and the Republican Party's failure to adequately address both during the Hyde administration. But, Democrats and the press still managed continually to bring up the Ku Klux Klan.[117] As the *Jefferson City Daily Capital News*, attempting to highlight the other issues of the campaign, put it: "Most decidedly, the issue is NOT whether Arthur W. Nelson, in company with friends, attended, largely out of curiosity, a meeting of the Ku Klux Klan, held in the open air, in California, Missouri, in June, 1923, regardless of whether one C. S. Burns makes any affidavits or not."[118]

Failing to move the campaign's theme back to the original issues, the Democrats sought out Klan opponents to defend Nelson's character. Congressman Harry Hawes, who declared, "I will not vote for Dr. Nelson or any other candidate for office who I believe is a klansman [*sic*]" when the affidavit news first broke, soon began to speak favorably of Nelson.[119] Henry Priest, former Democratic gubernatorial candidate and a known anti-Klan politician, expressed his belief that Nelson was being truthful in the matter.[120] Monsignor Timothy Dempsey, a prominent Catholic priest from St. Louis, issued a statement defending Nelson and confirming his close relationship with Nelson's family.[121] H. T. Zuzak, a Jewish businessman from Cooper County, referred to Nelson as a "capable and honest official" in a letter to the *Modern View*.[122] In reviewing the recent move by politicians and community leaders to defend Nelson, Judge A. H. Balkenbusch of Osage County told the press, "Either C. S. Burns . . . was not telling the truth or else Ed Patterson, Dr. Gray, Senator Reed, Harry Hawes, Governor Gardner, Judge Priest, and hundreds of other prominent Missourians were lying."[123]

To give the final word on the matter, the Democrats turned to the popular and fiery Senator James A. Reed to save Nelson and the party. Reed defended Nelson in a series of speeches in Kansas City, St. Louis, and Jefferson City in the final days before the election. At each stop, he returned to the alleged Hyde-Phares Conspiracy when discussing the claims against Nelson and informed voters that he would not support Nelson if the rumors were true.[124] Delivering a powerful speech at the state capitol building the night before the election, Reed denounced the Klan and defended Nelson. "When a group of men, wrapped in sheets and pillowcases for blinders, assembled in a pasture lot under a fiery cross, Nelson went along with hundreds of other sight seers to witness the proceedings," Reed told the assembled crowd, "[but] when the public ceremonies were over, he went about his business. . . . He was no more a party to that ceremony than a man that stands on the street and watches a circus parade is a member of the circus."[125]

While voters and the press could question the validity of the contents of an unknown page in an unknown book in an unknown location, it was much harder to find the truth when both the accuser and the accused admitted to being at the same place at the same time. It may not have been as damning in 1924 for one to say they heard a Klan lecture—in fact, it is quite possible that a large percentage of Missouri voters listened to a lecture on the Ku Klux Klan at some point between 1921 and 1924— yet A. W. Nelson's inability to separate fact from fiction, in the eyes of Missouri voters, contributed to his ultimate defeat in 1924. Did he meet the imperial wizard in Jasper County? Was he initiated as a Klansman in 1923? Did his name appear in the Tipton Klan ledger book? The answer to these questions may never be known. Still, it is nevertheless evident that the allegations that Nelson held Klan membership doomed his gubernatorial campaign and that the Klan issue significantly impacted the 1924 election at federal, state, and local levels.

The tension of the gubernatorial election continued through early November as the votes came in. While it soon became evident that Calvin Coolidge would continue as president, Missourians waited anxiously to find out who would become the next governor. Though the results awaited confirmation, the *St. Louis Globe Democrat* quickly declared that Nelson had little chance of catching Baker.[126] By November 7, the *Jefferson City Daily Capital News* reported that while there were still 157 precincts unaccounted, Nelson had won more counties than Baker and had a slight lead in Kansas City. Despite claiming fewer counties, Baker

174   Chapter Four

overwhelmingly won St. Louis, a city that Nelson rarely bothered to visit during the campaign. Ultimately, Baker's margin of victory in St. Louis propelled him to the governor's mansion.[127]

While many issues concerned Missouri voters during the 1920s, ranging from agriculture, education, and good roads to taxation, corruption, and law enforcement, they also cared deeply about the presumed power of the Ku Klux Klan. As such, the Klan issue made and destroyed political campaigns as voters were curious about where candidates stood on the hooded order and what, if any, sympathies they held for the organization. The death of C. S. Burns only a few days after A. W. Nelson's defeat in 1924 provides perhaps the most extreme outcome of the Klan issue in Missouri politics, with the *St. Louis Post-Dispatch* alleging that "the fatality was due indirectly to the recent episode of the affidavit affecting Nelson . . . but for that, the gun, in all probability, would not have been in use at the Burns home."[128] Yet Burns's affidavit, combined with the discussion of the Invisible Empire's political influence at the county, state, and federal levels, indicates that the Klan issue weighed heavily on the minds of individual voters from across the political spectrum during the 1920s.

Ultimately, the Klan was successful in some localities in Missouri. Still, when Election Day arrived, the hooded order suffered stiff repudiation at the polls in many state-level campaigns in 1922 and 1924. This rejection was far from the final nail in the Klan's coffin, but the organization entered the latter half of the 1920s severely fractured. Despite claims that the organization was nonpartisan, rumors and direct orders from senior Klan officials to vote for certain candidates for municipal, county, state, and federal office did not sit well with some Klansmen and -women who favored more local autonomy, particularly in Missouri. Tensions soon arose within various klaverns, and the anger, frustration, and disillusionment of many Klansmen and -women soon boiled over. The hooded order may have been partially rejected nationwide as voters went to the polls in 1922 and 1924, but the rollback of the Ku Klux Klan was only just beginning. Just as C. S. Burns had left the hooded order, whether due to philosophical or financial reasons, so too would fellow members soon cast off the robe and the hood as political defeat combined with headline-making scandals involving prominent Klansmen pushed many Klan supporters, especially in Missouri, to flee the Invisible Empire.

CHAPTER FIVE

"Behind the Mask"
Fraud, Bribery, and Scandal in Missouri's Invisible Empire

ON THE AFTERNOON of July 10, 1926, a seemingly endless caravan of automobiles, buses, and trains stopped in Elvins, Missouri, to drop off passengers. By suppertime, the crowd numbered in the thousands as people mingled along the railroad tracks waiting for a special train from St. Louis. A cheer rang out when the train arrived on schedule, and its occupants joined those already assembled. Departing Elvins at sunset, the large group marched through the community before visiting the neighboring towns of Desloge and Flat River. From end to end, the assembled mass spanned more than two miles. In each town along the nearly five-mile parade route, cheering spectators greeted the marchers and encouraged them on to the Flat River fairgrounds. While parades were not uncommon in the mining towns that surrounded the hulking structures and underground operations of the St. Joseph Lead Company, one of the United States' largest suppliers of lead and zinc, residents expressed the sentiment that the events of that day were "one of the most beautiful processions" in recent memory. At the head of the procession, William M. Campbell received the loudest roars of approval as he waved to the crowd while on horseback. Behind him, bands performed familiar songs, and drill teams executed marching maneuvers that identified their organizational affiliation, including members carrying red lights that joined together at a moment's notice to form a fiery cross.[1]

The Ku Klux Klan was unstable in the latter half of the 1920s. While the organization found success in communities across Indiana and Colorado, among others, states like Missouri largely rejected the Invisible Empire as its voters refused to elect high-profile candidates sympathetic to the Klan.[2] Despite defeat, the Missouri Klan refused to admit that it was on the path to irrelevance. Appointed as the new grand dragon of Missouri after serving as exalted cyclops of St. Joseph

177

Klan No. 4, William M. Campbell started his tenure to revitalize and expand the Invisible Empire in the state.[3] Within his own community, Campbell had little to worry about the scale of the Klan. St. Joseph not only boasted one of the largest klaverns in Missouri, but it also held chapters of the WKKK, Kamelia, and Junior Klan.[4] Additionally, the local Klan held weekly events in St. Joseph and utilized the *Missouri Valley Independent* to broadcast the principles of Klankraft to readers in Missouri, Iowa, Nebraska, and Kansas. As he singlehandedly became the highest-ranking Klansman in Missouri, Campbell relied more and more on the *Missouri Valley Independent* to assure supporters that the Invisible Empire was growing and that talk of the organization's decline voiced by Klan opponents, particularly the anti-Klan press, was out of touch with what he claimed was the upward trajectory of the hooded order.[5]

To counter claims of the Klan's decline, Campbell embarked on an ambitious reclamation plan to bring old and new members back to the group. The state organization was greatly aided in this goal on three fronts. First, despite assurances from some state lawmakers that they would push for anti-Klan bills in the Missouri General Assembly, newly elected governor Sam A. Baker indicated that he had no intention of backing such legislation.[6] Second, Imperial Wizard Hiram Evans selected Missouri for several important Klan events, including a well-publicized, though eventually canceled, parade in 1926 in St. Louis and the annual meeting of the Women of the Ku Klux Klan in 1927.[7] Finally, after the state received official incorporation as a "realm," Klan officials divided it into provinces. They began to hold regional meetings and events and a statewide conference known as a klorero. With Klan officials turning their eyes to Missouri, Campbell felt confident that his visits to klaverns across the state would galvanize support for the order. By organizing the provincial meetings, or klonverses, Campbell hoped to draw attention to the Klan's work from members and nonmembers by setting up rallies with music, parades, and speakers.[8] These meetings, however, were not devoid of the Klan's usual fiery rhetoric, as Campbell told those assembled in Flat River that there was a "danger of our great 'melting pot' degenerating into a 'garbage can' unless American citizens keep on the alert to prevent it."[9]

Based on attendance, Campbell's reclamation plan was a rousing success that showed the Klan was in a "sound and healthy condition."[10] The provincial meetings drew thousands of Klan members from different corners of the state. Once there, they gave their unwavering support to the grand dragon.[11] At the close of meetings in Independence, Excelsior Springs, Bowling Green, Flat River, Poplar Bluff, Columbia, and Springfield, as well as the state klorero in Clinton in 1926, the *Missouri Valley Independent* declared that membership had increased 65 percent since 1925 and that "every Klansman in attendance . . . returned home determined to do his utmost during the coming year to erect an edifice as strong as the Rock of Gibraltar on the sturdy foundation which results from the past year's efforts."[12] Initially, the meetings also reinforced Campbell's charge that opponents of the Klan were deeply mistaken in their claims that the organization was in decline. The *Missouri Valley Independent* declared, after Province No. 1 met in Independence, that "the size of the congregation was positive proof to the 'doubting Thomases' that the flame of Klankraft still burns brightly in the breasts of the Klansmen of Jackson county."[13]

Yet while hooded members joined Ozark Klan No. 3, St. Joseph Klan No. 4, Springfield Klan No. 12, Poplar Bluff Klan No. 48, Bowling Green Klan No. 127, St. Louis Klan No. 162, and many other klaverns, the state organization proved ineffective at mobilizing support for major social and political reform.[14] Outside of a few minor political victories in counties and municipalities, the Klan could claim little, if any, control over the state's governing bodies, especially the Missouri General Assembly. As the 1920s wore on, the Klan existed largely in name only in many communities. This point was reinforced by the change in coverage for the provincial meetings between 1926 and 1927 in the pages of the *Missouri Valley Independent*. While the provincial meetings and klorero held in 1926 garnered front-page billing and lengthy articles in each subsequent issue after the festivities, the 1927 events in St. Joseph, Carthage, Bowling Green, St. Louis, and California, as well as the klorero in Joplin that featured two speeches from Hiram Evans, received far less coverage, and descriptions of the large crowds, similar to the retelling of the parade in St. Francois County, were absent.[15] If Klan members and sympathizers hoped to read coverage of the 1928 meetings, they were disappointed when the *Missouri Valley Independent* ceased publication at the end of 1927.[16] Ultimately, Campbell could dismiss rumors of the order's demise as the 1920s wore on, but eventually, the grand dragon had

180   Chapter Five

to concede the inevitable: internal scandals, along with electoral failures, had destroyed the Invisible Empire in Missouri.

The Missouri Klan, much like the national organization, portrayed itself as strong and undivided in the 1920s, but the hooded order continued to lose members as scandals deepened during the decade. While not as damning as accusations against prominent Klansmen like D. C. Stephenson, who put several politicians in key positions of power in Indiana before eventually being charged with a range of crimes, including rape and murder, four notable scandals involving Missouri members deeply affected the state's hooded population.[17] C. C. Crawford, minister, lecturer, and editor of the St. Louis Klan-sympathetic newspaper the *Patriot*, engineered a fake slogan contest to bring in more subscribers for the publication. When the contest's dubious goals were revealed, Klan officials rushed to get out in front of a potential investigation of mail fraud by the US Postal Service. To manage negative attention from the fallout, particularly in the anti-Klan press, the Klan moved quickly to banish Crawford from the Invisible Empire, but in doing so severed ties with one of the most popular recruiters in the Midwest. Soon after, Heber Nations, state labor commissioner and close adviser to Governor Arthur Hyde, found himself at the center of a graft scandal alleging that he allowed St. Louis breweries to violate the Volstead Act in exchange for financial kickbacks. Nations appealed to clear his name, but the scandal ruined him personally and led him eventually to step down from a leadership position within the Klan. O. L. Spurgeon, a Baptist minister who rose from exalted cyclops of Poplar Bluff Klan No. 48 to become an imperial lecturer, was publicly banished from, and later sued, the hooded order after it was discovered that he attempted to recruit disillusioned Klansmen into a rival organization called the Independent Klan of America. Finally, Pierre Wallace, onetime exalted cyclops of Ozark Klan No. 3, faced a series of accusations concerning interference in municipal affairs as well as domestic violence. These revelations hurt the Klan's claims of respectability and confirmed anti-Klan fears of an invisible government in Jasper County.

From the periphery, the scandals involving C. C. Crawford, Heber Nations, O. L. Spurgeon, and Pierre Wallace seem pale compared to the

"Behind the Mask" 181

crimes of D. C. Stephenson. Yet each man found himself in a situation that compromised his image as a respectable Klansman and broke laws that members of the Invisible Empire and citizens in general were supposed to protect, follow, and defend. Together with allegations involving Klansmen and -women in other states, these scandals, in many ways, justified anti-Klan activists' claims that the organization was un-American, turned alleged hooded sympathies into political liabilities for potential candidates, and emphasized to those that had once donned the hood and robe, but were now fleeing the group, that the organization was not the bastion of 100 percent Americanism that they had assumed.

The dark clouds of scandal in Missouri began with just ten words: "Let only native-born American citizens enjoy the suffrage right." That short sentence won Howard K. Bowers of St. Louis a farm valued at nearly $25,000. Bowers had seen an advertisement in the *Patriot* about a subscription contest in the fall of 1923.[18] According to the ad, the author of the best slogan about Americanism would win a "beautiful Country Estate" generously donated by an "Illinois citizen who is 100 percent American every day [of] the year."[19] After learning of his victory, Bowers admitted that he had little farming experience but would rely upon his family for agricultural advice. When asked where the farm was located, Bowers admitted that he had few specifics about the property but believed it to be somewhere in central Illinois. Despite his ignorance of the rigors of agriculture, Bowers appeared ready to wave good-bye to city life and his career in the insurance business and head for greener acres.[20]

Reporters of the *St. Louis Post-Dispatch*, a bitter rival to the *Patriot*, felt that something did not add up about Bowers and his new farm and decided to investigate. The first question mark surrounding the contest dug up by the *Post-Dispatch* centered on Bowers's employment as a clerk at a downtown office building with alleged ties to the Klan.[21] In further reviewing the farm story, the *Post-Dispatch* reported that there were at least two mortgages tied to the land in question, one held by Mary and Lincoln Slick, who had owned the farm since 1912, and another claimed by an unknown man living on the East Coast. Reporters' interests were also piqued when they discovered that Lincoln Slick worked as the circulation manager of the *Patriot* and that both Slick and Bowers were given jobs at the newspaper around the same time that the farm subscription contest ended.[22] When pressed for details, C. C. Crawford and Frederick Barkhurst, editors and operators of the *Patriot*, confessed ignorance of the entire contest and claimed that Bowers already owned the farm. After this answer was deemed insufficient, the editors wilted under pressure and turned on one another.[23] Though he denied allegations of fraud, Crawford's plan for the slogan contest had been a calculated money grab to boost subscribers and revenue for the *Patriot*. Starting in August 1923, the Slicks were hired to supervise a group of men scouring portions of Illinois and Missouri with the goal of obtaining one hundred thousand new subscribers. If they reached their goal, the Slicks would receive $100,000 for their work with a pledge of an additional $60,000 if they could get two hundred thousand subscribers. As the *Patriot* was conducting the slogan contest at the same time, the money the Slicks received would have easily paid off the mortgages on their farm, which they could then transfer to the contest winner.[24]

While Crawford and the Slicks envisioned a major financial windfall from the slogan contest, the number of new subscribers lagged behind expectations, particularly after US Postal Service officials required that the contest be open to subscribers and nonsubscribers.[25] By December 1923, it was obvious that the anticipated total was out of reach, and with the announcement of the grand prize looming, Crawford had to make a tough decision to either give away the farm to the rightful winner and hope to break even financially from the fiasco or rig the results to ensure damage control. In the end, Crawford decided to "save the klan [*sic*] publication."[26] He brought Lincoln Slick and Howard Bowers into his office and worked out a deal where he wrote out several possible slogans for the contest, Bowers signed the official paperwork, and Slick picked his favorite slogan from the list. When the group reached its decision, the slogan was announced in the newspaper, attributing Bowers as the author. Slick and Bowers were then tasked with working out the transfer of the farm on their own—if they wanted to continue with that part of the plan. Both men, however, kept their jobs with the newspaper.[27] Crawford could claim the contest was legitimate while also ensuring that the newspaper avoided financial ruin.

The revelation that the contest was a fraud must have been satisfying for the *Post-Dispatch* staff as the newspaper had been the frequent target of fiery commentaries in the *Patriot*. In arguing why "the St. Louis Post-Dispatch must go," the *Patriot* found the newspaper to be "debased of morals and more or less a menace to public good."[28] The feud between the *Post-Dispatch* and the Klan dated back to the hooded order's arrival in the state in 1921. Soon after, the *Post-Dispatch* linked arms with other opposition newspapers to form an anti-Klan press that not only published stories on alleged Klan atrocities but also issued resounding calls to action against the Klan from their editorial pages. In reviewing the alleged fraud undertaken by C. C. Crawford and the Klan, the *Post-Dispatch* compared the entire contest to another example of "scoundrelism cloaked under a mask of whining hypocrisy."[29] Facing editorial heat from the *Post-Dispatch*, Crawford used nearly the entire front page of the *Patriot* to answer the newspaper's "campaign of malicious propaganda." He accused the newspaper of trying "to make me out a liar" by assigning a reporter involved in the *Post-Dispatch*'s coverage of the Mer Rouge massacre to cover the story.[30] The *Post-Dispatch* dismissed the condemnations of the *Patriot* and, mocking Crawford's ministerial work, asked God to be "merciful to the deluded followers of such a cause and such a leader."[31]

The *Post-Dispatch* was not the only newspaper to go after Crawford and the Klan over their fraud. Several state newspapers, including the *Church Progress* and the *Vienna Home-Advisor*, reprinted commentaries on the scandal from the *Post-Dispatch* and the *St. Louis Star*.[32] In its own review, the *Star* compared Crawford's farm-slogan campaign to a con man's shell game in an editorial cartoon and denounced the Klan because it attacked "all misgovernment, all acts that tend to destroy faith in government, and yet its members are often guilty of the things it assumes to condemn."[33] The *Washington Citizen* reminded its readers of Crawford's recent lectures in Franklin County and implied a loss of faith in the Klan editor: "People had heard of other Klan speakers getting out of the straight and narrow path, but they didn't think Dr. Crawford could do it."[34] In Jefferson County, the *Republican* filtered through reports of the scandal to ascertain why Crawford had not shown up for a scheduled speech in DeSoto and expressed concern over rumors in the county of

184 Chapter Five

increased tensions between pro- and anti-Klan factions.[35] The *Kansas City Catholic Register* filled its editorial page on March 13, 1924, with a dismissive and mocking tone regarding the growing scandals within the Invisible Empire:

> The Ku Klux Klan is in pretty bad shape. Consider the review of one day's activity. One of the founders of the Klan was convicted of violation of the Mann Act; a preacher who publicly espoused the Klan and used his pulpit for preaching the gospel of Kluxism was indicted for fraudulent use of the mails to increase the circulation of the official organ of the invisible empire; a public official who turned over a State Capitol for a Klan meeting is under fire for prostitution of his oath of office and bribery for the alleged protection of a brewer who violated the Eighteenth Amendment; a prominent Saint Louis Klansman was arrested after driving about the city for several days in a state of intoxication, distributing Ku Klux Knives. A tree is known by its fruits. It is a mystery that good and intelligent people can stick to such an organization and under such leaders.[36]

As news of the fraudulent slogan contest spread across the state and the country, Crawford resigned as minister of St. Louis's Fourth Christian Church. Despite his admittance of lying and defrauding potential subscribers, the church's board of governors refused to accept his resignation and passed a resolution defending Crawford and expressing confidence in his leadership.[37] When reporters reminded congregants that several Klan events had taken place at the church while Crawford served as pastor, church members denied that the KKK influenced church decisions. "The attitude of the congregation is to stand by the pastor till hell freezes over, then skate around on the ice," one church member defiantly told the press.[38] Given a chance to speak before his congregation, Crawford used his sermon to plead forgiveness and remind his followers that his "allegiance has always been and always will be to the Church of Christ."[39] "If I have sinned," he told those assembled, "remember it was my eagerness to that great cause, which is second only to the cause of God."[40] Despite his connection to the scandal, Crawford's congregation forgave him, and he remained the pastor of the Fourth Christian Church for the remainder of the 1920s. He even hosted Governor Sam A. Baker for the dedication of a new church building in 1926, though Baker later denied knowing about Crawford's Klan ties.[41]

Crawford's congregation may have continued to back him as news of the scandal filled newspapers, but Klan leaders were not so eager to forgive and forget. Upon learning of the contest, Imperial Representative George C. McCarron began his own investigation into the matter. He consulted prominent Klansman Heber Nations, and the two decided that all involved in the scandal needed to be reprimanded. After reviewing the statements of Bowers and Crawford, McCarron submitted information about the *Patriot* to the US District Attorney's Office.[42] Klan members were also quick to point out that the newspaper was not an official Klan publication, though Crawford did try to sell the newspaper to the local order.[43] The Klan rejected the sale, and various stockholders in the newspaper sued, claiming misappropriation of funds.[44] Though rumors circulated that he faced banishment from the Invisible Empire, Crawford was suspended from the Klan while officials in Atlanta reviewed his case.[45] The outcome of this hooded review is unknown, but Crawford never again served as a Klan leader in St. Louis.

Crawford's fall is significant because the Klan willingly sacrificed one of its own to save face during the scandal. Additionally, Crawford was not a minor Klansman who got into trouble but a well-known Protestant minister and one of the most popular Klan recruiters in the region. While assisting in the day-to-day operations of the *Patriot*, Crawford extensively toured Illinois and Missouri as a coveted speaker who brought the message of Klankraft and Americanism to cities and small towns throughout the Mississippi River valley. He also actively challenged Klan opponents on the speaker's circuit and in the pages of the *Patriot*.[46] He wrote and spoke often about the anti-Klan coalition, and in an address before nearly two thousand hooded members at St. Louis's Maxwelton Race Track, he defiantly told the crowd that "I hope I will see the Ku Klux Klan march down Grand boulevard and to see the opposition press beaten to its knees."[47] Yet despite his loyalty to the Klan, Crawford was expendable. In its review of the incident, the Klan-affiliated *Missouri Valley Independent* praised the actions of McCarron to show that "the

186   Chapter Five

Klan does not indorse any act by anybody that is a violation of our Nation's laws."[48]

McCarron's decision to consult with Heber Nations regarding punishment for the participants of the slogan contest must have seemed insulting to Crawford, considering Nations's own problematic record. In February 1924, while serving as state labor commissioner, Nations admitted to orchestrating the rental of the house chamber at the Missouri state capitol building for a Klan event. The incident brought denouncements from both Republicans and Democrats.[49] Around the same time, Heber's brother, Gus Nations, was involved in a raid on the Griesedieck Brothers' Brewery in St. Louis after federal Prohibition officials accused the company of selling beer in defiance of the Volstead Act. After a series of arrests for the liquor violation, employees admitted their guilt and told Prohibition agents they were part of a protection relationship between St. Louis brewers and state officials. Raymond Griesedieck confessed that the company had paid a state official roughly $15,000 to ensure protection from potential raids as the brewery produced real beer alongside legal near beer.[50] About a month before the raid, federal agents received a tip and soon discovered that employees met with unknown individuals while continually making phone calls between St. Louis, Kansas City, and Jefferson City. News of the mysterious circumstances surrounding the Griesedieck Brothers' Brewery soon reached Washington, DC, and Assistant US Attorney General Mabel Willebrandt, who ordered local officers to collect the confessions of employees in advance of an impending trial.[51]

As the Griesedieck employees detailed the protection plan to federal investigators, it was not long before the identities of the alleged state officials came to light. According to the *St. Louis Post-Dispatch*, the allegations of graft were like a "thundershower on a Fourth of July picnic," and the confessions were so damning that Governor Hyde canceled his planned European vacation to rush back to Missouri. Charles Prather, the first official to be named, immediately resigned as state food and drug commissioner after meeting with Hyde and officers of the Federal Internal Revenue Department. However, he told the press he planned to fight the charges as a private citizen. Nevertheless, Prather's departure shook state

Republicans as some political leaders considered him "the brains of the party." Originally from Advance, a small town bordering the Bootheel, Prather was appointed as state food and drug commissioner in 1922 by Hyde after being passed over, ironically, for a position as Missouri's federal Prohibition director.[52] After Prather's resignation, Heber Nations emerged as the possible second unnamed state official connected to the protection plan. With Hyde threatening to "clear the smell of beer out of the State Capital," many expected him to fire Nations.[53] Instead, Hyde kept Nations, widely considered another one of the governor's trusted advisers, as state labor commissioner, but he warned Nations that he would demand a resignation if evidence connected him to the scandal.[54] As Prather had done before, when Nations was indicted for his alleged role in the protection plan a few weeks later, he resigned but assured his supporters that he planned to "make vigorous war" against his accusers.[55]

With the case headed to trial in the spring of 1925, Nations most likely felt confident that Prather would unite with him to fight the allegations, but when Prather announced his intention to plead guilty, Nations soon realized that it would be his word against federal investigators, Griesedieck Brewery employees, and Charles Prather.[56] Nations, however, was not completely alone as his brother, Gus, agreed to serve as a possible witness for the defense. Additionally, members of the Anti-Saloon League and Woman's Christian Temperance Union initiated a letter-writing campaign to pressure federal officials and President Calvin Coolidge to halt the trial because they felt that Nations was unfairly targeted for his support of Prohibition and its enforcement.[57] When the trial opened in May 1925, Charles Prather and officials of the Griesedieck Brothers' Brewery immediately pleaded guilty as part of a plea deal to allow them to become witnesses for the prosecution. With members of the WCTU watching from the gallery, Heber Nations pleaded not guilty.[58] Called to testify, Charles Prather and Raymond Griesedieck discussed their encounters with the state labor commissioner and how he instructed the brewery employees to make monetary arrangements primarily with Prather because Nations was already doing a similar protection plan with another brewery. The second brewery remained anonymous, but Prather outlined how Nations received most of the payoff from the Griesediecks' protection arrangement. When pressed by prosecutors, the witnesses continually discussed how Heber Nations controlled beer protection in St. Louis due to his influence over his brother, Gus. Perhaps trying to splinter the Nations brothers, Raymond Griesedieck testified that Heber viewed Gus as "just a kid, with no mind of his own."[59]

Given a chance to cross-examine Prather and Griesedieck, Nations's defense team repeatedly inquired about a special arrangement with the prosecutor for their testimony. When the judge ruled the questioning unnecessary, Nations's attorney pressed Prather about whether Nations was ever in a meeting with the Griesediecks during a money exchange. Prather acknowledged that Nations was never part of the money transactions as he always collected his share after the meetings.[60] Not getting a desired answer and perhaps feeling the stares of WCTU members in the gallery, the defense attorney shifted the focus to Nations's dry record and asked Prather if he was aware that Nations was "as dry, if not dryer than Gus." A grin emerged on Prather's face as he replied, "Heber got dry at times."[61]

With little to celebrate at the start of the trial, the defense turned to Heber Nations to take the witness stand and clear his name. When pressed for details by both the prosecution and the defense about his knowledge of the Griesedieck Brewery, Nations made a habit of slamming his hand down on the witness box to punctuate his points. In his version of events, Nations was the hero seeking to keep St. Louis dry while aiding his brother, Gus, and other federal Prohibition agents. Nations argued that it was not a protection plan he and Prather were involved in but rather an organized scheme to catch the Griesedieck brewery violating the Volstead Act. Asked about Prather's comments that he claimed most of the protection money, Nations denied that he received bribe money. "I would say not," he loudly declared.[62]

In closing arguments, prosecutors compared the Nations brothers to the biblical characters Cain and Abel. Heber, serving as Cain, may not have killed his brother like his counterpart did, but he used his influence over Gus to betray him and the law. The defense, in its closing statement, portrayed the case as a conspiracy to slander and ruin the Nations family. Both brothers visibly wept as their defense attorney accused the "enemies of law enforcement" of trying to disgrace the Nations name.[63] The theory of a conspiracy against the Nations brothers put forth by the defense was not a new allegation, however, as both Heber and Gus had made similar claims in the lead-up to and during the trial.[64] Assistant US Attorney General Mabel Willebrandt quickly dismissed this claim by pointing out that Raymond Griesedieck could have made a similar claim of a frame-up on the witness stand but instead implicated Nations in the protection scheme.[65]

Sent to their private chambers to consider the evidence of the case, the jury deliberated for nearly twenty-seven hours before returning to the courtroom and informing the stunned gallery that Heber Nations was guilty of conspiracy to violate the Volstead Act. The judge sentenced Nations to eighteen months in federal prison and levied a fine of $3,333.[66] When asked for a statement regarding their support for the former state labor commissioner, the ASL and WCTU declined to comment.[67] The *St. Louis Post-Dispatch*, in its review of the case, did not mince words:

> Heber Nations was a bright and shining light among the leaders of the host of reformers who put over the Eighteenth Amendment and the Volstead act and who have been ardent advocates of the rigid enforcement of the prohibition laws. He was the plumed crusader of the cause of prohibition. His profession of devotion to the cause was perhaps the loudest and most insistent in the State of Missouri. His denunciation of other law breakers and of all those who opposed prohibition and the extreme methods of enforcing it was unbridled. He himself, after his indictment, is credited with 100 raids of alleged violators of the Volstead Act. He was the model of the political clergy, the pride of the Anti-Saloon League, and the pet of the W.C.T.U. His newspaper in Jefferson City was the recognized organ of high morality and law enforcement. Under Nations' cloak of righteousness, however, was the greasy hand of boodle. He had an itching palm. He used his vociferous professions of high moral purpose and civic righteousness to betray his cause and cheat the State. Under cover of zealous activity in the enforcement of the law and in the councils of prohibitionists, he entered into conspiracy to have the law violated by a brewery, and to protect the brewery in its violation of the law, for bribes. He stabbed the cause to which he professed the greatest devotion.[68]

190   Chapter Five

Almost immediately following the verdict, Nations and his defense team pushed for an appeal before the US Court of Appeals, but further scandal plagued him later in 1925.[69] Back in Cole County, a recently called grand jury investigated a series of controversial liquor raids undertaken by the sheriff's department and local citizens, including Nations. Jefferson City residents knew of Nations's federal trial, and the local *Tribune* devoted a lengthy editorial to the active work of the ASL and a "certain un-American secret organization" in aiding his defense. It was curious, the newspaper noted, that these "so-called victims," referring to the Nations brothers, were trying so hard to fight the same enforcement laws that they traditionally relied upon in their liquor raids.[70] The *Tribune* also found it curious that Sheriff L. C. Withaup allowed Heber Nations to participate in liquor raids despite his recent conviction. Less than a month after his initial trial ended, Nations accompanied Withaup and his deputies on a raid of a farm in rural Cole County.[71] "To the ordinary citizen," the *Tribune* asserted, "it would seem that it is Nations's cue to lay low and not indulge in cleaning up until he has swept before his own door." As for his participation in the raid, the newspaper advised the sheriff that "if Nations's thirst for riding is so insatiable that he cannot restrain himself . . . Withaup should do it for him."[72]

Since L. C. Withaup's election as sheriff in 1924, area residents had voiced concerns over his use of private citizens in liquor raids. Withaup's involvement with the Klan and his reliance upon fellow Klansmen to participate in raids left many to wonder who really ran the sheriff's office. This sentiment was shared by the *Tribune*, which felt that the "loyalty of Louis to Heber is touching though strange . . . joined as they were by the bonds of brotherhood in the Knights of the Ku Klux Klan."[73] The newspaper was concerned, however, that such a relationship threatened the enforcement of the law in Cole County. "Is the law of the klan [*sic*] above the law of the land?" the *Tribune* pondered. This question was especially pertinent after allegations surfaced that Withaup, in addition to using private citizens as part of his liquor-raiding party known as the "Four Horsemen," had granted certain prisoners in the county jail extreme leniency when it came to their confinement.[74] One prisoner later claimed that deputies allowed him to participate in a liquor raid.[75] Though the *Tribune* was willing to give Withaup the benefit of the doubt when it came to these charges, it warned the sheriff that county residents had "no patience with a system which permits enforcement by a certain group of citizens . . . a certain secret organization."[76]

FIGURE 14. Merchants Bank Building (*left*) in Jefferson City during the parade dedicating the new state capitol building, 1924. The top floor of the building served as a meeting place for the Jefferson City Klan. Courtesy of Van Gundy Photograph Collection (MS313). Missouri State Archives.

While Cole County residents may have objected to Nations's participation in liquor raids, the Klan initially stood behind him. At a Klan picnic on the outskirts of Jefferson City, four hundred attendees, including sheriff's department deputies, cheered as a speaker gave a rousing address expressing confidence in Nations and calling upon those assembled to "do their bit toward a vindication" as he pushed for an appeal.[77] Despite the support, Nations's relationship with the Invisible Empire disintegrated by the end of 1925. In November, he resigned as exalted cyclops of the Jefferson City klavern, though he refused to clarify whether this decision was the Klan's or his own.[78] Instead, in a public statement, Nations suggested that there was little need for a Klan in the capital city:

192   Chapter Five

There has been no quarrel between me and the Ku Klux Klan. I have only the highest respect for the men and women of Cole county who joined the organization, as I did, because we believed it the most powerful organized force for law enforcement in the community. But, the law enforcement in the community is a pretty well established fact. All of the soft drink parlors have been closed and we have elected a prosecuting attorney and sheriff who will make it hot for the law breakers.[79]

Out as leader of the Jefferson City Klan, Nations focused on his impending appeals case. In July 1926, the US Court of Appeals reversed Nations's conviction, citing that the judge should have recused himself in the first trial because of potential bias. Though not declaring Nations innocent, the Court of Appeals left the decision to seek a new trial to federal prosecutors.[80] Federal officials pursued such an option after the US Supreme Court ruled it would not review the appeals court's reversal.[81] When Nations's second trial came up in 1928, prosecutors again relied on Charles Prather and Raymond Griesedieck to testify on Nations's role in the protection plan. Seeking to strengthen his defense, Heber called on his brother, Gus, who was withheld as a witness originally, to testify about their efforts to suppress illegal alcohol in St. Louis. As it had done in 1925, the jury again found Nations guilty of conspiracy to violate the Volstead Act. The new judge showed Nations some leniency and reduced the fine to $2,000 while still upholding the eighteen-month prison sentence.[82] Nations and his attorneys once more pushed for an appeal.[83]

In what would become a successful trend for Heber Nations, the US Court of Appeals sided with the former state labor commissioner in 1929 and 1931 in his bid for a retrial.[84] The Court of Appeals ruled in both hearings that evidence was withheld in 1928 and again at Nations's third trial in 1930. By 1930, the trial and the Great Depression took a serious toll on Nations. He admitted that he had moved from Jefferson City to Farmington since the second appeal and had a hard time finding work due to the country's economic troubles and his own damaged reputation.[85] When federal prosecutors again used Charles Prather and Raymond Griesedieck to connect Nations to the beer protection plan, the former Klan leader lashed out on the witness stand and demanded to know why he was the target while guilty men like Prather and Griesedieck faced little punishment.[86] Despite an impassioned plea for leniency and the testimony of several current and former state officials brought in to vouch for his character, Nations was again found guilty of conspiracy to violate the Volstead Act.[87] When Nations won his third appeal in 1931, federal prosecutors debated the merits of a fourth trial, while the *St. Louis Post-Dispatch* demanded that the prosecution finish what it started.[88] After three successful convictions, the prosecution knew it still had a strong case, but the world was a much different place in 1932 than it had been in 1925. By the early 1930s, sentiment against the Eighteenth Amendment had grown stronger as the Depression deepened. Additionally, key witness Raymond Griesedieck had died. Federal officials declined when asked if the prosecution would pursue a fourth trial, citing that "the eighteenth amendment is now on its last legs."[89] Heber Nations was a free man, but little was left of the Invisible Empire.

While Heber Nations was mired in scandal following his departure from the hooded order, J. H. Wolpers of the *Poplar Bluff Republican* expressed hope that the former state labor commissioner's fall would be a valuable warning to other Klansmen and -women to get out of the Invisible Empire while there was still time. If not, a similar fate might befall them, or their reputations ruined by their association with the organization. When Nations tried to resurrect his public image by claiming that he had seen the light and vowing to vote for a Catholic candidate for mayor of Jefferson City, Wolpers questioned Nations's sincerity: "It is strange that brother Nations did not think of these high ideals when he led the blindfolded cohorts of the capital city . . . [w]hen he tried to ram the klan [*sic*] down the throat of the Republican party wherever he could reach into its organization."[90] Nevertheless, Wolpers felt that the burgeoning scandals within the Invisible Empire had hastened the exit of many former members because "the men and women who had been drawn into the klan [*sic*] under one pretext or the other saw the foolishness of the thing and refused to be further Spurgeonized or Nationized."[91]

If Heber Nations's role within the Klan had "Nationized" certain segments of Missouri's population, Wolpers's assessment of those who were

"Spurgeonized" served as a thinly veiled commentary on Poplar Bluff's O. L. Spurgeon. Arriving in Butler County in 1921, Spurgeon rose to local prominence as the pastor of Poplar Bluff's First Baptist Church.[92] From his pulpit, Spurgeon began to preach about 100 percent Americanism and praised the Klan for its activities across the country.[93] Spurgeon was very familiar with the Klan's tenets as he had been a lecturer and organizer for the group in Iowa and Minnesota before settling in Missouri.[94] Within two years of moving to First Baptist Church, Spurgeon became the exalted cyclops of Poplar Bluff Klan No. 48.[95] Toward the end of 1923, however, Spurgeon's climb within the ranks of the Klan was just too lucrative to pass up. He resigned his pastorate at First Baptist Church in October and stepped down as exalted cyclops a few weeks later.[96] Soon after, he packed up his family and moved to Collierville, Tennessee, a town roughly twenty miles southeast of Memphis near the Mississippi state line. Once in Collierville, Spurgeon became closely connected with the Memphis Klan while also expanding his role as a lecturer for the national organization. To this end, he made repeated trips back across the Mississippi River into Missouri to speak in towns throughout the Bootheel.[97]

In June 1924, Spurgeon returned to Poplar Bluff to dedicate the local chapter's new headquarters just north of town. Called Klandale, the stucco facility boasted a vestibule, two anterooms, storage space, and a large auditorium. The grounds that surrounded the new building featured a park, picnic grounds, and access to a spring. On the day of the festivities, Spurgeon welcomed Klansmen and -women from neighboring communities in Missouri, Illinois, and Arkansas. Totaling more than three thousand, the assembled crowd filled Poplar Bluff for a parade followed by a picnic and initiation of fifty new members at Klandale. Spurgeon and the local Klan also paid tribute to their fallen brethren by intentionally leaving six chairs empty during the event, including one dedicated to Dr. C. W. Williamson, whose funeral had occurred earlier in the day.[98] Not long after the dedication, Spurgeon returned to town to deliver what would become one of his most well-known addresses, "Behind the Mask," which argued that the Klan's use of masks and secrecy were not for "dark doings" but rather patriotic actions comparable to Paul Revere's famous ride and the Boston Tea Party.[99]

After proclaiming the goals of Klankraft to thousands of Missourians in the summer of 1924, O. L. Spurgeon's life took a dramatic turn within a matter of weeks. In August 1924, Spurgeon was arrested for disorderly conduct in Memphis. The arrest stemmed from a fight that broke out between J. D. Jones, a Birmingham, Alabama, police officer and Klansman, and Klan officials at the hooded order's headquarters in Memphis when Jones attempted to gain access to organizational records. Jones told the assembled Klansmen that he would take the records despite their protest, and after a scuffle ensued, Jones pulled his gun and fired a shot toward the group. W. A. Blankenship, the leader of the Memphis men, immediately called police, who arrested all involved.[100] Within a matter of days, as police investigated the incident, Klan officials in Atlanta quickly issued an edict banishing Spurgeon and the other Memphis Klansmen from the Invisible Empire.[101]

On its surface, the banishment of Spurgeon and the others appeared to be a decision by the Klan to save face after the negative publicity surrounding the shooting. The *Missouri Kourier* suggested as much when it touted a reorganization of the Memphis Klan in the weeks after the incident.[102] In reality, however, Jones made the trip from Birmingham to Memphis to root out a revolution within the hooded ranks. Since William Simmons's ouster in 1922, various Klan factions vied to control their fiefdoms. Simmons formed his Kamelia. D. C. Stephenson, originally a Hiram Evans backer, exerted his influence over the Realm of Indiana and frequently sparred with officials in Atlanta.[103] In 1924, a group of Midwestern klaverns in Indiana, Illinois, and Iowa banded together to form the Independent Klan of America (IKA). The Independent Klan of America's plan was to secede from the Invisible Empire because, as they argued, high-ranking officials, particularly Hiram Evans, had turned the hooded order into a moneymaking venture in violation of the organization's original goals.[104]

It is not known when O. L. Spurgeon joined the Independent Klan of America movement, but at the time of his ouster in August 1924, newspapers reported that he was part of a faction trying to form an IKA chapter in Memphis. Within weeks of his removal from the hooded order, Spurgeon organized a meeting of Klansmen in the Mississippi River valley and called on them to renounce their membership and join

196 Chapter Five

the IKA. When asked why he broke with the Klan, Spurgeon declared that he was "tired of imperialism and tyranny" and wanted a voice in the organizations in which he was a member. To this end, Spurgeon soon traveled throughout the region, recruiting for the IKA.[105] To produce a groundswell of support among disenchanted Klansmen, the IKA advertised that members of the Klan could transfer to the new group for a fee of one dollar or less.[106] The organization also quickly got to work forming auxiliaries, much like the Klan, including an African American branch called the Abraham Lincoln Auxiliary.[107] Hoping to stem the tide of revolution, Klan publications like the *Missouri Valley Independent* largely ignored the IKA or compared its activities to anti-Klan groups that were "typical enemy units organized to wage the destructionist propaganda within the ranks of the great Protestant order."[108] By 1926, the IKA claimed to have eighteen thousand members in Indiana with a growing presence throughout the Midwest.[109]

Soon after becoming a national representative for the IKA in Tennessee and Alabama, Spurgeon brought multiple lawsuits against the Klan, hoping to recoup financial losses from his banishment. He sued the *Kourier*, a Tennessee Klan publication, for $60,000, claiming that the newspaper ran multiple negative articles about him. Spurgeon followed this lawsuit with a second, where he argued that the Klan owed him back wages from his original contract as an imperial lecturer. Totaling up his lost compensation, Spurgeon alleged that his original agreement of $100 a week plus expenses entitled him to $2,053.20 from the hooded order, but the case was later dismissed.[110] These two trials were not Spurgeon's only legal battles with Klan officials. In addition to the disorderly conduct charge, he was charged with grand larceny following a lengthy disagreement with the Bolin family over a farm property in Collierville. When Spurgeon first moved to Tennessee, he bought the farm from E. E. Bolin, a local Klan official, but after his standing in the local Klan dissipated, the Bolins claimed that Spurgeon moved and tried to sell items that were not part of the farm sale. The feud came to literal blows when a fight between members of the Bolin family and Spurgeon broke out during the trial in magistrate court.[111]

No one was more pleased to report on Spurgeon's fall from grace than J. H. Wolpers at the *Poplar Bluff Republican*. Both during and after

Spurgeon's time at the First Baptist Church, Wolpers repeatedly called attention to the Klansman's activities, particularly when the headlines were less than positive. When Spurgeon visited Wayne County to preach on the Klan, the newspaper asserted that he was "much better qualified to represent the cause of the ku klux than he is the cause of Christ." In an editorial that praised Cape Girardeau and Sikeston for their booming businesses and lack of Klan chapters, Wolpers lamented that Poplar Bluff "had all those things that our neighboring towns had before we traded with Spurgeon and now we have the klan [sic] and the other towns have the other things." As Spurgeon struggled through his eviction from the Invisible Empire, the Republican eagerly splashed his legal troubles across the front page.

While fighting Spurgeon's efforts to gain financial compensation, the Klan turned its attention to the Independent Klan of America. Though the organization had appeared to largely ignore the IKA's recruiting campaign, it aimed to put a stop to its main rival via legal action. In 1925, the Klan sued the IKA for $500,000, claiming that the new organization did not have the right to use the word Klan in its title.[112] A federal judge ruled in the hooded order's favor, allowing the group to claim exclusive naming rights to the phrases "Klan," "The Knights of the Ku Klux Klan," "The Invisible Empire, Knights of the Ku Klux Klan," and "The Ku Klux Klan." When the dust settled, the Independent Klan of America restructured under the new title of "K.A.P.," though the meaning of the initials was not disclosed.[113] It is not known if Spurgeon stayed on with the new K.A.P. By the late 1920s, he had moved to Kansas City to take up the pastorate at Garfield Avenue Church.[114] After Spurgeon's departure, Poplar Bluff Klan No. 48 quietly sold Klandale in 1928 to a business owner who later turned the facility into a roadhouse.[115]

While the controversial exits of C. C. Crawford, Heber Nations, and O. L. Spurgeon affected the Missouri Klan, hooded members in the southwestern part of the state continued to achieve unrivaled recruiting success and political power. Perhaps no hooded member wielded more power in the region than Pierre Wallace, but just as Crawford, Nations, and Spurgeon before him, the Webb City Klansman was embroiled in significant scandals that led to his own departure from the Klan, impacted the

Invisible Empire's control of the region, and ultimately culminated in his death. Wallace was born in Webb City in 1887 and lived his entire life in Jasper County. After completing his education in the local school system, Wallace worked in the tobacco business for nearly twenty-five years, including a period as the manager of the Joplin Tobacco Company.[116] In addition to his role in the business community, Wallace was also active, along with his wife, Flora, in the Parent-Teacher Associations of Jasper County, with Flora serving as president of the Webb City PTA and as a member of the state board of Parent-Teacher Associations.[117]

When the Klan came to Jasper County in 1921, Wallace became one of the organization's most vocal supporters and used his standing in the community to rise to the rank of exalted cyclops.[118] In donning the white robes, Wallace hoped to make the local Klan into both a philanthropic organization, as evidenced by numerous hooded donations to local causes, as well as a powerful political machine.[119] Such an opportunity presented itself in the administration of Taylor Snapp, and the hooded order quickly tied itself to Joplin's new mayor. As a result, multiple anti-Klan organizations soon emerged in Jasper County to counter the Klan's political strength, though Snapp, Wallace, and Ozark Klan No. 3 initially kept the opposition at bay. Yet just as the national Klan entered a decline following 1924, so too did Jasper County Klansmen experience a similar collapse, particularly Wallace.

By the mid-1920s, Wallace not only claimed control over Ozark Klan No. 3 but also significantly influenced Jasper County politics. Sheriff Guy T. Humes appointed Wallace as one of his deputies, and though it was an unpaid position, the local press hinted that Humes answered to Wallace and not the other way around.[120] Soon after, however, Wallace mysteriously separated from the Klan. No clear explanation of his ouster was given because Jasper County newspapers did not cover the story as other publications did over the departure of C. C. Crawford, Heber Nations, and O. L. Spurgeon. Like Nations, it is unknown if he was forced out or voluntarily stepped down. The records of the Joplin Anti-Klan Organization, Carthage Anti-Klan Association, and Jasper County Anti-Klan Association (JCAKA) also offer little indication about what occurred within the rank and file of the hooded order. The *Kansas City Times* later claimed that Wallace "retired from active participation in klan

"Behind the Mask"   199

[*sic*] affairs."[121] Nevertheless, Wallace's life took a notable turn from the moment he left the Klan, as his wife later claimed that he began drinking heavily following his departure. Additionally, he lost his managerial job in 1927 when the Joplin Tobacco Company closed down. Wallace recovered slightly from economic disaster by finding work in the insurance business, but his drunkenness never subsided.[122]

While his drunken actions ultimately ended up on the front page of Jasper County newspapers, the biggest scandal connected to Wallace was an allegation by a former police officer that the exalted cyclops controlled Joplin's city hall during the Snapp administration. While Snapp never openly campaigned in favor of the Klan, he was not one to turn down hooded support. When he ran for reelection in 1926, the newly unified Jasper County Anti-Klan Association (also sometimes called the Anti-Klan Association of Jasper County or simply the Anti-Klan Organization) launched a full-scale campaign to elect J. F. Osborne over Snapp. A Joplin resident for more than thirty years, Osborne had risen from a young local attorney to a four-time mayor of the city.[123] While Osborne assured voters that the Klan would no longer influence municipal affairs, the "Klan issue," much like it had in statewide political campaigns in 1922 and 1924, quickly soured the mayoral race, with the *Globe* positing that the budding rivalry between J. F. Osborne and Taylor Snapp would be "the most bitter and strenuous campaign of [Osborne's] career."[124]

Allegations by anti-Klan supporters that the voices of hooded leaders like Wallace were constantly in Snapp's ear gained traction as the Invisible Empire experienced its greatest period of growth in Joplin during the mayor's administration. The Joplin Anti-Klan Organization unsuccessfully campaigned against this alleged invisible government during the 1924 municipal elections. Now faced with the prospect of four more years of Snapp-Klan leadership, Joplin's anti-Klan forces organized a counterattack and approached Osborne about running for mayor. Though he had retired when his term concluded in 1922, the growing influence of the Jasper County Klan convinced Osborne to reenter the political arena.[125] Initially, Osborne framed his campaign as an effort to reform allegedly corrupt law-enforcement institutions in Joplin to ensure that the city was the "'Gateway to the Ozarks'. . . not the gateway

200   Chapter Five

to jail."[126] Not surprisingly, Osborne's words received strong pushback from local law enforcement, particularly those associated with the Snapp administration.[127]

In addition to campaigning against corruption, Osborne also realized that the Klan's control of Jasper County was a pivotal talking point. At first, he cautiously referenced the Klan by suggesting that residents wanted city hall "free from the domination of sinister influences from the outside."[128] Yet as Snapp supporters bit back against charges of police corruption, Osborne laid the issue bare: "I am not a Klansman, never have been, and never will be. . . . I am opposed by the Klan, and I oppose the Klan and its insidious meddling in municipal affairs."[129] To wed these two points together, Osborn reminded voters that "people know things are wrong at city hall; and they have now to say whether the bold intermeddling and dictatorship there of the Boss from Webb City is to be approved for another term."[130] Osborne's accusations were quite clear to Joplin residents as people throughout Jasper County knew that Wallace was the exalted cyclops of Ozark Klan No. 3. What these potential voters were not prepared for, however, was definitive proof that Wallace controlled municipal affairs. Much like what C. S. Burns did to A. W. Nelson in October 1924, former Joplin police officer Glenn Skoggman upended Snapp's campaign when he alleged that the mayor and Wallace had personally reviewed a case that eventually led to his dismissal from the police force.[131] While Snapp had a right to investigate the case, Wallace's participation would have raised eyebrows, as Skoggman's claims placed the head of the local Klan and the mayor in the same room reviewing city affairs.[132]

When Joplin voters went to the polls in April 1926, the image of Snapp and Wallace side by side was firmly established in their minds. In the end, allegations of police corruption and Klan ties in the Snapp administration, combined with Osborne's own political record, produced a victory for the former mayor. It was not just Osborne who won on Election Day, however, as the Joplin press noted a decided repudiation of the Klan—only one Klan-backed candidate won in the municipal campaigns, and he was even deemed acceptable by anti-Klan supporters.[133] Osborne moved quickly to cleanse Joplin of the Klan soon after his victory. He expressed the expectation that city workers would show

"Behind the Mask" 201

loyalty to the new administration, but Osborne explicitly demanded that anyone who sided with the Klan should resign. When Osborne demoted fire chief Henry Wondell, arguing that his "membership and active participation in klan [*sic*] activities precluded me from considering him as a member of my cabinet," the city council launched an investigation, and more than thirty firefighters and police officers resigned in protest.[134] Osborne and his anti-Klan supporters—many of whom now occupied key positions in city government—never forgot the mass resignations and continued to purge officials tied to the former administration, citing that "no man could hold office under Snapp who did not belong to the Ku Klux Klan."[135]

Osborne's victory in the mayoral campaign galvanized anti-Klan sentiments throughout Jasper County, as many political candidates began to speak out against the hooded order. By November 1926, roughly twenty candidates campaigning for offices ranging from constable to congressman publicly denounced the Klan or confirmed that they were not members.[136] In an editorial titled "Frankness on the Klan," the *Globe* told its readers that "recent announcements by county candidates concerning their stand on the Ku Klux Klan is a development of the campaign that will be appreciated by voters. . . . [C]andidates who do not state their position against the Klan are taking chances on being accepted as klansmen [*sic*]."[137] In its efforts to turn voters against candidates with Klan ties, the Jasper County Anti-Klan Association experienced modest success on Election Day.[138] Though the JCAKA could not tout a rout of Klan forces in the county, it was nevertheless apparent that the wave of anti-Klan sentiment had continued from spring into autumn. Added to this, the Klan was rejected once more in December 1926 when Charles Patterson defeated Dr. A. B. Clark in a special mayoral election following Osborne's unexpected death.[139]

With an anti-Klan mayor occupying Joplin's city hall and his own ties with the Invisible Empire severed, Pierre Wallace lived out the rest of his life in a drunken stupor. His family tried to quell Wallace's drinking, but their efforts brought physical resistance. On more than one occasion, Wallace allegedly assaulted and verbally berated his wife, Flora. Wallace's son later claimed that his father "came home drunk nearly every night, except on Sundays."[140] This toxic turn brought about a final clash between

Pierre and Flora in 1929 when, during an argument with their son, she gunned him down in their home. Flora claimed self-defense and argued that she feared for her son's safety.[141] A coroner's jury agreed and decided to withhold charges against her, citing that the shooting was justified.[142] Wallace family attorneys concluded that "it wasn't Pierre Wallace who was killed but a man possessed by the demon, Rum."[143]

For men who originally donned white robes to stamp out liquor violations, protect the home, defend white womanhood, and end government corruption, C. C. Crawford, Heber Nations, O. L. Spurgeon, and Pierre Wallace all met their end in the Invisible Empire in defiance of the very laws they swore to promote. While most of the previously highlighted incidents involved Missouri Klansmen, arguably the biggest scandal to rock the Klan nationwide involved D. C. Stephenson of Indiana. Stephenson helped bring Indiana into the Invisible Empire in the early 1920s and made his home territory into one of the strongest regions for Klanism. His ambition greatly expanded the Klan Empire, yet his desire for power brought him at odds with Imperial Wizard Hiram Evans. Stephenson had been instrumental in removing William Simmons and replacing him with Evans. Still, a series of clashes between the two resulted in Stephenson's removal as grand dragon of the Indiana Klan. However, while Walter Bossert became Indiana's new leader, Stephenson was largely still in charge.[144]

As a result of Stephenson's ouster as grand dragon, the Indiana Klan divisively split into Bossert and Stephenson factions. The Klan still controlled the state, but the leadership divide created problems. While Bossert navigated the Klan toward upcoming elections, Stephenson eyed his own political career. It was during this period of political maneuvering that Stephenson decided to take a group of associates, including Madge Oberholtzer, a twenty-eight-year-old office clerk who had recently caught his eye, to Chicago.[145] On the train ride, Stephenson drank heavily and sexually assaulted Oberholtzer. Unsure about what to do with Oberholtzer, Stephenson kept her under close surveillance before relenting and allowing her to buy medical supplies. Out of Stephenson's sight, Oberholtzer bought poison, consumed it, and waited for death.[146] After initially withholding medical treatment from her, Stephenson took Oberholtzer back to Indianapolis and had his lieutenants dump her at her parents' home. She languished in agony for a few weeks before eventually dying. As she was unable to testify against Stephenson in a criminal trial, Oberholtzer's deathbed confession nevertheless served as the chief piece of evidence to convict the former grand dragon. In November 1925, Stephenson was found guilty of murder and sentenced to life in prison.[147]

From his jail cell, Stephenson waited for his political allies to come to his rescue. Despite many politicians owing their electoral success to Stephenson, many state Republicans distanced themselves from him in the wake of the scandal. Even Ed Jackson, whose election as governor was due in large part to Stephenson, refused to offer any help. When it became obvious that he would not receive the pardon he felt he deserved, Stephenson began to leak incriminating information to prominent state newspaper editors, who then pushed Governor Jackson to launch an investigation.[148] In response, Jackson tried to hold back the tide of allegations and control the release of possibly damaging information. Fearing that Jackson's plan for committee hearings would result in a cover-up, advocates pushed for a congressional investigation. Since part of Stephenson's allegations centered on the Indiana senatorial campaigns of James E. Watson and Arthur Robinson, the focus soon shifted to Missouri US senator James A. Reed.[149]

Stephenson's rise and fall is important not only because he violated laws that fellow Klansmen like Crawford, Nations, Spurgeon, and Wallace were supposed to defend but also because Missouri's anti-Klan press tied all of these scandals together to demonstrate hooded hypocrisy. Additionally, few scholars have offered analysis about the role of Missouri's anti-Klan senator James A. Reed in investigating Stephenson and the Klan. The hearings led by Reed connected Stephenson to political corruption, revealed secrets within the Invisible Empire, and gave rise to the senator's presidential aspirations. At the time of the Stephenson allegations, Reed was the chairman of the Senate Campaign Fund Investigating Committee, whose main job was to investigate irregularities and corruption in political campaigns involving current or potential US senators.[150] Initially, Reed told the press that he was hesitant to investigate the claims of graft in the Indiana Republican Party due to the impact that the midterm election of 1926 would have on the availability of committee members and potential witnesses. Finally, and most

204 Chapter Five

important, Reed indicated that there might not be enough evidence to warrant a congressional investigation.[151]

The mere possibility of Reed probing Indiana politics sent a shock wave through the Republican Party. Even if no substantial evidence was uncovered, party leaders worried about the damage daily press updates of the investigation would do to them in the midterm election. Additionally, Reed's reputation as a fiery opponent of the Klan, who frequently denounced the Invisible Empire, concerned many members of the hooded order.[152] However, as his name circulated in connection to a possible investigation, Reed kept quiet about the Klan. Knowing the damage his committee could do to the Republican Party and the Klan, Reed gave little indication of his plans for an inquiry, but by mid-October, he called his fellow committee members to Chicago.[153] Reed's earlier concerns about election conflicts proved true, as several committee members, including William King of Utah, Robert La Follette Jr. of Wisconsin, Charles McNary of Oregon, and Guy Goff of West Virginia, indicated they would have limited participation due to their campaign schedules.[154] Weighing his options, Reed decided to open the hearings by himself and called high-ranking officials from both the Indiana Republican and the Indiana Democratic Parties to testify regarding the recent Senate primaries, particularly the allegation that the Klan had thrown its overwhelming support behind James E. Watson and Arthur Robinson. While Watson had served in the US Senate since 1917, Governor Jackson recently appointed Robinson to Congress following the death of Senator Samuel Ralston.[155]

As with many politicians in Indiana, both Watson and Robinson had deep ties to D. C. Stephenson and the Klan. Stephenson expressed support for Watson's reelection bid, no doubt aware of the favors he could receive from such an endorsement. Robinson, on the other hand, was a lieutenant of Stephenson. If he could not have the seat himself, Stephenson wanted to ensure that someone he could trust would fill it. As such, Robinson's election served as a de facto victory for the now incarcerated ex-grand dragon.[156] After a parade of politicians and Klansmen made their way through Reed's one-man jury in Chicago, it quickly became obvious that the Republican Party and the Klan had struck a bargain when it came to electing Indiana's senators. Nevertheless, Reed was cautious since the Klan could technically back whatever candidate it preferred for public office. This brand of electioneering was not a crime, but what promises or arrangements were made to earn that support was a different matter.

Reed grilled witnesses for several days in Chicago about the alleged bargain but, citing pressing engagements back home, shifted the location of the hearings to Kansas City, where he could continue the investigation while also serving as the primary political orator for the Missouri Democratic Party.[157] When not interrogating witnesses, Reed spent his evenings denouncing the tactics and policies of the national Republican Party. After giving speeches throughout western Missouri, Reed decided to move the hearings to St. Louis so that he could canvass the eastern side of the state.[158] In an interesting twist, Reed's comments on the campaign trail were in support of senatorial candidate Harry Hawes, who was running against Republican George H. Williams, an incumbent whose name had come up during the hearings. Reed repeatedly pushed witnesses to explain how Williams was connected to Indiana politics and, in the process, uncovered shocking revelations about the senator's campaign.[159]

George H. Williams was no stranger to the Klan. In fact, in 1924, he had played a pivotal role in helping craft an anti-Klan plank at the Republican State Convention in Springfield. A year later, following the death of Senator Selden Spencer, Williams was appointed by Governor Sam Baker to fill the remainder of Spencer's term.[160] In 1926, as Williams faced serious challenges from fellow Republican candidates in the primary, the Ku Klux Klan extended a helping hand. While Grand Dragon William M. Campbell suggested "it would be unwise for Missouri Klansmen to make any concerted bid for activity in the primary," he nevertheless indicated his support for Williams.[161] Both Williams and Campbell dismissed the idea that the grand dragon's comments constituted an endorsement, but Williams did admit later that he had unknowingly met and spoken to Campbell during a train ride from St. Joseph to St. Louis.[162]

As Williams fought off Klan allegations in his own Senate campaign, Reed called on Vivian Tracy Wheatcraft to testify about her role in the campaign of James E. Watson and what, if any, connections she had to Williams. As the vice chairwoman of the Indiana Republican Committee,

Wheatcraft had worked closely with Senator Watson, and Reed wanted to know about her possible connection to the Klan. While not listed as a prominent member of the WKKK, Wheatcraft allegedly orchestrated a statewide mobilization effort to get women to support Watson. Labeled as "poison squads" in the press and by contemporary scholars like Kathleen Blee, these women's groups actively campaigned for Watson while also spreading vile rumors about his opponents.[163] The tactic had been so successful in Indiana that rumors swirled that Williams had enlisted Wheatcraft to do the same with women in Missouri for his own senatorial campaign.[164]

Reed had to wait to hear Wheatcraft's side of the story, however, as her associates informed him that she was confined to a hospital bed and unable to testify.[165] While he waited on her recovery, Reed pushed deeper into the Klan's involvement in Indiana politics and found that the hooded order originally intended to unite behind the state's Republican senate candidates, but pressure to do so from high-ranking Klan officials in Atlanta caused a further split in the Indiana Klan as Walter Bossert refused to support Watson. Hoping to prevent a similar schism as the Stephenson-Bossert split a few years earlier, Hiram Evans quickly removed Bossert as grand dragon and replaced him with another Klansman. With new leadership, most Indiana Klansmen and -women united behind Watson, Robinson, and the Republicans.[166]

With rumors swirling that Watson, Robinson, or both were Klansmen, Reed brought the initial hearings to a close at the end of October 1926. He tried once more to bring in Vivian Tracy Wheatcraft for testimony, but she had disappeared. Reed demanded answers since one of the reasons he moved the hearings to St. Louis, besides his speaking engagements, was to be closer to Wheatcraft's hospital. He soon discovered that she had left for Indiana in the middle of the night and, upon arriving in Indianapolis, was quickly readmitted to a new hospital, citing that she was too sick to testify.[167] Without Wheatcraft, Reed could not investigate possible connections between the political influence of Indiana's poison squads and their sisters in Missouri, though records indicate that Wheatcraft and Williams were familiar with one another. Several newspapers noted that Wheatcraft had taken up temporary residence in Princeton, Missouri, while working for the Williams campaign, and the *St. Louis Star* reported that both had served as speakers at a rally in Gallatin.[168]

With the election drawing near, Reed halted the hearings for the foreseeable future.[169] Though he was unable to draw a direct connection between the Klan's political activities in Indiana and Missouri, Reed's hearings nevertheless severely damaged Stephenson and the Invisible Empire. Additionally, in his own state, while Harry Hawes ran a strong Reed-esque campaign that tapped into white ethnic urban voters as well as members of the anti-Klan coalition, Reed's investigation and its subsequent coverage in state newspapers played a key role in George H. Williams's reelection defeat. Finally, Reed used his role as a Senate corruption investigator to lay the foundation for a campaign for the White House in 1928 as a candidate who favored states' rights, agricultural relief, and honest government.

By 1928, James A. Reed and the Ku Klux Klan both had their eyes set on the White House. Reed's dream would go unfulfilled, while Klan officials gloated that the organization's influence had secured the presidency for Herbert Hoover over the anti-Klan Al Smith. Yet, at the very moment the Klan claimed a sizable influence over American life, the very foundation of the organization, its solid rock, was crumbling. In Missouri, as well as nationwide, the ever-growing list of Klan scandals, combined with continued poor showings at the ballot box, served as perhaps the biggest point of repudiation of the hooded order. Whereas the anti-Klan press had mistakenly and prematurely declared the Klan's demise earlier in the 1920s, the latter half of the decade served as one of the darkest times for the group. "Goodbye nightshirts," the *Kansas City Call* declared as it noted that "the Invisible Empire [is becoming] invisible indeed."[170]

The scandals that rocked the Klan rolled back the remaining momentum of the organization, and the corruption and immorality that surrounded Klansmen like D. C. Stephenson, Heber Nations, C. C. Crawford, O. L. Spurgeon, Pierre Wallace, and many others reminded hooded members that the Invisible Empire had grown increasingly political and less moral over the 1920s. This was especially evident in the cases of corruption that far outpaced reform legislation pursued by Klan politicians in states where the organization wielded considerable sway.

Ultimately, as the Klan's membership numbers dipped dangerously low during the Great Depression, the organization's leaders tried to right the ship through new recruitment techniques and alliances with new right-wing groups. Such efforts stabilized elements of the organization but forever shaped the legacy of the Ku Klux Klan.[171]

CHAPTER SIX

"Kampaigning"

Activism, Lily-Whitism, and the
Political Realignment of Missouri's Black Voters

IN OCTOBER 1952, vaudevillian turned gossip columnist Walter Winchell premiered his new show on ABC television. Though it was a repackaging of his weekly radio program, Winchell, originally an avid backer of Franklin D. Roosevelt only to turn and embrace McCarthyism by the 1950s, opened his television show with a bang by directing his ire at the White House. According to Winchell, President Harry S. Truman, then wrapping up his second and final term in office, had secretly joined the Ku Klux Klan thirty years prior in Kansas City. On air, Winchell produced signed affidavits claiming that Truman had been a member of the Klan, even if only briefly. When asked why he had targeted a retiring president, Winchell asserted that his efforts were a direct response to claims that Dwight D. Eisenhower, the Republican presidential candidate running against Adlai Stevenson, had a history of racial prejudice.[1]

A few days after the television program, the *Kansas City Call* hit back against Winchell's claims, noting that "records of the county were diligently searched by Republicans," and even the *Call*'s own investigation into the matter had turned up "not one bit of evidence to link Harry S. Truman with the Ku Klux Klan." The *Call* also claimed that even if Truman had joined the Klan, he most likely would have admitted his error and explained why he no longer held membership.[2] The *St. Louis Argus*, though not directly discussing Winchell's claims, nevertheless pushed back against the allegations by highlighting Truman's upcoming visit to the city on behalf of Adlai Stevenson as well as featuring an editorial cartoon depicting a Klan hood draped over Republican vice-presidential candidate Richard Nixon's home with text suggesting that Nixon supported a restrictive covenant in his neighborhood.[3] By the time of the general election, both newspapers followed up their commentaries by issuing endorsements for the Democratic Party.

210   Chapter Six

Winchell's allegations against Truman were not new. Truman had already weathered the gossip storm eight years earlier when Roosevelt selected him as his running mate in 1944. That year, as he crisscrossed the country, Truman was bombarded with questions about his alleged membership in the Klan. Like the rumors that doomed A. W. Nelson in the 1924 Missouri gubernatorial race, Truman had to answer regarding his whereabouts concerning the Kansas City Klan. Multiple former Klansmen signed affidavits claiming that they saw Truman at Klan events as early as 1922 in Kansas City, with one man, L. H. Goddard, even going so far as to allege that the then young politician had given a speech in front of hooded members. With the election hanging in the balance and Republicans offering up the allegations as a prime example of why Truman and Roosevelt could not be trusted, the Missourian felt compelled to offer a rebuttal.[4]

Just as his White House press staff would in 1952, Truman addressed the rumors directly. No, Truman claimed, he had not joined the Klan or participated in any meetings. "I have driven by them on my way to my own campaign meetings while I was fighting the Klan," Truman exclaimed. If his political credentials were not enough to knock down the story, Truman went on to tie himself to efforts by Grand Lodge Masons in September 1921 to expel any members with Klan affiliations. Finally, the then vice-presidential candidate argued the only time he engaged with the Klan at all in the 1920s was to rally against the hooded order: "Some of us fought the Klan to a standstill and finally licked them."[5]

While Truman as president eventually sought a wider, if complicated, embrace of civil rights policy, his fighting of the Klan on behalf of the Pendergast Machine and the larger Democratic Party ushered in not only his own political career but also helped lay the foundation for a seismic realignment for voters in Missouri as part of the larger New Deal coalition. According to most historians of the twentieth-century United States, the formation of the New Deal coalition was set in place by the mid-1930s, roughly around the time of Franklin Roosevelt's reelection bid. In Missouri, however, efforts at such a coalition developed earlier than national trends. One of the chief architects given credit for this coalition is Tom Pendergast, Kansas City's Democratic boss and leader of the Goat faction of the party in the city. Pendergast and his allies' promise of patronage and public works, as well as their criticism of Republican policies, brought increasing numbers of new voters into the Democratic camp.[6]

By the mid-1920s, the Democratic Party of Missouri had to make a tough decision about its political future. The year 1924 had been a particularly bad one for Missouri Democrats as not only were they continued to be shut out of every statewide office, but the party also lost two seats in the state's congressional delegation and the majority in the Missouri House of Representatives. The party had long been splintered between rural and urban factions on several issues, but it tended to unify on Election Day. This was not the case in 1922 when pro–Woodrow Wilson opponents of James A. Reed unsuccessfully tried to undercut his reelection bid for the US Senate. Similarly, a tug-of-war for political control in Kansas City resulted in a tenuous relationship between the factions of the city's Democratic political machines led by Joseph Shannon and Tom Pendergast. Additionally, the state party had trouble distancing itself from a seemingly close relationship with the Klan in key elections, most notably the 1924 gubernatorial campaign of A. W. Nelson. Finally, state Democrats were splintered over the prospects of recruiting African American voters into the party.

While far from unified on these issues, state Democrats realized by the mid-1920s that Missouri's growing African American population was key to the party's political fortunes. Urban party members had appealed to Black voters as early as the late nineteenth century, but Democrats in other parts of the state, particularly rural areas, were less open to African American inclusion. The state legislature had narrowly rejected efforts to pass stronger Jim Crow laws to replicate states of the Deep South, and the movement toward such legislation by rural Democrats kept the issue constantly at the forefront, as open appeals to white supremacy hurt efforts to recruit Black voters.[7]

Beginning in the 1920s, the state Democratic Party launched a multifaceted appeal to Black voters during the interwar period. Though the party did not hold major power in statewide offices or in the city of St. Louis, Democrats nevertheless promised African Americans positions of patronage if electoral victory was achieved. The blueprint for such a plan was laid out through the efforts pursued by the Pendergast Machine in Kansas City before the 1920s. Democrats also reached out to African Americans by critiquing the failings of Republican municipal and state officials. While this proved difficult during the administration of Arthur Hyde, an active member of the NAACP, his successor, Sam A. Baker, did not have a strong civil rights record. Though he won the governor's seat on a campaign denouncing the Klan, Baker quickly made it clear that he would not support civil rights or anti-Klan legislation. Additionally, Baker's meddling with the funding and administration of Lincoln University brought severe retaliation from the African American press. Finally, they accused the Republican Party as a whole of rejecting Black voters in favor of southern white voters and opposing civil rights policies under the banner of lily-whitism.

For Missouri Democrats, the accusation of Republican lily-whitism served as one of the major campaign messages circulated to Black voters. Considering the frequency in which the "Klan issue" had been used earlier in the 1920s, particularly in the 1924 gubernatorial election, against political figures, it is not surprising that Missouri Democrats continued its use through the remainder of the decade. In the latter half of the 1920s, however, it took on a new form: "kampaigning." For every Democratic candidate accused of questionable ties to the Klan, including Harry S. Truman, Democratic Party leaders and their allies in the press asserted that many Republicans—from the White House to a town mayor—were actively kampaigning for hooded support.

Initially, the kampaigning accusation threatened to further splinter the anti-Klan coalition. While major white anti-Klan political leaders such as James A. Reed and Harry Hawes, both Democrats, alleged that Klansmen were enthusiastically welcomed in the GOP, prominent Black anti-Klan leaders, including George L. Vaughn of the NAACP, J. E. Mitchell of the *St. Louis Argus*, and C. A. Franklin of the *Kansas City Call*, all Republicans, disputed these claims. Added to that, the Democratic strategy proved to be difficult since key state Republicans, such as Arthur Hyde, Sam Baker, and L. C. Dyer, had already spoken out in opposition to the Klan. Nevertheless, Democrats enlisted William J. Thompkins of Kansas City and George B. Vashon and Joseph L. McLemore of St. Louis, notable Black leaders within the party, to ratchet up Black voter-recruitment efforts and target Republican kampaigning.

As the 1920s concluded, the anti-Klan coalition came to a crossroads. Largely due to opposition, internal scandals, and political failures, the Klan was dwindling in influence, both locally and nationwide. Yet the political realignment seedbed planted through the "Klan issue" and kampaigning allegations continued to prove fertile, and with Herbert Hoover seemingly kowtowing to the hooded order as the Klan experienced a brief but limited resurgence in opposition to the presidential candidacy of Catholic Al Smith, Vaughn, Mitchell, and Franklin all reevaluated their political positions relative to the respective parties. During the 1930s, the Missouri Democratic Party, now joined by several notable former Black Republicans, including members of the anti-Klan coalition, still hurled Klan accusations at opposing candidates, even as the party regained control of state politics and the Missouri Klan shrank into obscurity, but, by that time, however, these efforts played little outcome in these elections. Instead, the party had to grapple with its own failures to recruit and retain Black voter support as it fell into the same pattern of broken promises that it had previously charged against Republicans. Ultimately, while Black voters increasingly backed Democratic candidates statewide and nationally during the 1930s, it was not until after World War II that the realignment effort begun in the 1920s was complete.

In early 1924, a political realignment, at least for one man, was on the horizon, but his shift in local allegiances, as well as coordinated efforts with fellow politically active Black leaders, deeply impacted the Democratic Party. William J. Thompkins, an African American doctor in Kansas City, had grown weary of Joseph Shannon's Rabbit faction of the city Democratic Party. However, he was unwilling to throw his support to the Republican Party, as many of his fellow Black Kansas Citians did at the time. Born in Jefferson City, Missouri, in 1879, Thompkins grew up in the capital city, only a few blocks away from the seat of government at a time of Democratic dominance. As such, Thompkins long claimed that his family had supported the Democratic Party since the Civil War. In adulthood, he put himself through college, working various jobs. He earned a degree from Jefferson City's Lincoln Institute in 1901, and, after briefly enrolling at the University of Colorado, he earned a medical degree from Howard University in 1906. After completing an internship at Howard University's Freedmen's Hospital, Thompkins returned to Missouri, received his medical license, and opened a private practice in Kansas City. Almost immediately, Thompkins made a name for himself as a respected doctor in the community. His reputation and acclaim soon earned him an appointment as superintendent of the city's General Hospital No. 2, a segregated medical facility. Despite his quick rise in status, Thompkins repeatedly tried to use his local connections to depart the city for more prestigious patronage jobs back in Washington, DC, including as chief of surgery at Freedmen's Hospital. When these attempts failed, he turned increasingly to politics.[8]

Figure 15. Doctors of General Hospital No. 2, date unknown. Though not identified in the photograph, it is believed that William J. Thompkins is the man seated in the dark suit. Courtesy of Williams Photo Studio Collection (AC27). Black Archives of Mid-America.

While Kansas City's African American population was largely tied to the Republican Party, Thompkins saw growing possibilities for patronage and prestige through the city's Democratic machines. Besides showing support for Democratic presidential candidates, he also initially aligned himself with the city's Rabbit faction of the party controlled by Joseph Shannon as part of the Negro Central Democratic Organization. This relationship was sometimes challenging, as Shannon and his lieutenant

Casimir Welch jostled with Thompkins over their influence within the city's Black population. When Frank Cromwell was elected mayor in 1922, Welch and Shannon used their political influence to remove Thompkins as hospital superintendent.[9] Thompkins's allegiance to the Democratic Party was no doubt tested in the wake of his ouster as hospital superintendent by Shannon and Welsh, and with Cromwell running for reelection in 1924, it is understandable why Thompkins would keep a low profile. Yet the doctor seemingly continued to rally for Democratic candidates, even presenting a loving cup to presidential candidate John W. Davis when he visited Missouri in September 1924.[10]

Not wavering from the Democratic Party, Thompkins nevertheless reevaluated his political alliances. When Joe Shannon threw Rabbit support behind the Republican Party to undercut the Pendergast Machine and thus allow GOP victory in the city's mayoral race and other statewide offices in 1924, Thompkins joined Pendergast's Goat faction. He was not alone in this shift, as several Shannonites, including Casimir Welch, also joined the Pendergast ranks. Before he served under Pendergast, Welch made a name for himself due to his physical prowess, fighting skills, and intimidating demeanor, which caught Shannon's attention. Under Shannon's direction, Welch rallied African American voters in Kansas City's Sixth District to the Democratic Party by any means necessary. He achieved political success by winning several terms as a municipal judge, though rumors circulated that voter fraud played a significant role in his victories. Not long after switching sides, Welch expanded his activities to convince Kansas City Black voters, especially those in "Little Tammany," to vote Democratic and Pendergast.[11]

With Welch exerting increasing control over Little Tammany, Thompkins waited for the next opportunity to use his influence to gain a lucrative patronage position. In 1926, he completed a survey of tuberculosis in the city's African American neighborhoods, which won him acclaim. He convinced Pendergast to reward his loyalty with an appointment with the city hygiene department.[12] In 1928, Thompkins paired with Black nightclub owner and fellow Pendergast supporter Felix Payne to start a newspaper called the *Kansas City American*. Strongly backed by Pendergast, the *American* quickly became a Democratic-leaning alternative to C. A. Franklin's Republican-supporting *Kansas City Call*.

216   Chapter Six

Almost immediately, Thompkins went to work trying to convince the city's Black voters that there was no place for them in an increasingly lily-white Republican Party.[13]

Through the *Kansas City American*, Thompkins circulated key Pendergast talking points so that readers were well versed in the triumphs of Democratic city management and the follies of Republican rule statewide. This point was particularly popular in the pages of the *American* where the Republican mayoral administration of Albert Beach received sizable criticism for allegations of police brutality and being "so long on promises to the Negroes and so poor on performance" when it came to public works projects like a new segregated City Hospital No. 2.[14] The *American's* critique of Republicans took on a nuanced approach as a 1925 antibossism voter referendum for a new city charter, as well as a brokered deal between the Rabbit and Goat factions, had actually put Democrats back in power over many city affairs, including through the office of city manager Henry McElroy, but since Beach was the face of Kansas City as mayor and Governor Sam Baker controlled the city's police board, the newspaper went on the attack for municipal mismanagement.[15]

When not criticizing the Beach and Baker administrations for their broken promises to Black voters, Kansas City Democrats and the *American* accused the Republican Party of kampaigning, an attack angle that was replicated by Democrats across the state. One of the earliest examples of such tactics occurred during Albert Beach's successful campaign for mayor in 1924. City Democrats denounced the hooded order in their party platform and later claimed that Republicans were purging specific residents from the city's voter rolls because they were foreign born or had names that were assumed to be foreign.[16] When Republicans pushed back against the allegations, Sam B. Strother, chair of the Democratic City Committee and a former mayor, warned that the issue was a prime example that "the election of Mr. Beach would stamp Kansas City as a klan [*sic*] city."[17] Later, the Democratic City Committee placed a carefully crafted ad in the *Kansas City Call* featuring an image of Klansmen assembled under a lynching victim with text proclaiming, "Kansas City Negroes you are selling your future, your unborn children's future, if you vote for a party that endorses the Ku Klux Klan."[18]

Though it was a damning claim, Beach deflected the charges by issuing a front-page statement in the *Kansas City Star* denying membership in the hooded order or that it held any influence over his candidacy.[19] Additionally, in the *Kansas City Call*, C. A. Franklin referred to the Klan accusations as a "dud" and assured Black voters that the "list of Republican candidates includes Catholic, Jewish, and Negro nominees, an indisputable fact which answers charge of Klan dictation."[20] Instead, Republicans focused on examples of graft and corruption by Shannon and Pendergast allies, particularly the recent placement of a garbage dump in an African American neighborhood, as their chief counterattack as Beach claimed a victory of roughly five thousand votes.[21] Incumbent Frank Cromwell won more total wards than Beach, including some with sizable Black populations, but his challenger ran up a significant vote advantage in the predominantly African American Fourth Ward. Yet Democrats, despite the defeat, saw potential in attracting African Americans by alleging Klan influence within the Republican Party.[22] This point was not lost on C. A. Franklin, who warned Republicans that "while the Klan is southern born and therefore of Democratic origin, their political strategy will be to connect it to Republicans now."[23]

After the implementation of the new city charter in 1925, Albert Beach easily won reelection and faced few charges of Klan influence during the remaining years of the 1920s, but his tenure was nevertheless obstructed by Democratic control of the city council and the city manager's office. When Beach decided not to run for reelection in 1930, Republicans supported George E. Kimball, a former comptroller and county court judge who campaigned as a "clean man with a clean record" who would break the Democratic machine's stranglehold on power.[24] City Democrats settled on Bryce B. Smith, a member of Shannon's Rabbit faction who made a fortune on a multimillion-dollar baking empire. On the campaign trail, Smith touted the accomplishments of Democratic city leaders, particularly city manager Henry McElroy, and emphasized plans to expand patronage and build much-needed institutions in Black neighborhoods, including the construction of a new City Hospital No. 2.[25]

Once Kimball emerged as the leading contender on the Republican side, the *American* focused on the candidate, often tying his role in the Beach administration to allege Republican broken promises and mismanagement. While Kimball largely avoided the Klan and actively worked to convince Black voters to stay in the Grand Old Party (GOP), he faced a daunting challenge when the campaign shifted after a fiery cross was reportedly lit on the grounds of the Paseo school. The origins of the cross were never identified, but the *American* repeatedly accused local Republicans of influencing the Klan to display the cross. The newspaper went so far as to suggest—incorrectly—that the Klan had not been an issue locally for several years until the mayoral campaign resurrected it. In retrospect, the newspaper most likely was referring to the McElroy administration keeping large-scale Klan activities, such as parades and major meetings, from taking place in the city, as even the *American's* own editorial page was full of Klan commentaries dating back to its establishment in 1928. A few weeks after the fiery-cross story first appeared, the *American* again brought the issue to the forefront when it ran an editorial cartoon on the front page of its March 20, 1930, edition depicting Kimball speaking to an audience while Klansmen stood behind a stage curtain whispering talking points to the candidate. Interestingly, the *American's* articles and commentaries on the fiery cross near Paseo school were the only coverage of the incident in Kansas City newspapers, including the *Call*.[26]

Despite Republican efforts to claim that Bryce B. Smith was the hand-picked candidate of a Pendergast, Shannon, and McElroy Democratic Party that had done more in power to line their pockets with government contracts than provide jobs to impoverished Black laborers, Smith ran up a sizable advantage over Kimball on Election Day. He even drew a soft endorsement of his candidacy from C. A. Franklin of the *Kansas City Call*.[27] The margin was so large that the press and contemporary scholars have questioned the validity of the total. Kimball himself alluded to such an outcome when he expressed his hope that his victory would be a "funeral of ghosts," referring to the use of fake voter-registration information by city Democrats to pad totals in select wards. According to the *Kansas City American*, Smith had garnered roughly 70 percent of the African American vote in the city, the highest recorded share at the time. The *Call* estimated this number to be closer to 50 percent. Overall, Smith claimed a vote majority of more than twenty-three thousand over his challenger.[28]

Now controlling the entire city political apparatus, Democrats enacted an ambitious ten-year plan through the city council that led to countless jobs and city-improvement projects and the construction of facilities such as city hall and the Jackson County Courthouse that still dot the Kansas City skyline.[29]

William Thompkins's efforts to bring Black voters into the Democratic Party were not confined to just Kansas City, nor was his kampaigning rhetoric restricted to the pages of the *Kansas City American*. Thompkins traveled the country rallying audiences to Democratic policies. For African American voters, this included a specific focus on promises of sound policy and patronage, as well as warnings about the lily-white leanings of the Republican Party. In St. Joseph, he touted a pamphlet he had written featuring a tiny Calvin Coolidge puppet controlled by a Klansman.[30] Visiting Missouri, Nebraska, Oklahoma, and Kentucky on behalf of Democratic candidates, he warned of a "Ku Klux Klan spirit" in the Republican Party and advised Black voters that their trips to the ballot box would counteract those of Klansmen.[31]

As he traveled through Missouri, Thompkins also interacted with other African Americans, both Democrats and Republicans, who supported his kampaigning tactics. The most notable were J. E. Mitchell, George B. Vashon, and Joseph L. McLemore of St. Louis. While Thompkins's Kansas City quickly became a Democratic stronghold, especially among Black voters, St. Louis was a different story. Except for Rolla Wells's eight-year tenure between 1901 and 1909, no Democrat had served as mayor since the mid-1890s. Representation in the Missouri General Assembly was not much better, as Republicans held a majority of the city's seats in both chambers. Drawing from German American and African American residents, many of whom had supported the party since the Civil War, the city Republican Party had long dominated municipal affairs.[32] Nevertheless, using tactics similar to those of Kansas City Democrats, St. Louisans eventually swung the city into the Democratic column. To do so, however, Democrats hit on the same issues that had brought their Kansas City counterparts into power, including promises of patronage, criticisms of Republican policies, and tying their opponents to the Ku Klux Klan.

While St. Louis had been a predominately Republican city, Democrats felt they had a good chance in the 1925 mayoral campaign with William Igoe, a lawyer and former congressman.[33] Igoe's electoral chances seemed positive after a nasty Republican primary between Louis Aloe, a well-respected Jewish businessman who had made a name for himself as the onetime president of the city's Board of Aldermen, and Victor Miller, a former police commissioner fresh off a defeat in the 1924 gubernatorial primary. Miller emerged victorious in the primary, but his past ties to a police department plagued with allegations of brutality, as well as accusations by Aloe supporters and J. E. Mitchell's *St. Louis Argus* that the Klan strongly backed his candidacy, left Igoe with plenty of campaign material. Miller repeatedly mentioned that he never joined the Klan—even going so far as to offer a $25,000 reward for anyone who could provide evidence to prove this claim wrong—but the *Argus* countered that he did not openly denounce the hooded order.[34] Having long supported Republican candidates, Mitchell was in a tough position: rally to a candidate he was obviously at odds with, or back a candidate of a party he fiercely opposed. In a particularly stunning series of editorials, the *Argus* advised readers to forsake party loyalty in favor of candidates serving their interests: "We believe that the election of Mr. Igoe as mayor will be a death blow to the Ku Klux Klan in this city. Such a blow, at this time, will help all parties in the future because it is the Klan influence that is threatening to rend the Republican Party to pieces in this city at this time."[35]

Seizing on the *Argus* editorials, George B. Vashon and his St. Louis Colored Democratic Club utilized Mitchell's hesitancy over Miller to recruit potential voters.[36] Born in 1862 in Pittsburgh, Pennsylvania, George B. Vashon, named for his father, abolitionist George Boyer Vashon, moved to St. Louis in the 1880s with his brother, John, to teach in the city's schools after completing his studies at Spencerian Business College and Alcorn University. Originally involved in Republican politics, Vashon joined the Democratic ranks in the 1890s. He quickly became a city Democratic political leader in the African American neighborhoods and later served as president of the Negro Democratic League in Missouri. After John's death in 1924, St. Louis's second Black high school, Vashon, honored the family's name.[37]

Warning of the dangers of a Miller victory, George B. Vashon declared that the "election of Mr. Igoe will be the most stunning blow to the Ku Klux Klan that can be delivered, and it will undo the Jim Crow deviltry of the only Jim Crow city administration that has ever disgraced St. Louis."[38] The *Argus* followed Vashon's lead by pointing out how prominent Black Republican leaders such as Homer G. Phillips and George L. Vaughn were opposed to Miller.[39] The *Argus* also accused Miller of using white men to corral African American support.[40] In addition to promoting negative perceptions of Miller in the African American press, Democrats also attacked the candidate for his weak stance on several issues, including his uncompromising stance on Prohibition, past confrontations between the Black community and Miller's police force, and his noncommittal stance on the Klan.[41]

Attempting to counter Democratic efforts to court African Americans, Republicans relied on prominent African American leader Jordan Chambers to keep Black voters in line with the party.[42] Born in Tennessee in 1896, Chambers moved with his family to St. Louis at the dawn of the twentieth century. He attended Sumner High School, and though Chambers did not graduate, scholar Mary Welek argues that his connections with his classmates proved extremely crucial later in life. Before owning and managing Peoples Undertaking Company, Chambers worked odd jobs in St. Louis and slowly developed an interest in politics. At first, he aligned with the Republican Party at the ward level. Through his connections, Chambers helped sustain Black support for the GOP, including thwarting Democratic attempts to peel away voters from the Republican Party.[43]

Building on Chambers's local influence, Republicans paid for strategic ads in the *Argus* promoting Miller's qualifications and his denial of Klan affiliation. One particular ad, featuring Chambers's name at the top of a list of supporters, asked voters to back the straight Republican ticket and pointed out discrepancies in the Klan charges against Miller.[44] A group of African American clergymen were also called upon to write an op-ed in the *St. Louis Star* in support of Miller.[45] Finally, Congressman L. C. Dyer, who had authored a failed federal antilynching bill only a few years prior, crisscrossed the city stumping for Miller. Beloved in his home district, Dyer spoke of Republican efforts to expand rights for African

FIGURE 16. Jordan Chambers (center) seated behind a desk with Elmer Mosee (left) and David M. Grant (right), 1941. Courtesy of David Grant Papers (S0552). The State Historical Society of Missouri.

Americans and reminded Black voters that Democrats were responsible for disenfranchisement in other parts of the country.[46] Ultimately, Dyer, along with Louis Aloe, put any differences they had with Miller aside to campaign on behalf of the party.[47]

Though he had a perceived unfavorable reputation in the city, Victor Miller won the St. Louis mayoral race over William Igoe by three thousand votes.[48] Miller managed to keep Republicans strongly in line with his candidacy while also not losing a significant portion of the African American vote. However, while Democrats could not topple the entrenched Republicans in St. Louis, they did make inroads in the African American community as an estimated 30 percent of Black voters in the city cast their ballot for Igoe.[49] The *Argus* noted this when it declared that "Negroes voted against Mr. Miller as they had never before voted in this city against a man on the Republican ticket."[50] Yet despite the potential electoral swing, African Americans, including J. E. Mitchell of the *Argus*, were not ready to switch parties. Nevertheless, they realized that the big tent of the GOP now made room for Klansmen. This point was not lost on the *Argus* when it reported a fiery cross lit in front of St. Louis City Hall allegedly celebrating Miller's mayoral victory.[51]

In the four years that progressed from Miller's victory in 1925 and his subsequent reelection campaign in 1929, St. Louis Republicans tried to address the divisions that had caused the desertion of roughly one-third of Black voters. While the *Argus* critiqued Miller on what the newspaper saw as his administration's failings, it seemingly gave the mayor a brief pass when it came to the Klan. When Klan officials made repeated announcements that St. Louis would be the site of future hooded events and parades, the *Argus* acknowledged that many people thought the Klan would have significant influence over the Miller administration but that the hooded order had declined locally. At the same time, though, the *Argus* made it clear that any public Klan event in the city needed a permit and that the Miller administration approved the permits.[52]

Despite outreach efforts to gauge support for Republican candidates after 1925, a group of Black Republicans in Missouri's twelfth congressional district, which made up a sizable portion of St. Louis African American population, rejected the party's preference of seven-term incumbent L. C. Dyer and pushed for either Homer G. Phillips or George L. Vaughn, both local attorneys, to challenge Dyer in the primary the following year. J. E. Mitchell thanked Dyer for his congressional service in the *Argus* but declared that a new voice was needed for the Twelfth District and backed Vaughn in the primary.[53] On the Democratic side, George B. Vashon unsuccessfully faced off against hotelier David Israel in a bid to see who could rally the larger support base and out-anti-Klan the other, with Israel going so far as to claim that Dyer, who had spoken out against the hooded order since 1921, had been silent on the issue.[54] Hinting at Democratic outreach in Black neighborhoods, supporters of Vashon warned voters that "a vote for Mr. Vashon says to the colored citizen, 'come in;' a vote for Mr. Israel says to these citizens, 'not wanted.'"[55] Despite the challengers from all comers, L. C. Dyer easily won reelection.[56]

Dyer returned to Congress in 1927, but his Twelfth District increasingly evolved over his final years in office as Democrats continually appealed to his Black constituents and supported African American candidates to run against him. After Vashon, the choice in 1928 was Joseph L. McLemore, a Louisiana-born attorney who headed the Mound City Bar Association and was proclaimed as the first Black Democrat from Missouri nominated for Congress.[57] While continuing to advise readers to choose candidate over party, the *Argus* was nevertheless enthusiastic at the prospect of McLemore in Congress and issued an endorsement of the candidate.[58] Not to be outdone, Dyer published a statement in the *Argus* defending his record, suggesting to McLemore that it was Republicans who helped men like him earn an education, and calling the Democratic Party the party of "slavery, lynching, disfranchisement, peonage, Jim-crow-ism, segregation, ignorance and persecution."[59] Dyer won by nearly seven thousand votes, a margin more than two thousand votes larger than his 1926 total against David Israel.[60] Aware of Republican strength in the city and across the country, the *Argus* warned the GOP not to revel in these victories or forget the critical role Black voters played in their continued success.[61]

While there were many notable defectors from the Republicans within the St. Louis African American community as the 1920s faded into the 1930s, arguably none proved to be more significant than Jordan Chambers. He played a sizable role in keeping voters in the Republican column during each of Victor Miller's mayoral campaigns and proved to be such a political kingmaker that the *St. Louis Post-Dispatch* heralded him as the "Negro Mayor of St. Louis" in 1931. Yet by the early 1930s, Chambers had grown frustrated with the Republican Party. Like his fellow St. Louisans, he listened with growing impatience as Republicans accumulated a list of unfulfilled promises to the Black community, including a new hospital. As the Great Depression deepened and Franklin Roosevelt won election to the White House, Chambers organized the nonpartisan Co-operative Civic Association. Initially, the association served as an introductory forum for Black voters to assess all political parties. Chambers was cautious to commit to a specific party and advised voters to weigh the benefits offered in exchange for their votes. Though Chambers's ties to the GOP were fraying, Democrats hesitated to form an alliance, particularly regarding patronage. Instead, Democrats formed a tenuous relationship with the association through William Igoe, whom Chambers admired.[62]

"Kampaigning" 225

The delicate relationship between Igoe, Chambers, and the Democratic Party solidified in 1933. In that year's mayoral race, Victor Miller opted not to seek reelection, and Republicans selected Walter J. G. Neun, a local attorney and president of the Board of Aldermen who had served as acting mayor during Miller's health struggles. After brokering a deal to end a strike between workers and streetcar companies, Neun used his newfound political fame to campaign against Roosevelt's New Deal as "the worst deal we have ever had."[63] To challenge Neun, Democrats turned to Bernard Dickmann, onetime president of the St. Louis Real Estate Exchange. Dickmann initially provided little spark to Black voters, and the *Argus* was less than enthusiastic about his candidacy.[64] The trajectory of his campaign took a notably different turn, however, when Jordan Chambers's Co-operative Civic Association issued a show of support for Dickmann calling Republicans "arrogant, intolerant and 'cock sure' of themselves" and adding that party officials had "mistreated the Negro vote, brow beaten and sought to 'kill off' Negro leaders who had courage enough to ask for a square deal for their people."[65]

The Co-operative Civic Association's announcement produced a powerful response across the city. George L. Vaughn echoed the endorsement and noted that "for more than thirty years I have fought the battles of the Republican party. The net results have been little or nothing besides broken promises."[66] The *Argus* acknowledged the association's position, but cautioned voters to consider whether a Dickmann administration would truly bring about "a new deal for Negroes in politics."[67] Republicans, likewise, questioned if the association's endorsement was unanimous, especially for a man who chaired the powerful St. Louis Real Estate Exchange, notorious for its role in ensuring that many city neighborhoods remained segregated. Republicans expressed confidence that Dickmann's past alleged transgressions, plus Neun's promises of continued patronage and completion of City Hospital No. 2, would keep the party in power in St. Louis. Yet Chambers's shift into the Dickmann camp produced a groundswell of support for the candidate. In the campaign's final days, the *Argus* firmly moved toward Dickmann. At a large meeting of Black voters, Vaughn and Mitchell spoke of the Republican Party's broken promises before Dickmann stood up and laid out plans for how he would meet the expectations that his rivals had ignored. Finally,

226 Chapter Six

in public speeches and editorials in the *Argus*, Dickmann supporters tied him to Franklin Roosevelt's New Deal.[68]

In April 1933, the *Argus* headlined that "Negro votes turn tide in epochal St. Louis election."[69] Dickmann crushed Neun at the polls by more than 15,600 votes, including running up majorities in all the sizable African American wards. Dickmann had done what no St. Louis Democrat had done before, winning a majority of the city's Black voters. The *Argus* celebrated Dickmann's victory by noting that Republicans had much to learn in defeat and that Black voters could potentially come back to the party if promises made were promises kept. Perhaps noting the mayor-elect's promises to voters, the newspaper reminded Democrats that a similar fate would befall them if they did not do right by city residents: "We are going to take the mayor at his word, look for and expect a new deal."[70]

While local Democrats launched a slow but ultimately successful campaign not only to win power at the municipal level but also to convince a majority of African American voters to back the party, state Democratic leaders noted the cracks forming in the foundation of the Republican Party. Considering how bad the 1924 election had been for Missouri Democrats, the midterm election in 1926 could be considered a moderate success. Though Democrats were unable to reclaim the majority in the Missouri House of Representatives, they still controlled the Missouri Senate. At the top of the ticket, Democrats gained four seats in the state's congressional delegation, despite L. C. Dyer holding off David Israel in the predominantly African American twelfth congressional district.[71]

The biggest success for Missouri Democrats in 1926 was Harry Hawes's election to the US Senate. Though far from a household name to the average voter outside of St. Louis, Hawes nevertheless launched an ambitious campaign for the US Senate based on his political legacy. Hawes helped organize the gubernatorial career of Joseph Folk in 1904 as a member of St. Louis's Jefferson Club. Likewise, Hawes's time in the state legislature was marked by bipartisan successes, including a program to modernize Missouri's roadway system through the State Highway Act of 1917. He also sidestepped the friction between the pro–Woodrow

FIGURE 17. Harry Hawes, date unknown. Courtesy of Bernard Dickmann Photograph Collection (S0555). The State Historical Society of Missouri.

Wilson and pro–James A. Reed factions of the state Democratic Party in the early 1920s by appealing to both sides without alienating either group. Opting to take a noncommittal stance on issues like the League of Nations, World Court, and Prohibition, Hawes built a white ethnic urban voting base in St. Louis that elected him to the US House of Representatives in 1920, 1922, and 1924.[72]

Similar to Reed, Hawes also rallied voters to his anti-Klan stance. This proved especially significant as George H. Williams faced allegations of Klan influence, including coordination with Vivian Tracy Wheatcraft and her "poison squads" of women. Hawes's anti-Klan position won him cross-state support from the Pendergast and Shannon machines of Kansas City, and it also played a key role in his appeal to Black voters.[73] Yet though J. E. Mitchell of the *St. Louis Argus* had revolted against Victor Miller a year prior over his alleged Klan ties, the newspaper endorsed Williams over Hawes and said little about the rumored connections between Williams, Wheatcraft, or Grand Dragon William Campbell. Where the *Argus* lacked in Klan coverage—connecting Williams to

228 Chapter Six

the hooded order only after the election—the *St. Louis Post-Dispatch* made its feelings explicitly clear on the Williams allegations when it ran an editorial cartoon titled "Kampaigning" depicting a Klansman with "Williams for Senator" written on the back of his white robe.[74]

Having the Democratic bases of Missouri's major metropolises behind him, Hawes collected enough rural support to ensure victory on Election Day.[75] Republicans carried most of the Black vote in rural areas, particularly the Bootheel. Kansas City African Americans—boosted by C. A. Franklin's editorial in the *Call* that "Williams [is] no good for Negroes"—nearly split among the parties, with an estimated 42 percent casting votes for Democrats.[76] In St. Louis, Democrats collected increased Black voting totals through George B. Vashon's grassroots efforts, particularly in the Twelfth District. While he failed to gain J. E. Mitchell's endorsement, Hawes helped Democrats in their continuing efforts to make inroads in Black neighborhoods and win over African American voters. Hawes may not have yet convinced a majority of African Americans to back the Democratic Party, but his victory, backed by an increasing Black vote, served as yet another crushing blow for the Missouri Klan's political ambitions. With Hawes joining Reed in Washington, DC, Missouri now had the distinction of having two anti-Klan senators. Yet just as James A. Reed was no doubt happy to see a fellow member of the Democratic Party in the Senate chamber, his own tenure was nearing its end. During the 1926 campaign, Reed surprised many supporters by announcing his decision not to seek reelection. While some supporters assumed that the senator planned to return home to Missouri, he showed his intentions to seek the presidency. Despite Republican dominance of the White House during the 1920s, Reed's path to the Democratic nomination was not easy.[77] First, his prior verbal jabs at Woodrow Wilson continued to bring him stiff opposition from supporters of the now deceased president. Second, his fiery rhetoric alienated some rural Democrats, particularly drys. Finally, Reed's ascendancy to the nomination was blocked by the groundswell of support for New York governor Al Smith.

Hoping to muddy the waters to force a compromise nomination at the Democratic National Convention, Reed toned down his fiery rhetoric and took more moderate stances on key issues, including backing

"Kampaigning" 229

limited government, states' rights, rural infrastructure programs, and an end to political corruption. At the Democratic National Convention, when Al Smith quickly emerged as the perennial favorite but failed to garner enough votes to secure the nomination, Reed saw his chance and encouraged his supporters to tout his sentiments in favor of upholding the Eighteenth Amendment. The tactic failed, and Al Smith eventually won the party's nomination. When he was allegedly offered the opportunity to serve as Smith's running mate, Reed turned it down. He campaigned hard for Smith's election in 1928, but privately, Reed confided to friends that the candidate had little chance of winning because of his Catholicism.[78]

When Reed failed to garner the nomination and opted not to seek reelection, Missouri Democrats faced a daunting yet potentially lucrative election cycle in 1928. Much to his dismay, Reed's onetime rival Charles M. Hay secured the Democratic primary for his Senate seat. In the gubernatorial primary, Pendergast forces successfully elevated Francis M. Wilson, a former state legislator and US district attorney from Kansas City, as the Democratic challenger to St. Louis Republican Henry Caulfield. Two years after his failed bid to secure a primary victory in the twelfth congressional district, George B. Vashon watched as fellow Black Democrat Joseph L. McLemore faced off against L. C. Dyer.[79]

As Al Smith, Charles Hay, Francis M. Wilson, and Joseph L. McLemore took to the campaign trail, the *Post-Dispatch* pondered how a potential shift of African American voters to the Democratic Party would impact Republicans in future election cycles. When posed the question, St. Louis Republicans scoffed at the suggestion and pointed out that six of the fifty-six members of the Republican City Committee were African Americans. Despite this initial confidence, Republicans had much to fear about Democratic efforts. Though Jordan Chambers's shift into the Democratic camp was still a few years away, George B. Vashon continued to organize local Black voters through his Association of Negro Democratic Clubs, which claimed to have several thousand members.[80] Likewise, building upon his success in Kansas City, William J. Thompkins took to the lecture circuit to rally Black voters to the Democratic cause nationwide under the banner of the Smith-for-President Colored League, where he confidently told all who would

230   Chapter Six

listen that 65 percent of the state's African American voters would cast ballots for the Democrats in November 1928.[81]

Statewide recruiting efforts by Vashon and Thompkins received sympathetic and sometimes supportive commentaries in the *Argus* but found initial opposition from the *Call*, which opposed Democratic efforts to recruit African Americans, including expanded patronage opportunities and the construction of several notable projects.[82] The *Call* also continually overlooked rumors that local Republicans had built an alliance with the Klan in Jackson County.[83] By the end of the 1920s, C. A. Franklin wavered in his support for some Republicans but did not abandon the party. Instead, he began to express further doubts about the trajectory of the Republican Party. The cause for this reevaluation was the 1928 Republican National Convention in Kansas City. When party officials opted to segregate delegates by race, Franklin unleashed his outrage in the pages of the *Call*. His commentary on lily-whitism did not sway Republicans, and after the convention ended without a major platform addressing civil rights, Franklin expressed doubts about the party's direction.[84] Despite his concerns about the Republicans after the national convention, Franklin nevertheless endorsed Herbert Hoover for president.[85]

While C. A. Franklin may have toed the line when it came to national politics, he surprised many fellow Missourians when he backed Francis M. Wilson for governor over Republican Henry Caulfield.[86] In fact, historian Thomas D. Wilson notes that by the late 1920s, the *Call* no longer advised its readers to vote the straight Republican ticket.[87] "Negro voters should vote for the party that promises best, and most looks like it will carry out its promises," the *Call* reminded readers in September 1928.[88] State and local Democrats, while never gaining the full backing of Franklin and the *Call*, received increasingly positive endorsements from the newspaper: "When the democrats of Missouri, through their platform makers, promised to help [African Americans] get education and employment, they then and there broke party precedent, and put the standard of equality before the law where all could see it."[89] Though he despised Tom Pendergast, Franklin could no longer overlook the efforts made by local Democrats to appeal to Black voters. He soon developed a friendly relationship with Harry S. Truman as the young politician actively worked within the Pendergast Machine to increase

"Kampaigning" 231

accessibility to jobs and institutions for African Americans. The two men corresponded regularly in the 1930s, but Franklin never abandoned the Republican Party.[90]

C. A. Franklin remained a Republican, but he nevertheless allowed the pages of the *Call* to be open to political advertisements from both parties. To dissuade African Americans from switching parties, Republicans tended to focus on the so-called myth of Black voter abandonment. "Negroes will never in any large numbers vote to put a Democrat at the head of this country," a Republican advertisement confidently proclaimed. Republicans were also quick to remind voters that the Democratic Party controlled the South in the midst of Jim Crow and lynchings. Finally, Republicans touted the campaigns of prominent politicians, including Herbert Hoover, Henry Caulfield, and L. Amasa Knox, an African American candidate for the Missouri General Assembly.[91]

To counter Republican attacks, state Democrats promoted the party's work in Black communities, particularly those tied to Vashon and Thompkins, including the establishment of Smith-for-President Colored League clubs in twenty-five towns across the state.[92] Democrats were also quick to point out how the failings of state Republicans influenced realignment. Not only had the Baker administration failed to promote civil rights statewide and autonomy for Lincoln University, but the Republican-controlled police boards in Kansas City and St. Louis were accused of brutality in several instances, including in the aftermath of a tornado that struck St. Louis in 1927.[93]

In addition to using the pages of the *Call* and the *Argus* to attack Republicans, Kansas City Democrats associated with the Pendergast Machine also trumpeted their policies and promises in the pages of the *Kansas City American*.[94] This was especially relevant in the carefully placed articles and editorials informing readers and potential voters that "Negroes who regard the Klan as the most important issue confronting their race will support Smith," Republicans were "joining hands with the Ku Klux Klan," and "Ask your Republican Candidate if the Klan in this city and county endorsed you when they endorsed them."[95] The *American* also accused Kansas City Klansmen of circulating sample ballots in Black neighborhoods advising voters to reject Democratic candidates.[96] Finally, in promoting the campaigns of men like Smith, Wilson, and McLemore, the *American* declared that the Democratic Party was

232   Chapter Six

the only safe home for African American voters going forward: "The Republican party's betrayal has been shown by their readiness to fall in with the sectarian bigotry of a narrowminded and illiterate theocracy, and their entire willingness to accept the support of that nocturnal power, the Ku Klux Klan."[97]

Added to this targeted focus on the hooded order in the press, men like Thompkins and Vashon were ever ready on the campaign trail to point out that African Americans were fleeing to the Democratic Party because of "the activity of the Ku Klux Klan for the Republican party and its candidates."[98] When asked how Black voters in St. Louis approached these allegations, Vashon, who worked with Thompkins in the Smith-for-President Colored League, told the press: "They think that when the Republican party welcomes the Ku Klux Klan, it's time to leave, just as a man runs from a room when a mad dog enters. . . . [T]here have been 10,000 other issues all along, but they have not been as clear to the Negro mind as this one."[99]

In a final effort to tie Republicans, particularly Hebert Hoover, to the Klan, Democrats launched perhaps their more audacious political advertisements only days before the general election in 1928. In one ad labeled "Now Git," a man identified as Herbert Hoover is seen kicking a group of prominent Black leaders out of the Republican Party while being encouraged by several individuals, including a Klansman and another man holding a lily-white flower.[100] In the second, under a bold headline proclaiming, "Threat to Negro in Ku Klux Klan Alliance with Republican Party," the ad laid out the various ways that "Awakened Negro Voters [Were] Turning to [the] Democratic Party." The text touted Democratic advances for African Americans wrapped around a large cartoon depicting Herbert Hoover alongside two advice-wielding Klansmen who reminded the candidate to keep his lily-white stance, while an African American man representing "15 Million Negroes" stands in the foreground. Underneath the image, the advertisement laid the Klan issue bare:

The Ku Klux Klan is working hand in hand with the Republican National Committee to elect Herbert Hoover president of the United States. The Klan again is riding in America and Hoover and [vice-presidential candidate Charles] Curtis are it's [*sic*] standard bearers. The hooded hordes called to arms from the remotest corners of this land are mobilized to elect the Republican candidates November 6th. The state and county Republican organizations are depending upon this same cowardly outfit to elect their tickets. Make no mistake about this. What price has Klan exacted of the Republican party for it's [*sic*] support? How safe will the Negro be in the event of a Republican victory with his avowed enemy the Ku Klux Klan firmly entrenched in Washington? Why is Candidate Hoover so silent about the Klan? Alfred E. Smith, Democratic candidate for president, has repeatedly denounced this un-American organization. His election will forever end this menace to the well being of Negroes. A vote for Hoover is a vote for the Klan and Lily Whites, a vote for Smith is a vote for Fair Play and Equal Opportunity.[101]

As the dust settled on Election Day, Republicans still laid claim to the White House, governor's mansion, and a majority of Missouri's African American voters. When the 1929 session of the Missouri General Assembly opened in Jefferson City, all three Black state representatives were Republicans. With James A. Reed opting to retire, Republicans even captured his old US Senate seat with Roscoe C. Patterson's victory over Charles M. Hay. It seemed, at the time, that Republicans had withstood repeated attempts by Democrats to flip Black votes. Yet for the first time since 1888, Democrats carried St. Louis in the general election.[102] Added to this, it was estimated that nearly half of Kansas City's Black voters backed Democratic candidates in 1928.[103] Though their brethren in rural sections of the state were not yet ready to defect from the Republicans, Black voters across Missouri seriously weighed their options within the Democratic Party. Under the heading "The Negro in Politics," J. E. Mitchell editorialized in the *Argus* that a new day might be on the horizon: "The Negro is experiencing more difficulty in finding himself than ever before in his political history.... [T]his unholy alliance with the K.K.K. [and the Republican Party] shakes out confidence and clips our sails and leaves us still to wonder where our future haven shall be.... [I]f there is any deflection of Negro voters from the G.O.P. in large numbers, that party alone will be responsible."[104]

234   Chapter Six

The failure of state Republicans to reestablish strong relationships with
Black voters came to a head by the early 1930s. Though Governor Henry
S. Caulfield was well respected among African Americans for patronage
and notable opposition to the Klan, his attempts to win back key voters
by working against Democrats proved a mistake. Following the 1931
lynching of Raymond Gunn in Maryville, legislators from both parties
pushed for a state antilynching law. When the Democrats' version passed
the Missouri General Assembly, Caulfield vetoed it. Caulfield denied
it was a partisan decision, citing that the bill was too lenient toward
law-enforcement officials who failed to stop the lynching. Nevertheless,
state Democrats had a field day with Caulfield's veto, and the African
American press fumed at the decision.[105] State Republicans also felt the
heat over Herbert Hoover's nomination of Judge John J. Parker of North
Carolina to the US Supreme Court. Parker drew heavy opposition from
African Americans for his comments against Black voting rights. Parker
ultimately failed in the US Senate to be seated on the Supreme Court,
but Black Missourians took note that Republican Roscoe Patterson
voted in favor, while Democrat Harry Hawes voted against the judge.[106]

   While state Democrats experienced limited success in convincing
African Americans to vote against the Republican Party during the
1920s, the shift in voter allegiance continued as the Great Depression
deepened. When Bryce B. Smith was elected mayor of Kansas City in
1930, voting totals suggested that a sizable majority of Black voters in
the city backed Democratic candidates.[107] By the 1932 federal and state
elections, conditions were ripe for a Democratic landslide. Alongside
the presidential election that year, every major statewide office, which
Republicans had held for more than a decade, was up for grabs.
Additionally, since Governor Henry Caulfield had vetoed a Democrat-
friendly redistricting bill a year prior, each of the state's congressional
districts was categorized as at-large versus the traditional geographic
regions. As such, Missouri voters held tremendous power in determining
the party in power, which proved detrimental for Republicans during the
early years of the Great Depression.[108]

   Though Democrats readily applied the label of Klan affiliation to
Republicans during the 1920s and 1930s, Francis M. Wilson also dealt
with rumors of kampaigning during his second bid for the governorship

in 1932. This time, however, the alleged infiltration was from within the party and attached to his primary opponent, Russell Dearmont. An attorney and state senator from Cape Girardeau, Dearmont mounted a primary challenge to Wilson that promoted his legislative record and community ties to southeast Missouri. Dearmont was a strong opponent and frequently attacked Wilson by questioning his health and ties to Pendergast. Seeking to counter these charges, Wilson learned from supporters that the attorney had significant Klan backing. Soon after, the Pendergast-affiliated *Missouri Herald* made Dearmont's alleged Klan ties public. For his part, Dearmont quickly swatted away the allegations, including rumors spread by Pendergast allies that he had even joined the Klan during the 1920s. According to Dearmont and his supporters, not only had the senator never joined the Klan, but he was among a group of Cape Girardeau citizens who actively worked to prevent the Klan from holding meetings in the city. In response, Dearmont went on the offensive, charging that Wilson had no position on the Klan because he wanted both Klan and anti-Klan votes.[109]

While Dearmont hit back at Wilson, the candidate and his closest supporters debated how to respond. Though the Klan was far from the membership levels it had had even four years earlier, Wilson was wary of efforts to galvanize current and former Klansmen, particularly in Dearmont's home territory of southeast Missouri. In letters to several supporters, Wilson warned of circulars distributed specifically to former Klansmen attacking him and championing Dearmont. Wilson's supporters were divided on how to respond to the circulars. Some emphasized the need to expose Dearmont's close ties to the Klan, particularly the allegation that one of the senator's publicity managers had "led nightriders in many raids on helpless and defenseless persons." Yet others felt it was a nonissue and that some of the more vocal former Klan members supporting Dearmont had more enemies than friends. Ultimately, Wilson followed the advice of S. E. Juden of Caruthersville, who warned that Democratic-affiliated Klansmen "may do great damage to the party" and monitored the situation but never openly drew attention to it during the campaign.[110]

In the Democratic primary in August, Wilson topped Dearmont by roughly 150,000 votes, but he never reached the governor's mansion.

On October 12, 1932, Wilson died suddenly from illness. Having put so much time and publicity into a Roosevelt-Wilson ticket, state Democrats frantically searched for a viable candidate. Guy Brasfield Park, a circuit-court judge from Platte County, was soon selected, and the campaign marched on at a quick pace to introduce voters to the relatively unknown Park. Though the new candidate did not have the same level of support among Black voters as Wilson, Park and the Democrats were nevertheless able to organize around previous inroads in cities and ride Roosevelt's coattails.[111] In the 1932 election, scholar Larry Grothaus posits that a slim majority of Black voters supported the Democratic Party in Missouri, though results were mixed in rural communities, particularly in the Ozarks and Bootheel.[112]

Though it had gained majority support and risen back into power thanks to African American voters, the Missouri Democratic Party found itself in trouble with these same voters as the 1930s wore on. The threat of the Klan had subsided significantly by the early 1930s. While it was not uncommon to see Democratic politicians and the press attempt to tie their opponents back to the Klan, the warning rang hollow as the Depression deepened and the Klan fell into obscurity. Additionally, Democrats had failed to honor promises of patronage, political power, and protection from police brutality, just as the Republicans had. Thrust into power on such pledges, Democrats soon found that they were not immune from the same scandals that doomed Republicans with African American voters. By the decade's end, the state and its African American residents threatened to swing back to the Republican column.[113]

Initially, Democrats had seemed happy to divide the spoils. Upon gaining office in 1933, Governor Park quickly established an interracial committee to address concerns among African Americans. For their loyalty to the party and key role in attracting Black voters, Park placed William Thompkins and Joseph McLemore on the committee as well as on the Board of Curators of Lincoln University. Park also made sizable efforts to grant patronage across the state. As the administrators and liaisons for state and federal aid, Democrats proved adept at steering programs to supporters and areas of the state important to keeping the party in power. Not surprisingly, local fiefdoms gained added importance for securing such aid and ensuring that African American residents received a set amount of it. In Pendergast's Kansas City, this amounted to roughly 10 percent of patronage jobs since Black residents were 10 percent of the city's population.[114]

Additionally, in African American neighborhoods and wards, Democrats allowed an element of local control and close ties to state and federal politicians. As such, African Americans lobbied and campaigned for local office, neighborhood leaders secured patronage jobs for supporters, and elected officials attempted to secure major relief programs in their districts. Grothaus notes that Congressman Thomas C. Hennings Jr. became especially notable for his efforts to help Black residents in his district. Surprisingly, early on, Black voters turned their ire to federal officials when patronage- and relief-program promises fell through instead of blaming local and state Democrats. This was especially true in rural Missouri, where African Americans were largely denied the benefits of backing the winning party. Nevertheless, the Democratic apparatuses in St. Louis and Kansas City kept their voters housed, clothed, fed, and employed—within reason.[115]

While state and local Democrats wielded patronage and relief to stay in power, they also sought to ensure victory at the top of the ticket as support for Franklin D. Roosevelt's New Deal meant continued funding for those very relief programs. In each of his elections, Roosevelt carried Missouri and most of the state's Black voters, while local leaders reminded voters of what the entire Democratic Party could do for them. At the same time, Roosevelt wasn't immune from dissension within the ranks. For starters, while C. A. Franklin did offer support at times in the pages of the *Call* for Harry S. Truman, Guy Park, and the Pendergast Machine, he reserved few positive comments for Roosevelt. Not only was Franklin an avid anti–New Dealer, but he also argued that the programs did little to help African Americans. Additionally, while he may have pushed Black Kansas Citians to support local Democrats, Franklin always promoted the Republican candidate during presidential elections.[116]

By the latter half of the 1930s, Roosevelt had won reelection, Harry S. Truman had joined the US Senate, Lloyd Stark had succeeded Guy Park in the governor's mansion, and Democrats had firm control of the Missouri General Assembly. Yet, by all accounts, support among

African American voters began to slip. Beginning with deepening scandals surrounding Tom Pendergast, his machine's eventual destruction brought about a fissure within the city's Democratic voters that allowed Republicans to slowly gain back a portion of Black voters. In St. Louis, the administration of Bernard Dickmann, though winning reelection in 1937, soon found an evaporation of Black support. The city's Sixth Ward, which had only recently flipped from Republican to Democrat, turned back to the Republicans in the next election cycle. This was due largely to a reinvigorated strategy pursued by the Republicans in African American neighborhoods that was buoyed by criticisms that Dickmann had not done enough to address Black concerns, particularly when it came to patronage. Though Dickmann had completed Homer G. Phillips Hospital, as promised, Republicans countered with their own promise to provide new updates to the facility. Finally, Black residents opted to vote with their pocketbooks after a Dickmann-backed ordinance on smokeless coal saw prices skyrocket through the fall and winter. In 1941, Dickmann lost reelection.[117]

While the failings of the Pendergast and Dickmann machines were localized, the administration of Lloyd Stark provided another significant blow to Democratic support among Black voters. Stark was unable to replicate the success of Guy Park, who not only used government programs to attract African Americans but also largely received a pass from voters on issues that had sunk other officeholders, including patronage, racial violence, and political influence at Lincoln University. Stark, on the other hand, drew the ire of Black voters. First, he was unpopular for his role in bringing down elements of the Pendergast Machine. Second, Stark did little to stop rural efforts to pass legislation to stop the US Supreme Court's ruling in the *Gaines v. Canada* case that would have integrated the University of Missouri. Stark's inaction, alongside rural Democrats' support for such legislation, was not forgotten by Black voters. Finally, Stark was criticized for his heavy-handed reaction to the 1939 sharecroppers strike in southeast Missouri when he called in the Missouri State Highway Patrol and forcefully disbanded the sharecroppers' camps in the dead of winter. Not surprisingly, Stark's bid in 1940 to unseat Harry S. Truman as US senator was unsuccessful, as Truman gained a sizable advantage among Black voters.[118]

"Kampaigning" 239

Though Truman had triumphed over Stark to secure the Democratic nomination on his way to the US Senate, his strong showing among African American voters was the exception to the rule at the start of the 1940s. In addition to Stark's and Dickmann's defeats, Roosevelt experienced sizable defections among the state's Black voters, even as he repeatedly won the state and presidency. By 1943, Republicans had regained the governor's mansion, controlled the general assembly, and held a majority of the state's congressional seats. Except for the general assembly, which they controlled until the start of the 1949 term, Republicans' hold over state offices was brief. Yet African Americans were still apprehensive about realigning with the Democrats. Even after selecting Truman to be his running mate in 1944, Roosevelt still faced stiff criticism in the African American press for what many interpreted as Jim Crow control over the Democratic Party and efforts at kampaigning to attract southern Democrats. Truman himself was not immune from this and, in the presidential campaign, faced one of the toughest critiques of his character since his earliest days in politics when the Klan allegations surfaced.[119]

As Truman successfully fought off Republican efforts to kampaign against him, he helped Roosevelt win an unprecedented fourth term as president. When Roosevelt died a year later, the Missourian was thrust into the presidency as World War II concluded and a new world order emerged. His actions as president, particularly executive orders integrating federal employment and the military, proved significant for the future of the Democratic Party nationally and within Missouri. After experiencing further dissension from Black voters in the 1945 St. Louis mayoral race and the 1946 general election, both dominated by Republicans, Democrats carefully rallied around Truman's Fair Deal and civil rights efforts. The result was a significant victory in 1948 that ushered in an era of absolute dominance for the state Democratic Party. From inauguration day in 1949, a Republican would not win election as governor until 1972. In the Missouri General Assembly, with the exception of the 1953–54 sessions, Republicans would not hold a majority in either chamber until 2001.[120]

The 1948 election also started a wave of unrivaled support for Democratic candidates among African American voters that continues into the twenty-first century. Scholars Lorenzo J. Greene, Gary R. Kremer, and Antonio F. Holland have noted the stark shift in Black support for Democratic candidates in the postwar era. Starting with Walthall Moore's victory in 1920, at least sixty-five Black candidates won election to the general assembly or the state's congressional delegation over the next seventy-two years. Reflecting on their respective tenures, this political realignment becomes clear. Before 1948, nine African American candidates served at various times in the Missouri House of Representatives. Of those representatives, six of the nine were Republicans, while the three Democrats all served terms in the 1940s. After J. Clayborne Bush and Josiah C. Thomas were not reelected in 1948, only two African American Republican candidates would win election to the general assembly through 1992. In that same time frame, however, Missouri voters sent more than fifty Black Democrats to Jefferson City or Washington, DC. Though the Republican Party has had control of both chambers of the Missouri General Assembly since the early 2000s, Black political leaders in the state capitol have remained overwhelmingly Democratic.[121]

CHAPTER SEVEN

"The Spirit of the Klan"
The Fracturing of the Anti-Klan Coalition

IN AUGUST 1946, *Cosmopolitan Magazine* ran an article by Harry T. Brundidge titled "The Klan Rides Again," which detailed recent activities of the hooded organization across the United States, including "recruiting thousands of followers in the South and the Midwest for a new drive against refugees and labor unions." The article was brought to the attention of William G. Pinsley of the Anti-Defamation League of B'nai B'rith, who urgently sent a memorandum to the Jewish Community Relations Council of St. Louis highlighting Brundidge's findings about Klan activity in Missouri.[1] According to Brundidge, "In St. Louis, there is plenty of Klan activity. There are three organized Klaverns in the city and St. Louis county. Kleagles working out of St. Louis are busy in Springfield, Jefferson City, Cape Girardeau, Hayti, Carthage, Webb City and in areas where the Amalgamated Clothing Workers have been successful in consolidating gains." In response to Pinsley's request for confirmation regarding the article's details, Myron Schwartz, executive secretary of the Jewish Community Relations Council, tried to assuage Pinsley's fears and noted that the Klan was "very quiescent locally." Schwartz continued that the only alleged Klan activity in the city had been a cross burning at the recently integrated Buder Park a few weeks prior. Schwartz mailed newspaper clippings about Buder Park to Pinsley, but for the most part pointed out that the Klan activity highlighted in the article was more so related to rural Missouri than the city of St. Louis.[2]

Myron Schwartz's response to the Buder Park cross burning is notable because the incident not only fueled a summer-long saga over the integration of the neighborhood facility that still simmered at the time of Pinsley's letter, but also served as a key marker in the evolution between the interwar-years Klan and its post–World War II offspring. By the summer of 1946, members of the St. Louis Civic Improvement

241

242   Chapter Seven

Association had grown tired of broken promises from city officials about expanded recreational access for local Black children. The group was particularly interested in Buder Park, a neighborhood green space with a playground, pool, and public baths because it was in a racially integrated neighborhood southwest of St. Louis's Union Station. When the association brought Black children to the park in June 1946, they were initially met by a park attendant who informed them that the park was for whites only. Returning a few days later, the group found the park's amenities closed off, its pool drained, and the playground swings locked in place. As the *St. Louis Argus* fumed about segregation at Buder Park, city officials announced their intent to shift the space from whites-only to an African American park. Soon after, a petition circulated among white residents of the area seeking to return the park to its prior status.[3]

On June 18, 1946, Thelma Watson, a member of the St. Louis Civic Improvement Association, saw what appeared to be something on fire not far from her home and rushed toward Buder Park. Arriving at the park, she saw a cross engulfed in flames with a white hood over the top labeled "K.K.K." In the distance, she saw several white males fleeing the scene. Once the fire was extinguished, a photograph of the cross and mask appeared in all the major city newspapers. Soon after, the press pages filled with letters to the editors regarding the incident.[4] "Fed by kerosene and hate," the *St. Louis Star-Times* declared, the fiery cross stood in a place "turned over only 24 hours before to Negro children who had no other place to play." Most newspapers noted that the cross could have been set by Klansmen or by vigilantes seeking to emulate the hooded order, but, as the *Star-Times* concluded, "It makes little difference really . . . [f]or it was the spirit of the Klan that set torch to it, and it is that spirit even more than the agency that must be quenched."[5]

In the wake of the cross burning, city officials faced protests over the park's status. Groups in favor of integrating the park, such as the St. Louis Civic Improvement Association, asked Mayor Aloys Kauffman, as well as director of public welfare and former governor Henry Caulfield, not to reverse course or bend to public pressure. Opponents of the integration held meetings and circulated petitions throughout the neighborhood to rally support.[6] At a meeting at St. Henry's Catholic School, one protester declared, "If we permit the city and the Negroes to take the park away from our children, it will be the forerunner of similar encroachments all over the city in the future."[7] In a surprise move, a group of two hundred white students, along with a few teachers and parents, marched from Choteau School to city hall to protest the park's integration nearly four months after the start of tensions.[8]

The *St. Louis Argus* did little to mask its conclusions about who erected the cross and thus ignited not only the gasoline-soaked burlap that encased it but also the city of St. Louis at large. Within days of the incident, the *Argus* named Gerald L. K. Smith, a Wisconsin-born minister and political organizer, the guilty party.[9] Smith had recently set his sights on St. Louis as he sought to expand his Christian Nationalist Crusade, an offshoot of the pre–World War II America First movement. Though the earlier iteration had dissolved not long after Pearl Harbor, Smith's efforts combined isolationist sentiments with support for white supremacy, anti-Semitism, and fascism. The timing of Smith's arrival in St. Louis and the Buder Park incident was not lost on the *Argus*, which was in the midst of a years-long editorial crusade against him. "As has been said time and again," the *Argus* thundered, "in times like these, when the true patriots of America are looking for a new and better world, there is no place in the new scheme of things for rabble-rousing, race baiting, Hitlerism or Ku Klux Klanisms."[10]

The *Argus*'s attempts to tie men like Gerald L. K. Smith to groups like the Ku Klux Klan were not isolated to just that newspaper. As the *Argus* noted when it alleged that the "Gerald L. K. Smith crowd are the pilots and the seed sowers for the spirit of the Ku Klux Klan," many movements aligned with demagoguery, fascism, and white supremacy formed, fractured, and failed during the 1930s and the 1940s.[11] At the exact moment when the hooded order's membership was at one of its lowest levels during the interwar period, these various groups bubbled up to attract new members, including current and former Klansmen and -women, and build on the foundation laid by the 1920s Klan. As scholars have noted, despite their individual identities, these groups overlapped with one another on key issues and, at times, coordinated their efforts during the Great Depression and World War II. Considering this, Nancy MacLean argues that any study of the second Klan that does

244   Chapter Seven

not examine it from a global perspective of simultaneous right-wing and fascist movements is "bound to yield a limited understanding of its place in history.[12] However, Leo Ribuffo, in his pioneering work *The Old Christian Right*, cautions against easy assumptions about the connections between various right-wing groups of this era, noting that while they may have appeared alongside one another at rallies or had at least been in communication, they were far from an organized juggernaut ordering their adherents to take over the United States.[13]

At the same time, just as they had done during the height of the Invisible Empire during the 1920s, various anti-Klan groups and individuals turned their attention to these new organizations during the 1930s and 1940s to destroy them before they gained similar membership levels and political power. This task proved surprisingly easier than it had been in the 1920s due to the fringe nature of several of these organizations. Simultaneously, however, many of these anti-Klan activists soon found themselves on opposing sides. Gone was the tenuous but, at times, united effort to curtail the hooded order, replaced by groups whose cultural, racial, and religious heritage, as well as their own intolerance, caused a serious strain on previous relationships. For example, Father Charles Coughlin had made a name for himself in the 1920s as a wildly popular radio minister and led an all-out assault by Catholics on the Klan. By the end of the 1930s, however, Coughlin's increasingly vitriolic and anti-Semitic broadcasts inspired a segment of his followers to align with American groups interested in anticommunism, segregation, fascism, and working alongside the Klan.

While Coughlin's position deeply affected the sentiments of his radio listeners, particularly among Catholics, it was just one element that splintered support among old allies from the anti-Klan days. The realignment of Black voters in Missouri severed political relationships that dated back multiple generations. Additionally, with the deterioration of conditions in Nazi Germany during the 1930s, Missouri Jews increasingly found the state's German American population divided over what truly was happening in the fatherland. Finally, as the Buder Park incident demonstrates, though some residents may have objected to the Klan for personal reasons two decades prior, supporting efforts to integrate public facilities was a different matter. Even Archbishop John J. Glennon, who had warned those in attendance at Dedication Day in 1924 not to let bigotry darken the halls of the new state capitol building, was far from opposed to segregation and even went to great lengths to stall attempts to integrate parochial schools in Missouri.[14]

The evolution and, at times, dissolution of the already tenuous anti-Klan coalition during the final years of the interwar period and the subsequent revival of the Klan after World War II are important topics. Various fascist and white supremacist organizations grew in Missouri and nationwide during the 1930s and 1940s that appealed to both Klan and anti-Klan supporters. It is critical to look at the remnants of the anti-Klan coalition that continued to challenge not only the Klan but also these various groups that targeted their identities during what Leo Ribuffo defines as the "Brown Scare." Finally, in showing the battles that raged, both overseas and on the home front in the early years of World War II, it is important to highlight how these various fascist and white-supremacist groups aligned in these years and ultimately contributed to the growth of the Klan's third generation during the postwar civil rights movement.

By the 1930s, the Ku Klux Klan was a shell of its former self. Having peaked with an estimated membership in the millions, the organization entered the 1930s with roughly one hundred thousand Klansmen and -women. Even the fervent anti-Catholicism surrounding Al Smith's presidential campaign in 1928 was not enough to resurrect sinking numbers. As the Great Depression deepened, numbers dipped still lower as membership dues proved too costly for the downtrodden and unemployed. A decade into his reign as imperial wizard, Hiram Evans traveled the country extensively to rally members back into the fold. Yet there were few promising leads outside of places like Georgia, Florida, New York, and the Upper Midwest. In an era of high unemployment, the Klan was unable to increase its membership, even as it altered its principal message to focus on calls to remove immigrants and foreigners from the country to open up jobs for American-born workers. On top of this message, the group also increased its antiunion sentiments, arguing that foreign influence and communism had seeped into organized labor.[15]

Despite the drop in membership, St. Joseph still held considerable sway over the shrinking Invisible Empire in Missouri. In 1929, Grand Dragon William M. Campbell resigned his post to serve on the national Klan's imperial kloncilium where he told a St. Joseph newspaper that his

246   Chapter Seven

role was to "take the radicalism out of the organization."[16] In his place, Harry C. Spratt, who had worked under Campbell as the secretary of St. Joseph Klan No. 4, took over as grand dragon of the realm that contained Missouri and Kansas. Spratt was a dedicated acolyte involved in the hooded order for nearly a decade. After serving as secretary of St. Joseph Klan No. 4, Spratt became a traveling auditor for the organization in Missouri, Kansas, and Nebraska and then was transferred to Imperial Headquarters in Atlanta. Klan officials shuffled him between Atlanta and an office in Washington, DC, during the latter half of the 1920s before promoting him to grand dragon.[17]

Owing to Campbell's and Spratt's influence, Hiram Evans visited St. Joseph during a tour of the Midwest in 1930. He spoke before a crowd estimated at fifteen hundred, where he warned against US involvement in the World Court, claimed that enfranchisement of African Americans should end via repeal of the Fifteenth Amendment, and touted the strength of the hooded order.[18] Evans undoubtedly painted a rosier picture than reality on the ground. While efforts were made to build upon earlier recruiting successes, coverage of Klan activities in statewide newspapers was relatively stagnant during the 1930s. When a fiery cross was set in Scott County in the Bootheel in 1931, the *Chaffee Signal* viewed it as more of a nuisance than a call to action: "In the midst of our depression there is no need for a revival of this secret organization."[19] By the middle of the decade, Spratt left the hooded order, though some confusion exists about the exact time line as he later claimed that it was around 1933, but the *St. Joseph Union Observer* listed an H. C. Spratt as imperial kligrapp in 1936.[20]

Though his son Heber and thousands of other Missourians left the Klan by the 1930s, Gilbert O. Nations refused to cease his efforts to summon Protestant America to the battlefield on behalf of what he saw as the continuing threat of Catholicism in the United States. For Nations, men like 1928 Democratic presidential candidate Al Smith represented not just a threat to temperance and morality but an individual who fulfilled a prophecy he had warned about since the early 1910s. In Nations's mind, not only was Smith, as a Catholic, ineligible for office, but his potential election as president also raised the specter of pontifical control of the White House. To counter this threat, Nations published extensively in sympathetic newspapers to spearhead a revival of the Klan.

"The Spirit of the Klan" 247

He also quickly went to work on a book, *The Political Career of Alfred E. Smith*, where he argued that "it would be an appalling calamity to clothe [a Catholic] with the Presidency of the United States."[21]

Nations and his supporters may have won the battle when Herbert Hoover defeated Al Smith in 1928, but the holy war destroyed the so-called patriotic movement. Just as the Klan declined by the 1930s, so too did the market for such publications. Nations had a hand in creating the *New Menace*, an anti-Catholic newspaper based in Aurora, Missouri. However, though it had a similar name, content, and list of backers as its predecessor, the *Menace*, the publication struggled during the 1920s and found itself repeatedly asking for donations and pressing subscribers to pay their bills to keep the newspaper afloat.[22] Nations continued contributing material to the *New Menace*, but he soon turned his interests to another publication, the *Protestant*. Published in Washington, DC, the *Protestant* advertised itself as a "militant but scholarly magazine" that was a "concise monthly digest of EXCLUSIVE FACTS that concern all Protestants."[23] Nations hoped that his new venture would provide an even larger pulpit by which to peddle his continued anti-Catholic views, and his gamble proved correct—at least initially—as his writings on temperance and religion found a new home in the pamphlets and lecture circuit of the Klan.

At the end of the 1920s, the *New Menace* still shipped out from Aurora and proudly proclaimed itself "The Great National Protestant Weekly Newspaper," but by the mid-1930s, the publication was forced to reorganize as the *Monitor*, which announced that it would be "Devoted to Free Discussion of Great National Issues."[24] Nations followed suit with his own publishing empire by merging the *Protestant* with *Fellowship Forum*, a fellow 1920s-era newspaper that once claimed more than a million subscribers and promoted anti-Catholicism and the Klan. While these moves were proclaimed as a consolidation of newspapers to better serve an army of subscribers, critics, like the *Brooklyn Torch*, saw a decline in readership due to "bilious, sour, uninteresting, long-winded and flat contributions from their pencils," adding that since the early years of the *Menace*:

> They would trot out an ex-Monsignor and make him dance through column after column of racy stories. The Pope would be treated as

248   Chapter Seven

a punching bag; he would be hit severely, but only to spring back
to the same position for a further swat in the proceeding issue. If a
priest appeared at some beach in a bathing suit, a story of serial pro-
portions would be invented. If the crops were bad in North Dakota,
Margaret Tilly, the well-known ex-nun, formerly of California—but
in reality Billy Parker—would explain to readers that it was due to
a visitation from God, because of the sins of some Bishop who died
several years previously from the gout.[25]

By the latter half of the 1930s, Nations parted ways with *Fellowship
Forum*, and the Klan was back in national headlines. Like many Americans,
Klan members were initially swept up in Franklin Roosevelt's promises
of a New Deal and looked favorably on his acquiescence to segregationist
southern Democrats to earn their votes. However, their infatuation with
Roosevelt ended when the new president included Jewish and Catholic officials within his administration, including Henry Morgenthau Jr., James
Farley, and later US Supreme Court justice Felix Frankfurter. Following
the retirement of Willis Van Devanter from the US Supreme Court in
1937, Roosevelt nominated Hugo Black, a pro–New Deal US Senator
from Alabama, to replace him. Not long after his nomination, however,
Black was embroiled in scandal when allegations surfaced that he had
previously been a member of the Klan. Black did little to challenge these
rumors and admitted that he had since separated from the hooded order.
Opponents found Black's admission damning and protested his placement on the nation's highest court. Black's supporters, including NAACP
president Walter White, defended the Alabama senator's statements that
he was no longer connected with or influenced by the Klan. Black ultimately weathered the storm and served on the US Supreme Court until
1971, but the publicity from the scandal allowed the future justice and
others to vilify the hooded order to distance him from the Klan.[26]
    When Hugo Black's Klan ties became public, the organization was also
dealing with the fallout over its rumored connection to a group called the
Black Legion. Originally a paramilitary arm of several Klan chapters in
Ohio during the 1920s that donned black robes instead of the traditional white, the Black Legion soon split off to form its own organization,
though ties between both groups continued. By the 1930s, the Black

"The Spirit of the Klan" 249

Legion's strength was based in the Midwest, particularly factory towns in Ohio and Michigan, with membership estimated in the thousands. Though flying largely under the radar, the group made headlines in the mid-1930s when Charles Poole, a Works Progress Administration organizer, was kidnapped and murdered in Detroit by Black Legion members, twelve of whom would later be convicted of murder. Soon after, Warner Brothers adapted a fictionalized version of the crime into a major motion picture starring Humphrey Bogart called *Black Legion* (1937).[27]

As the Black Legion's involvement in Poole's death, as well as other crimes, became public, Hiram Evans denounced the group. It was one of Evans's final acts as leader of the Invisible Empire. By the mid-1930s, the Great Depression, eroding membership, and losing members to other groups, such as the Black Legion, had left Evans with little path forward for the Klan. At a particularly low point, the Klan authorized the sale of the Imperial Headquarters in Atlanta. An insurance company bought it and immediately sold it to a local Catholic parish to use as a rectory. By the end of the decade, Evans retired and was replaced by James Colescott, a Klan official responsible for the Midwest realms. The group continued to have outposts in the Midwest and South, with its largest concentration of strength in Florida. To stay relevant, mend fences, and draw in new areas of support, the Klan soon aligned itself with various like-minded organizations.[28]

While the Klan's membership dipped from highs in the millions down into the thousands, and the organization was relatively powerless outside of a few locations, the group's impact on the Jazz Age nevertheless shaped how many Americans interpreted the growing upheaval of the interwar period. Scholars have long debated the significance of the financial crisis of the 1930s, Franklin D. Roosevelt's response, and why such an economic calamity did not lead to widespread political revolution in the United States as it did in other countries. Instead, what animosity did bubble up centered on labor strife, opinions regarding Roosevelt's New Deal, and various firebrands who vied for supporters among the hungry and the hopeless. At the same time, a nation of immigrants cast its eyes toward conflicts around the globe, particularly in Europe and Asia, and questioned not only how to address the refugee crisis but also what, if

250   Chapter Seven

any, intervention needed to be pursued by the US government. In the lead-up to Franklin D. Roosevelt's 1933 inauguration and initial planning for his New Deal administration, the situation overseas jockeyed for position on the front page of local newspapers as Americans kept a close eye not only on the deepening Depression but also on the rise of fascism in Europe, particularly in Mussolini's Italy and Hitler's Germany.[29]

When the plight of German Jews under the Hitler regime hit Missouri newspapers, editors and publishers quickly framed what was happening in terms that would be easy for readers to understand. Referring to Hitler as a "Ku Klux Chancellor," the *Kansas City Journal-Post* offered its readers an eerie comparison: "Hitler sounds like a grand kleagle elevated to the chancellorship, and his followers make statements very much like the sentiments muttered through white sheets a decade ago in this country."[30] Upon reading the *Journal-Post's* sentiments, the *Kansas City Jewish Chronicle* touted the comparison to its readers.[31] Soon after, the *Kansas City Star* ran a series of articles on the situation in Germany that compared Hitler's rise to power to a scenario of the Klan gaining control of the White House in the 1920s.[32] Echoing this assessment, Henry J. Haskell, editor of the *Star*, sent a dispatch from Germany calling Nazism "a combination of old-fashioned Populism, the Ku Klux Klan and 'Hello, World' Henderson's crusade against the chain store."[33] In St. Louis, the *Modern View* and the *Globe-Democrat* documented similarities between Nazi and Klan tactics. At the same time, the *Argus* expressed solidarity with Jews in Germany, noting a "Ku Klux Klan Spirit" that targeted both groups.[34] If this imagery was not graphic enough, the *Kansas City Call* put its stamp on the subject by featuring an editorial cartoon depicting Hitler holding a swastika and whip while his illuminated shadow displayed a Klansman holding a fiery cross and whip under the title "Another Klansman."[35]

Missouri newspaper staff were not the only ones to make a connection between Nazism and the Klan. Echoing former presidential candidate Al Smith's sentiments that the best way to combat anti-Semitism was to "drag it out in the open sunlight and give it the same treatment we gave the Ku Klux Klan," state political leaders, particularly Arthur Hyde and James Reed, issued similar statements supporting German Jews and attacking Nazi policies.[36] At an anti-Nazi rally in Kansas City, Reed told the assembled crowd that "no man ever sought dictatorial power who was not in his heart a monster." Hyde warned listeners that "persecution of Jews by those who call themselves Christians does Christianity an evil service."[37] Later, Reed told the Committee for the Defense of Human Rights against Nazism that he planned to attack fascism and its supporters, both in the United States and abroad, just as he had done against the Klan a decade earlier because "today, it is the Jew who is the particular victim. But tomorrow, and tomorrow, and tomorrow, the waves may break higher and higher upon the shores, until they may engulf all lands and all peoples."[38]

While the denouncement of Hitler's agenda was nearly universal, particularly in the Jewish press, there was also a hint of caution toward directing anger at German Americans. Only a generation prior, Missouri's German population, which dated back to the first years of statehood, experienced a period during World War I when German identity was severely curtailed, German-language schools and newspapers shuttered, names Americanized, and even beer gardens closed under Prohibition.[39] In the aftermath of the war, another sizable exodus of Germans arrived on American soil, eager to experience prosperity unattainable in defeated and war-ravaged Germany. Just as their ancestors had done in prior generations, they set up roots in their new communities and attempted to keep their German culture alive. Despite an ocean separating them from the fatherland, German Americans kept close contact with family and friends back home. As such, it is not surprising that they would have been relatively well versed in the political transition occurring in Weimar Germany.[40]

Though it was still nearly a decade before Adolf Hitler was appointed chancellor and seized power, news of the political activism of the Nazi Party slowly seeped into American newspapers by the mid-1920s. By all accounts, Nazi leaders cared little initially about what support might exist for the party in the United States. Yet as early as 1924, the National Socialist Teutonia Association had formed with members eager to show their support for the Nazis in Germany. By the 1930s, the NSTA had chapters in several American cities, including Detroit, Chicago, Los Angeles, New York, and Cincinnati. Eager to earn the distinction of being christened as an official National Socialist German Workers' Party

252 Chapter Seven

organization in the United States, NSTA leaders were greatly dismayed when Hitler gained power and did little to address his supporters across the Atlantic Ocean. When NSDAP leaders did opt to recognize the recruitment efforts occurring in the United States, they chose a New York–based organization called the National Socialist German Workers' Party, or Gauleitung-USA. This decision cratered support for the NSTA, and members quickly merged with Gauleitung-USA.[41]

Though the merger of NSTA and Gauleitung-USA seemingly brought harmony among the various Nazi-sympathizing groups in the United States, it also created additional fissures and internal disputes that threatened to destroy all involved. While German diplomats and sympathizers flooded the United States with propaganda aimed at altering the image of Hitler and Nazis as well as propping up key talking points regarding wartime grievances, infighting among the groups proved so severe that NSDAP leaders officially disbanded Gauleitung-USA. Out of the rubble emerged a new organization, the Friends of New Germany, headed by Heinz Spanknobel. Originally part of the NSTA, Spanknobel traveled to Germany during the infighting to gain official recognition for his efforts to promote National Socialism in the United States. He made connections with Rudolph Hess, deputy führer of the Nazi Party. He returned to the United States eager to bring together former members of NSTA, Gauleitung-USA, Swastika League, and other smaller Nazi-sympathetic groups.[42]

With the city's sizable German population that dated back to the nineteenth century, it is not surprising that Nazi sympathizers and propagandists focused their attention on St. Louis. By the mid-1930s, a chapter of the Friends of New Germany was organized in the city with an estimated membership of seventy-five. To grow the group in the region, the German Consul in St. Louis personally contacted Heinz Spanknobel with the names of individuals it thought worthy of consideration for membership. Within a year of its founding, the local chapter's activities, including meetings and events, received coverage in the national organization's newspaper, *Deutsche Zeitung*. It also worked to distribute propaganda and emulate Nazi tactics, particularly boycotting Jewish businesses by claiming that Jews had caused the Great Depression. One local official, Otto Gruendler, was so enamored with Nazism that

"The Spirit of the Klan"   253

he allegedly kept a shrine to Hitler in his home and sent his family to
live in Germany. The Friends of New Germany also quickly infiltrated
the German House, a community center constructed in 1929 featuring
meeting rooms, a tavern, a restaurant, a bowling alley, and a large auditorium that had become the nerve center for St. Louis's German American
heritage groups in the 1930s.[43]

Heinz Spanknobel's plan to unite American and German Nazi supporters under the banner of the Friends of New Germany proved to be
brief. Like earlier infighting among the various groups, Spanknobel's efforts to consolidate and take over his rivals met with sizable opposition.
Given his ties to Rudolph Hess and the Nazi Party in Germany, it's not
surprising that he was soon charged with being an unregistered foreign
agent. Spanknobel fled the United States for Germany to avoid the
charges, and more infighting occurred as Spanknobel's chosen successor,
Ignatz Griebl, vied with the NSDAP-preferred Fritz Gissibl for the official title of *bundesleiter*. Gissibl eventually won out, but his time as leader
was marked by congressional investigations into Nazi sympathizers and
propaganda in the United States. After congressional scrutiny of the alleged un-American activities of the Friends of New Germany, NSDAP
officials decided to rebrand the group. All German nationals were ordered
out or told to work toward naturalization. Additionally, the group more
closely wedded itself to German heritage in the United States. While
these efforts culminated with the dissolution of the Friends of New
Germany, it laid the foundation for the Amerikadeutscher Volksbund.
The Amerikadeutscher Volksbund, or German-American Bund, fed off
of Hitler's rise to power in Germany as well as the rapid distribution of
pro-Nazi propaganda in the United States.[44]

The Volksbund was led by Fritz Julius Kuhn, a Munich-born World
War I veteran and chemical engineer. After serving in France as a machine gunner and later joining the Freikorps, Kuhn became a follower of
the NSDAP. In his own probably fictitious origin story, Kuhn later used
his early support for the NSDAP to suggest that he had served alongside
Adolf Hitler during the notorious Beer Hall Putsch in 1923.[45] Kuhn's
path to the United States led through Mexico, where he spent four years
as a chemist before crossing the border into Texas. He moved to New
York but ultimately settled in Michigan and quickly became connected

254 Chapter Seven

with members of the Friends of New Germany. From there, Kuhn quickly rose through the ranks, first as a regional gauleiter in 1935, then as the handpicked successor of Fritz Gissibl to be *bundesleiter*. However, Kuhn desired a grander title, and when the Amerikadeutscher Volksbund formed in 1936, he styled himself American Fuehrer. To emphasize his title's status, Kuhn mimicked Hitler in his speeches and appearance. Despite his eccentric attitude, Kuhn did provide an initial period of stability to the Bund since the organization found financial backing and launched a publicity campaign targeting supporters of fascism in the United States. A carefully crafted image Kuhn had reproduced of meeting with Hitler in Germany during the 1936 Olympics bolstered this campaign. However, Kuhn was among thousands of visitors who exchanged small talk with the Fuehrer as he showed off Nazi Germany to the world. Nevertheless, the photograph and a generic comment from Hitler to keep up the good work in the United States were repackaged as an official endorsement of Kuhn and the Bund.[46]

Just as the Friends of New Germany transitioned into the German-American Bund, so too did local members make the switch in allegiance. While Fritz Kuhn became the so-called American Fuehrer, Anton Kessler rose to similar stature among Missouri Bundists who had started out in the Friends of New Germany, and much like Kuhn, Kessler frequently wore uniforms to local events to stand out. Kessler was born in Wiesbaden, Germany, in 1895 and immigrated to the United States in 1910. Not long after that, he made his new home in St. Louis, where he worked as a painter and interior decorator during the 1920s and 1930s. Kessler's naturalization status in the United States was questioned while he was a member of the Bund. Sources confided that he had applied for full citizenship twice since moving to St. Louis, but neither time completed the paperwork. Having lived in St. Louis for more than twenty years by the 1930s, Kessler was well connected with the city's various German societies. Eager to join the original Friends of New Germany, Kessler eventually transitioned into the German-American Bund by the mid- to late 1930s, becoming leader of the local chapter of the Ordnungs Dienst, a militant police force within the Bund that wore uniforms not unlike the German SS.[47]

Not simply interested in continuing their work just in St. Louis, local Nazi sympathizers soon set up two recreation and educational facilities outside of the city. Along the Meramec River south of St. Louis, the German-American Bund bought a two-story clubhouse called Camp Deutsch Horst in 1937 as a weekend gathering place for members and their families. The next summer, a youth camp was established near Stanton, Missouri, roughly sixty miles from St. Louis, by the German-American Commercial League. The camp started with little fanfare, but when neighbors claimed a Nazi flag was flown over the grounds and a reporter for the *St. Louis Post-Dispatch* was turned away at the gate, the facility gained widespread publicity, causing officials to clarify that it was intended as a retreat for children learning German heritage and cultural traditions. Nevertheless, rumors continued about the small camp surrounded by a barbed-wire fence and adorned with German insignia in the middle of the Missouri Ozarks. Despite these efforts to spread beyond the boundaries of St. Louis, there is little evidence to suggest that the Missouri Bund had any semblance of additional activity outside the city.[48]

While Fritz Kuhn had hoped to grow the German-American Bund off of the publicity surrounding his meeting and photo with Hitler, the following years saw decline. Continuing congressional investigations into state and national leaders and a deteriorating diplomatic relationship between Germany and the United States convinced many German nationals among the ranks to leave for the fatherland. Additionally, as the Dies Committee and the House Un-American Activities Committee turned up more and more damning and, at times, sensational, information about the inner workings of Nazi-sympathetic groups in the United States, events in Germany also soured many Americans against the Bund. After Kristallnacht, a series of violent riots across Germany that targeted Jewish businesses, schools, and synagogues in November 1938, the American press portrayed Nazism with increasing hostility.[49]

Hoping to head off what seemed like a growing certainty, Fritz Kuhn traveled back to Germany in a last-ditch effort to gain the authorization and endorsement he desperately sought. He returned disappointed and soon took his frustrations out via the lecture circuit and Bund publications with material that grew increasingly anti-Semitic. As internal rumors spread that the Bund's finances were grossly mismanaged, Kuhn tried to stabilize the failing organization by reaching out to other right-wing organizations in the hopes of drawing in new support and

256   Chapter Seven

members, including the Friends of Progress, a California-based isola-tionist group led by Robert Noble and Ellis Jones, as well as the Father Charles Coughlin–inspired Christian Front. In a particularly daring decision, Bund members in New Jersey invited local Klansmen to attend events at Camp Nordland. Initially, Klan members, particularly in the South, were suspicious of the Bund's ambitions, but members in New Jersey soon flocked to Camp Nordland. The relationship was brief. After the appearance of Klansmen alongside uniformed Bund members drew negative publicity in the press, Imperial Wizard Colescott and the *Fiery Cross* denounced the Bund.[50]

One of the most notable groups to link up with the Bund, as well as with former members of the Friends of New Germany, was William Dudley Pelley's Silver Legion, better known as the Silver Shirts.[51] Born the son of a Southern Methodist minister in 1890, Pelley eschewed his New England upbringing for the life of a journalist and screenwriter. However, he later grew disillusioned with the glitz and glamour of Hollywood. His youthful experiences embittered him, and he soon developed strong opposition to communism as well as what he saw as Jewish influence in Hollywood. With Hitler's rise to power in Germany, Pelley sought to start his own movement centered on spiritualism and fascism. He called this movement the Silver Legion, and his recruits, donning uniforms reminiscent of Hitler's Brown Shirts and Benito Mussolini's Black Shirts, soon numbered in the thousands, earning the name Silver Shirts. Pelley traveled the country lecturing Americans about the dangers of Franklin Roosevelt's New Deal. Much like other fascist groups of the era, Pelley's Silver Legion cloaked itself in anticommunism, anti-Semitism, and isolationism. He also ran for president in a direct, if long-shot, challenge to Roosevelt under the banner of his self-created Christian Party.[52]

In a final act to resurrect the Bund and show Americans and Germans that he was the American Fuehrer, Fritz Kuhn planned a large rally at New York's Madison Square Garden. Aware that the organization's fi-nances could probably not handle the sheer expense of such an event, Kuhn initially hoped that New York City leaders would shut the rally down, thus giving him a financial out and a recruiting cry of censorship. Instead, the rally proceeded with city officials citing Kuhn's freedom of

"The Spirit of the Klan" 257

speech and their hope that the event would bolster calls for further crackdowns against the Bund. Positioned in the rear of the stage, a giant image of George Washington gazed down upon the swastika-draped festivities as Kuhn and others touted Hitler and Nazi Germany and pledged hope for similar actions in the United States. Kuhn may have received the headlines he wanted from the rally, including when a Jewish protester

FIGURE 18. Editorial cartoon by Daniel Fitzpatrick titled *The Bund-Klan Axis* depicting the alleged alliance between the Ku Klux Klan and the German-American Bund, 1939. Courtesy of the St. Louis Post-Dispatch Editorial Cartoon Collection (P0077). The State Historical Society of Missouri.

258 Chapter Seven

rushed the stage, but the misappropriation of event funds would be the last nail in the Bund's coffin. In late 1939, Kuhn was found guilty of forgery and larceny. The Bund sputtered on as he sat in prison, but it was never the same.[53]

Just as the German-American Bund declined nationwide, so did its influence in St. Louis wane. At the end of 1937, grand plans were made for St. Louis to host the convention for midwestern chapters of the Bund featuring Fritz Kuhn as the main speaker. After a series of protests and negative publicity, the convention was moved from the German House, but after other venues refused to accommodate the event, it was canceled. Not long after the cancellation, Anton Kessler departed Missouri for a lengthy stay in Germany. When he returned in the winter of 1939, conditions had deteriorated further due to continuing protests against the group. The local Bund secured a visit from Fritz Kuhn in the summer of 1939, but Kuhn's scandals, combined with a targeted opposition campaign to out members and get them fired from their jobs, sealed the fate of the St. Louis group.[54]

As the propaganda distributed by pro-Nazi organizations slowly filtered through the American landscape in the 1930s, it found receptive audiences beyond the meetings and rallies of groups like the Friends of New Germany, German-American Bund, Silver Legion, Christian Front, and the Ku Klux Klan. Though he publicly admitted that he strongly detested the Bund, Charles Coughlin nevertheless embraced some of the group's main arguments concerning economics, politics, and global affairs. Born in Hamilton, Ontario, Canada, in 1891 to a devout Catholic family, Coughlin was inspired by his mother to enter the ministry. He was ordained a priest in 1916, but after developing concerns over the restructuring of the Basilian Fathers, Coughlin relocated to a parish in the Archdiocese of Detroit in the 1920s. By 1926, he had made a home in the newly formed Shrine of the Little Flower in Michigan. In what would eventually become his trademark, Coughlin began to broadcast his sermons from a local radio station by the late 1920s, partially to help secure funding for his church's loans. After a cross burning at the site of his church in 1926, Coughlin increasingly used his amplified pulpit to rally fellow anti-Klan activists to defeat the Invisible Empire.[55]

"The Spirit of the Klan"   259

Coughlin's sermons gained a national following after CBS opted to distribute the radio show, but this affiliation was short-lived due to the divisive nature of his topics. Nevertheless, Coughlin soldiered on with his own financed radio program that reached millions of people via more than fifty affiliates by the end of the 1930s. Initially devoting his sermons to issues concerning Catholics, particularly denouncements of the Klan, Coughlin's weekly broadcasts soon morphed into social and political commentaries. In addition to critiquing Prohibition, communism, and free-market capitalism, Coughlin soon turned his attention to the presidency of Franklin Roosevelt. At first, Coughlin rallied to the president as a savior during the Great Depression. Yet by 1934, when Roosevelt ignored Coughlin's advice and influence, he turned against him and shifted further and further to the right of the political spectrum.[56]

While distancing himself from Roosevelt, Coughlin nevertheless found a sizable population of adoring supporters in Missouri thanks to radio stations like WHB in Kansas City as well as KSD and the far-reaching KMOX in St. Louis airing Coughlin's broadcast weekly starting in the 1930s.[57] In a letter to the editor in the *St. Louis Post-Dispatch*, an Edina, Missouri, resident applauded Coughlin as someone with "the courage to present facts as they are, the Americanism to lift up his mighty voice in defense of the humble citizens who are oppressed by privilege and by greed, and the Christianity to bring the trust of the people back to God."[58] The *St. Louis Western Watchman* echoed these sentiments noting, that the priest "displays breathtaking courage" in his work to "tear the mask from the pious hypocrite."[59] Even as Coughlin began to critique Roosevelt's New Deal through his National Union for Social Justice, the *Tri-City Independent* found that local residents responded favorably to the pastor's radio sermons, noting that "Festus [Missouri] will be ably represented in the National Union for Social Justice."[60] Not long after, several branches of the National Union for Social Justice were established in Missouri.[61]

In this early period, however, Coughlin was not without his controversies. Initially celebrated as a religious leader who stood up for the downtrodden during the Great Depression, Coughlin's comments on the Roosevelt administration and global affairs soon brought criticism. As Adolf Hitler gained power in Germany and news reports circulated of

260   Chapter Seven

crackdowns on Jews, Coughlin denounced these Nazi policies while also tying them to other autocratic governments, including the Soviet Union and Mexico. In each case, Coughlin noted the plight of Catholics in these locations as being comparable to the Jews in Nazi Germany. This stance was not much different from the editorial sections of prominent Catholic newspapers in Missouri at the time, but as Coughlin's commentaries began to display elements of anti-Semitism, criticism of the popular priest soon followed.[62] While still applauding Coughlin for discussing the struggle of Jews in Germany in his broadcasts, the *Kansas City Jewish Chronicle* nevertheless could not understand "how any Catholic lay or clerical leader in America could even conceive of utilizing the vicious weapon of race or religious prejudice to gain any advantage, moral or material; for that poisonous weapon has been just as damaging to the Catholic in America as it has been to the Jew."[63]

Given the charges of anti-Semitism directed at Charles Coughlin, one of his strongest advocates in St. Louis was an unlikely source. Rabbi Ferdinand Isserman, a recent transplant from Canada, found Coughlin's calls for social reform admirable. Born in Antwerp, Belgium, in 1898, Isserman immigrated with his family to the United States when he was eight and settled in Newark, New Jersey. In 1914, he enrolled at Hebrew Union College in Ohio and received a bachelor's degree. A few years later, he completed his studies at the University of Cincinnati for a second bachelor's degree. He was ordained as a rabbi in 1922 and initially served as assistant rabbi at Rodeph Shalom Congregation in Philadelphia. While there, he earned a master's degree from the University of Pennsylvania. After spending four years at Toronto Hebrew Congregation, Isserman moved to St. Louis in 1929 to serve as rabbi at Temple Israel. Isserman remained at Temple Israel for the next thirty-four years.[64]

Though Coughlin's broadcasts could be found on local radio stations, Isserman used his sermons and editorial role in the *Modern View*, a local Jewish newspaper, to introduce St. Louisans to the celebrity pastor. By the mid-1930s, he devoted multiple sermons to modern interpretations of Coughlin, such as "Is the Radio Pulpit of Father Coughlin an Asset or a Liability to Religion?" Isserman also critiqued what he saw as "fascist jitters" in the United States, including those who claimed that Roosevelt or Coughlin would soon wield dictatorial power.[65] Though he never

FIGURE 19. Ferdinand Isserman, date unknown. Courtesy of Metropolitan Church Federation Records (S0618). The State Historical Society of Missouri.

officially joined Coughlin's National Union for Social Justice, Isserman did defend the organization's aims, including delivering an address at a meeting in Detroit in 1935.[66] After Isserman's show of support, Coughlin thanked him, noting that "your excellent address on the fundamental principles of social justice accomplished much in reducing the criticisms of those who consistently have been trying to build up a spirit of antipathy between the members of your race and religion and myself."[67] In response, Isserman reprinted excerpts from his correspondence with Coughlin in the *Modern View* to show that "Father Coughlin not only personally promised me to fight any attempt to foster antisemitism in America, but that without hesitancy he put that promise in writing."[68]

While the basis for promoting Isserman's speech at a meeting of the National Union for Social Justice was to defend Coughlin against growing claims of anti-Semitism, critics increasingly denounced his fierce opposition to Roosevelt's New Deal policies as well as his rabid isolationism and overt sympathy for fascism. Instead of aligning with New Deal liberals, Coughlin seemingly made a home among conservatives, isolationists, and elements of the Far Right.[69] In the months leading up to Isserman's address, however, the *Modern View* rarely published articles or commentaries critical of Coughlin.[70] Across the state, the *Kansas City Jewish Chronicle* was perplexed by Isserman's defense of a man with a "palpable anti-semitic attitude." Noting Coughlin's shift from a Klan fighter to an anti-Semite, the newspaper wondered what had happened to the priest given that "he certainly is familiar with the history of the Know-nothing and the A.P.A. movements in former times and of the Ku Klux Klan and the Black Legion in the present."[71]

By 1936, Coughlin had reached the zenith of his power and moved quickly to capitalize on it to unseat Franklin Roosevelt from the White House. To do so, Coughlin aligned with several prominent anti–New Dealers to spearhead a political movement under the banner of the Union Party. In addition to Coughlinites, the Union Party also contained supporters of Francis Townsend's old-age pension plan that would later morph into Social Security as well as Gerald L. K. Smith's faction of Huey Long's Share Our Wealth campaign, which had fizzled after Long's assassination in 1935. While Coughlin, Townsend, and Smith each saw themselves as the rightful heir to the Union Party's nomination, they also realized how the ascension of one might alienate the others. To keep the coalition together, party leaders selected William Lemke, a Republican congressman from North Dakota, as their presidential candidate. From the start, however, the campaign was doomed, primarily because most anti–New Dealers still favored their traditional political parties over a third-party movement. Additionally, as the campaign progressed, both Coughlin's and Smith's public comments turned increasingly anti-Semitic. Lemke collected nearly nine hundred thousand votes but finished a distant third to Roosevelt and Republican candidate Alf Landon.[72]

The charges of anti-Semitism leveled against Coughlin prior to the formation of the Union Party increased following the 1936 presidential campaign. By 1938, Coughlin's radio broadcasts regularly denounced Roosevelt in favor of political leaders like Hitler and Mussolini. That same year, his *Social Justice* publication reprinted "The Protocols of the Elders of Zion," an anti-Semitic text that had been previously distributed through Henry Ford's *Dearborn Independent*. Finally, his words over the air and in print inspired a group made up largely of Catholics called the Christian Front to distribute propaganda, boycott Jewish businesses,

"The Spirit of the Klan"   263

and closely align with other right-wing groups in the region, including the German-American Bund. In the aftermath of Kristallnacht in November 1938, Coughlin's radio address downplayed what had occurred to the Jewish population in Nazi Germany and likened it to earlier persecution of Catholics and Christians under communist governments.[73] Shocked by Coughlin's comments, the *Kansas City Jewish Chronicle* called on Catholic leaders to intervene because "every Catholic ought to know that Coughlin is brandishing a torch that may well fire the flames of a much more devastating anti-Catholic hatred than can be visited upon the lesser minority of Jews."[74]

Not long after his Kristallnacht broadcasts, Coughlin's radio empire began to unravel. Several radio stations cut his programming or asked for advance copies of scripts. The federal government also began to issue or deny permits to radio stations based on content. The denial of permits related to Coughlin programming temporarily removed him from the air. Additionally, internal debates within the Catholic Church finally turned against him. Coughlin long had had the support of Bishop Michael Gallagher, his direct superior, and thus church officials could put pressure on the bishop, but only Gallagher could remove Coughlin. Gallagher held firm in his support for Coughlin. However, after Gallagher's death in 1937, a new superior, Bishop Edward Mooney, was less than enthusiastic. Even Pope Pius XI sent representatives to the United States to inquire about what could be done regarding Coughlin. In 1940, with Europe engulfed in World War II and Coughlin calling on listeners to chart a path of isolationism, the radio priest was removed from the airwaves due to public pressure and the decision by the National Association of Broadcasters to enforce a new code regulating limits on airtime to controversial figures.[75] With Coughlin's tenure ending, the *Modern View* celebrated: "We know the stock arguments in advance—The Jews, Communists, Reds, Bolsheviks, Atheists, International Bankers, C.I.O., A.F.L. and the New Deal were the cause of it all! However we believe that the Detroit radio priest has cried wolf once too often and the public will no longer be fooled by the smoke screen which he sets up to cover the fact that he has done more to inflame passions and prejudices, set man against man, and religion against religion, than any living human being, not excluding Adolf Hitler."[76]

264   Chapter Seven

Much like the internal debates among Catholic leaders on how best
to rein in Coughlin's broadcasts without causing a schism within the
church, so too did the Missouri Catholic press respond with caution
over the matter. As Coughlin slipped deeper and deeper into fascism
and anti-Semitism, the *St. Joseph Catholic Tribune* and the *Kansas City
Catholic Register* continued to reprint national articles about Coughlin
but offered no serious critiques in their editorial pages. Such a policy
was most likely to keep in step with national Catholic publications, such
as the Knights of Columbus's *Columbia*, which scholar Christopher
Kauffman notes never spoke out in favor or against Coughlin and remained "entirely aloof" on the subject during the 1930s.[77] However, there
were notable exceptions. When Ray E. Krings, a St. Louisan involved
with the Federation of Catholic Alumni against Communism, Fascism,
and Nazi-ism, discovered that a local branch of the National Union for
Social Justice sold copies of "The Protocols of the Elders of Zion" at one
of their events, he wrote to Coughlin, warning, "Failure on your part to
publicly condemn this disparagement of Jews as Jews must, of necessity,
mean a parting of the ways between you and thinking individuals who, in
the past, have been sympathetic to your cause."[78]

While the Catholic press may have hesitated to denounce Coughlin,
Ferdinand Isserman's support deteriorated quickly in the latter half of
the 1930s. Though he had appeared alongside Coughlin at the National
Union for Social Justice rally in Detroit in 1935, Isserman grew increasingly wary of the relationship. Noting that "many of our friends have
become of the opinion that because Father Coughlin no longer enters
their homes via the radio that he is entering no home and influencing no
one," Isserman warned that efforts to curtail the radio broadcasts must
continue because "Father Coughlin has hundreds of thousands of listeners. Most of them are decent, kindly, fair-minded, perhaps, suffering
Americans who believe in fair play. If week after week, he pours the vials
of his vitriolic abuse upon Jews with all the eloquence and imagery at
his command; if week after week, Jews remain silent and do not answer
these spurious arguments, Jews stand condemned by default."[79] To this
end, Isserman and the *Modern View* touted efforts by local organizations
to distribute pamphlets on Coughlin, including *Father Coughlin, His
Facts and Arguments* and *Father Coughlin, Priest and Politician.*[80] Isserman

also delivered his own thoughts on the matter in a sermon titled, "What Should Jews Do about Father Coughlin?"[81]

Though Isserman may have been receptive to Father Coughlin initially, he never wavered from his concern and opposition to the Nazi seizure of power in Germany. Like other rabbis in St. Louis, Isserman used his pulpit as well as the editorial page of the *Modern View* to speak out regarding Nazism.[82] As Coughlin's reign over the radio airwaves came to an end and Hitler's war machine spread out across Europe, the *Modern View* reminded, "If our readers sometimes become impatient with our reiteration of articles on the deeds of these two gentlemen, let them remember that we are just as weary of commenting on the subjects as they are reading about them. But so long as Hitler, Coughlin, et al, mold world affairs and public opinion as they do by their acts and utterances, so long will the 'Modern View' continue to comment on their activities."[83]

Isserman also made three heralded trips to Germany in 1933, 1935, and 1937 to see firsthand the plight of Jews in Europe and subsequently spoke on and published accounts of his visits. In 1933's *Sentenced to Death!* Isserman argued that there was no hope for Jews under Nazi rule in Germany, and soon after returning to the United States, he called on St. Louis Jews to locate and identify Nazi-sympathetic activities in the city, particularly those associated with the Friends of New Germany and the German-American Bund.[84] While his call to action was met with support, Isserman also had to deal with internal factions within various Jewish organizations regarding how to respond to fascism. Though all groups were in favor of shutting down the distribution of Nazi propaganda, the American Jewish Committee balked at plans for more direct action outlined by the American Jewish Congress, Jewish War Veterans, B'nai B'rith, and the Anti-Defamation League, including targeted boycotts of German goods and businesses. Isserman was no doubt aware of earlier failed attempts to unite these various Jewish groups together under one banner, yet he supported contemporary efforts to create the Jewish Coordinating Council and the St. Louis Council for American Democracy.[85]

The Jewish Coordinating Council was formed in 1938 and brought together the previously mentioned groups as well as the Jewish Federation, Anti-Nazi League, Vaad Hoir, and Zionist Organization. The Jewish

266   Chapter Seven

Coordinating Council was led by Samuel Sievers, a local attorney and member of B'nai B'rith who also served as a field representative for the Anti-Defamation League. Originally from St. Louis, Sievers knew the city well and was primarily responsible for investigating local cases of anti-Semitism dating back to the efforts of the Klan during the 1920s. Seeking to target the largest contingent of Nazi sympathizers, the Jewish Coordinating Council rallied around efforts to stop the German-American Bund in St. Louis. In doing so, it created a speakers bureau to educate the masses about the dangers of fascism and Nazism, especially the views espoused by the Bund. Additionally, with Father Coughlin's shift into outright anti-Semitism, the Jewish Coordinating Council also spoke out against the radio priest.[86] In 1945, members of the Jewish Coordinating Council voted to change the organization's name to the Jewish Community Relations Council to reflect its commitment to promote education and interracial understanding.[87]

Formed a year prior to the Jewish Coordinating Council, the St. Louis Council for American Democracy was the brainchild of several local religious leaders, including Isserman and Rev. Dr. Truman B. Douglass, an Iowa-born minister at Pilgrim Congregational Church. In October 1937, Douglass's pastoral study at the Pilgrim Congregational Church became the organization's founding headquarters as members of the American Legion, Veterans of Foreign Wars (VFW), Congress of Industrial Organizations (CIO), Urban League, German Liberty Union, and American League against War and Fascism met to discuss the upcoming midwestern convention of the German-American Bund in St. Louis. The group initially outlined plans for a brief time line that would solely focus on protesting the Bund's planned convention. To this end, the council issued a resolution calling on Mayor Bernard Dickmann to shut down any public parade conducted by the Bund during the convention. While the veterans groups within the council feared riots breaking out along the parade route, Isserman voiced his opposition to the plan, arguing that such actions would be "using the methods of Fascism in a democracy."[88]

Almost immediately, however, the St. Louis Council for American Democracy had to fend off accusations that it was a front for communist sympathizers. The local Daughters of the American Revolution asked council leaders how many "reds" it had within its membership.[89] Anton

Kessler found the group to be composed of "patriotic, loyal organizations that have been poisoned against us by the press."[90] To dissuade fears, Douglass invited various German societies in the city to join the council's ranks and participate in protests against the Bund, citing that the group "is in no sense an anti-foreign movement."[91] The council's relationship with the German societies was tenuous, as many of these groups blamed the organization for smaller crowds at German Day festivities due to protests.[92] Likewise, the council made major headlines when it called on Secretary of State Cordell Hull to investigate the German youth camp at Stanton, Missouri.[93]

Though the Bund ultimately decided not to hold its midwestern convention in St. Louis, the council continued its planned counterprotest at the downtown armory. A crowd of nearly two thousand gathered to hear a range of speakers denounce the Bund and fascist elements within the United States. Applauding the activism of St. Louis residents, Paul Hoegen, president of the German Press Club, told the assembled masses that "it is to our credit that [the Bund] hasn't made much headway here, despite the large German population." Noting that political and social opinions varied among attendees, Rev. George M. Gibson of Webster Groves's First Congregational Church nevertheless felt that "we believe in American democracy, with its freedom, rather than the totalitarian state." Yet Gibson also warned listeners to consider the hysteria that had befallen the nation in the wake of World War I and advised them not to become anti-German or repeat the earlier "post-war red-hunts."[94]

The November 1937 armory rally served as a high-water mark for anti-Nazi and anti-Bund activity in St. Louis. Even the organizers of the Council for American Democracy admitted that though the group's rallies brought together the "blue and khaki overseas caps of the veterans' organizations . . . many of the city's outstanding liberals, some members of the Socialist party, a few Communists, and a few members of the Volksbund," it was only meant to be a temporary organization.[95] Once the Bund canceled the midwestern convention, it set off a chain of events— many of which were influenced by opposition protests—that marked the death knell of the Bund. The Council for American Democracy picketed alongside the CIO and VFW outside of a Bund event in March 1938, but soon after, activity went dormant as local Bund leaders, including

Anton Kessler, departed the city for Germany. In 1939, an investigation by the Department of Justice found Bund activity minimal in Missouri, with only a few dozen members in St. Louis. A few months later, in a dramatic display analogous to the status of the Missouri Bund, Camp Deutsch Horst, the group's recreational clubhouse on the Meramec River, burned down after unknown assailants set fire to the building.[96]

While the Missouri Bund certainly faced sizable opposition from St. Louis residents affiliated with the Council for American Democracy, Jewish Coordinating Council, and other local groups, a former St. Louisan spent the latter half of the 1930s slowly building up his own anti-Nazi organization in Kansas City. Born in Lincoln County in 1885, Leon Milton Birkhead grew up on a farm near Winfield, Missouri, fifty miles northwest of St. Louis. At the turn of the twentieth century, Birkhead enrolled at McKendree College before eventually becoming a Methodist minister in St. Louis. Realizing that his liberal views were not widely shared within the Methodist Church, including his support for women's suffrage and his opposition to Prohibition, Birkhead switched denominations around 1917 to the Unitarian Church. This move brought him first to Wichita before settling in Kansas City, where he helped establish All Souls Unitarian Church, also known as the Liberal Center. Though he developed a faithful following, Birkhead's early years in Kansas City were not without controversy. He famously supported Clarence Darrow's cross-examination of William Jennings Bryan during the 1925 Scopes Trial. Sinclair Lewis also consulted Birkhead for Lewis's 1927 novel that satirized evangelicalism, *Elmer Gantry*. In addition to his liberal views, he was also known for opening the doors of the church to attendees of all backgrounds, including racially and religiously integrated services. He drew further ire for his denouncements of the political machine of Tom Pendergast. While his opposition to Pendergast was potentially rooted in his support for Republicans, he eventually lost faith in the Grand Old Party after witnessing the anti-Catholicism directed at presidential candidate Al Smith.[97] In reflecting on Birkhead's tumultuous 1920s, the *St. Louis Post-Dispatch* concluded, "Having been charged with being a blue-nosed Puritan, a Red, a rumpot, an atheist, an advocate of free love, he was now to hear himself denounced as a puppet of the pope."[98]

FIGURE 20. Leon Birkhead, date unknown. Courtesy of Leon Milton Birkhead Papers (K0280). The State Historical Society of Missouri.

For much of his ministerial career, Birkhead was, as the *Post-Dispatch* dubbed him, "A Lifelong Fighter Against Oppression."[99] Having opened his church to members of all faiths, it is not surprising that Birkhead challenged those who preached religious intolerance. During the 1920s, when the Ku Klux Klan arrived in Kansas City, Birkhead devoted several sermons to what he saw as reactionaries in religion. Singling out the Klan by name, Birkhead referred to the group's tenets as "un-American, it is bigotry, it is littleness to oppose any religious organization in America. Instead of being 100 percent American it is not 1 percent American."[100] Yet in seeking to tamp down bigotry, he wrote to fellow community leaders in Kansas City in 1923, inquiring if they might reach out to various groups to join together for a talking session about their differences: "Do you think it would be possible to get together representatives of the Jewish people and some of those who have been carrying on anti-Jewish propaganda, the Catholics, the Ku Klux Klan, the Fundamentalists and the Liberals of the Protestant groups?"[101]

Birkhead's plans for unity and understanding met with mixed results, and by the early 1930s, he turned his attention to a new threat on the

270 Chapter Seven

horizon. During a trip to Germany in 1931, Birkhead took note of growing Nazi sentiments. He returned to Kansas City concerned but cautious and slowly began collecting materials related to fascism. Soon after Hitler came to power in 1933, Birkhead's lectures and sermons shifted to the growing dangers of Nazi propaganda circulating in the United States. He also surveyed the influence of controversial figures, such as Huey Long, Charles Coughlin, and Gerald B. Winrod, a notorious anti-Semitic evangelist from Kansas dubbed the "Jayhawk Nazi." In 1935, Birkhead made a second trip to Germany. This time, his previous concerns about fascism were verified. Meeting with Paul Wurm, who was an editor of the German anti-Semitic newspaper *Der Stürmer* and close associate of Julius Streicher, Birkhead was informed of various Nazi sympathizers in the United States who eagerly distributed and promoted Nazi propaganda. Birkhead quickly wired his findings back to the United States, where his information appeared in several national newspapers.[102]

Convinced more than ever of the danger of what he had previously called "Hitlerism in America," Birkhead returned from Germany in 1935 to establish a new organization aimed at destroying homegrown fascism. This new group was called the Friends of Democracy and, for most of its existence, was headquartered in Kansas City. Initially, his staff collected pamphlets and publications of fascist propaganda, which Birkhead displayed on the lecture circuit and in congressional hearings. Not satisfied with just newspaper clippings, Birkhead quickly went to work interviewing the individuals Paul Wurm had identified as Nazi sympathizers in the United States. Finally, after promoting the need to defeat fascists in the United States, Birkhead built Friends of Democracy into a sizable fighting force. During the latter half of 1936, newspapers such as the *Kansas City Jewish Chronicle* carried Birkhead's multiple-part series on what he perceived as threats within the United States titled "Fascism at Our Gates."[103] When Gerald B. Winrod ran for Congress in 1938, Birkhead rallied the group toward his eventual defeat. After Charles Coughlin's anti-Semitic remarks culminated in his fiery rhetoric following Kristallnacht, Birkhead called the radio priest a demagogue and pressured Catholic officials to remove him from the airwaves. In *The Attack on Democracy*, published in 1939 by the Institute for Propaganda Analysis, Birkhead warned readers about nearly eight hundred fascist

"The Spirit of the Klan"	271

organizations in the United States ranging from those associated with Winrod and Coughlin to George Deatherage's Knights of the White Camelia, William Dudley Pelley's Silver Shirts, and Fritz Kuhn's German-American Bund.[104]

By 1939, though he had played a part in successfully defeating the threats of men like Winrod and Coughlin, Birkhead decided that he could no longer split his time between Friends of Democracy and All Souls Unitarian Church. Soon after, he retired from the pulpit and devoted himself exclusively to fighting fascism. Having grown Friends of Democracy from a small Kansas City–based group to a national organization with a membership estimated at roughly ten thousand, including a sizable women's division, Birkhead decided to depart his midwestern home of the last twenty-two years for the strategically located Friends of Democracy branch office in New York. From there, he continued to warn against not only the continuing threat of fascism but also what he interpreted as a growing merger between fascist groups and isolationists, particularly the America First Committee and its chief spokesperson, Charles Lindbergh. When the America First movement collapsed after the bombing of Pearl Harbor in 1941, Friends of Democracy kept an anxious watch regarding what it hoped would be a dual victory over fascism at home and abroad.[105]

During the postwar years, Birkhead and Friends of Democracy turned their attention to Cold Warriors, who rabidly denounced communism and continued to monitor the policies previously pursued by isolationist and fascistic groups during the Great Depression.[106] At the same time, Birkhead also issued a stark warning regarding the future: "Friends of Democracy knows of at least 100 instances of Klan cross burnings in different parts of the country."[107] When asked who or what was responsible for the Klan's revival, Birkhead pointed to increasing racial tensions following the war that were fed by figures like Eugene Talmadge, the multiterm segregationist governor of Georgia, and Gerald L. K. Smith, a Wisconsin-born minister who spent time in Indiana and Louisiana before joining the ranks of Huey Long's Share Our Wealth campaign. Noting that Talmadge and Smith took advantage of racial tensions, Birkhead called on their opponents to protest against both but directed particular scorn for Smith: "Some argue that the best way to get rid of

272 Chapter Seven

Smith is to ignore him by giving him 'thunderous silence.' But this policy is wrong. H. L. Mencken calls Smith the great living rabble-rouser. To oppose him gives him temporary publicity, but unfavorable publicity hurts him."[108]

The Gerald L. K. Smith that Birkhead was so concerned about in 1946 was a more dynamic but no less charismatic figure than the man who first gained publicity as a minister in Shreveport, Louisiana. Though the *St. Louis Argus* later dubbed him Gerald "KKK" Smith, he initially denied any direct connection to the Invisible Empire as he rose to prominence as a Disciples of Christ minister in the Klan hotbed of 1920s Indiana.[109] After completing his coursework at Valparaiso University, Smith pastored in Wisconsin and Indiana but eventually moved to Shreveport at the end of the 1920s. While in Louisiana, Smith met and became closely aligned with Governor Huey P. Long, though his connections to the Kingfish did not sit well with some in his congregation, and he was forced to resign from his pastorate by 1933. Soon after, he fully embraced Long's vision for political realignment and became a lead campaigner for the governor's Share Our Wealth program. When Long was assassinated in 1935, Smith's influence within his mentor's political apparatus quickly vanished. He tried briefly to become the new leader of the Share Our Wealth movement, but without Huey Long, the momentum stalled.[110]

As war in Europe and Asia loomed on the horizon during the 1930s, Smith hitched his wagon to a seemingly endless list of isolationists and anti–New Dealers, each vying to unseat Franklin Roosevelt, including Eugene Talmadge, Francis Townsend, Charles Coughlin, and William Lemke. Smith rallied his supporters around the Union Party in 1936, but after suffering a sizable defeat to Roosevelt in that year's election, the political movement dissolved. Smith also flirted with the idea of joining William Dudley Pelley's Silver Legion, and evidence suggests that he did appear alongside Silver Shirt members at rallies. Finally, Smith tried to merge his isolationist movement, later called the Christian Nationalist Crusade, with the budding America First Committee. When his efforts failed, and the America First Committee diminished in influence after Pearl Harbor, Smith co-opted the name and created the America First Party in 1943. Critics later charged that Smith set up his America First Party in Michigan to attract former Coughlinites, Klansmen, and Black Legion members. Within a year of the party's establishment, Smith

"The Spirit of the Klan"   273

quickly looked for new cities in which to rally support for his anticommunist and political ambitions, with St. Louis soon becoming a hotbed of activity.[111]

Don Lohbeck led Gerald L. K. Smith's forays into St. Louis. Born in St. Louis in 1917, Lohbeck was the son of an electrician. By his late teens, Lohbeck was an experienced concert pianist who gave performances across the city. After graduating from Cleveland High School and enrolling in classes at Eastman School of Music in Rochester, New York, and the Chicago Musical College, Lohbeck used his connections with the St. Louis Symphony to book a concert tour in France in 1939. Heralded as a new student of the famed French composer Isidor Philipp, Lohbeck was set to start his tour at the American embassy in France when Germany invaded Poland. The cascading effects of the French-Polish alliance brought about military preparation in France and the cancellation of Lohbeck's scheduled performances. Instead, he assisted the Red Cross with the increasing number of war refugees arriving in France. When he returned to St. Louis several weeks later, deeply impacted by what he had seen on his long trip back to the United States, Lohbeck told the *St. Louis Globe Democrat* that it seemed like "the end of the world," at least for his career aspirations.[112] More than destroying his musical career, World War II also deeply embittered him toward those he saw responsible for the war—communists, autocrats, war profiteers, and Jews. Soon after, Lohbeck drifted into the America First movement and openly expressed his isolationist sentiments. In several letters to the editors of the *St. Louis Post-Dispatch*, he complained about government censorship, called for voters to elect reform candidates to clean up the Missouri General Assembly, and defended the isolationism promoted by Charles Lindbergh.[113]

In 1944, Lohbeck came into the orbit of Gerald L. K. Smith, who needed assistance after his longtime office manager, Bernard Doman, had grown disillusioned with his work and quit. Lohbeck's previous tenure as an organizer for the American First Committee proved lucrative for Smith, as his new assistant had information on thousands of isolationists. At first, Smith put Lohbeck to work as a temporary chairman of efforts to create an America First Party branch in St. Louis.[114] He also slowly transitioned into an editorial role on Smith's *Cross and the Flag*. Founded in 1942, the *Cross and the Flag* was originally intended as a religious

274   Chapter Seven

and isolationist publication. Over time, however, it increasingly became more racist and anti-Semitic, often reprinting speeches, editorials, and articles from other extremist newspapers. In his editorials featured on the last page of each edition, Lohbeck frequently attacked what he perceived to be communist and Jewish influence in global affairs.[115] After William Dudley Pelley was arrested following his release from federal prison, Lohbeck alleged that he was a "victim of New Deal–Zionist vengeance."[116] The publication also frequently expressed opposition to integration due to what it alleged to be ties between civil rights activists and communists and depicted African Americans as uncivilized, lascivious, and animalistic. By the early 1950s, the publication had grown to more than ten thousand subscribers, but it was often deemed too controversial for inclusion on most American newsstands.[117]

Though largely national in focus, the *Cross and the Flag* also devoted extensive coverage to matters specific to St. Louis. When a group of local residents publicly bragged that Smith should be arrested, tried, and executed for treason, the *Cross and the Flag* featured a multipage review of the threat and reminded readers, "The self-respecting white people of America must take steps immediately to safeguard our cities and our Nation against the revolutionary trickery of the Communists, the New Dealers, and the mongrelizers in general."[118] One of its frequent targets through the 1940s and 1950s was Rabbi Ferdinand M. Isserman, whom the publication referred to as a "loud-mouthed enemy of Gerald L. K. Smith and the Christian Nationalist Crusade."[119] In addition to critiquing Isserman for his support of the American Civil Liberties Union and the Civil Rights Congress, and efforts to "force St. Louisans under the yoke of F.E.P.C. [Fair Employment Practices Committee] and race-mixing legislation," most articles connected him to his brother's prior court cases and legal work on behalf of communist groups in New York.[120]

Beyond his work on the editorial page, Lohbeck's grassroots efforts to recruit members to Smith's America First Party had a rocky beginning. Though historian Glen Jeansonne argues that a portion of St. Louis's white working-class residents certainly responded to Smith's views as the city's Black population steadily increased during the Great Depression and Great Migration, opposition to his rallies and speeches, particularly by veterans groups and Jewish organizations, made Lohbeck's work challenging. During a speech in February 1944, Smith was interrupted by Fred Emig, an early supporter of the Council for American Democracy, who inquired why Lohbeck, who was around twenty-six at the time, was not serving in World War II and instead had registered as a conscientious objector.[121] While Smith defended his assistant, the US Army soon sent Lohbeck to a labor camp for conscientious objectors in New York. Lohbeck was able to get classified as unfit to work not long after arriving in camp and returned to St. Louis, but when officials discovered that he went back to the full-time job of managing Smith's affairs and editing the *Cross and the Flag*, he was sent back to New York. Smith and Lohbeck used the situation to justify their claims that the government targeted them.[122]

After the war, Smith began considering plans to move the America First Party's headquarters to St. Louis. Given Don Lohbeck's increasing presence within the organization, the relocation in 1947 is not surprising. Yet despite local support from those connected with Lohbeck, numerous individuals and groups within the city vehemently opposed the plan. When Smith spoke alongside Father Arthur Terminiello, dubbed the Father Coughlin of the South, at Kiel Auditorium in April 1946, a group of World War II veterans crashed the rally and briefly took control of the microphone to denounce the speech. Lohbeck tried to commandeer the PA system to shut down the protest, but the veterans group drowned his voice out with shouts of "draft dodger." Outside, picketers conducted a counterdemonstration and held up signs declaring, "Boycott Hitler Hate Makers" and "Stop the Hiel at Kiel."[123] A month later, when Smith held a national convention of his supporters in the city, four hundred attendees convened inside Kiel Auditorium while more than fifteen hundred protesters listened to Leon M. Birkhead at the neighboring Soldiers Memorial declare, "We can't ignore Smith and hide our heads in the sand. Such methods were unsuccessful against Hitler in Germany."[124] By the end of the summer, as Smith continued to hold rallies in the city, the *St. Louis Argus* as well as members of the NAACP, Jewish Community Relations Council, and various veterans groups banded together to picket his rallies and called on the mayor and Board of Aldermen to shut down future gatherings.[125] When he returned to St. Louis in July 1946, Birkhead surveyed the racial animosity bubbling up in the city alongside

276 Chapter Seven

Smith's rallies and the cross burning at Buder Park and concluded that the examples were more evidence that "the Ku Klux Klan is reviving everywhere in the United States."[126]

While facing heat for expanding his Christian Nationalist Crusade into St. Louis under the direction of Don Lohbeck, Smith also utilized the young organizer as a political operative to gauge interest in nationalist policies in both political parties. Smith lobbied Republicans in 1944 not to support Wendell Wilkie, the party's presidential candidate four years earlier, and threatened to run a nationalist third-party candidate if they did.[127] At the start of the Cold War, Smith dispatched Lohbeck to the Republican and Democratic National Conventions in 1948 and 1952 and even to check in with Dixiecrats at the States' Rights Democratic Convention in Mississippi.[128] When he found few takers, Smith reorganized the America First Party into the Christian Nationalist Party (CNP) and put Lohbeck in charge of making sure the party had candidates on the ballot. Lohbeck chaired the party's 1948 convention in St. Louis, where Smith was nominated for president. The party's platform included pledges to reevaluate the nation's atomic program, establish better relations with Francisco Franco in Spain and Chiang Kai-shek in China, oppose organized labor and its alleged communist ties, take the United States out of the United Nations, and strengthen segregation laws at the federal level. The most controversial plank centered on Smith's plan to deport all noncitizens and nondesirable aliens, particularly Jews, as well as send all African Americans back to Africa with a small stipend.[129] In 1952, Lohbeck made headlines when, to convince Republican delegates to back General Douglas MacArthur, he distributed literature claiming that Dwight D. Eisenhower had substantial Jewish support. After Republicans backed Eisenhower, the Christian Nationalist Party nominated MacArthur as its presidential candidate. MacArthur refused to acknowledge the nomination, and after having his name placed on the ballot in just five states, including Missouri, he collected fewer than 2,000 votes.[130]

With his extensive experience in the political arena, it is not surprising that Lohbeck eventually decided to run for office. Before being sent off to the conscientious-objectors camp at the end of 1944, he filed as a Republican candidate in Missouri's twelfth congressional district, though he finished a distant third in the primary.[131] In 1949, Lohbeck

"The Spirit of the Klan" 277

launched a bid to become mayor of St. Louis, but after the Christian Nationalist Party was barred from the ballot, he unsuccessfully took his appeal to the Supreme Court of Missouri.[132] A year later, under the Christian Nationalist Party banner, Lohbeck lost a long-shot race in Missouri's eleventh congressional district, then lost the subsequent special election for the same district following the death of John B. Sullivan not long after he began his new term.[133] In 1952, as he faced scrutiny for his involvement in distributing Eisenhower anti-Semitic smear literature, Lohbeck announced plans to run for governor. In a campaign that saw more than 1.8 million ballots cast, Lohbeck finished fifth with just under 200 votes.[134]

In addition to his own efforts to gain office, Lohbeck also tried to turn the Christian Nationalist Party into a viable state-level political machine. His efforts were initially blocked by state officials who questioned the intentions and goals of the party. When Lohbeck's bid for mayor was halted in 1949, the CNP ticket also included candidates for alderman and comptroller.[135] Acknowledging that his efforts to win election to Congress in 1950 hinged on whether election officials deemed the CNP legitimate, Lohbeck announced that candidates on the party ticket would enter their respective Republican primaries if need be.[136] After state officials reversed course and allowed the CNP on the ballot, the party ran candidates for US Senate, state auditor, St. Louis collector of revenue, and three state congressional districts.[137] Lohbeck and the CNP's 1950 and 1951 campaigns proved so vitriolic that the Missouri General Assembly debated a bill to ban political parties from the ballot in future elections unless they garnered at least 2 percent of the previous vote total of the gubernatorial race.[138] The bill failed to pass, and Lohbeck unsuccessfully tried his luck in the 1952 governor's race along with CNP candidates Alva Jernigan vying for a seat in Congress, O. M. Tanner seeking to become lieutenant governor, and Christian Frederick running for US Senate.[139]

By the 1950s, the CNP slowly began to fracture as an organization. Smith's stay in Missouri lasted only a few months, and when he departed, he left the headquarters under the direction of his St. Louis staff.[140] In his place, a power struggle developed between local leaders, particularly Lohbeck and John W. Hamilton, another Smith aide. Initially, the two put their differences aside to promote Smith and the

278   Chapter Seven

Christian Nationalist Party. As Lohbeck took on more responsibilities for Smith's national work, Hamilton became the St. Louis chairman of the CNP.[141] The two shared the CNP ticket several times in their bid for political office, but by 1951, Hamilton split from the group. While still frequently identified in the press as a Smith supporter, Hamilton joined Forest W. Wolf, another St. Louis–based former CNP member, to form the Citizens Protective Association, which focused largely on protesting attempts to integrate public facilities in the city.[142] Lohbeck himself was no stranger to segregationist sentiments, as he had actively collected signatures for the Racial Purity Committee for several petitions seeking to stop integration and entrench segregation laws statewide.[143] He also tried to align his faction of the CNP with Harold Loomis Jr. and his Columbians, a Georgia-based white-supremacist organization, though the relationship was brief.[144]

The growing segregationist and white-supremacist sentiments emerging among Smith adherents in St. Louis came to a head when Lohbeck and Hamilton launched their respective political campaigns in 1950. The CNP received negative publicity for circulating a local publication called *Attack!* whose subheading featured the biblical passage: "I come not with Peace, but a Sword." With article titles such as "Is This What You Want in St. Louis" (featuring an image of an interracial group at a party), "Jews against America," and "Keep the Black and White Races Separate," it was not hard for readers to decipher the message within its pages. In his editorial in the November 1, 1950, edition, Lohbeck promised that if elected to Congress, he would "stop the mongrelization of our children . . . expose the Jewish conspiracy to dominate our nation and abolish our Christian faith . . . [and] oppose with all my power the superstate idea of world-government." Below the editorial, Lohbeck touted his anticommunist stance by reprinting a notorious image of him taken a few years prior when he placed hostile signs at the Russian embassy in Washington, DC.[145]

The segregationist stance of Lohbeck, Hamilton, and the CNP contributed to arguably the largest protest against the group. Beyond *Attack!* and its open call for white supremacy, Lohbeck took to the air on radio and television to broadcast his message during his 1950 and 1951 congressional campaigns. As a result, city newspapers were flooded with editorials and letters expressing opposition.[146] The *St. Louis Post-Dispatch*, which owned KSD-TV, defended the station's decision to let Lohbeck speak by pointing to the opportunity being extended to other candidates, but the letters continued.[147] Not long after, the bill to bar fringe political parties from appearing on statewide ballots was debated in the Missouri General Assembly. Considering that the party threatened to be removed from the ballot, the *Columbia Missourian*'s editors wondered aloud who would choose to join such a movement: "That that Christian Nationalist doctrine is suspiciously fascistic, or that its aims are akin to those of the K.K.K. and the Columbians, or that Smith has been proven to be a rabble-rouser of the Father Coughlin stripe does not seem to bother its followers."[148] In surveying the need for action against the Christian Nationalist Crusade, one frustrated St. Louisan lamented that Lohbeck's incendiary oratory "could do more harm in this country than an atomic bomb."[149]

The Christian Nationalist Party ceased operations in Missouri by the mid-1950s, largely due to internal tensions and Lohbeck's split from Smith.[150] Hamilton led the Citizens Protective Association for a few more years before his legal troubles caught up to him and landed him in the penitentiary.[151] In his place, Forest W. Wolf continued the activities of the Citizens Protective Association and its publication, the *White Sentinel*, through the latter half of the 1950s.[152] Having been the local focal point for the Christian Nationalist Crusade for several years, Lohbeck left St. Louis for New Mexico, where he tried to cobble together a career in uranium mining. Governor John Burroughs appointed him chairman of the citizens' state advisory committee on atomic affairs, but accusations regarding his earlier work with Smith led to an investigation for subversive activities.[153] Having spent only a few months in St. Louis, Smith headed west to continue to build up his Christian Nationalist Crusade during the 1950s. In the early 1960s, he moved a portion of his operations to Eureka Springs, Arkansas, roughly ten miles from the Missouri border, and commissioned the construction of both an amphitheater for showings of a recurring passion play as well as a large sculpture of Jesus called Christ of the Ozarks. After he died in 1976, Smith was buried in Eureka Springs.[154]

Contemporary scholars debate how close a relationship existed between Gerald L. K. Smith, the Christian Nationalist Crusade, and the Klan. However, evidence that post–World War II Klansmen in parts of

280   Chapter Seven

the South had previously been followers of Smith makes clear that the beliefs and core goals of both groups, including racial segregation, anti-communism, and anti-Semitism, were closely aligned in this era.[155] This is especially relevant as it relates to Donald Lohbeck. While Lohbeck may have never actively donned the hood and robes of the Klan, his involvement with Smith's Christian Nationalist Crusade kept him and his supporters close to the epicenter of mid-twentieth-century white-supremacist discourse and like-minded organizations. One prime example is the relationship between Lohbeck and prosegregationist groups like the Racial Purity Committee, Citizens Protective Association, and Harold Loomis Jr.'s Columbians.

Another key connection point between Lohbeck, Smith, and the Klan is Wesley Swift, a New Jersey minister who rose to prominence within the Angelus Temple of the well-known evangelist Aimee Semple McPherson. While in California, Swift first heard lectures from Gerald Burton Winrod, who deeply impressed the young preacher with his interpretations of British Israelism. After World War II, Swift founded his own church, later called Church of Jesus Christ-Christian, which focused on Christian Identity theology wherein white Christians, not Jews, are claimed to be the true descendants of the Israelites and thus God's chosen people. Around the same time, Swift became closely involved with the Klan's revival in California.[156] By 1950, Swift shared the stage of the Christian Nationalist convention with Smith and Lohbeck, and the *Cross and the Flag* championed his cause.[157] Among the white-supremacist leaders who later claimed to be influenced by Swift included Oren Petito of the National States' Rights Party, William Potter Gale of Posse Comitatus, and prominent Klan leaders David Duke and Tom Metzger. After Swift died in 1970, his church relocated to Idaho under the leadership of Richard Butler and was renamed Aryan Nations. By the 1980s, the compound at Hayden Lake, Idaho, became a pilgrimage site for various leaders and groups within the growing white-power movement.[158]

As the Depression deepened and war loomed on the horizon, American newspapers of the 1930s and 1940s, as well as what remained of the

"The Spirit of the Klan"   281

earlier anti-Klan coalition, expressed the sentiment that the "spirit of the Klan" existed in various charismatic leaders and organizations who not only built their crusades off of the foundation laid by the 1920s Klan but also kept the ground fertile and well sown for the hooded order and similar groups to sprout up after World War II. While some, particularly Jewish and African American organizations, continued to challenge the hooded order as well as groups they felt embodied the "spirit of the Klan," the actions of many coalition members fell within the parameters of what Leo Ribuffo has dubbed the "Brown Scare," a series of investigations and exposés, from the halls of Congress to American newsrooms, that sought to prove that far-right groups actively attempted to overthrow the US government, and eventually led to several individuals being indicted and facing jail time for what was deemed subversive activities, including William Dudley Pelley and Gerald B. Winrod.[159]

Nevertheless, while Ribuffo's warning about the dynamics of the Brown Scare should be heeded, and later evidence has shown that some of these organizations were in communication with one another but not deeply interconnected, their activities did influence later far-right, anti-Semitic, fascist, and extremist groups in the latter half of the twentieth century, including the Ku Klux Klan, both in ideology as well as in membership. At the same time, there was also a notable shift in the anti-Klan coalition, particularly as it relates to the relationship between white Catholics and various far-right organizations. Catholics and their institutions had a history of supporting elements of anti-Semitism, white supremacy, and segregation, including Luke E. Hart, whom scholar Christopher Kauffman has called "far from an enthusiastic integrationist," and the Knights of Columbus, which dealt with internal and external pressure to enforce an end to segregated councils well into the 1960s.[160] Yet as the Catholic Church, as well as its leaders and parishioners, debated issues such as religious toleration, civil rights, integration, and communism, the outright objection of Catholics to their onetime enemies softened by the mid-twentieth century from animosity to ambivalence. One of the prime examples is Father Charles Coughlin's followers who formed the Christian Front, which aligned with fascist, white supremacist, and anti-Semitic organizations, such as the German-American Bund, at the same time that these groups were courting the Klan.[161] Additionally, C. Daniel Kurts, head of the Christian Front, appeared onstage at the same Christian Nationalist convention that featured Smith, Lohbeck, and Swift.[162] Finally, as white-supremacist leaders seemingly had few quarrels with white Catholics joining their ranks, the National Knights of the Ku Klux Klan voted to accept white Catholics as members in 1974.[163]

EPILOGUE

The chorus of "We Shall Overcome" could be heard echoing from the pews of the historic Eighth and Center Streets Baptist Church. On the evening of April 23, 1982, attendees prepared for the uncertainty that dawn would bring the next day. A few weeks prior, James L. Betts and Mary Carr, St. Louis residents who claimed the titles of grand wizard and grand genie of the New Order, Knights of the Ku Klux Klan, announced plans for a recruiting rally in Mark Twain's boyhood hometown of Hannibal, Missouri. In response, the National Association for the Advancement of Colored People sent national deputy executive director Charles Smith to Missouri. In front of a crowd of roughly two hundred, Reverend Smith preached a message of brotherhood, declaring, "I love every Ku Klux Klansman in the country," but he also warned that "We ain't got time for hate."[1] Joining Smith at the pulpit, Hannibal mayor John Lyng advised those assembled to cooperate with and uplift those around them for the betterment of the community: "If you can do this while the cameras are turned our way, perhaps there can be some benefit in the ordeal that confronts us."[2] Though not in attendance, Stanley Anderman, a representative of the St. Louis Anti-Defamation League advised curiosity seekers and the media to stay away because their presence would only give the Klan more publicity.[3]

Residents of Hannibal were notably uneasy about Betts and Carr's plan to bring carloads of Klan members and supporters to the town of roughly eighteen thousand. A little more than three years earlier, in 1979, the Klan and American Nazi Party had made national headlines when gunshots erupted at a rally in Greensboro, North Carolina, between hooded supporters and protesters connected with the Communist Workers Party. When the dust settled, several attendees were wounded, and five protesters lay dead.[4] To prevent a similar outcome, Mayor Lyng and law-enforcement agencies held planning meetings and attempted to separate the Klan rally from scheduled protest events. Protesters were given Nipper Park, a small park along the banks of the Mississippi River. Betts and Carr's rally was assigned to Clemens Field, a baseball facility a few blocks away that had briefly housed German prisoners of war during World War II. Lyng and law-enforcement officials felt that the walls and fences enclosing Clemens Field would prevent any confrontation.[5]

When the day of the rally dawned, Hannibal was filled with more than one hundred law-enforcement officers, several dozen protesters, a contingent of journalists, and anxious city residents—a sizable crowd for a town with only one known Klansman, a twenty-year-old named Don McLeod who had filed for the rally permit. At the appointed hour, a caravan of vehicles rolled into view. Emerging from their cars, roughly thirty Klan members and supporters headed into Clemens Field. Donning satin robes and armbands featuring swastikas, Klan members distributed flyers and other paraphernalia while speakers prepared their remarks.[6] Betts later explained to the press that he selected Hannibal for the rally because "in Hannibal, they have no way now to help white people, no organization."[7] McLeod echoed the sentiment, declaring, "I'm looking for others who agree with me."[8]

In nearby Nipper Park, counterprotesters, including members of the NAACP, International Committee against Racism (IN-CAR), Operation PUSH, and United Front against the Klan, a group that described itself as a coalition of "women, blacks, homosexuals, socialists and others," gathered, hoping to direct attention away from Clemens Field. Initially, protesters waved signs reading "Stop Klan Terror" and "Lesbians and Gays Love—the Klan Hates," and the press noted that those assembled outnumbered Klansmen nearly two to one, with most of the groups coming from St. Louis. However, as the events in Clemens Field kicked off, members of the International Committee against Racism began marching from Nipper Park headed in that direction. Chanting "Death to the Klan," a statement like what was uttered by protesters before the 1979 shoot-out in Greensboro, the group soon arrived at the fence surrounding the baseball facility, where they were met with Nazi salutes and cries of "white power." A man, later identified as IN-CAR member Paul Gomberg, broke through the barricades placed to keep the crowd back and charged toward the Klansmen. A photograph of two IN-CAR members being restrained by police while kicking a fallen Klansman was splashed across newspapers the following day. Law enforcement in riot gear soon broke up the fight, and the Klan supporters hurried to their vehicles and left town.[9] Surveying the scene, Andy Harding, a retired railroad worker living in Hannibal, told the *St. Louis Post-Dispatch*, "I think people around here just wish they'd all go away—both sides."[10]

FIGURE 21. Anti-Klan protesters in Hannibal, Missouri, April 1982. Courtesy of Marion County, Missouri, Photograph Collection (P1147). The State Historical Society of Missouri.

In the sixty years that elapsed between J. F. Craig's call to action for Klansmen and -women who were "catching hell from all quarters" and the clash between Klan and anti-Klan groups on the streets of Hannibal, the scope and power of the Invisible Empire changed dramatically. What started out as a small fraternal organization that promoted nativism, racism, and moral reform under the control of William Simmons had morphed into a white-robed juggernaut during the Jazz Age, only to see

286   Epilogue

its numbers dwindle during the waning years of the interwar period due to scandals, economic hardships, and the rise and fall of like-minded groups who eagerly welcomed wary Klan members. Yet the sheer fact that there was a Ku Klux Klan left in 1982—albeit one of the many localized offshoots—to organize a rally in Hannibal speaks to the legacy of the Klan and its ability to revive itself over generations.

At the same time, counterprotesters in Hannibal indicate that a fractured anti-Klan coalition continued to monitor hood activity. However, the lofty goals of an interracial, interdenominational, and bipartisan anti-Klan coalition that circulated in the interwar period never fully materialized. Originating in the editorial pages of several newspapers in Missouri and nationwide, calls for anti-Klan activism and coalition building found receptive audiences among subscribers, politicians, and community leaders. Supporters circulated these newspapers' commentaries and other publications denouncing the Klan, and quickly went to work rallying like-minded individuals and groups to their cause. Yet, just as quickly as these efforts organized, so too did early warning signs emerge. Most prominent among these were concerns about who should lead these anti-Klan activists. Though each producing sizable numbers of speeches, editorials, and political pressure, Catholics, Jews, and African Americans differed greatly in their individual approaches. While locking arms at times and coordinating their efforts, all three seemingly came to the agreement that others should lead, particularly Protestant groups and denominations whose membership closely overlapped with the Klan.

The budding anti-Klan coalition was also sidetracked by political infighting among supporters. With Klan and anti-Klan members populating both major political parties, coalition participants were uneasy with the idea of fleeing their long-standing political homes for the opposition party, even if seemingly pro-Klan candidates led the ticket. Instead, they sought to reform the parties from within by utilizing the "Klan issue," where potential candidates were pressured to speak out against the hooded order, or at the very least give their position on the Klan. These efforts met with surprising success in Missouri, and it is noteworthy that anti-Klan elements in both parties kept Klan support to a minimum at the statewide level. Additionally, efforts by Missouri Democrats to attract African American voters through promises of patronage and claims that Republicans supported Klan members and lily-white politics brought the party back into power in Missouri and formed a key element of the burgeoning New Deal coalition. However, the allegations, name-calling, and mud-throwing of campaign season, particularly by way of the "Klan issue" and rumored "kampaigning," strained bipartisan ties in the anti-Klan coalition.

By the 1930s, the anti-Klan coalition celebrated the seeming decline of the Invisible Empire. Yet as the prelude to World War II began and fascism threatened to sweep across the globe, the coalition underwent a final fracturing. Building on bipartisan breakdowns at the end of the 1920s, some members felt that other issues were more important than protesting a greatly diminished hooded order. For those that remained, they anxiously surveyed the "spirit of the Klan" that existed in several right-wing groups of the day, including the German-American Bund, Christian Front, Silver Legion, and Christian Nationalist Crusade. While these groups had short life spans, the anti-Klan coalition watched as some of its members aligned with these organizations over concerns ranging from isolationism and anti–New Deal rhetoric to civil rights and integration. As the civil rights movement dawned in the postwar era, anti-Klan coalition members found themselves on both sides of the picket line.

The Ku Klux Klan—largely due to an Internal Revenue Service tax investigation—emerged from World War II in shambles. James Colescott tried to keep the organization together, but by the end of the war, it seemed as if the Invisible Empire would truly fade away. Nevertheless, Dr. Samuel Green, an Atlanta obstetrician, sought to revive the hooded order once more. Green encapsulated the Klan's second life span. Having first joined the organization in the 1920s, Green slowly worked his way up into a leadership role, particularly as members deserted during the Great Depression. By the end of the 1930s, he not only served as grand dragon of the Georgia Klan, but he also held considerable influence with Colescott, who saw him as a valuable lieutenant. When the tax inves-tigation forced the Klan to cease its operations—at least as an official

288   Epilogue

organization—Green kept in close contact with associates throughout the South. By the end of 1946, Green relaunched the hooded order under the title of the Association of Georgia Klans.[11]

Under Samuel Green's leadership, this revived Klan inspired national headlines, such as the one in *Cosmopolitan Magazine*, declaring "The Klan Rides Again." The organization proclaimed the same tenets as its earlier iteration, particularly its distrust of Jews and African Americans, but it also focused on the bubbling cauldron of racial tension that emerged out of World War II. What had been termed as a Double V campaign to defeat racism at home and fascism abroad by the *Pittsburgh Courier* inspired Klansmen to oppose federal policies regarding civil rights, including the Fair Employment Practices Committee, as well as the integration of the US military in 1947. Additionally, discussions over organized labor and the integration of public facilities, such as St. Louis's Buder Park, spawned warnings from the Klan that communism had infiltrated the United States.[12]

Much like the interwar years, the postwar period also brought sizable opposition to the Klan's plans for reforming American society. Though newspaper editors and publishers had come and gone since the end of World War II, an anti-Klan press remained potent in the late 1940s. Media figures like Drew Pearson and Walter Winchell denounced the hooded order in the pages of national publications. Stetson Kennedy, a folklorist and former Works Progress Administration writer, went one step further when he and a few other individuals infiltrated the Georgia Klan and relayed information discussed in local meetings to law enforcement, journalists, and creators of the radio program *The Adventures of Superman*. Confused Klan members struggled to find the leaker, even as their home radios blared programs where the man of steel bravely defeated villainous Klansmen. Kennedy also wrote *I Rode with the Ku Klux Klan* (later retitled as *The Klan Unmasked*).[13]

If media opposition was not enough, the Klan also found that state governors were less inclined to support the group than they had been a generation prior. Outside of a few segregationist politicians, such as Eugene Talmadge, a sizable portion of southern governors went on the record with their negative sentiments about the Klan, particularly as night riding plagued local communities and fiery crosses illuminated the

Epilogue 289

night skies. Congress and state legislatures soon followed with their own attempts to curtail Klan activity while not actively trying to roll back Jim Crow. Georgia officials even went so far as to pursue efforts to revoke the Klan's charter, citing the organization's ties to subversive groups like Gerald L. K. Smith's Christian Nationalist Crusade, Harold Loomis Jr.'s Columbians, and the German-American Bund.[14]

Just as the postwar Klan existed without a charter, so too was it soon without a leader when Samuel Green died unexpectedly in 1949. Though it carried the name Association of Georgia Klans, Green's organization was a single entity spread out over several states, much like its predecessor. In the wake of his death, however, the group splintered under the leadership of Sam Roper, an Atlanta police officer. Now, one Klan became many Klans, each promoting similar tenets and vying for power over local fiefdoms. William Morris started the Federated Ku Klux Klans of Alabama. Tom Hamilton led the Association of Carolina Klans. Robert Shelton split off and founded United Klans of America. Original Southern Klans, Inc., soon sprang up and was followed by Dixie Klans, Inc.; National Knights Federation; and Northern and Southern Knights of the Ku Klux Klan.[15] In reviewing the rival Klans that spawned during the 1950s and 1960s, scholar David Chalmers characterizes the various leaders as "marginal fanatics and mercenary opportunists." He argues, "Most Wizards and Dragons, like Bill Hendrix, were concerned with the Klan as a money-making organization. Many, like the Bryan brothers in North Carolina, had considerable criminal records. Some, like Ace Carter, were emotionally unstable and prone to sudden violence. Few, as shown most notably by Rev. Alvin Horn of Alabama, were inclined to practice the morality they publicly preached. Most, like Reverend James Cole, who took on the Lumbee Indians, were prone to the fault of bad judgment. Although they dreamed big, they thought small."[16]

The factionalism that enveloped the Klan in the aftermath of Samuel Green's death also slowly filtered into Missouri. However, the organization had a seemingly tiny following during the 1940s and 1950s, with some conservative estimates placing the hooded membership as low as forty. When Klan activity did pick up in the mid-1960s, the state's grand dragon bragged that new klaverns were established in Dexter, Jefferson City, Cape Girardeau, Springfield, and St. Louis under the banner of

290 Epilogue

the National Knights of the Ku Klux Klan and that "numerous Missouri counties where people who sympathize with our objectives have indicated they will co-operate with us."[17] Yet the state grand dragon's claims that he had built up a new Missouri Klan to several hundred members were dubious at best. When the Klan held a rally in Sullivan, a former hotbed of hooded activity decades prior near the famed Route 66, Walter Brake, the chief of police, told the press, "I didn't think there were any Klansmen left around here, but I guess there are."[18]

The postwar Klan that emerged in Missouri was sporadic at best and largely unorganized. Gone were the days forty years earlier when the impending arrival of a Klan lecturer or recruiter was front-page news in local newspapers, when an organized headquarters in Atlanta could disperse pamphlets, robes, and membership cards nationwide, and when most communities had well-placed and -respected individuals ready to lead their communities into the Invisible Empire. The major leaders who had led the group through the 1920s and 1930s had long since departed the hooded ranks, whether by renouncing their membership or by simply passing away. Heber Nations experienced a brief return to political relevance in the 1940s before dying in 1948. He was outlived by his father, Gilbert O. Nations, who died two years later. Little is known of George McCarron's final years, but by all accounts, he had passed by the 1950s. When William M. Campbell died in 1953, he was remembered more for being a respected doctor than the former grand dragon.[19]

In addition to losing some of its most significant power brokers, the Missouri Klan also saw its membership scattered over the postwar years to countless rivals, including White Citizens Councils, National States Rights Party, Gerald L. K. Smith's Christian Nationalist Crusade, John Birch Society, and other anticommunist and white-supremacist organizations that provided an air of respectability that hooded robes and fiery crosses did not.[20] For those who were still interested in joining the Klan, recruiting efforts became highly territorial and nonunified by the 1960s due to struggles for control of the state organization. Benjamin Franklin Gibson, a machinist and welder from Jefferson County who had spent time in prison on a counterfeiting charge, became the state's new grand dragon after a group aligned with Robert M. Shelton's United Klans of America pushed for more secrecy regarding local activities. Gibson succeeded Gilbert S. Gillespie, a St. Louisan affiliated with James R.

Venable's National Knights of the Ku Klux Klan, who favored more open recruitment, including distributing flyers and pamphlets in public places.[21] A third group, dubbed the Ozark Klan, pushed for a statewide organization that was independent of outside control and warned Missourians that if federal officials, civil rights leaders, and anti-Klan activists wielded their influence in the region, "They can make [your town] a Selma, Alabama, anytime they want."[22]

While Missouri's Klans had largely become fringe groups by the 1960s, they still received considerable attention from the remnants of the former anti-Klan coalition. When Klan activity was rumored in the Bootheel county of Stoddard, Rev. Arthur C. Fulbright, pastor of the Dexter First Methodist Church and a member of the Missouri Commission on Human Rights, told the press that "we don't have room for a hate organization like that here or anywhere in southeast Missouri."[23] Much like former state Klan leaders, prominent coalition boosters had also passed away by the 1960s, including George L. Vaughn, Cora J. Carter, J. E. Mitchell, James A. Reed, Harry Hawes, Arthur Hyde, and L. M. Birkhead.[24] Some members, however, still remained active. Allen McReynolds used his connections in the Jasper County Anti-Klan Association to launch a successful bid for the Missouri General Assembly. He was eventually appointed to the University of Missouri's Board of Curators during the university's integration in 1950.[25] Samuel Sievers and Ferdinand Isserman held prominent roles in St. Louis Jewish organizations that worked to combat anti-Semitism, particularly the Jewish Community Relations Council.[26] Having fought anti-Catholicism since the early twentieth century, Luke E. Hart continued to advise local chapters of the Knights of Columbus on how best to combat distribution of the bogus oath well into the 1960s, even after his promotion to supreme knight (the highest position in the organization) in 1953.[27] Though his mentor, C. A. Franklin, died in 1955, Roy Wilkins rose through the ranks of the NAACP in the postwar years, eventually becoming executive director, and he led the organization during the heart of the civil rights movement.[28]

In the late 1970s, when the *St. Louis Post-Dispatch* sat down to interview James L. Betts and Mary Carr, only a few years before their infamous rally in Hannibal, they spoke of an evolving Klan much different from its brethren even a decade prior. Though Klan leaders in the 1960s had

292   Epilogue

claimed that membership was steadily rising in many communities, Betts alleged that only about twenty-five members were active in St. Louis when he joined in 1974. In his midtwenties at the time, Betts said he had grown disillusioned with traditional political activism and sought a new outlet. Originally a Republican, Betts feuded with his more liberal family members and rallied to George Wallace in 1968 and 1972 before breaking away when the Alabama presidential aspirant began to hire African Americans on his campaign staff and refused to denounce Jews. In 1976, he was ordained as a minister in the Florida-based white supremacist Church of the Creator. At the time of the 1978 interview, Betts claimed to be the leader of more than two thousand members of the New Order of Knights of the Ku Klux Klan in Missouri. However, it is not entirely clear if this was just within Betts and Carr's faction of the group, a total of all Missourians who were aligned with various Klan chapters, or a fabricated number to suggest strength.[29]

If Betts claimed the title of grand dragon, Mary Carr introduced herself as the grand genie of the state. Much like Betts, Carr had slowly transitioned into the Klan in early adulthood. She was originally from Kansas City, Kansas, but called St. Louis home since the late 1950s. Politically active, she campaigned for Christopher "Kit" Bond and Gene McNary before growing frustrated with the Republican Party. She appeared at a city council meeting in 1974 in Nazi apparel to denounce a planned shopping center because it might attract Black customers. She later ran unsuccessfully to be city marshal and mayor of Black Jack, Missouri, a small suburb in north St. Louis. In the *Post-Dispatch*'s photo spread from the interview, Carr looked the part of a suburban wife and mother. Not surprisingly, Carr spoke of issues she felt connected the Klan to anxious suburbanites, particularly what she saw as the unchecked flow of immorality, drugs, and Black residents into the city's outer-ring communities. At the same time, Carr proclaimed it to be a radically different Klan. This new Klan, while still promoting anticommunism and opposition to African Americans and Jews, seemingly struck a somewhat moderate tone when it came to religious affiliation, as Carr admitted that she was Catholic, a fact that would have been unheard of in previous Klan generations. When presented with charges of the Klan's notorious past, Betts and Carr pushed back against claims of vigilantism, noting that the Klan

Epilogue   293

tried to quell violence rather than commit it. Instead, they argued, the new Missouri Klan was more concerned with stopping busing, aiding law enforcement, and keeping children morally responsible. As for the typical cross burnings and rallies, Carr confessed that most were done in secret now, lest curious passersby or anti-Klan activists snap photographs or write down license plates for public identification.[30]

By the early 1980s, Betts's and Carr's names appeared so frequently in Missouri newspapers related to Klan recruitment that it seemed like the Invisible Empire of more than five decades prior had descended again over the Show-Me State. Yet despite obvious callbacks to the interwar Klan, it was another set of military conflicts—the Cold War and Vietnam War—that radically shaped the Klan that Betts, Carr, and other Missourians joined. Scholar Kathleen Belew argues that surges in Klan membership more closely aligned with "the aftermath of war than with poverty, anti-immigration sentiment, or populism."[31] In media interviews, both Betts and Carr alluded to as much when they pointed out that the civil rights movement and the Vietnam years had galvanized a movement among younger people to join the Klan. Carr confessed to working her way through various groups before deciding that she needed something on the "right-wing, extreme side."[32] In the years leading up to the Hannibal rally, Betts and Carr carefully cultivated an image for Missouri residents of a new Klan with working-class roots but a white-collar persona. When Joel Shatto, a Klansman from Brookfield who worked alongside Betts and Carr, told the *Post-Dispatch* that his followers were part of Bill Wilkinson's Louisiana Klan faction, Carr was quick to claim that they were actually aligned with David Duke's seemingly more nonviolent group.[33] To emphasize this new image, Klan members distributed literature on college campuses, held rallies in small towns across Missouri, and campaigned for local political office to show that "people here are ready to accept racism."[34]

Yet despite their efforts to portray themselves, as their group's name suggested, as a new order, Betts and Carr recruited in an evolving landscape. In the lead-up to, and in the immediate aftermath of, the 1982 Hannibal rally, the Missouri State Highway Patrol launched a series of internal investigations into white-supremacist activity across the state. While they only found reliable information on a handful of Klansmen

294   Epilogue

and -women in ten counties, including the previously mentioned James Betts, Mary Carr, and Benjamin Franklin Gibson, as well as a Bootheel motorcycle gang called the Pharaohs, the reports showed key facets of overlap in the evolving white-power movement.[35] An investigation into the activities of the Lexington-based National Conservative Party found that the group attempted to rally supporters, including frustrated farmers amid the agricultural crisis and conservative voters of both major political parties, to "make America great again" and attend rallies near Kansas City, including one that would feature Thomas Robb, a Klan leader from Harrison, Arkansas, who had spoken in Hannibal.[36] The patrol also received a 1983 report from the Kansas Bureau of Investigation on the Posse Comitatus movement that found that several groups with similar philosophies operated in Missouri. Beyond the Klan, these groups included the Liberty Lobby; Citizen Council; National Alliance; Minutemen; Committee of Ten Million; National Emancipation of Our White Seed; Christian Patriots Defense League; Farmer's Liberation Army; Our Savior Church, led by Gordon Winrod, the son of the "Nazi Jayhawker," Gerald Burton Winrod; Church of Israel, a Schell City Christian Identity community led by Dan Gayman; and the Covenant, the Sword, and the Arm of the Lord, a paramilitary organization based in Arkansas with a training facility in Ozark County.[37]

The Hannibal rally also demonstrated that anti-Klan adherents were still active in making their voices heard. The Missouri State Highway Patrol consulted with Stanley Anderman, regional director for the Anti-Defamation League of B'nai B'rith, in preparation for the rally. He spoke of the organization's long history of tracking extremist groups.[38] Though not always in complete coordination, both the ADL and groups like the NAACP had protested against Klan activity in Missouri since the 1920s. Anderman told protesters to stay away from Hannibal, but the NAACP had personnel on the ground, including national deputy executive director Charles Smith.[39] By the 1980s, the NAACP was well seasoned when it came to addressing the Klan, and its members in Missouri had repeatedly spoken out and counterprotested against the actions of the hooded order in countless communities. One relatively new anti-Klan organization, though not in attendance in Hannibal, was the Southern Poverty Law Center. Founded in Montgomery, Alabama,

Epilogue   295

in 1971 by Morris Dees, Joseph Levin Jr., and Julian Bond as a civil rights organization, the Southern Poverty Law Center was young but well established by the Hannibal rally. Beginning in 1979 and continuing to the present day, the organization filed lawsuits against Klan members, chapters, and other white-supremacist groups seeking monetary damages for those impacted by the Klan. In 1981, the Southern Poverty Law Center launched Klanwatch, now called Hatewatch, to monitor extremism in the United States.[40]

By the 1980s, despite more than fifty years of activity, the anti-Klan coalition was as tenuous as it had been in the 1920s. Before the Hannibal rally, Stanley Anderman of the Anti-Defamation League of B'nai B'rith warned law enforcement that "problems could arise if one of several other groups or movements come to Hannibal to counter-demonstrate against the Klan and therefore create a confrontation." Anderman's biggest concern, beyond the Klan, was the possible activities of Paul Gomberg, a University of Missouri–St. Louis professor, and his involvement with local chapters of the Progressive Labor Party and the International Committee against Racism.[41] Additionally, when a group called United Concerned Citizens repeatedly pressured city officials to postpone Klan rallies and enact an antimask law for parades in Columbia, the actions were met with criticism from civil liberties supporters within the anti-Klan ranks.[42] Similar legal battles ensued over years-long efforts to remove Carr's personalized "ARYAN-1" license plate and prevent the Klan from participating in the state's Adopt-a-Highway program.[43]

Only a year after the Hannibal rally, a significant turning point in the trajectory of the Klan and other organizations emerged. According to scholar Kathleen Belew, a meeting of the minds at Hayden Lake, Idaho, in the summer of 1983 fomented a revolution that "shifted nationwide to call for revolution against the Zionist Occupational Government (ZOG), bombing of public infrastructure, undermining of national currency, assassination of federal agents and judges, and attempts to break away into a white separatist nation."[44] This rhetoric slowly seeped into the talking points of Betts, Carr, and other Missourians soon after the killing of Jimmie Linegar and wounding of Allen Hines, two Missouri State Highway Patrol troopers, by David Tate, a member of the Order,

296   Epilogue

a secret extremist offshoot of the Idaho-based Aryan Nations, near Branson in 1985.[45] In 1988, when the *Post-Dispatch* approached Betts and Carr regarding their work with a new group called the White American Freedom Fighters, Carr allegedly called Tate "a religious, wonderful boy" and declared that "I am in this to the death. . . . I am giving my life to the white racist movement," though she later tried to sue the newspaper for libel, claiming the article misrepresented her views.[46]

Across the state in Kansas City, David Tate also became a significant figure for J. Allen Moran, and he developed a yearning to head out west to what he hoped would soon be a white-nationalist homeland. At the time that an extensive manhunt was under way in the Ozarks looking for Tate, Moran was a young veteran training to become a law-enforcement officer in Platte County, Missouri, just north of Kansas City. By his own admission, Moran was introduced to white-supremacist discourse through Tate's eventual conviction on murder charges and his own efforts to understand why someone would gun down a fellow law officer. His search for answers initially led him to David Duke's National Association for the Advancement of White People. Later, when the *Kansas City Star* rejected his efforts to put an advertisement for the NAAWP in its pages, Moran sought out more like-minded individuals and slowly worked his way through information on Christian Identity, Posse Comitatus, Neo-Nazis, and the Klan. In a chance meeting at a gun show, Moran was introduced to Dennis Mahon, a fellow veteran and recent Oklahoma transplant who relocated to the Kansas City area and recruited for the Klan. Mahon was initially suspicious of Moran, and for good reason, considering the US Bureau of Alcohol, Tobacco, and Firearms allegedly tried to coax him into turning informant against Mahon and other Klan officials, but when Moran was fired from his job as a Platte City police officer, Mahon welcomed him into the Klan.[47]

By the mid-1990s, Moran, Mahon, Betts, and Carr had all departed to various corners of the growing white-power movement. While Mahon had introduced Moran to *The Turner Diaries*, an incendiary novel of race war and revolution, and initiated him into the Klan, the two had an eventual falling-out.[48] Moran continued to hold firm to his beliefs, but he also spoke to the *Kansas City Star* about efforts to artificially boost membership numbers to make groups like the Klan seem more popular to the general public.[49] Such a claim was not unusual to the Klan's critics, as Betts and Carr announced that membership was in the thousands in 1978. One law-enforcement official responded that "if you dropped two zeroes and divided by two you might be closer to it."[50] In the more than fifteen years since the 1978 article, Betts and Carr had both shifted into the camp of the White American Freedom Fighters. However, they did join with Moran and Mahon in the late 1980s and early 1990s to get Klan programming on local public-access television.[51] In 1992, Betts announced his plan to create an all-white city in Franklin County, southwest of St. Louis.[52] From there, the trail goes cold on all four except for Dennis Mahon. Though he resigned from the Klan in 1989 amid fallout over confessing to urinating on seats in Air Force One when the plane was receiving routine maintenance in Wichita, Kansas, Mahon stayed in close contact with many in the white-power movement.[53] By the 1990s, he was a recruiter for White Aryan Resistance and actively targeted young skinheads in the region. Soon after a truck bomb exploded in front of the Alfred P. Murrah Federal Building in Oklahoma City in 1995, killing 168, Mahon was a person of interest related to his possible ties between white-supremacist organizations in Missouri, Arkansas, Kansas, and Oklahoma and a young Gulf War veteran named Timothy McVeigh.[54]

Today, the Klan/anti-Klan battles of a century ago still rage, though the key talking points and terminology have been altered for the modern era. Now, banner terms such as *alt-right* and *antifa* dot the media landscape, and propaganda circulates on social media at a pace unfathomable to their 1920s predecessors. At the same time, the language and rhetoric of political and organizational leaders of today have changed little. It is not unheard of to hear the words of Hiram Evans at the 1924 Second Imperial Klonvokation repackaged in the mainstream media in reference to debates over immigration, public education, and civil rights. In this regard, it appears all too apparent that despite their best efforts more than a century ago, anti-Klan activists failed to prevent the spread of the Invisible Empire across the United States. Scholar Kathleen Blee has hinted as much in her book *Women of the Klan* where, during interviews with former Klanswomen more than fifty years after their time in the Invisible Empire, she found that many expressed "pride, not regret,"

298 Epilogue

because they found "their membership in one of U.S. history's most vicious campaigns of prejudice and hatred primarily as a time of friendship and solidarity among like-minded women."[55]

Ultimately, many Americans shared the Klan's views on racial and religious issues, even if they refused to show overt support for the Klan. Instead of cross burnings, they participated in book burnings or wrote scorching newspaper editorials against civil rights and integration. Instead of speaking on behalf of the hooded order in public venues, they secretly passed incendiary literature to friends, confidants, and coworkers. Instead of visibly joining the ranks of the Invisible Empire, they hid their beliefs behind a veneer of respectability. Through all of this, and because of all of this, the Klan and similar groups remain active in American society even as membership numbers stay relatively small. Yet though the Klan continues to rise like a phoenix out of the ashes of its own burned crosses, anti-Klan activists have continually organized and mobilized to challenge it.

NOTES

Preface

1. *Jefferson City Democrat-Tribune*, 6 August 1924, 23 October 1924, 25 October 1924; *Jefferson City Daily Capital News*, 3 August 1924; *Cole County Weekly Rustler*, 8 August 1924; *Official Manual of the State of Missouri, 1921–1922*, 868; *Official Manual of the State of Missouri, 1925–1926*, 902.

2. *Jefferson City Daily Capital News*, 26 September 1924.

3. *Jefferson City Daily Capital News*, 8 June 1941.

4. *Kansas City Times*, 27 October 1924; *Jefferson City Democrat-Tribune*, 25 October 1924, 27 October 1924, 28 October 1924, 4 November 1924, 6 November 1924; *Jefferson City Daily Capital News*, 6 November 1924; *Cole County Weekly Rustler*, 7 November 1924.

Introduction

1. *St. Louis Post-Dispatch*, 10 October 1922.

2. *St. Louis Post-Dispatch*, 10 October 1922.

3. *St. Louis Star*, 10 October 1922; *St. Louis Post-Dispatch*, 31 October 1934; *Kansas City Times*, 17 July 1944.

4. *St. Louis Star*, 8 October 1922, 10 October 1922; *St. Louis Post-Dispatch*, 10 October 1922; *St. Louis Globe-Democrat*, 10 October 1922.

5. *St. Louis Star*, 8 October 1922, 10 October 1922; *St. Louis Post-Dispatch*, 10 October 1922; *St. Louis Globe-Democrat*, 10 October 1922.

6. *St. Louis Star*, 8 October 1922, 10 October 1922.

7. *Kansas City Star*, 2 December 1922; *Kansas City Journal*, 7 December 1922, 14 January 1923; *Independence Examiner*, 15 January 1923, 16 January 1923.

8. *Kansas City Journal*, 17 January 1923, 20 January 1923; *Independence Examiner*, 19 January 1923; *Kansas City Times*, 17 January 1923, 22 January 1923.

9. *Kansas City Times*, 22 January 1923.

10. John M. Mecklin, *The Ku Klux Klan: A Study of the American Mind*, 99; Henry P. Fry, *The Modern Ku Klux Klan*; Stanley Frost, *The Challenge of the Klan*; Felix Harcourt, *Ku Klux Kulture: America and the Klan in the 1920s*, 52–74.

11. Frederick L. Allen, *Only Yesterday: An Informal History of the 1920s*, 57.

12. David M. Chalmers, *Hooded Americanism: The History of the Ku Klux Klan*, 329–30; David Cunningham, *Klansville, U.S.A.: The Rise and Fall of the Civil Rights–Era Ku Klux Klan*, 27.

Notes to Introduction

13. Charles Alexander, *The Ku Klux Klan in the Southwest*; Chalmers, *Hooded Americanism*; Kenneth T. Jackson, *The Ku Klux Klan in the City, 1915–1930*.

14. Robert A. Goldberg, *Hooded Empire: The Ku Klux Klan in Colorado*; Shawn Lay, ed., *The Invisible Empire in the West: Toward a New Historical Appraisal of the Ku Klux Klan of the 1920s*; William D. Jenkins, *Steel Valley Klan: The Ku Klux Klan in Ohio's Mahoning Valley*; Leonard J. Moore, *Citizen Klansmen: The Ku Klux Klan in Indiana, 1921–1928*; Shawn Lay, *Hooded Knights on the Niagara: The Ku Klux Klan in Buffalo, New York*; Kathleen M. Blee, *Women of the Klan: Racism and Gender in the 1920s*; Nancy MacLean, *Behind the Mask of Chivalry: The Making of the Second Ku Klux Klan*; Larry R. Gerlach, *Blazing Crosses in Zion: The Ku Klux Klan in Utah*; Wyn C. Wade, *The Fiery Cross: The Ku Klux Klan in America*.

15. Kelly J. Baker, *Gospel according to the Klan: The KKK's Appeal to Protestant America, 1915–1930*; Linda Gordon, *The Second Coming of the KKK: The Ku Klux Klan of the 1920s and the American Political Tradition*; Harcourt, *Ku Klux Kulture*; Thomas Pegram, *One Hundred Percent American: The Rebirth and Decline of the Ku Klux Klan in the 1920s*; Kenneth Barnes, *Anti-Catholicism in Arkansas: How Politicians, the Press, the Klan, and Religious Leaders Imagined an Enemy, 1910–1960*; Kenneth Barnes, *The Ku Klux Klan in 1920s Arkansas: How Protestant White Nationalism Came to Rule a State*; Rory McVeigh, *The Rise of the Ku Klux Klan: Right-Wing Movements and National Politics*; Craig Fox, *Everyday Klansfolk: White Protestant Life and the KKK in 1920s Michigan*; Miguel Hernandez, *The Ku Klux Klan and Freemasonry in 1920s America: Fighting Fraternities*; James H. Madison, *The Ku Klux Klan in the Heartland*.

16. Lay, *Invisible Empire in the West*; W. Jenkins, *Steel Valley Klan*; L. Moore, *Citizen Klansmen*; Lay, *Hooded Knights on the Niagara*; David J. Goldberg, "Unmasking the Ku Klux Klan: The Northern Movement against the KKK, 1920–1925"; Lynn Dumenil, "The Tribal Twenties: 'Assimilated' Catholics' Response to Anti-Catholicism in the 1920s"; Harcourt, *Ku Klux Kulture*; Madison, *Ku Klux Klan in the Heartland*.

17. Dumenil, "Tribal Twenties," 22.

18. *St. Louis Star*, 12 May 1921.

19. *Jefferson City Democrat-Tribune*, 24 August 1923.

20. *St. Louis Post-Dispatch*, 18 October 1922; *St. Louis Argus*, 13 October 1922.

21. *St. Louis Star*, 11 October 1922.

22. *St. Louis Argus*, 13 October 1922; *Kansas City Call*, 26 January 1923.

23. *Kansas City Call*, 26 January 1923.

24. Chalmers, *Hooded Americanism*, 34; L. Gordon, *Second Coming of the KKK*, 29–30. For a monograph that focuses on the ties between the Klan and the Masons, see Hernandez, *Ku Klux Klan and Freemasonry in 1920s America*.

25. *Kansas City Catholic Register*, 1 February 1923. Hart's comments caught the attention of Missouri Klansmen who warned about efforts to solicit Hart into rallying anti-Klan groups into a singular organization. *Klan Kourier*, 8 May 1924.

26. *St. Louis Post-Dispatch*, 13 October 1922; *Joplin Globe*, 13 October 1922.

27. *St. Louis Star*, 14 October 1922; *Kansas City Times*, 14 October 1922.

28. *St. Louis Post-Dispatch*, 4 November 1922.

29. *Independence Examiner*, 16 January 1923.

Notes to Chapter One 301

30. Timothy Rives, "The Second Ku Klux Klan In Kansas City: Rise and Fall of a White Nationalist Movement."

31. *Independence Examiner*, 19 January 1923. For monographs on the origins of the Second Klan, see MacLean, *Behind the Mask of Chivalry*, 4–5; Lay, *Hooded Knights on the Niagara*, 2–4; Lay, *Invisible Empire in the West*, 3–8; Baker, *Gospel according to the Klan*, 4–5; Chalmers, *Hooded Americanism*, 28–38; Gerlach, *Blazing Crosses in Zion*, 4–7; Wade, *Fiery Cross*, 140–66; W. Jenkins, *Steel Valley Klan*, 1–4; Blee, *Women of the Klan*, 17–21; L. Gordon, *Second Coming of the KKK*, 11–16; Harcourt, *Ku Klux Kulture*, 2–4; R. Goldberg, *Hooded Empire*, 3–5; and Pegram, *One Hundred Percent American*, 5–10.

32. Chalmers, *Hooded Americanism*, 100–108; L. Gordon, *Second Coming of the KKK*, 15–16; Harcourt, *Ku Klux Kulture*, 4–5.

33. Chalmers, *Hooded Americanism*, 304–42; Cunningham, *Klansville, U.S.A.*, 26–31.

34. Baker, *Gospel according to the Klan*; L. Gordon, *Second Coming of the KKK*; Harcourt, *Ku Klux Kulture*.

Chapter One
"The Black Clouds of Bigotry"
The Origins of the Ku Klux Klan in Missouri

1. *St. Louis Post-Dispatch*, 6 October 1924, 7 October 1924; *St. Louis Star*, 6 October 1924, 7 October 1924; *Kansas City Star*, 6 October 1924; *Kansas City Times*, 7 October 1924. For a detailed history of Dedication Day, see Gary R. Kremer, *Heartland History*, 2–5.

2. *Jefferson City Daily Democrat-Tribune*, 24 September 1924.

3. Kremer, *Heartland History*, 2–5; *St. Louis Post-Dispatch*, 7 October 1924; *St. Louis Star*, 7 October 1924; *Kansas City Times*, 7 October 1924.

4. Kremer, *Heartland History*, 2–5; *St. Louis Post-Dispatch*, 6 October 1924, 7 October 1924; *St. Louis Star*, 6 October 1924, 7 October 1924; *Kansas City Times*, 7 October 1924.

5. *Kansas City Star*, 6 October 1924; *St. Louis Globe-Democrat*, 7 October 1924.

6. *St. Louis Post-Dispatch*, 6 October 1924, 7 October 1924; *St. Louis Star*, 6 October 1924, 7 October 1924; *St. Louis Argus*, 10 October 1924, 17 October 1924; *Kansas City Times*, 7 October 1924.

7. *St. Louis Post-Dispatch*, 7 October 1924; *Jefferson City Democrat-Tribune*, 8 October 1924; *St. Louis Argus*, 10 October 1924, 17 October 1924.

8. St. Louis *Post-Dispatch*, 7 October 1924.

9. MacLean, *Behind the Mask of Chivalry*, 4–5; Lay, *Hooded Knights on the Niagara*, 2–4; Lay, *Invisible Empire in the West*, 3–8; Baker, *Gospel according to the Klan*, 4–5; Chalmers, *Hooded Americanism*, 28–38; Gerlach, *Blazing Crosses in Zion*, 4–7; Wade, *Fiery Cross*, 140–66; W. Jenkins, *Steel Valley Klan*, 1–4; Blee, *Women of the Klan*, 17–21; L. Gordon, *Second Coming of the KKK*, 11–16; Harcourt, *Ku Klux Kulture*, 2–4; R. Goldberg, *Hooded Empire*, 3–5; Pegram, *One Hundred Percent American*, 5–10.

10. Lay, *Hooded Knights on the Niagara*, 2–.

11. MacLean, *Behind the Mask of Chivalry*, 4–5; Lay, *Hooded Knights on the Niagara*, 2–4; Lay, *Invisible Empire in the West*, 3–8; Baker, *Gospel according to the Klan*, 4–5;

302 Notes to Chapter One

Chalmers, *Hooded Americanism*, 28–38; Gerlach, *Blazing Cross in Zion*, 4–7; Wade, *Fiery Cross*, 140–66; W. Jenkins, *Steel Valley Klan*, 1–4; Blee, *Women of the Klan*, 17–21; L. Gordon, *Second Coming of the KKK*, 11–16; Harcourt, *Ku Klux Kulture*, 2–4; Pegram, *One Hundred Percent American*, 5–10.

12. Chalmers, *Hooded Americanism*, 100–108; L. Gordon, *Second Coming of the KKK*, 15–16; Harcourt, *Ku Klux Kulture*, 4–5.

13. Blee, *Women of the Klan*, 23–28; Chalmers, *Hooded Americanism*, 105–7; L. Gordon, *Second Coming of the KKK*, 109–38.

14. Blee, *Women of the Klan*, 26–28; Baker, *Gospel according to the Klan*, 135–38; K. Barnes, *Anti-Catholicism in Arkansas*, 122–23; L. Gordon, *Second Coming of the KKK*, 109–38.

15. Blee, *Women of the Klan*, 28.

16. Blee, *Women of the Klan*, 28, 34–35, 39–40; L. Gordon, *Second Coming of the KKK*, 109–38.

17. *Imperial Night-Hawk*, 1 August 1923.

18. Blee, *Women of the Klan*, 25–60; Baker, *Gospel according to the Klan*, 125–61; K. Barnes, *Anti-Catholicism in Arkansas*, 122–24; Chalmers, *Hooded Americanism*, 57–58, 240–41; L. Gordon, *Second Coming of the KKK*, 109–38; K. Barnes, *Ku Klux Klan in 1920s Arkansas*, 24–31, 95–96, 159–63.

19. *Patriot*, 27 July 1923.

20. *Missouri Valley Independent*, 7 June 1923, 5 July 1923, 26 July 1923, 9 August 1923, 27 September 1923, 4 October 1923, 12 February 1925, 26 March 1925.

21. *Patriot*, 12 July 1923, 20 July 1923, 27 July 1923, 3 August 1923, 10 August 1923, 17 August 1923, 11 October 1923, 1 November 1923, 15 November 1923, 29 November 1923, 6 December 1923, 20 December 1923; *Missouri Fiery Cross*, 28 February 1924, 20 March 1924; *Klan Kourier*, 22 May 1924, 5 June 1924, 12 June 1924, 19 June 1924, 26 June 1924, 3 July 1924, 10 July 1924, 17 July 1924; *Missouri Kourier*, 1 August 1924, 5 September 1924; *Missouri Valley Independent*, 4 October 1923, 8 January 1925, 15 January 1925, 26 February 1925, 28 May 1925, 4 June 1925, 10 March 1927, 3 November 1927, 10 November 1927; *Jefferson City Democrat-Tribune*, 16 August 1924; *Jefferson City Daily Capital News*, 25 October 1924; *Jefferson City Daily Post*, 15 December 1924; *Marion County Herald*, 22 August 1924; *Macon Daily Chronicle Herald*, 2 May 1925; *Joplin Globe*, 22 September 1926;

22. *Missouri Valley Independent*, 4 October 1923, 8 January 1925, 15 January 1925, 26 February 1925, 28 May 1925, 4 June 1925, 10 March 1927, 3 November 1927, 10 November 1927. These are specific examples of summaries of WKKK events. The *Missouri Valley Independent* had a section in each edition that listed the dates, times, and locations of KKK and WKKK weekly meetings.

23. *Patriot*, 12 July 1923, 20 July 1923, 27 July 1923, 3 August 1923, 10 August 1923, 17 August 1923, 11 October 1923, 1 November 1923, 15 November 1923, 29 November 1923, 6 December 1923, 20 December 1923; *Missouri Fiery Cross*, 28 February 1924, 20 March 1924, *Klan Kourier*, 22 May 1924, 29 May 1924, 5 June 1924, 12 June 1924, 19 June 1924, 26 June 1924, 3 July 1924, 10 July 1924, 17 July 1924; *Missouri Kourier*, 1 August 1924, 5 September 1924. During its life span, the *Patriot* also changed its name to the *Missouri Fiery Cross*, *Klan Kourier*, and *Missouri Kourier*.

Notes to Chapter One

303

24. *Patriot*, 11 October 1923, 15 November 1923.

25. *Missouri Kourier*, 1 August 1924, 8 August 1924, 16 August 1924, 23 August 1924, 30 August 1924, 5 September 1924, 12 September 1924, 19 September 1924, 26 September 1924, 3 October 1924, 10 October 1924, 17 October 1924, 31 October 1924, 7 November 1924, 14 November 1924, 21 November 1924, 28 November 1924, 5 December 1924, 12 December 1924, 19 December 1924.

26. L. Gordon, *Second Coming of the KKK*, 133–34; K. Barnes, *Ku Klux Klan in 1920s Arkansas*, 34; *Missouri Valley Independent*, 1 May 1924.

27. L. Gordon, *Second Coming of the KKK*, 133–34; K. Barnes, *Ku Klux Klan in 1920s Arkansas*, 34; *Missouri Valley Independent*, 25 November 1926.

28. K. Barnes, *Ku Klux Klan in 1920s Arkansas*, 34; *Missouri Valley Independent*, 1 January 1925.

29. L. Gordon, *Second Coming of the KKK*, 133–34; *Missouri Valley Independent*, 1 January 1925.

30. *Missouri Valley Independent*, 1 January 1925.

31. *Missouri Valley Independent*, 1 January 1925, 20 August 1925, 23 September 1926.

32. Knights of the Ku Klux Klan, Inc., *Proceedings of the Second Imperial Klonvokation: Held in Kansas City, Missouri, Sept. 23, 24, 25 and 26, 1924*, 54.

33. Knights of the Ku Klux Klan, Inc., *Proceedings of the Second Imperial Klonvokation*, 54.

34. Knights of the Ku Klux Klan, Inc., *Proceedings of the Second Imperial Klonvokation*, 145–46.

35. Knights of the Ku Klux Klan, Inc., *Proceedings of the Second Imperial Klonvokation*, 61.

36. Knights of the Ku Klux Klan, Inc., *Proceedings of the Second Imperial Klonvokation*, 222.

37. Knights of the Ku Klux Klan, Inc., *Proceedings of the Second Imperial Klonvokation*, 63.

38. Knights of the Ku Klux Klan, Inc., *Proceedings of the Second Imperial Klonvokation*, 79.

39. Knights of the Ku Klux Klan, Inc., *Proceedings of the Second Imperial Klonvokation*, 100–101. The 81.9 percent of the Klan's population resided in Louisiana, Texas, New Mexico, Arizona, Arkansas, Oklahoma, Mississippi, Alabama, Georgia, Florida, South Carolina, North Carolina, Virginia, Kentucky, Tennessee, West Virginia, Illinois, Indiana, Wisconsin, Ohio, and Michigan (twenty-one states). The 18.1 percent of the Klan's population resided in California, Nevada, Utah, Colorado, Oregon, Washington, Idaho, Wyoming, Montana, North Dakota, South Dakota, Minnesota, Iowa, Missouri, Nebraska, Kansas, Pennsylvania, Delaware, Maryland, New Jersey, New York, Connecticut, Rhode Island, Massachusetts, New Hampshire, Vermont, and Maine (twenty-seven states).

40. *Missouri Valley Independent*, 2 October 1924.

41. *Joplin Globe*, 8 March 1921.

42. *Joplin Globe*, 8 March 1921.

43. *Joplin Globe*, 8 March 1921.

44. For monographs on slavery, emancipation, and Reconstruction in Missouri, see Perry McCandless, *A History of Missouri*; Stephen Aron, *American Confluence: The*

304 Notes to Chapter One

Missouri Frontier from Borderland to Border State; Kristen Epps, *Slavery on the Periphery: The Kansas-Missouri Border in the Antebellum and Civil War Eras*; Lorenzo J. Greene, Gary R. Kremer, and Antonio F. Holland, *Missouri's Black Heritage*; Diane Mutti Burke, *On Slavery's Border: Missouri's Small Slaveholding Households, 1815–1865*; Aaron Astor, *Rebels on the Border: Civil War, Emancipation, and the Reconstruction of Kentucky and Missouri*; William E. Parrish, *Missouri under Radical Rule, 1865–1870*; Fred DeArmond, "Reconstruction in Missouri"; William E. Parrish, *A History of Missouri*; Alison Clark Efford, *German Immigrants, Race, and Citizenship in the Civil War Era*; Lawrence O. Christensen, "Race Relations in St. Louis, 1865–1916"; Lawrence O. Christensen and Gray Kremer, *A History of Missouri*; Sherry Lamb Schirmer, *A City Divided: The Racial Landscape of Kansas City, 1900–1960*; David Thelen, *Paths of Resistance: Tradition and Democracy in Industrializing Missouri*; and Sydney J. Norton, ed., *Fighting for a Free Missouri: German Immigrants, African Americans, and the Issue of Slavery*.

45. Elaine Frantz Parsons, *Ku-Klux: The Birth of the Klan during Reconstruction*, 30; Eric Foner, *Reconstruction: America's Unfinished Revolution, 1863–1877*, 425.

46. Parsons, *Ku-Klux*, 7–8, 27–71; Foner, *Reconstruction*, 425–40; Wade, *Fiery Cross*, 31–79; Chalmers, *Hooded Americanism*, 8–21.

47. Astor, *Rebels on the Border*, 140–41, 168–69, 178, 181, 191; John Starrett Hughes, "Lafayette County and the Aftermath of Slavery, 1861–1870," 54–58; Aaron Astor, "The *Lexington Weekly Caucasian*: White Supremacist Discourse in Post–Civil War Western Missouri," in *Bleeding Kansas, Bleeding Missouri: The Long Civil War on the Border*, ed. Jonathan Earle and Diane Mutti Burke, 189–203.

48. Parrish, *A History of Missouri*, 282; Astor, *Rebels on the Border*, 190–92, 230; Hughes, "Lafayette County and the Aftermath of Slavery," 58; DeArmond, "Reconstruction in Missouri," 377; Thelen, *Paths of Resistance*, 60–61.

49. The aptly named Ku Klux Klan Act, originally crafted with the intent to designate certain criminal offenses as punishable under the federal government, held that if states did not uphold key elements of the Fourteenth Amendment, they would be subject to federal prosecution and even military intervention. As such, the act brought forth more rigorous suppression of violence at the state level, with governors like Missouri's B. Gratz Brown warning residents that if local officials did not address alleged atrocities, then state and federal intervention would follow.

50. For Brown's response to alleged Klan activity, see Parrish, *A History of Missouri*, 282; E. M. Lick to B. Gratz Brown, 20 June 1871, Benjamin Gratz Brown Collection, Missouri State Archives, Jefferson City (hereafter cited as BGB, MSA-JC); A. J. Barker to B. Gratz Brown, 29 June 1871, BGB, MSA-JC; Edmund S. Woog to Albert Sigel, 4 October 1871, BGB, MSA-JC; James Shelton Alsup to B. Gratz Brown, 21 January 1872, BGB, MSA-JC; W. Lawson to B. Gratz Brown, 14 March 1872, BGB, MSA-JC; E. K. Cooper to B. Gratz Brown, 3 April 1872, BGB, MSA-JC.

51. Astor, *Rebels on the Border*, 191.

52. E. M. Lick to B. Gratz Brown, 20 June 1871, BGB, MSA-JC.

53. Edmund S. Woog to Albert Sigel, 4 October 1871, BGB, MSA-JC.

54. Edmund S. Woog to Albert Sigel, 4 October 1871, BGB, MSA-JC.

55. E. K. Cooper to B. Gratz Brown, 3 April 1872, BGB, MSA-JC.

Notes to Chapter One 305

56. *Lexington Intelligencer*, 10 January 1872, 17 January 1872.

57. For information on Congress and the Grant administration's response to Klan atrocities, see Foner, *Reconstruction*, 454–59; Parsons, *Ku-Klux*, 184–86, 215–302; and Wade, *Fiery Cross*, 83–90, 99–101.

58. Foner, *Reconstruction*, 455–57; Parsons, *Ku-Klux*, 159, 162, 167; Efford, *German Immigrants, Race, and Citizenship in the Civil War Era*, 183–85.

59. L. Greene, Kremer, and Holland, *Missouri's Black Heritage*, 104–17; Christensen and Kremer, *A History of Missouri*, 147–49.

60. *Joplin Globe*, 8 March 1921.

61. Greg Olson, *Indigenous Missourians: Ancient Societies to the Present*; Benjamine E. Park, *Kingdom of Nauvoo: The Rise and Fall of a Religious Empire on the American Frontier*; Michael Fellman, *Inside War: The Guerilla Conflict in Missouri during the Civil War*; Joseph M. Beilein Jr., *Bushwhackers: Guerilla Warfare, Manhood, and the Household in Civil War Missouri*; Matthew J. Hernando, *Faces Like Devils: The Bald Knobber Vigilantes in the Ozarks*; Kimberly Harper, *White Man's Heaven: The Lynching and Expulsion of Blacks in the Southern Ozarks, 1894–1909*; Brent M. S. Campney, *Hostile Heartland: Racism, Repression, and Resistance in the Midwest*. Walter Johnson, *The Broken Heart of America: St. Louis and the Violent History of the United States*.

62. L. Greene, Kremer, and Holland, *Missouri's Black Heritage*, 107–9; Harriet C. Frazier, *Lynchings in Missouri, 1803–1981*, 105–62, 198–201; Campney, *Hostile Heartland*, 92–135; Harper, *White Man's Heaven*.

63. *Joplin Globe*, 8 March 1921, 11 March 1921, 12 March 1921.

64. *Patriot*, 10 August 1923.

65. *Patriot*, 10 August 1923.

66. *Joplin Globe*, 8 March 1921.

67. *St. Louis Star*, 25 September 1921; *St. Louis Post-Dispatch*, 25 September 1921.

68. McCandless, *A History of Missouri*, 38–41; Frederick E. Brock, "The American Party in Missouri, 1854–1860," 20–22; Astor, *Rebels on the Border*, 18–19; Aron, *American Confluence*, 202–3, 237–38; Epps, *Slavery on the Periphery*, 80–82; Efford, *German Immigrants, Race, and Citizenship in the Civil War Era*, 56–57, 73, 92; US Bureau of the Census, *Fourteenth Census of the United States: 1920*, vol. 2, *Population*, 546. For larger works that survey nativism in the nineteenth century, see Tyler Anbinder, *Nativism and Slavery: The Northern Known Nothings and the Politics of the 1850s*; Luke Ritter, *Inventing America's First Immigration Crisis: Political Nativism in the Antebellum West*; John Higham, *Strangers in the Land: Patterns of American Nativism, 1860–1925*; and Ray Allen Billington, *The Protestant Crusade, 1800–1860: A Study of the Origins of American Nativism*.

69. Walter Ehrlich, *Zion in the Valley: The Jewish Community in St. Louis*, vols. 1–2; Howard F. Sachs, "Development of the Jewish Community of Kansas City, 1864–1908"; Joseph Schultz, ed., *Mid-America's Promise: A Profile of Kansas City Jewry*; Lee Shai Weissbach, *Jewish Life in Small-Town America*; Shari Rabin, *Jews on the Frontier: Religion and Mobility in Nineteenth Century America*; Anne Hessler, "German Jews in Small Towns in Missouri, 1850–1920"; Sandra Rubinstein Peterson, "'One Heart, Many Souls': The National Council of Jewish Women and Identity Formation in St. Louis, 1919–1950"; *The Lead Belt Jewish Oral History Project*; Mara Cohen Ioannides and Rachel Gholson,

306   Notes to Chapter One

Jews of Springfield in the Ozarks; Mara Cohen Ioannides, *Creating Community: The Jews of Springfield, Missouri*.

70. James Neal Primm, *Lion of the Valley: St. Louis, Missouri, 1764–1980*, 91–94, 143–44, 164, 314–15; Brock, "American Party in Missouri," 17–22; McCandless, *A History of Missouri*, 39–41; Efford, *German Immigrants, Race, and Citizenship in the Civil War Era*, 34.

71. Anbinder, *Nativism and Slavery*, 9–21, 28–29; Brock, "American Party in Missouri," 3–8, 23–27, 143–45; William Barnaby Faherty, "Nativism and Midwestern Education: The Experience of St. Louis University, 1832–1856," 447–58; Primm, *Lion of the Valley*, 166–69; Joseph H. Schmidt, "Recollections of the First Catholic Missions in Central Missouri," 90; Donald L. Kinzer, *An Episode in Anti-Catholicism: The American Protective Association*, 33–35, 47–48; Higham, *Strangers in the Land*, 35–105; David H. Bennett, *The Party of Fear: The American Far Right from Nativism to the Militia Movement*, 174; Ritter, *Inventing America's First Immigration Crisis*, 1–173.

72. Bennett, *Party of Fear*, 171–73.

73. Kinzer, *Episode in Anti-Catholicism*, 81–83; Bennett, *Party of Fear*, 171–76; Higham, *Strangers in the Land*, 84–85. In reviewing anti-Catholic literature from the 1890s, Bennett cites the reprinting of Maria Monk's convent exposé from the 1830s as well as the emergence of several similar pamphlets and books, particularly related to Margaret Shepherd, that detailed alleged atrocities within the Catholic Church. For more information on anti-Catholicism literature in the nineteenth century, see Cassandra Yacovazzi, *Escaped Nuns: True Womanhood and the Campaign against Convents in Antebellum America*.

74. Kinzer, *Episode in Anti-Catholicism*, 85; *St. Joseph Herald*, 4 April 1894. The three APA-linked nativist newspapers included the *Kansas City American*, *Springfield Protestant American*, and *St. Louis True American*. *APA Magazine*, December 1895. For comments by the *Western Watchman* about APA influence in St. Louis, see *Western Watchman*, 16 May 1895.

75. Kinzer, *Episode in Anti-Catholicism*, 140; Bennett, *Party of Fear*, 178.

76. *Menace*, 11 November 1911.

77. Justin Nordstrom, *Danger on the Doorstep: Anti-Catholicism and American Print Culture in the Progressive Era*, 10, 56, 183; Matt Pearce, "A Century Ago, a Popular Missouri Newspaper Demonized a Religious Minority: Catholics," *Los Angeles Times*, 9 December 2015; *Menace*, 11 November 1911; *Springfield News & Leader*, 21 February 1960.

78. Pearce, "Century Ago"; Nordstrom, *Danger on the Doorstep*, 80–82.

79. Pearce, "Century Ago"; Nordstrom, *Danger on the Doorstep*, 80–82.

80. Pearce, "Century Ago"; Nordstrom, *Danger on the Doorstep*, 80–82; *Kansas City Star*, 29 September 1929; *Joplin Globe*, 29 September 1929; *Springfield News & Leader*, 21 February 1960.

81. *Menace*, 10 October 1914, 28 November 1914, 27 February 1915, 10 April 1915, 4 December 1915, 8 January 1916, 13 May 1916, 10 March 1917, 14 April 1917, 5 May 1917, 25 August 1917, 1 September 1917, 22 September 1917, 29 September 1917, 6 October 1917, 3 November 1917; *Springfield News & Leader*, 21 February 1960. For more information on legal challenges to the *Menace*, including the banning of the

Notes to Chapter One 307

publication in Canada, see Nordstrom, *Danger on the Doorstep*, 1–2, 76–77, 114–17, 129–42, 176, 182–85; Pearce, "Century Ago"; and Christopher Kauffman, *Faith and Fraternalism: The History of the Knights of Columbus*, 268–89.

82. Robert Sidney Douglass, *History of Southeast Missouri: A Narrative Account of Its Historical Progress, Its People and Its Principal Interests*, 571–72. On Nations's years as a schoolteacher, see *Ste. Genevieve Fair Play*, 30 March 1889, 8 August 1891, 25 March 1893, 1 July 1893, 16 February 1895, 13 April 1895.

83. On Nations's congressional campaigns and his splintering from the Republican Party, see *Greenville Sun*, 12 May 1904, 7 February 1908, 18 February 1908, 9 July 1908; *St. Louis Globe-Democrat*, 27 July 1906, 6 August 1908, 31 July 1912; *Kansas City Times*, 27 May 1908; *Grandin Herald*, 6 February 1908, 2 July 1908; *Iron County Register*, 16 July 1908, 31 October 1912; *Ellington Press*, 16 July 1908, 23 July 1908, 30 July 1908; *Jefferson County Republican*, 31 July 1908; *Perry County Sun*, 6 August 1908; *Jefferson Democrat*, 29 October 1908; *Ellington Press*, 13 June 1912; *Fredericktown Democrat-News*, 22 August 1912; *Chillicothe Constitution-Tribune*, 9 May 1914; and *Bloomfield Vindicator*, 7 April 1916.

84. For Nations's involvement with temperance and the Constitutional Amendment Association, see *St. Louis Globe-Democrat*, 29 June 1909, 4 August 1909, 18 October 1910; *Chillicothe Constitution*, 14 October 1909; *Mexico Missouri Message*, 21 October 1909; *Chariton Courier*, 22 October 1909; *Kansas City Star*, 24 October 1909; *Jackson Herald*, 25 November 1909, 9 December 1909; *Fredericktown Democrat-News*, 16 December 1909, 8 July 1915; *St. Louis Post-Dispatch*, 12 March 1910, 6 October 1910; *Kansas City Word and Way*, 10 March 1910, 19 May 1910, 2 June 1910, 16 June 1910; *Bloomfield Vindicator*, 24 June 1910; *Poplar Bluff Weekly Citizen-Democrat*, 21 October 1910; *Macon Republican*, 22 October 1910; *University Missourian*, 3 November 1910; *Canton Press*, 4 November 1910; and *Piedmont Weekly Banner*, 22 July 1915.

85. Robbi Courtaway, *Wetter than the Mississippi: Prohibition in St. Louis and Beyond*, 93; Gilbert O. Nations, *The Blight of Mexico; or, Four Hundred Years of Papal Tyranny and Plunder*; Gilbert O. Nations, *Papal Sovereignty: The Government within Our Government*; Gilbert O. Nations, *Papal Guilt of the World War*.

86. *Menace*, 24 March 1917, 7 April 1917, 14 April 1917, 19 May 1917, 26 May 1917, 2 June 1917, 23 June 1917, 28 July 1917, 4 August 1917, 11 August 1917, 29 September 1917, 10 November 1917, 17 November 1917, 16 February 1918, 23 February 1918, 16 March 1918, 23 March 1918, 6 April 1918.

87. *Menace*, 20 May 1916, 22 June 1918.

88. Nordstrom, *Danger on the Doorstep*, 194–96; *Menace*, 9 February 1918, 19 March 1918, 15 October 1918, 26 October 1918; *Springfield News & Leader*, 21 February 1960.

89. *St. Louis Post-Dispatch*, 14 February 1950; *Joplin Globe*, 29 September 1929.

90. *Kansas City Journal*, 11 October 1922, 12 October 1922, 29 October 1922; *Kansas City Star*, 11 October 1922, 29 October 1922.

91. *Kansas City Journal*, 17 January 1923, 20 January 1923; *Independence Examiner*, 19 January 1923; *Kansas City Times*, 17 January 1923, 22 January 1923; *New Menace*, 24 February 1923.

92. Lisa McGirr, *The War on Alcohol: Prohibition and the Rise of the American State*, 132–42; L. Gordon, *Second Coming of the KKK*, 95–96.

308 Notes to Chapter One

93. For detailed histories of the Anti-Saloon League and Woman's Christian Temperance Union, see K. Austin Kerr, *Organized for Prohibition: A New History of the Anti-Saloon League*; Thomas R. Pegram, *Battling Demon Rum: The Struggle for a Dry America*; McGirr, *War on Alcohol*; Ruth Bordin, *Woman and Temperance: The Quest for Power and Liberty, 1873–1900*; Ian Tyrrell, *Woman's World, Woman's Empire: The Woman's Christian Temperance Union in International Perspective, 1880–1930*; Ruth Bordin, *Frances Willard: A Biography*; and B. Blanche Butts-Runion, "Through the Years": A History of the First Seventy-Five Years of the Woman's Christian Temperance Union of Missouri, 1882–1957.

94. Chalmers, *Hooded Americanism*, 31–32; L. Gordon, *Second Coming on the KKK*, 13.

95. Pegram, *Battling Demon Rum*, 170–73; McGirr, *War on Alcohol*, 6–13; Kerr, *Organized for Prohibition*, 230–31.

96. *Missouri Valley Independent*, 4 October 1923.

97. For more information on the WCTU and its stance on issues of bigotry, see Bordin, *Woman and Temperance*, 85–87; Tyrrell, *Woman's World, Woman's Empire*, 4–8, 81–113; Bordin, *Frances Willard: A Biography*, 54–65; Glenda Elizabeth Gilmore, *Gender and Jim Crow: Women and the Politics of White Supremacy in North Carolina, 1896–1920*, 45–59; McGirr, *War on Alcohol*, 139–42; MacLean, *Behind the Mask of Chivalry*, 40, 106, 110, 116; Blee, *Women of the Klan*, 25–28, 40, 103–4; *Union Signal*, 22 May 1924; *Missouri Counselor*, December 1922; and *St. Louis Post-Dispatch*, 9 September 1925, 10 September 1925, 14 September 1925.

98. *St. Louis Star*, 21 May 1924.

99. Courtaway, *Wetter than the Mississippi*, 88–105.

100. *Joplin Globe*, 8 March 1921.

101. Christensen and Kremer, *A History of Missouri*, 24; Richard S. Kirkendall, *A History of Missouri*, 67–74, 152–61; Franklin D. Mitchell, *Embattled Democracy: Missouri Democratic Politics, 1919–1932*, 15.

102. Lawrence O. Christensen et al., eds., *Dictionary of Missouri Biography*, 601–4.

103. Christensen et al., *Dictionary of Missouri Biography*, 601–4. For monographs that survey Pendergast's life, see Lawrence H. Larsen and Nancy J. Hulston, *Pendergast!*; Robert H. Ferrell, *Truman and Pendergast*; Lyle W. Dorsett, *The Pendergast Machine*; William M. Reddig, *Tom's Town: Kansas City and the Pendergast Legend*; and Diane Mutti Burke, Jason Roe, and John Herron, eds., *Wide-Open Town: Kansas City in the Pendergast Era*.

104. Christensen et al., *Dictionary of Missouri Biography*, 687–89.

105. Gary R. Kremer, "William J. Thompkins: African American Physician, Politician, and Publisher," 170–71; Thomas D. Wilson, "Chester A. Franklin and Harry S. Truman: An African-American Conservative and the 'Conversion' of the Future President," 53–54; Schirmer, *City Divided*, 153, 160–61; Mutti Burke, Roe, and Herron, *Wide Open Town*, 36–41.

106. Christensen et al., *Dictionary of Missouri Biography*, 418–19; *Kansas City Times*, 3 November 1922; Arthur M. Hyde to A. D. Spencer, 25 October 1924, folder 369, Arthur Mastick Hyde Papers, State Historical Society of Missouri, Columbia (hereafter cited as AMH, SHSMO).

Notes to Chapter One

309

107. Christensen et al., *Dictionary of Missouri Biography*, 25–26; *St. Louis Post-Dispatch*, 14 October 1924, 29 October 1924; *Kansas City Call*, 31 October 1924.

108. *Missouri Kourier*, 5 September 1924.

109. *St. Louis Post-Dispatch*, 11 May 1921, 6 September 1921; *Kansas City Times*, 20 October 1921.

110. *St. Louis Star*, 25 September 1921; *St. Louis Globe-Democrat*, 25 September 1921; *St. Louis Post-Dispatch*, 25 September 1921.

111. *St. Louis Post-Dispatch*, 11 April 1922; *St. Louis Star*, 11 April 1922; *St. Louis Globe-Democrat*, 11 April 1922.

112. *Patriot*, 12 July 1923, 27 July 1923, 17 August 1923, 24 August 1923, 7 September 1923, 28 September 1923, 5 October 1923, 17 October 1923, 1 November 1923, 15 November 1923, 22 November 1923, 13 December 1923, 27 December 1923, 3 January 1924, 10 January 1924, 7 February 1924; *St. Louis Post-Dispatch*, 10 October 1922, 31 May 1923, 25 June 1923, 5 August 1923, 26 February 1924.

113. *St. Louis Star*, 2 December 1922, 26 December 1922, 7 May 1923, 2 June 1923, 8 June 1823, 12 June 1923; *Missouri Valley Independent*, 3 May 1923, 7 June 1923; *St. Louis Post-Dispatch*, 5 June 1923, 14 June 1923.

114. For issues of the *Patriot*, see reel 41734, Columbia Research Center, State Historical Society of Missouri, Columbia. Born in 1875 near Des Moines, Iowa, Frederick Barkhurst began his career in newspapers while still a teenager. Barely out of school, he bought a weekly newspaper in Stanhope, Iowa, before moving on to Chicago. Eventually, he relocated to Missouri to work at newspaper offices in Forest City, Maryville, Carthage, Springfield, and St. Joseph. After a brief period spent as a literary syndicate contributor to newspapers on the East Coast, Barkhurst moved back to Missouri to work with the *St. Louis Evening Times*. *Springfield Daily Leader*, 8 October 1923; *St. Louis Globe-Democrat*, 17 January 1944.

115. For issues of *Missouri Fiery Cross*, *Klan Kourier*, and *Missouri Kourier*, see reel 41734, Columbia Research Center, State Historical Society of Missouri, Columbia.

116. "Minutes of Proceedings of Investigating Committee on Methodist Episcopal Church, South versus Charles D. McGehee," n.d., folders 68–71, William Fletcher McMurry Papers, State Historical Society of Missouri, Columbia (hereafter cited as WFM, SHSMO); *St. Louis Post-Dispatch*, 20 June 1923, 25 June 1923, 24 September 1923. For census data on McGehee, see Year: 1920; Census Place: Indianola, Sunflower, Mississippi; Roll: T625_894; Page: 7B; Enumeration District: 119.

117. *St. Louis Post-Dispatch*, 12 March 1923, 16 April 1923, 25 June 1923, 1 September 1923, 2 September 1923, 3 September 1923.

118. *St. Louis Post-Dispatch*, 25 June 1923.

119. "Minutes of Proceedings of Investigating Committee on Methodist Episcopal Church, South versus Charles D. McGehee," n.d., folders 68–71, WFM, SHSMO; *St. Louis Post-Dispatch*, 1 September 1923.

120. *St. Louis Post-Dispatch*, 3 September 1923.

121. "Minutes of Proceedings of Investigating Committee on Methodist Episcopal Church, South versus Charles D. McGehee," n.d., folders 68–71, WFM, SHSMO; *St. Louis Post-Dispatch*, 2 September 1923.

310 Notes to Chapter One

122. "Minutes of Proceedings of Investigating Committee on Methodist Episcopal Church, South versus Charles D. McGehee," n.d., folders 68–71, WFM, SHSMO; *St. Louis Post-Dispatch*, 3 September 1923.

123. *St. Louis Post-Dispatch*, 1 September 1923, 2 September 1923, 3 September 1923.

124. *St. Louis Post-Dispatch*, 24 September 1923.

125. "Minutes of Proceedings of Investigating Committee on Methodist Episcopal Church, South versus Charles D. McGehee," n.d., folders 68–71, WFM, SHSMO; *St. Louis Post-Dispatch*, 13 February 1924.

126. *St. Louis Post-Dispatch*, 13 February 1924, 26 October 1924.

127. Alexander, *Ku Klux Klan in the Southwest*, 43–44; *St. Louis Globe-Democrat*, 8 March 1928; *Kansas City Times*, 27 December 1951.

128. *Missouri Valley Independent*, 27 September 1923.

129. *Kansas City Star*, 13 July 1924.

130. *Poplar Bluff Interstate American*, 17 July 1924.

131. *Missouri Kourier*, 10 October 1924, 17 October 1924.

132. Knights of the Ku Klux Klan, Inc., *Proceedings of the Second Imperial Klonvokation*.

133. Rives, "Second Ku Klux Klan in Kansas City."

134. *Missouri Valley Independent*, 22 February 1923.

135. Rives, "Second Ku Klux Klan in Kansas City."

136. *Kansas City Journal*, 24 July 1921.

137. *Kansas City Journal*, 11 October 1922, 29 October 1922; *Kansas City Star*, 11 October 1922, 29 October 1922, 16 January 1924; *Kansas City Times*, 11 July 1923.

138. *Kansas City Journal*, 12 October 1922, 12 December 1923; *Kansas City Star*, 29 October 1922, 8 November 1922.

139. *Kansas City Times*, 11 July 1923.

140. *Kansas City Star*, 22 August 1948, 15 February 1959.

141. *Kansas City Journal*, 2 November 1922; *Kansas City Times*, 30 April 1924, 4 November 1924; *St. Louis Post-Dispatch*, 27 October 1944; *Kansas City Star*, 14 April 1924, 26 October 1944.

142. *Missouri Valley Independent*, 15 February 1923, 22 February 1923, 1 March 1923, 5 April 1923, 17 March 1923, 7 June 1923, 19 July 1923, 26 July 1923, 9 August 1923, 16 August 1923, 23 August 1923, 30 August 1923, 6 March 1924.

143. *Missouri Valley Independent*, 31 May 1923.

144. *Missouri Valley Independent*, 9 August 1923.

145. *Kansas City Times*, 11 July 1923; *Missouri Valley Independent*, 7 February 1924, 14 February 1924, 17 April 1924.

146. *Missouri Valley Independent*, 6 March 1924.

147. *Blackwell Daily News*, 30 June 1914; *Missouri Valley Independent*, 22 March 1923; *St. Louis Star*, 14 February 1924; *Blackwell Morning Tribune*, 29 September 1939; *Daily Oklahoman*, 29 September 1939.

148. *Missouri Valley Independent*, 1 March 1923, 22 March 1923, 24 May 1923, 14 June 1923, 21 June 1923, 19 July 1923, 2 August 1923, 9 August 1923.

149. *Missouri Valley Independent*, 14 June 1923.

150. Wallace Klan #60 to Arthur Hyde, 25 January 1923, folder 367, AMH, SHS-MO; Willow Springs Klan Number Thirty Five Realm of MO to Arthur Hyde, Western

Union Telegram, 26 January 1923, folder 367, AMH, SHSMO; W. M. Campbell to Arthur Hyde, Western Union Telegram, 27 January 1923, folder 367, AMH, SHSMO; John E. Slater to Arthur Hyde, Western Union Telegram, 28 January 1923, folder 367, AMH, SHSMO; Isaac Shambaugh Klan #7 Neosho, Granby Provisional Klan, Diamond Provisional Klan to Arthur Hyde, Western Union Telegram, folder 367, AMH, SHSMO; Higginsville Klan No. 36 to Arthur Hyde, 27 January 1923, folder 367, AMH, SHSMO; Washburn Klan No. 25 to Arthur Hyde, 23 January 1923, folder 367, AMH, SHSMO; Holden Klan No. 30 to Arthur Hyde, N.D., folder 367, AMH, SHSMO; Independence Klan No. 27 to Arthur Hyde, 27 January 1923, folder 367, AMH, SHSMO; Pleasant Hill Klan No. 54 to Arthur Hyde, 28 January 1923, folder 367, AMH, SHSMO.

151. *Joplin Globe*, 10 April 1921.

152. *Joplin Globe*, 30 October 1921, 7 February 1923, 8 February 1923, 20 January 1924, 5 October 1924, 23 November 1924, 16 July 1929, 27 July 1929.

153. *Joplin Globe*, 20 December 1921, 25 December 1921, 16 July 1929, 27 July 1929. For articles that focus on alleged Klan violence in the South, see *Joplin Globe*, 23 July 1921, 2 October 1921, 6 October 1921, 2 November 1921, 6 November 1921, 24 November 1921, 4 December 1921.

154. Isaac Shambaugh Klan #7 Neosho, Granby Provisional Klan, Diamond Provisional Klan to Arthur Hyde, Western Union Telegram, folder 367, AMH, SHSMO; *Springfield Daily Leader*, 26 August 1922, 21 July 1923, 28 September 1923; *Springfield Missouri Republican*, 27 August 1922; *Missouri Valley Independent*, 26 April 1923.

155. *Springfield Missouri Republican*, 26 April 1921.

156. *Springfield Daily Leader*, 26 March 1921.

157. *Springfield Daily Leader*, 1 May 1922, 30 July 1922; Campney, *Hostile Heartland*, 123–24.

158. *Springfield Daily Leader*, 20 August 1922; *Springfield Missouri Republican*, 20 August 1922, 25 August 1922, 27 August 1922.

159. *Springfield Daily Leader*, 26 June 1922; *Springfield Missouri Republican*, 27 June 1922; Willow Springs Klan Number Thirty Five Realm of MO to Arthur Hyde, Western Union Telegram, 26 January 1923, folder 367, AMH, SHSMO; Campney, *Hostile Heartland*, 123–24.

160. *Poplar Bluff Weekly Citizen-Democrat*, 27 July 1922; *Fredericktown Democrat-News*, 22 February 1923, 19 July 1923.

161. *Word and Way*, 12 May 1910, 24 November 1910, 14 September 1911; *Poplar Bluff American*, 22 August 1921, 22 October 1923.

162. *Word and Way*, 28 December 1911, 29 January 1914.

163. *Menace*, 18 April 1914, 25 April 1914, 2 May 1914, 9 May 1914, 27 June 1914.

164. *Des Moines Evening Tribune*, 4 September 1921, 16 September 1921; *Des Moines Register*, 18 September 1921.

165. *Memphis Commercial Appeal*, 9 September 1923; *Missouri Valley Independent*, 1 February 1923, 27 September 1923; *Poplar Bluff Weekly Citizen-Democrat*, 25 January 1923; *Wayne County Journal*, 22 February 1923; *Poplar Bluff Interstate-American*, 27 February 1923, 24 March 1923, 5 June 1924, 6 June 1924, 7 June 1924, 24 June 1924, 16 July 1924.

312 Notes to Chapter One

166. *Poplar Bluff Interstate-American*, 22 October 1923; *Poplar Bluff Weekly Citizen-Democrat*, 15 November 1923.

167. *Poplar Bluff Interstate-American*, 5 June 1924, 6 June 1924, 7 June 1924, 24 June 1924, 16 July 1924.

168. *Memphis Commercial Appeal*, 19 August 1924; *Poplar Bluff Republican*, 20 August 1924, 27 August 1924.

169. "Daily Reminder 1924," "Daily Reminder 1925," "Daily Reminder 1926," folders 29–30, Charles Merlin Barnes Papers, State Historical Society of Missouri, Columbia (hereafter cited as CMB, SHSMO).

170. *Missouri Valley Independent*, 15 March 1923.

171. *Missouri Valley Independent*, 15 March 1923.

172. *One Hundred Years of Medicine and Surgery in Missouri: Historical and Biographical Review of the Careers of the Physicians and Surgeons of the State of Missouri, and Sketches of Some of Its Notable Medical Institutions*, 228; *St. Joseph News-Press*, 13 June 1953.

173. *St. Joseph News-Press*, 14 December 1910, 15 December 1910, 16 December 1910.

174. *Missouri Valley Independent*, 3 January 1924.

175. *St. Joseph Gazette*, 2 October 1921.

176. *Missouri Valley Independent*, 23 October 1924, 30 October 1924.

177. *Missouri Valley Independent*, 23 August 1923.

178. *Missouri Valley Independent*, 4 December 1924.

179. For issues of the *Missouri Valley Independent*, see reels 37680–82, Columbia Research Center, State Historical Society of Missouri, Columbia.

180. *St. Joseph News-Press*, 20 April 1934.

181. *Fulton Sun-Gazette*, 21 August 1965.

182. *St. Joseph News-Press*, 10 January 1941; *Kansas City Times*, 10 January 1941; *Missouri Valley Independent*, 1 March 1923, 8 March 1923, 15 March 1923, 17 May 1923, 31 May 1923, 30 August 1923, 18 October 1923, 7 August 1924, 21 August 1924.

183. *Missouri Valley Independent*, 18 January 1923, 7 February 1923, 15 February 1923, 22 February 1923, 22 March 1923, 29 March 1923, 5 April 1923, 24 May 1923, 31 May 1923, 21 June 1923, 26 July 1923, 2 August 1923, 23 August 1923.

184. Jason McDonald, "'Watch Adair County Klan Grow': The Second Ku Klux Klan in Kirksville, Missouri, 1923–1925"; *Missouri Valley Independent*, 24 May 1923, 31 May 1923, 26 July 1923, 2 August 1923.

185. *Missouri Valley Independent*, 14 June 1923; *Palmyra Spectator*, 19 July 1923.

186. *Official Manual of the State of Missouri for the Years 1909–1910*, 15–16; *St. Louis Post-Dispatch*, 7 October 1924; *Jefferson City Democrat-Tribune*, 8 October 1924; *St. Louis Argus*, 10 October 1924, 17 October 1924; *Jefferson City Tribune*, 25 July 1925, 27 July 1925.

187. Courtaway, *Wetter than the Mississippi*, 88–105; *Jefferson City Democrat-Tribune*, 25 October 1916; *St. Louis Globe-Democrat*, 4 September 1918; *St. Louis Post-Dispatch*, 18 December 1920; *Nevada Southwest Mail*, 25 February 1921; *Kansas City Times*, 7 May 1923; *Farmington Times*, 27 January 1910.

Notes to Chapter Two

188. *Patriot*, 12 July 1923.

189. Kremer, *Heartland History*, 32–34; *Jefferson City Daily Capital News*, 22 August 1923, 23 August 1923, 24 August 1923, 2 October 1923; *Jefferson City Democrat-Tribune*, 1 October 1923.

190. *Patriot*, 12 July 1923, 21 September 1923, 22 November 1923.

191. Kremer, *Heartland History*, 32–34; *St. Louis Post-Dispatch*, 14 February 1924, 15 February 1924; *St. Louis Star*, 14 February 1924; *Kansas City Star*, 14 February 1924; *Jefferson City Democrat-Tribune*, 15 February 1924. For letters opposing the Klan's use of the capitol, see W. S. O'Brien to Arthur Hyde, 15 February 1924, folder 368, AMH, SHSMO; Vincent M. Carroll to Arthur Hyde, Western Union Telegram, 14 February 1924, folder 368, AMH, SHSMO; Fred E. Kies to Hiram Lloyd, Western Union Telegram, 16 February 1924, folder 368, AMH, SHSMO; and *St. Louis Post-Dispatch*, 14 February 1924, 15 February 1924, 16 February 1924, 22 February 1924. For letters supporting the Klan's use of the capitol, see Sam J. Corbett to Arthur Hyde, 23 February 1924, folder 368, AMH, SHSMO; Harry Houck to Arthur Hyde, 25 February 1924, folder 368, AMH, SHSMO; and Guy Davis to Arthur Hyde, 26 February 1924, folder 368, AMH, SHSMO.

192. *St. Louis Star*, 15 February 1924.

193. Kremer, *Heartland History*, 32–34; *Jefferson City Democrat-Tribune*, 12 July 1924, 14 July 1924, 15 July 1924; *Jefferson City Daily Capital News*, 13 July 1924, 15 July 1924; Jerry Butcher, *Ku Klux Klan: The "Invisible Empire" in the Missouri Capital, Governor Arthur M. Hyde versus the Ku Klux Klan*.

194. Hugh Q. Miller to Arthur Hyde, 13 July 1924, folder 368, AMH, SHSMO.

195. Kremer, *Heartland History*, 32–34; *Fulton Daily Sun*, 21 August 1923, 23 August 1923, 12 May 1924; *Fulton Gazette*, 23 August 1923, 20 September 1923, 8 November 1923, 29 November 1923, 27 December 1923, 15 May 1924; *Fulton Missouri Telegraph*, 15 May 1924; *Mokane Missourian*, 30 November 1923, 28 December 1923.

196. J. D. Whitman to Arthur Hyde, 24 July 1924, folder 368, AMH, SHSMO.

197. *Centralia Courier*, 6 April 1923, 17 July 1923; *Columbia Missourian*, 31 July 1923.

198. Kremer, *Heartland History*, 32–34; *Jefferson City Tribune*, 25 July 1925, 27 July 1925. For details on the Washington, DC, Klan parade, see Pegram, *One Hundred Percent American*, 185; and Chalmers, *Hooded Americanism*, 285–88.

199. *Jefferson City Tribune*, 27 July 1925.

200. *Jefferson City Tribune*, 25 July 1925.

Chapter Two
"Masked Malcontents"
Violence, Vigilantism, and the Anti-Klan Press

1. *Springfield Republican*, 19 June 1921; *Kansas City Post*, 20 June 1921; *Greenfield Vedette*, 30 June 1921.

2. *Springfield Republican*, 19 June 1921; *Kansas City Post*, 20 June 1921; *Kansas City Kansan*, 20 June 1921; *Lincoln Journal*, 20 June 1921; *New York Daily News*, 21 June 1921; *Greenfield Vedette*, 30 June 1921.

314   Notes to Chapter Two

3. *Springfield Daily Leader*, 24 June 1921.

4. *Springfield Republican*, 19 June 1921; *Kansas City Post*, 20 June 1921; *Greenfield Vedette*, 30 June 1921; *Springfield Daily Leader*, 27 June 1921; *St. Louis Globe-Democrat*, 1 July 1921.

5. *Springfield Republican*, 12 July 1921, 31 July 1921.

6. *Springfield Daily Leader*, 18 July 1921.

7. *Columbia Evening Missourian*, 9 April 1921; *Kansas City Star*, 13 May 1921.

8. *Southeast Missourian*, 2 April 1921; *Fulton Daily Sun*, 2 April 1921; *Fulton Gazette*, 7 April 1921; *Columbia Missourian*, 2 April 1921; *St. Louis Argus*, 20 May 1921; *Kansas City Star*, 13 May 1921, 22 July 1921, 23 July 1921, 24 July 1921, 26 July 1921, 31 July 1921; *Kansas City Journal*, 18 July 1921, 20 July 1921, 21 July 1921, 23 July 1921, 26 July 1921, 27 July 1921, 28 July 1921, 29 July 1921, 30 July 1921, 31 July 1921; *Kansas City Catholic Register*, 7 July 1921, 21 July 1921, 28 July 1921.

9. *Kansas City Star*, 31 July 1921.

10. *St. Louis Post-Dispatch*, 6 July 1921, 7 July 1921; *St. Louis Argus*, 15 April 1921; *Church Progress*, 7 July 1921, 14 July 1921; *Western Watchman*, 27 May 1921, 22 July 1921, 29 July 1921, 12 August 1921, 26 August 1921; *Southeast Missourian*, 22 July 1921; *Columbia Missourian*, 9 April 1921, 20 July 1921, 22 July 1921, 29 July 1921; *Joplin Globe*, 9 June 1921, 23 July 1921; *Fulton Daily Sun*, 22 January 1921, 20 June 1921; *Jasper County Democrat*, 24 June 1921.

11. *Church Progress*, 28 July 1921.

12. *Jewish Voice*, 6 October 1921.

13. *St. Louis Post-Dispatch*, 25 July 1921.

14. *Modern View*, 16 September 1921.

15. *St. Louis Star*, 8 July 1921.

16. *St. Louis Globe-Democrat*, 8 May 1921.

17. *St. Louis Argus*, 21 January 1921.

18. *St. Louis Argus*, 18 February 1921.

19. Debra Foster Greene, "Published in the Interest of Colored People: The *St. Louis Argus* Newspaper in the Twentieth Century," 9–12, 12–24.

20. D. Greene, "Published in the Interest of Colored People," 15–16, 14, 32–70, 45.

21. D. Greene, "Published in the Interest of Colored People," 44–45.

22. *St. Louis Post-Dispatch*, 6 September 1921; *St. Louis Argus*, 9 September 1921.

23. *St. Louis Argus*, 16 September 1921.

24. *St. Louis Argus*, 16 September 1921.

25. *St. Louis Argus*, 23 September 1921.

26. *St. Louis Argus*, 30 September 1921; *St. Louis Post-Dispatch*, 28 September 1921; *St. Louis Globe-Democrat*, 28 September 1921.

27. *St. Louis Argus*, 30 September 1921; *St. Louis Post-Dispatch*, 28 September 1921; *St. Louis Globe-Democrat*, 29 September 1921.

28. *St. Louis Argus*, 30 September 1921.

29. *St. Louis Argus*, 14 October 1921.

30. *St. Louis Post-Dispatch*, 8 October 1921; *St. Louis Globe-Democrat*, 8 October 1921; *St. Louis Star*, 8 October 1921; *St. Louis Argus*, 14 October 1921. Those who refused to vote in favor of the anti-Klan resolution were Gus A. Baur (Fourteenth Ward), Alfred

Bergmann (Eighteenth Ward), Ralph H. Eilers (Twenty-Sixth Ward), John Fett (Eleventh Ward), Charles A. Groeschel (Twenty-Fourth Ward), Joseph Heckel (Thirteenth Ward), Joseph Hirth (Eighth Ward), Hermann C. Kralemann (Twenty-Second Ward), Edward Kuhs (First Ward), Martin D. Lohman (Ninth Ward), George Meisinger (Tenth Ward), Charles A. Neumann (Twelfth Ward), August H. Niederluecke (Nineteenth Ward), William Otto (Fourth Ward), Adam Reis (Sixteenth Ward), Edward Scholl (Second Ward), Wilber C. Schwartz (Twelfth Ward), Clinton E. Udell (Twenty-Third Ward), William J. Studt (Twenty-First Ward), Harry Uhlemeyer (Fifteenth Ward), Henry Wander (Seventh Ward), Edward Wiehe (Fifth Ward), and Samuel L. Wimer (Twenty-Seventh Ward).

31. *St. Louis Argus*, 14 October 1921.

32. *St. Louis Argus*, 14 October 1921.

33. *St. Louis Star*, 8 October 1921.

34. *St. Louis Post-Dispatch*, 15 October 1921; *St. Louis Globe-Democrat*, 15 October 1921; *St. Louis Star*, 15 October 1921.

35. *Kansas City Catholic Register*, 2 June 1921.

36. *Kansas City Catholic Register*, 7 July 1921, 21 July 1921, 28 July 1921.

37. *Kansas City Journal*, 21 July 1921.

38. *Kansas City Call*, 29 April 1922.

39. *Kansas City Star*, 12 October 1921; *Kansas City Call*, 29 April 1922.

40. *Kansas City Call*, 29 April 1922.

41. For general resources on the Ku Klux Klan and anti-Semitism in the United States in the early twentieth century, see Jonathan D. Sarna, *American Judaism: A History*, 214–23; Jacob M. Sable, "Some American Jewish Organizational Efforts to Combat Anti-Semitism, 1906–30," 258–59; Leonard Dinnerstein, *Antisemitism in America*, 78–104; David A. Gerber, ed., *Anti-Semitism in American History*, 22–33; Lynn Dumenil, *The Modern Temper: American Culture and Society in the 1920s*, 214–17, 235–49.

42. Judith M. Firestone, "Jewish Journalism in Kansas City," in *Mid-America's Promise*, ed. Schultz, 185–98.

43. Firestone, "Jewish Journalism in Kansas City," in *Mid-America's Promise*, ed. Schultz, 186.

44. *Kansas City Catholic Register*, 27 April 1922, 11 May 1922, 22 June 1922; *Kansas City Jewish Chronicle*, 12 May 1922; Barbara J. Rush, "The Ku Klux Klan in Kansas City during the Twenties," 98–102.

45. *Kansas City Catholic Register*, 27 April 1922; *St. Louis Argus*, 5 May 1922; *Kansas City Call*, 13 May 1922, 20 May 1922; *Kansan*, n.d., Ku Klux Klan—April 1922, folder 17, box C-313, National Association for the Advancement of Colored People Records, Library of Congress (hereafter cited as NAACP, LOC).

46. *Kansas City Catholic Register*, 11 May 1922; *Shreveport Journal*, 7 May 1922, Ku Klux Klan—May, 1922, folder 18, box C-313, NAACP, LOC; Rush, "Ku Klux Klan in Kansas City during the Twenties," 90–91. For information on the Ku Klux Klan in Kansas City, Kansas, see Rives, "Second Ku Klux Klan in Kansas City"; and Rush, "Ku Klux Klan in Kansas City during the Twenties."

47. *Kansas City Jewish Chronicle*, 12 May 1922.

48. Wilson, "Chester A. Franklin and Harry S. Truman," 49–50.

316 Notes to Chapter Two

49. Wilson, "Chester A. Franklin and Harry S. Truman," 50–51, 52, 53–56.

50. Wilson, "Chester A. Franklin and Harry S. Truman," 57; Roy Wilkins, *Standing Fast: The Autobiography of Roy Wilkins*, 54–56; Yvonne Ryan, *Roy Wilkins: The Quiet Revolutionary and the NAACP*, 1–12.

51. Wilkins, *Standing Fast*, 56–110; Schirmer, *City Divided*, 115, 128–29; George A. McElroy, "Roy Wilkins as a Journalist," 21–42.

52. Wilkins, *Standing Fast*, 60.

53. *Kansas City Call*, 25 March 1922, 29 April 1922, 13 May 1922; 10 June 1922, 17 June 1922; 8 July 1922, 15 July 1922, 13 October 1922, 27 October 1922, 3 November 1922, 10 November 1922, 15 December 1922, 26 January 1923, 1 June 1923, 25 July 1924, 1 August 1924, 3 October 1924, 17 October 1924, 31 October 1924, 16 October 1925, 2 July 1926, 13 August 1926, 24 September 1926, 25 February 1927, 24 June 1927, 17 February 1928.

54. *Kansas City Call*, 29 April 1922, 13 May 1922, 10 June 1922, 17 Jun 1922, 8 July 1922, 15 July 1922.

55. *Kansas City Call*, 10 June 1922, 17 June 1922.

56. *Kansas City Call*, 10 June 1922.

57. *Kansas City Call*, 26 January 1923.

58. *Kansas City Jewish Chronicle*, 15 December 1922.

59. *Kansas City Jewish Chronicle*, 22 August 1924.

60. *Kansas City Catholic Register*, 29 June 1922.

61. *Kansas City Catholic Register*, 11 May 1922, 18 May 1922, 25 May 1922, 22 June 1922, 29 June 1922, 27 July 1922, 14 September 1922, 21 September 1922, 28 September 1922, 5 October 1922, 12 October 1922, 19 October 1922, 26 October 1922, 4 November 1922, 11 November 1922, 16 November 1922.

62. *Kansas City Catholic Register*, 18 May 1922, 25 May 1922.

63. For examples of *New York World* articles republished in the *Kansas City Catholic Register*, see 14 September 1922, 21 September 1922, and 28 September 1922.

64. *Kansas City Catholic Register*, 28 September 1922.

65. *Kansas City Journal*, 12 October 1922.

66. *Kansas City Catholic Register*, 5 October 1922, 12 October 1922, 19 October 1922, 26 October 1922, 2 November 1922, 9 November 1922, 16 November 1922.

67. *Kansas City Catholic Register*, 5 October 1922.

68. *St. Joseph News-Press*, 19 July 1921.

69. *Sikeston Standard*, 9 March 1923.

70. *Springfield Leader*, 3 October 1921.

71. *Jefferson City Democrat-Tribune*, 24 August 1923, 3 October 1923; *Jefferson City Daily Capital News*, 3 October 1923.

72. *Columbia Daily Tribune*, 26 March 1923.

73. *Poplar Bluff Daily American Republic*, 21 May 1951.

74. *Poplar Bluff Daily American Republic*, 21 May 1951.

75. *Poplar Bluff Republican*, 3 February 1921.

76. *Poplar Bluff Interstate-American*, 6 July 1922, 18 July 1922; *Poplar Bluff Republican*, 20 July 1922, 27 July 1922, 10 August 1922 7 September 1922, 14 September 1922, 28 September 1922.

Notes to Chapter Two

77. *Poplar Bluff Republican*, 21 September 1921.

78. *Poplar Bluff Republican*, 20 July 1922.

79. *Poplar Bluff Republican*, 27 July 1922.

80. *Poplar Bluff Republican*, 14 September 1922.

81. *Poplar Bluff Republican*, 31 August 1922, 28 September 1922, 9 November 1922, 30 November 1922, 4 January 1923, 11 January 1923, 8 February 1923, 8 March 1923, 20 September 1923, 18 October 1923, 10 January 1924, 24 January 1924, 12 June 1924, 21 August 1924, 16 April 1925, 30 April 1925, 15 April 1926.

82. *Poplar Bluff Republican*, 10 August 1922.

83. *Poplar Bluff Republican*, 21 August 1924.

84. *Poplar Bluff Republican*, 20 September 1923, 10 January 1924, 21 August 1924, 28 August 1924, 30 April 1925.

85. *Poplar Bluff Republican*, 21 February 1924, 20 March 1924, 27 March 1924, 3 April 1924, 9 October 1924, 16 October 1924.

86. *Poplar Bluff Republican*, 30 November 1922.

87. *Poplar Bluff Republican*, 15 February 1923, 1 March 1923, 18 October 1923, 9 October 1924, 16 October 1924.

88. *Vienna Home-Adviser*, 24 January 1924.

89. *Vienna Home-Adviser*, 15 November 1923.

90. *Vienna Home-Adviser*, 6 March 1924.

91. *Vienna Home-Adviser*, 13 March 1924.

92. *Vienna Home-Adviser*, 13 March 1924.

93. *Vienna Home-Adviser*, 24 January 1924.

94. *Vienna Home-Adviser*, 8 May 1924.

95. *Vienna Home-Adviser*, 13 March 1924.

96. *Vienna Home-Adviser*, 24 April 1924.

97. *Vienna Home-Adviser*, 19 June 1924.

98. *Vienna Home-Adviser*, 3 April 1924.

99. *Warrensburg Star-Journal*, 14 December 1943.

100. *Warrensburg Star-Journal*, 28 November 1922, 16 January 1923, 1 May 1923, 3 July 1923, 27 July 1923, 14 August 1923, 28 December 1923.

101. *Warrensburg Star-Journal*, 5 February 1924.

102. *Warrensburg Star-Journal*, 28 October 1924.

103. *Warrensburg Star-Journal*, 31 October 1924.

104. *Warrensburg Star-Journal*, 11 November 1924, 14 November 1924, 21 November 1924, 25 November 1924, 28 November 1924, 2 December 1924, 16 December 1924.

105. *Warrensburg Star-Journal*, 24 March 1925, 27 March 1925, 3 April 1925, 10 April 1925.

106. *Warrensburg Star-Journal*, 10 April 1925.

107. *Warrensburg Star-Journal*, 29 May 1925, 26 June 1925, 30 June 1925.

108. *St. Louis Globe-Democrat*, 13 August 1921.

109. *St. Louis Globe-Democrat*, 13 August 1921.

110. Lay, *Hooded Knights on the Niagara*, 4, 40–41; Chalmers, *Hooded Americanism*, 35–36; Wade, *Fiery Cross*, 160–61; W. Jenkins, *Steel Valley Klan*, 5–6; *St. Louis Post-Dispatch*, 6 September 1921, 7 September 1921, 8 September 1921, 12 September 1921,

318 Notes to Chapter Two

13 September 1921, 14 September 1921, 15 September 1921, 16 September 1921, 17 September 1921, 18 September 1921, 19 September 1921.

111. *St. Louis Post-Dispatch*, 7 September 1921; Baker, *Gospel According to the Klan*, 34–35.

112. *St. Louis Post-Dispatch*, 13 September 1921.

113. *St. Louis Post-Dispatch*, 8 September 1921, 14 September 1921, 4 October 1921. The Missouri Klan officers identified were Frank Crippen (grand goblin), G. A. Glasscock (king kleagle), Casey Jones (king kleagle), L. H. Scott (kleagle), A. Fischer Jr. (kleagle), W. H. Thompson (kleagle), and R. G. Allen Jr. (kleagle).

114. *St. Louis Post-Dispatch*, 16 September 1921.

115. *Jewish Voice*, 22 September 1921, 13 October 1921; *Church Progress*, 22 September 1921; *St. Louis Post-Dispatch*, 12 September 1921.

116. *St. Louis Post-Dispatch*, 18 September 1921, 2 October 1921; *St. Louis Argus*, 7 October 1921.

117. House Committee on Rules, *The Ku-Klux Klan: Hearing before the Committee on Rules*, 3–48.

118. House Committee on Rules, *Ku-Klux Klan*, 6.

119. House Committee on Rules, *Ku-Klux Klan*, 6–8.

120. House Committee on Rules, *Ku-Klux Klan*, 67–184; Lay, *Hooded Knights on the Niagara*, 4; W. Jenkins, *Steel Valley Klan*, 6.

121. House Committee on Rules, *Ku-Klux Klan*, 138.

122. House Committee on Rules, *Ku-Klux Klan*, 139.

123. Lay, *Hooded Knights on the Niagara*, 4; W. Jenkins, *Steel Valley Klan*, 6. For local coverage of the congressional investigation, see *St. Louis Post-Dispatch*, 11 October 1921, 12 October 1921, 13 October 1921, 14 October 1921, 15 October 1921, 16 October 1921, 17 October 1921, 18 October 1921; *St. Louis Globe Democrat*, 13 October 1921, 14 October 1921; *Church Progress*, 20 October 1921, 27 October 1921; *Joplin Globe*, 12 October 1921, 13 October 1921, 14 October 1921, 15 October 1921, 18 October 1921; *Joplin News-Herald*, 11 October 1921, 12 October 1921, 13 October 1921, 17 October 1921; *St. Joseph News-Press*, 12 October 1921, 14 October 1921; *St. Joseph Gazette*, 12 October 1921, 13 October 1921, 14 October 1921, 15 October 1921, 18 October 1921; *St. Joseph Catholic Tribune*, 22 October 1921, 29 October 1921, 5 November 1921; *Hannibal Courier-Post*, 10 October 1921, 11 October 1921, 12 October 1921, 13 October 1921, 17 October 1921; *Jefferson City Daily Capital News*, 12 October 1921, 13 October 1921, 14 October 1921; *Columbia Daily Tribune*, 11 October 1921, 14 October 1921; *Kansas City Journal*, 12 October 1921, 13 October 1921, 14 October 1921, 15 October 1921, 18 October 1921; and *Kansas City Star*, 11 October 1921, 12 October 1921, 13 October 1921, 14 October 1921.

124. Chalmers, *Hooded Americanism*, 98–108; W. Jenkins, *Steel Valley Klan*, 6–9; Alexander, *Ku Klux Klan in the Southwest*, 109–10; Lay, *Invisible Empire in the West*, 8–9; Blee, *Women of the Klan*, 23–27.

125. James Weldon Johnson to Arthur Hyde, 30 April 1923, Western Union Telegram, folder 107, Arthur Mastick Hyde Papers, State Historical Society of Missouri, Columbia (hereafter cited as AMH, SHSMO).

126. *St. Joseph News-Press*, 20 October 1922.

127. *St. Joseph News-Press*, 20 October 1922.

128. *St. Joseph News-Press*, 20 October 1922, 21 October 1922. John Bond and Verna Nye came forward as the occupants of the automobile being followed by police for suspected bootlegging activities, though no evidence was found to suggest they were law violators.

129. *St. Joseph News-Press*, 20 October 1922, 21 October 1922.

130. *St. Joseph News-Press*, 20 October 1922, 21 October 1922, 23 October 1922.

131. *St. Joseph News-Press*, 23 October 1922; George Wells shot Carl Schimpfesser following a disturbance at a local pool hall. Though witnesses said Schimpfesser was not involved in the fight, police decided to take him in for questioning, and he was shot when he allegedly tried to flee the officers. The *St. Joseph Observer* noted that "it has become an almost frequent occurrence for a police officer to kill someone." *St. Joseph Observer*, 30 September 1922.

132. *St. Joseph News-Press*, 21 October 1922.

133. *St. Joseph News-Press*, 23 October 1922.

134. *St. Joseph News-Press*, 21 October 1922

135. *St. Joseph News-Press*, 29 September 1921; *St. Joseph Gazette*, 29 September 1921, 1 October 1921, 2 October 1921; *St. Joseph Observer*, 1 October 1921; *St. Joseph Catholic Tribune*, 1 October 1921.

136. *St. Joseph Observer*, 28 October 1922.

137. *St. Joseph News-Press*, 23 October 1922.

138. News of the death of Nellie Margaret Hale reached a national audience. The following newspapers ran articles about her funeral: *St. Louis Post-Dispatch*, 23 October 1922, 24 October 1922; *Kansas City Journal*, 21 October 1922, 22 October 1922, 23 October 1922; *Atlanta Constitution*, 23 October 1922; *Des Moines Register*, 23 October 1922; *Tennessean* 23 October 1922; *Arkansas Gazette*, 23 October 1922; *Detroit Free Press*, 23 October 1922; *New York World*, 22 October 1922; *New York Herald*, 23 October 1922; and *New York Tribune*, 23 October 1922. Clippings from the *New York World*, *New York Herald*, *New York Tribune* can also be found in the National Association for the Advancement of Colored People Collection at the Library of Congress, which indicates that the NAACP was keeping a close eye on the Hale controversy as well. Ku Klux Klan—October 1922, folder 9, box C-314, NAACP, LOC.

139. *St. Louis Post-Dispatch*, 29 October 1922.

140. *St. Louis Post-Dispatch*, 29 October 1922; *St. Joseph Gazette*, 21 October 1922, 22 October 1922, 24 October 1922, 26 October 1922, 27 October 1922, 29 October 1922; *St. Joseph News-Press*, 21 October 1922, 23 October 1922. Willie Wright and Carl Schimpfesser were shot while allegedly fleeing from officers, while Dr. W. W. Wertenberger and patrolman John House were hit by stray bullets fired by police in pursuit of other suspects.

141. Neal Gallagher to Arthur Hyde, 20 October 1922, folder 630, AMH, SHSMO; H.J. Bowen to Arthur Hyde, 24 October 1922, folder 630, AMH, SHSMO; W. C. Pierce to Arthur Hyde, Western Union Telegram, 23 October 1922, folder 630, AMH, SHSMO; Unknown to Arthur Hyde, 23 October 1922, folder 630, AMH, SHSMO;

320 Notes to Chapter Two

Thomas Clark to Arthur Hyde, 23 October 1922, folder 630, AMH, SHSMO; John Downey to Arthur Hyde, 23 October 1922, folder 630, AMH, SHSMO; W. L. Mack to Arthur Hyde, 24 October 1922, folder 630, AMH, SHSMO; Brown to Arthur Hyde, 24 October 1922, folder 630, AMH, SHSMO; Zerbst Pharmaceutical Company to Arthur Hyde, 25 October 1922, folder 630, AMH, SHSMO; Buchanan County Republican Central Committee to Arthur Hyde, 25 October 1922, folder 630, AMH, SHSMO; Law Enforcement League to Arthur Hyde, Western Union Telegram, 23 October 1922, folder 630, AMH, SHSMO; H. P. Scruby to Arthur Hyde, 28 October 1922, folder 630, AMH, SHSMO; Maurice Ryan to Arthur Hyde, 30 October 1922, folder 630, AMH, SHSMO; C.E. Betts to Arthur Hyde, 10 November 1922, folder 630, AMH, SHSMO; John L. Barkley to Arthur Hyde, 23 November 1922, folder 630, AMH, SHSMO; John L. Barkley to Arthur Hyde, 4 December 1922, folder 630, AMH, SHSMO.

142. *St. Joseph News-Press*, 28 November 1922; *St. Joseph Gazette*, 1 November 1922, 29 November 1922; *Chillicothe Constitution* and *Nevada Mail* dated 2 December 1922 in folder 630, AMH, SHSMO.

143. *St. Louis Post-Dispatch*, 25 August 1921, 9 September 1921, 20 September 1921; *Joplin Globe*, 21 September 1921, 23 September 1921, 23 October 1921; St. Louis *Argus*, 23 September 1921.

144. Herbert Bayard Swope to Arthur Hyde, Western Union Telegram, 8 September 1921, folder 365, AMH, SHSMO; C. Anderson Wright to Arthur Hyde, 23 September 1921, folder 365, AMH, SHSMO; C. Anderson Wright to Arthur Hyde, 28 September 1921, folder 365, AMH, SHSMO; Arthur Hyde to C. Anderson Wright, 26 September 1921, folder 365, AMH, SHSMO; Arthur Hyde to C. Anderson Wright, 4 October 1921, folder 365, AMH, SHSMO.

145. T. S. Hardy to Arthur Hyde, 26 April 1921, folder 365, AMH, SHSMO.

146. Nat Spencer to Arthur Hyde, 30 July 1921, folder 365, AMH, SHSMO; *Kansas City Journal*, 30 July 1921; *Kansas City Times*, 30 July 1921.

147. Monen L. Gray to Arthur Hyde, 23 August 1921, folder 365, AMH, SHSMO.

148. Alexander, *Ku Klux Klan in the Southwest*, 68–75.

149. Alexander, *Ku Klux Klan in the Southwest*, 68.

150. Paul M. Angle, *Bloody Williamson: A Chapter in American Lawlessness*; Masatomo Ayabe, "Ku Kluxers in a Coal Mining Community: A Study of the Ku Klux Klan Movement in Williamson County, Illinois, 1923–1926."

151. *St. Louis Post-Dispatch*, 4 March 1923.

152. *St. Louis Post-Dispatch*, 4 March 1923; *Caruthersville Democrat-Argus*, 23 February 1923, 27 February 1923.

153. *Southeast Missourian*, 12 January 1923, 18 January 1923; *St. Louis Post-Dispatch*, 29 October 1922; James L. Jackson to Arthur Hyde, 6 November 1922, folder 366, AMH, SHSMO; Arthur Hyde to James L. Jackson, 9 November 1922, folder 366, AMH, SHSMO; Paul Burton to Arthur Hyde, 8 November 1922, folder 366, AMH, SHSMO.

154. Harper, *White Man's Heaven*, 1–234; Thelen, *Paths of Resistance*, 92–99; Bonnie Stepenoff, *Thad Snow: A Life of Social Reform in the Missouri Bootheel*, 21; Frazier, *Lynchings in Missouri*, 105–62; Campney, *Hostile Heartland*, 92–135.

Notes to Chapter Two   321

155. Jarod Roll, *Spirit of Rebellion: Labor and Religion in the New Cotton South*, 52, 56–58; Joel P. Rhodes, *A Missouri Railroad Pioneer: The Life of Louis Houck*, 254–73; Stepenoff, *Thad Snow*, 9–22.

156. Roll, *Spirit of Rebellion*, 52, 56–58; Stepenoff, *Thad Snow*, 53–60; Brent M. S. Campney, "'The Drift of Things in Southeast Missouri': Demographic Transformation and Anti-Black Violence, 1900–1930."

157. Isabel Wilkerson, *The Warmth of Other Suns: The Epic Story of America's Great Migration*, 8–15; Carol Anderson, *White Rage: The Unspoken Truth of Our Racial Divide*, 39–66; Leon F. Litwack, *Trouble in Mind: Black Southerners in the Age of Jim Crow*, 481–96; Steven Hahn, *A Nation under Our Feet: Black Political Struggles in the Rural South from Slavery to the Great Migration*, 455–68.

158. Roll, *Spirit of Rebellion*, 53; Hahn, *Nation under Our Feet*, 468–76.

159. Thad Snow, *From Missouri: An American Farmer Looks Back*, 123.

160. Snow, *From Missouri*, 123.

161. L. Greene, Kremer, and Holland, *Missouri's Black Heritage*, 140–51.

162. US Bureau of the Census, *Thirteenth Census of the United States: 1910*, vol. 2, *Population*, 1101–20; US Bureau of the Census, *Fourteenth Census of the United States: 1920*, vol. 2, *Population*, 551–61; US Bureau of the Census, *Fifteenth Census of the United States: 1930*, vol. 2, *Population*, 1339–46.

163. Roll, *Spirit of Rebellion*, 52–75; Campney, "'Drift of Things in Southeast Missouri,'" 185–205.

164. *Southeast Missourian*, 18 January 1923, 6 February 1923, 14 February 1924; *St. Louis Argus*, 2 February 1923, 2 March 1923; *Kansas City Call*, 9 February 1923, 2 March 1923; *St. Louis Star*, 1 March 1923, 2 March 1923; Campney, "'Drift of Things in Southeast Missouri,'" 185–205.

165. Arthur Hyde to W. P. Robertson, 28 February 1923, Western Union Telegram, folder 107, AMH, SHSMO; Arthur Hyde to J. W. Timberman, 28 February 1923, Western Union Telegram, folder 107, AMH, SHSMO; Arthur Hyde to C. D. Jackson, 28 February 1923, Western Union Telegram, folder 107, AMH, SHSMO; Arthur Hyde to W. E. Kirkendall, 28 February 1923, Western Union Telegram, folder 107, AMH, SHSMO.

166. Arthur Hyde to Edward Hays, 23 September 1923, folder 367, AMH, SHSMO; Edward Hays to Arthur Hyde, 26 September 1923, folder 367, AMH, SHSMO; Arthur Hyde to Harry Daugherty, 28 September 1923, folder 367, AMH, SHSMO; Assistant Attorney General to Arthur Hyde, 28 October 1923, folder 367, AMH, SHSMO.

167. *St. Louis Post-Dispatch*, 28 February 1923; Campney, "'Drift of Things in Southeast Missouri,'" 185–205.

168. *Southeast Missourian*, 14 March 1923; *Hayti Missouri Herald*, 9 March 1923; *Dunklin County News*, 9 March 1923; *New Madrid Weekly Record*, 16 March 1923; *Charleston Enterprise-Courier*, 22 March 1923; *St. Louis Star*, 15 March 1923.

169. J. W. Timberman to Arthur Hyde, 2 March 1923, Western Union Telegram, folder 107, AMH, SHSMO; W. E. Kirkendall to Arthur Hyde, 1 March 1923, Western Union Telegram, folder 107, AMH, SHSMO; C. D. Jackson to Arthur Hyde, 1 March 1923, Western Union Telegram, folder 107, AMH, SHSMO; W. P. Robertson to Arthur Hyde, 2 March 1923, Western Union Telegram, folder 107, AMH, SHSMO.

170. Arthur Hyde to Carl Bloker, 28 February 1923, Western Union Telegram, folder 107, AMH, SHSMO; Arthur Hyde to Joe Cash, 28 February 1923, Western Union Telegram, folder 107, AMH, SHSMO; Arthur Hyde to Simon Loebe, 28 February 1923, Western Union Telegram, folder 107, AMH, SHSMO; Arthur Hyde to C. F. Bloker, 2 March 1923, folder 107, AMH, SHSMO; Campney, "'Drift of Things in Southeast Missouri,'" 185–205.

171. H. P. Loebe to Arthur Hyde, 1 March 1923, Western Union Telegram, folder 107, AMH, SHSMO; Joe Cash to Arthur Hyde, 1 March 1923, Western Union Telegram, folder 107, AMH, SHSMO.

172. C. F. Bloker to Arthur Hyde, 1 March 1923, Western Union Telegram, folder 107, AMH, SHSMO; C. F. Bloker to Arthur Hyde, 1 March 1923, folder 107, AMH, SHSMO.

173. *St. Louis Post-Dispatch*, 2 March 1923, 3 March 1923.

174. J. S. Gossom to Arthur Hyde, 24 March 1923, folder 107, AMH, SHSMO; A. C. Thrower to Arthur Hyde, 24 April 1923, folder 107, AMH, SHSMO; *St. Louis Post-Dispatch*, 2 March 1923, 3 March 1923, 23 April 1923; *St. Louis Argus*, 2 March 1923; *Hayti Missouri Herald*, 16 March 1923; *Stoddard Tribune*, 26 April 1923; Campney, "'Drift of Things in Southeast Missouri,'" 185–205.

175. *St. Louis Post-Dispatch*, 24 April 1923; Campney, "'Drift of Things in Southeast Missouri,'" 185–205.

176. *St. Louis Post-Dispatch*, 11 May 1923; *Bloomfield Vindicator*, 11 May 1923.

177. *St. Louis Post-Dispatch*, 10 May 1923; Campney, "'Drift of Things in Southeast Missouri,'" 185–205.

178. *St. Louis Post-Dispatch*, 11 May 1923; *Southeast Missourian*, 10 February 1923; Campney, "'Drift of Things in Southeast Missouri,'" 185–205. C. D. Unsell told the *Southeast Missourian* that while the Klan was not organized in Cape Girardeau, it did have members in Poplar Bluff, Neelyville, Harviell, Doniphan, Naylor, Piedmont, Williamsville, Puxico, Dexter, Bernie, Bloomfield, Illmo, Fornfelt, Chaffee, Sikeston, Morley, Charleston, Morehouse, Lilbourn, Marston, Parma, New Madrid, Portageville, Gideon, Caruthersville, Hayti, Steele, Campbell, Malden, Kennett, and Senath.

179. *Dexter Statesman*, 9 February 1923, 23 February 1923, 9 March 1923, 23 March 1923; *East Prairie Eagle*, 23 February 1923; *Malden Merit*, 23 March 1923; *Charleston Enterprise-Courier*, 4 October 1923.

180. *Charleston Enterprise-Courier*, 18 October 1923, 25 October 1923, 1 November 1923, 29 November 1923, 29 November 1923, 30 October 1924, 6 November 1924, 20 November 1924, 4 December 1924; *Caruthersville Democrat-Argus*, 31 October 1924, 7 November 1924; *Hayti Missouri Herald*, 31 October 1924, 14 November 1924, 21 November 1924; Campney, "'Drift of Things in Southeast Missouri,'" 185–205.

181. *Kansas City Catholic Register*, 9 November 1922.

Chapter Three
"We Will Tear Off This Mask of Secrecy"
Building an Anti-Klan Coalition

1. George L. Vaughn to NAACP, 16 May 1921, folder 19, box 1: G109, National Association for the Advancement of Colored People Collection, Library of Congress (hereafter cited as NAACP, LOC).

Notes to Chapter Three

2. Christensen et al., *Dictionary of Missouri Biography*, 769–70; *St. Louis Argus*, 27 May 1921, 10 June 1921, 19 August 1949.

3. George L. Vaughn to NAACP, 16 May 1921, folder 19, box 1: G109, NAACP, LOC.

4. *St. Louis Argus*, 25 June 1915, 19 April 1918, 17 May 1918, 4 October 1918, 18 July 1919, 27 May 1921, 10 June 1921, 21 September 1921, 7 September 1923, 13 August 1926.

5. Cora J. Carter to James Weldon Johnson, 13 May 1921, Western Union Telegram, folder 19, box 1: G109, NAACP, LOC.

6. Walter White to Cora J. Carter, 13 May 1921, Western Union Telegram, folder 19, box 1: G109, NAACP, LOC.

7. Walter White to Cora J. Carter, 13 May 1921, folder 19, box I: G109, NAACP, LOC.

8. Cora J. Carter to Walter White, 1 June 1921, folder 19, box 1: G109, NAACP, LOC.

9. *St. Louis Argus*, 10 June 1921.

10. *St. Louis Argus*, 1 July 1921.

11. David Goldberg, *Discontented America: The United States in the 1920s*, 132.

12. Kauffman, *Faith and Fraternalism*, 280–85.

13. *Missouri Valley Independent*, 17 April 1924.

14. Kauffman, *Faith and Fraternalism*, 280–85.

15. Philip Gleason, *The Conservative Reformers: German-American Catholics and the Social Order*, 23–29.

16. Gleason, *Conservative Reformers*, 122–23, 69–89, 125–31, 102–15, 91–100.

17. Gleason, *Conservative Reformers*, 104–5, 117, 124.

18. *Central-Blatt and Social Justice*, September 1923, October 1923, April 1924, June 1924, July 1924, August 1924, July 1925.

19. *Central-Blatt and Social Justice*, September 1923, October 1923.

20. *Central-Blatt and Social Justice*, October 1923.

21. Official Report 1922, Missouri State Convention, folder 86, box 1, Catholic Central Verein of America: Printed Materials, Catholic Central Verein of America Records, University of Notre Dame Archives, Notre Dame, IN (hereafter cited as CCV-UNDA).

22. Official Report 1923, Missouri State Convention, folder 87, box 1, Catholic Central Verein of America: Printed Materials, CCV-UNDA.

23. Central Bureau of the Central Verein to Rev. G. E. Sommerhauser, 21 October 1926, folder 1, box 7, Central Bureau General Correspondence, Catholic Central Verein of America: Manuscripts, CCV-UNDA.

24. M. M. of St. John Evangelist to F. B. Kenkel, 29 April 1924, folder 2, box 7, Central Bureau General Correspondence, Catholic Central Verein of America: Manuscripts, CCV-UNDA.

25. Central Bureau of the Central Verein to Rev. John W. Keyes, 5 October 1929, folder 3, box 7, Central Bureau General Correspondence, Catholic Central Verein of America: Manuscripts, CCV-UNDA.

26. For correspondence on fake lecturers written between 1900 and 1960, see folders 1–3, box 7, Central Bureau General Correspondence, Catholic Central Verein of America: Manuscripts, CCV-UNDA.

324   Notes to Chapter Three

27. Kauffman, *Faith and Fraternalism*, 1–28; Christopher Kauffman, *Columbianism and the Knights of Columbus: A Quincentenary History*, 21.

28. Kauffman, *Columbianism and the Knights of Columbus*, 58–59; Kauffman, *Faith and Fraternalism*, 268–89; Nordstrom, *Danger on the Doorstep*, 176, 182–84.

29. Kauffman, *Faith and Fraternalism*, 261–73; Kauffman, *Columbianism and the Knights of Columbus*, 65.

30. Kauffman, *Faith and Fraternalism*, 275–77.

31. Kauffman, *Columbianism and the Knights of Columbus*, 91.

32. *St. Louis Argus*, 30 September 1921, 14 October 1921; *St. Louis Post-Dispatch*, 28 September 1921, 8 October 1921, 15 October 1921; *St. Louis Globe-Democrat*, 28 September 1921, 8 October 1921, 15 October 1921; *St. Louis Star*, 8 October 1921, 15 October 1921.

33. Kauffman, *Columbianism and the Knights of Columbus*, 91; *Kansas City Catholic Register*, 6 July 1922; *St. Louis Star*, 3 August 1921, 4 August 1921, 3 July 1922; *St. Joseph Catholic Tribune*, 5 August 1922.

34. *Mariner*, May 1922, March 1923.

35. *Mariner*, November 1922.

36. *Mariner*, December 1922.

37. James Garrity to Luke E. Hart, 28 September 1925, file 20, box 32, Collection 0005 Bogus Oath Collection, Knights of Columbus Supreme Council Archives, New Haven, CT (hereafter cited as BOC, KCSCA); James Garrity to Luke E. Hart, 1 October 1925, file 20, box 32, BOC, KCSCA; David F. Supple to Luke E. Hart, 30 September 1925, file 20, box 32, BOC, KCSCA; Luke E. Hart to David F. Supple, 6 October 1925, file 20, Box 32, BOC, KCSCA; Luke E. Hart to James Garrity, 6 October 1925, file 20, Box 32, BOC, KCSCA; Luke E. Hart to Robert R. Hull, 23 March 1926, file 20, box 32, BOC, KCSCA; Luke E. Hart to Mrs. P. G. Boyd, 10 October 1928, file 1, box 36, BOC, KCSCA; William J. McGinley to Luke E. Hart, 31 October 1928, file 1, box 36, BOC, KCSCA; Luke E. Hart to William J. McGinley, 3 November 1928, file 1, box 36, BOC, KCSCA; Luke E. Hart to Dr. J. W. King, 23 February 1923, file 6, box 39, BOC, KCSCA; Luke E. Hart to The New Menace, 7 March 1923, file 6, box 39, BOC, KCS-CA; Luke E. Hart to The New Menace, 20 March 1923, file 6, box 39, BOC, KCSCA; Walter A. Lynch to Luke E. Hart, 27 December 1923, file 6, box 39, BOC, KCSCA; Luke E. Hart to Walter A. Lynch, 31 December 1923, file 6, box 39, BOC, KCSCA; David Goldstein to William J. McGinley, 18 January 1924, file 7, box 39, BOC, KCSCA; William J. McGinley, 22 January 1924, file 7, box 39, BOC, KCSCA; Luke E. Hart to David Goldstein, 7 February 1924, file 7, box 39, BOC, KCSCA; David Tobin to Luke E. Hart, 27 August 1924, file 7, box 39, BOC, KCSCA; Luke E. Hart to David Tobin, 3 September 1924, file 7, box 39, BOC, KCSCA; Leo Firmin to Luke E. Hart, 7 February 1925, file 8, box 39, BOC, KCSCA; Luke E. Hart to Leo Firmin, 10 February 1925, file 8, box 39, BOC, KCSCA; T. J. Donovan to William J. McGinley, 18 July 1928, file 9, box 39, BOC, KCSCA; William J. McGinley to Luke E. Hart, 20 September 1928, file 9, box 39, BOC, KCSCA; James Favor to William J. McGinley, 18 September 1928, file 9, box 39, BOC, KCSCA; William J. McGinley to James Favor, 21 September 1928, file 9, box 39, BOC, KCSCA; William J. McGinley to Luke E. Hart, 21 September 1928, file 9,

Notes to Chapter Three 325

box 39, BOC, KCSCA; Robert R. Hull to Luke E. Hart, 1 October 1928, file 9, box 39, BOC, KCSCA; Luke E. Hart to Robert R. Hull, 3 October 1928, file 9, box 39, BOC, KCSCA; William J. McGinley to Luke E. Hart, 10 October 1928, file 9, box 39, BOC, KCSCA; William R. Hart to Luke E. Hart, 29 October 1928, file 9, box 39, BOC, KCS-CA; Luke E. Hart to William R. Hart, 30 October 1928, file 9, box 39, BOC, KCSCA.

38. Barney E. Reilly to Luke E. Hart, 15 March 1923, file 5, box 47, Record Group 0024, Sub-Group 4, Supreme Advocate Luke E. Hart Records, Knights of Columbus Supreme Council Archives, New Haven, CT (hereafter cited as SALEHR, KCSCA); Luke E. Hart to Barney E. Reilly, 16 March 1923, file 5, box 47, Record Group 0024, Sub-Group 4, SALEHR, KCSCA; Morgan Lawson to Luke E. Hart, 15 September 1922, file 1, box 67, Record Group 0024, Sub-Group 4, SALEHR, KCSCA; Luke E. Hart to Morgan Lawson, 18 September 1922, file 1, box 67, Record Group 0024, Sub-Group 4, SALEHR, KCSCA; Luke E. Hart to William J. McGinley, 18 September 1922, file 1, box 67, Record Group 0024, Sub-Group 4, SALEHR, KCSCA; Morgan Lawson to Luke E. Hart, 25 September 1922, file 1, box 67, Record Group 0024, Sub-Group 4, SALEHR, KCSCA; Luke E. Hart to William J. McGinley, 27 September 1922, file 1, box 67, Record Group 0024, Sub-Group 4, SALEHR, KCSCA; Morgan Lawson to Luke E. Hart, 3 October 1922, file 1, box 67, Record Group 0024, Sub-Group 4, SALEHR, KCSCA; W. H. Hurley to William J. McGinley, 12 February 1923, file 1, box 67, Record Group 0024, Sub-Group 4, SALEHR, KCSCA; William J. McGinley to Luke E. Hart, 16 February 1923, file 1, box 67, Record Group 0024, Sub-Group 4, SALEHR, KCSCA; Luke E. Hart to W. H. Hurley, 19 February 1923, file 1, box 67, Record Group 0024, Sub-Group 4, SALEHR, KCSCA; Luke E. Hart to William J. Mc-Ginley, 19 February 1923, file 1, box 67, Record Group 0024, Sub-Group 4, SALEHR, KCSCA; W. H. Hurley to Luke E. Hart, 20 February 1923, file 1, box 67, Record Group 0024, Sub-Group 4, SALEHR, KCSCA; Jno. McGaw to Luke E. Hart, 15 March 1923, file 1, box 67, Record Group 0024, Sub-Group 4, SALEHR, KCSCA; Luke E. Hart to Jno. McGaw, 17 March 1923, file 1, box 67, Record Group 0024, Sub-Group 4, SALEHR, KCSCA; Luke E. Hart to Festus J. Wade, 1 September 1923, file 1, box 67, Record Group 0024, Sub-Group 4, SALEHR, KCSCA; Rev. F. H. Dieckmann to Luke E. Hart, 23 February 1924, file 1, box 67, Record Group 0024, Sub-Group 4, SALEHR, KCSCA; Luke E. Hart to Rev. F. H. Dieckmann, 26 February 1924, file 1, box 67, Record Group 0024, Sub-Group 4, SALEHR, KCSCA; W. A. Franken to Luke E. Hart, 13 June 1924, file 1, box 67, Record Group 0024, Sub-Group 4, SALEHR, KCSCA; Luke E. Hart to W. A. Franken, 20 June 1924, file 1, box 67, Record Group 0024, Sub-Group 4, SALEHR, KCSCA; W. A. Franken to Luke E. Hart, 23 June 1924, file 1, box 67, Re-cord Group 0024, Sub-Group 4, SALEHR, KCSCA; O. R. Proctor to Luke E. Hart, 28 July 1924, file 1, box 67, Record Group 0024, Sub-Group 4, SALEHR, KCSCA; Luke E. Hart to O. R. Proctor, 8 July 1924, file 1, box 67, Record Group 0024, Sub-Group 4, SALEHR, KCSCA; Luke E. Hart to William J. McGinley, 31 July 1924, file 1, box 67, Record Group 0024, Sub-Group 4, SALEHR, KCSCA; Rev. R. E. Graham to Luke E. Hart, 30 July 1924, file 1, box 67, Record Group 0024, Sub-Group 4, SALEHR, KCSCA; Luke E. Hart to Rev. R. E. Graham, 31 July 1924, file 1, box 67, Record Group 0024, Sub-Group 4, SALEHR, KCSCA; C. T. Jameson to Luke E. Hart, file 1, box 67,

326 Notes to Chapter Three

Record Group 0024, Sub-Group 4, SALEHR, KCSCA; Luke E. Hart to C. T. Jameson, 8 July 1924, file 1, box 67, Record Group 0024, Sub-Group 4, SALEHR, KCSCA; Luke E. Hart to John Rogers, 27 July 1928, file 1, box 67, Record Group 0024, Sub-Group 4, SALEHR, KCSCA; Luke E. Hart to Everett Reeves, 26 October 1928, file 1, box 67, Record Group 0024, Sub-Group 4, SALEHR, KCSCA; A. W. Zimmer to Luke E. Hart, 7 November 1928, file 1, box 67, Record Group 0024, Sub-Group 4, SALEHR, KCSCA; Luke E. Hart to A. W. Zimmer, 8 November 1928, file 1, box 67, Record Group 0024, Sub-Group 4, SALEHR, KCSCA; Luke E. Hart to Joseph B. Lischwe, 14 July 1930, file 1, box 67, Record Group 0024, Sub-Group 4, SALEHR, KCSCA.

39. D. J. Woodlock to Luke E. Hart, 9 February 1923, file 1, box 67, Record Group 0024, Sub-Group 4, SALEHR, KCSCA; Luke E. Hart to D. J. Woodlock, 16 February 1923, file 1, box 67, Record Group 0024, Sub-Group 4, SALEHR, KCSCA.

40. Lee Hagood to Luke E. Hart, 20 August 1924, file 1, box 67, Record Group 0024, Sub-Group 4, SALEHR, KCSCA; Luke E. Hart to Lee Hagood, 25 August 1924, file 1, box 67, Record Group 0024, Sub-Group 4, SALEHR, KCSCA; Lee Hagood to Luke E. Hart, 29 August 1924, file 1, box 67, Record Group 0024, Sub-Group 4, SALEHR, KCSCA; Luke E. Hart to Lee Hagood, 5 September 1924, file 1, box 67, Record Group 0024, Sub-Group 4, SALEHR, KCSCA.

41. Luke E. Hart to T. E. Purcell, 13 June 1922, file 1, box 67, Record Group 0024, Sub-Group 4, SALEHR, KCSCA; T. E. Purcell to Luke E. Hart, n.d., file 1, box 67, Record Group 0024, Sub-Group 4, SALEHR, KCSCA; Luke E. Hart to T. E. Purcell, 5 June 1923, file 1, box 67, Record Group 0024, Sub-Group 4, SALEHR, KCSCA; T. E. Purcell to Luke E. Hart, 24 June 1924, file 1, box 67, Record Group 0024, Sub-Group 4, SALEHR, KCSCA; Luke E. Hart to T. E. Purcell, 25 June 1924, file 1, box 67, Record Group 0024, Sub-Group 4, SALEHR, KCSCA; Luke E. Hart to John Fugel, 30 November 1923, file 1, box 67, Record Group 0024, Sub-Group 4, SALEHR, KCSCA; John Fugel to Luke E. Hart, 9 February 1924, file 1, box 67, Record Group 0024, Sub-Group 4, SALEHR, KCSCA; Luke E. Hart to John Fugel, 11 February 1924, file 1, box 67, Record Group 0024, Sub-Group 4, SALEHR, KCSCA.

42. *St. Joseph Catholic Tribune*, 24 February 1923.

43. T. E. Purcell to James Flaherty, 21 April 1923, file 1, box 67, Record Group 0024, Sub-Group 4, SALEHR, KCSCA.; James Flaherty to T. E. Purcell, 11 May 1923, file 1, box 67, Record Group 0024, Sub-Group 4, SALEHR, KCSCA.; James Flaherty to Luke E. Hart, 11 May 1923, file 1, box 67, Record Group 0024, Sub-Group 4, SALEHR, KCSCA.; Luke E. Hart to James Flaherty, 14 May 1923, file 1, box 67, Record Group 0024, Sub-Group 4, SALEHR, KCSCA.

44. James Flaherty to Luke E. Hart, 14 May 1923, file 1, box 67, Record Group 0024, Sub-Group 4, SALEHR, KCSCA.

45. Luke E. Hart to John J. Glennon, 10 September 1921, file 1, box 67, Record Group 0024, Sub-Group 4, SALEHR, KCSCA.

46. John J. Glennon to Luke E. Hart, 12 September 1921, file 1, box 67, Record Group 0024, Sub-Group 4, SALEHR, KCSCA.

47. Chalmers, *Hooded Americanism*, 183–84; Blee, *Women of the Klan*, 119–20; D. Goldberg, *Discontented America*, 134–35; W. Jenkins, *Steel Valley Klan*, 77–78. Historian

Notes to Chapter Three

William Jenkins has claimed that the AUL began to recruit new members outside of Chicago only in December 1922, but the establishment of the St. Joseph chapter suggests that AUL branches may have been set up in outside communities shortly after the organization was created.

48. *Patriot*, 6 December 1923, 13 December 1923.

49. *St. Louis Star*, 14 August 1922.

50. G. K. Rutledge to Arthur Hyde, 19 July 1922, folder 366, Arthur Mastick Hyde Papers, State Historical Society of Missouri, Columbia (hereafter cited as AMH, SHS-MO); Arthur Hyde to G. K. Rutledge, 20 July 1922, folder 366, AMH, SHSMO.

51. *Patriot*, 24 August 1923, 21 September 1923, 6 December 1923, 20 December 1923; *Kansas City Catholic Register*, 16 August 1923; *St. Joseph Catholic Tribune*, 25 August 1923.

52. *Kansas City Times*, 13 August 1923; *St. Joseph Catholic Tribune*, 25 August 1923.

53. *St. Joseph News-Press*, 14 September 1922; *St. Joseph Catholic Tribune*, 16 September 1922.

54. *St. Joseph Observer*, 16 September 1922; *St. Joseph Catholic Tribune*, 9 September 1922.

55. *St. Joseph Gazette*, 24 September 1922; *St. Joseph News-Press*, 25 September 1922, 10 October 1922, 11 October 1922; *St. Joseph Catholic Tribune*, 30 September 1922.

56. *Kansas City Star*, 23 January 1923; *St. Joseph News-Press*, 23 January 1923; *The Modern View*, 2 February 1923.

57. *Missouri Valley Independent*, 19 April 1923, 16 August 1923.

58. Megan Ming Francis, *Civil Rights and the Making of the Modern American State*, 31–41; Patricia Sullivan, *Lift Every Voice: The NAACP and the Making of the Civil Rights Movement*, 1–24.

59. Sullivan, *Life Every Voice*, 100. For information on the formation of NAACP branches in Missouri, see J. H. Lawrie to W. E. B. Du Bois, 26 March 1919, folder 4, box 1: G107, NAACP, LOC; Myrtle Cook to James Weldon Johnson, 25 April 1921, folder 23, box 1: G107, NAACP, LOC; Annual Report of the St. Louis Branch of the National Association for the Advancement of Colored People, 2 January 1917, folder 19, box 1: G109, NAACP, LOC; A. L. Foster to Roy Nash, 3 October 1917, folder 17, box G111, NAACP, LOC; "Balance Sheet," 1922, folder 10, box G-222, NAACP, LOC; M. S. Smith to James Weldon Johnson, 22 May 1922, folder 19, box 1: G109, NAACP, LOC; M. S. Smith to Moorfield Story, 11 November 1922, folder 19, box 1: G109, NAACP, LOC; Ida Becks to James Weldon Johnson, 13 December 1921, folder 18, box G107, NAACP, LOC; Robert Bagnall to Robert S. Cobb, 20 May 1922, folder 18, box G107, NAACP, LOC; and *St. Louis Argus*, 9 June 1922, 23 June 1922. For more information on communities interested in establishing an NAACP branch during the 1920s, see H. D. Haney to Robert Bagnall, 26 April 1921, folder 6, box 1: G107, NAACP, LOC; and R. W. B. Hayes to Roy Nash, 7 September 1917, folder 16, box 1: G109, NAACP, LOC. The Missouri branches included St. Louis, Kansas City, Springfield, Cape Girardeau, Caruthersville, Kirkwood, and Jefferson City.

60. For examples of the NAACP campaign against the Klan, see Walter White to Bella Neumann Zilberman, 16 December 1920, folder 2, box 1: C312, NAACP, LOC;

328   Notes to Chapter Three

Walter White to John A. Melby, 31 January 1921, folder 5, box 1: C312, NAACP, LOC; Walter White to A. Clement Neal, 12 April 1921, folder 6, box 1: C312, NAACP, LOC; Nathan B. Young to Walter White, 5 January 1921, folder 3, box 1: C312, NAACP, LOC; Nathan B. Young to James Weldon Johnson, 7 January 1921, folder 3, box 1: C312, NAACP, LOC; Walter White to Nathan B. Young, 31 January 1921, folder 3, box 1: C312, NAACP, LOC; and Nathan B. Young to Walter White, 27 January 1921, folder 4, box 1: C312, NAACP, LOC. At the time that he was communicating with the National Branch of the NAACP, Nathan Young was the president of Florida A&M University. He became the president of Lincoln University in Jefferson City, Missouri, in 1923.

61. *St. Louis Argus*, 13 May 1921; St. Louis *Star*, 11 May 1921.

62. John Love to James Weldon Johnson, 17 May 1921, folder 23, box 1: G107, NAACP, LOC. For the Klan article featured in the *Star*, see *Kansas City Star*, 13 May 1921.

63. *St. Louis Argus*, 3 June 1921. The committee that composed the petition included Rev. S. M. Arthur, C. A. Curry, Rev. W. H. Hill, A. M. Oliver, R. Holloway, and Mrs. E. A. Drasdall.

64. H. N. Jones to NAACP, 16 December 1922, folder 4, box 1: G107, NAACP, LOC.

65. Springfield Klan No. 12 to James B. Clark, 17 July 1923, folder 2, box 1: C313, NAACP, LOC; James B. Clark to William Pickens, 19 July 1923, folder 2, box 1: C313, NAACP, LOC; Walter White to James B. Clark, 25 July 1923, folder 2, box 1: C313, NAACP, LOC; Walter White to Chief Inspector of Post Office Department, 26 July 1923, folder 2, box 1: C313, NAACP, LOC; Chief Inspector of Post Office Department to NAACP, 3 August 1923, folder 2, box 1: C313, NAACP, LOC; Walter White to James B. Clark, 8 August 1923, folder 2, box 1: C313, NAACP, LOC; Walter White to James B. Clark, 22 November 1923, folder 3, box 1: C313, NAACP, LOC.

66. "Colored Advancement Society Polls Congress on Ku Klux Klan," Press Release, 13 October 1921, folder 13, box 1: C312, NAACP, LOC.

67. Roscoe C. Patterson to James Weldon Johnson, 8 October 1921, folder 14, box 1: C312, NAACP, LOC.

68. T. W. Hukriede to James Weldon Johnson, 7 October 1921, folder 14, box 1: C312, NAACP, LOC.

69. I. V. McPherson to NAACP, 12 October 1921, folder 14, box 1: C312, NAACP, LOC.

70. For letters about Roy Hammonds lynching, see James Weldon Johnson to Arthur Hyde, 30 April 1921, folder 105, AMH, SHSMO; John L. Love to Arthur Hyde, 1 May 1921, folder 105, AMH, SHSMO; Walter White to Arthur Hyde, 26 May 1921, folder 105, AMH, SHSMO; Arthur Hyde to Walter White, 1 June 1921, folder 105, AMH, SHSMO; James Weldon Johnson to Arthur Hyde, 30 April 1921, folder 12, box C361, NAACP, LOC; James Weldon Johnson to Arthur Hyde, 26 May 1921, folder 12, box C361, NAACP, LOC; and Arthur Hyde to James Weldon Johnson, 1 June 1921, folder 12, box C361, NAACP, LOC. For letters on the Dyer Anti-Lynching Bill, see James Weldon Johnson to Arthur Hyde, 8 February 1922, folder 106, AMH, SHSMO; James Weldon Johnson to Arthur Hyde, 4 March 1922, folder 106, AMH, SHSMO; Executive Secretary of Arthur Hyde to James Weldon Johnson, 10 March 1922, folder 106, AMH, SHSMO; L. C. Dyer to Arthur Hyde, 13 March 1922, folder 106, AMH, SHSMO; and

Notes to Chapter Three   329

Executive Secretary of Arthur Hyde to L. C. Dyer, 15 March 1922, folder 106, AMH, SHSMO. For additional letters asking Hyde to aid the Dyer Bill, see J. M. Batchman to Arthur Hyde, 14 May 1922, folder 106, AMH, SHSMO; J. E. McCulloch to Arthur Hyde, 29 June 1922, folder 106, AMH, SHSMO; Edmund Koeln to Arthur Hyde, 10 July 1922, folder 106, AMH, SHSMO; and J. McCulloch to Arthur Hyde, 25 July 1922, folder 106, AMH, SHSMO.

71. Cora Carter to Arthur Hyde, 26 February 1922, folder 106, AMH, SHSMO.

72. Arthur Hyde to Cora Carter, 27 February 1922, folder 106, AMH, SHSMO; "Membership Certificate of Arthur Hyde," 1 March 1922, folder 106, AMH, SHSMO; *St. Louis Argus*, 23 June 1922.

73. Sullivan, *Life Every Voice*, 61–100; Mary G. Rolinson, *Grassroots Garveyism: The Universal Negro Improvement Association in the Rural South, 1920–1927*, 173.

74. Colin Grant, *Negro with a Hat: The Rise and Fall of Marcus Garvey*, 52–317.

75. Rolinson, *Grassroots Garveyism*, 72–102; Judith Stein, *The World of Marcus Garvey: Race and Class in Modern Society*, 108–52.

76. Rolinson, *Grassroots Garveyism*, 145; Stein, *World of Marcus Garvey*, 159; Grant, *Negro with a Hat*, 334–35.

77. *Negro World*, 21 February 1921, 9 April 21, 16 April 1921, 18 June 1921, 2 July 1921, 9 July 1921, 20 August 1921, 3 September 1921, 10 September 1921, 17 September 1921, 1 October 1921, 8 October 1921, 22 October 1921, 29 October 1921, 25 March 1922.

78. *Negro World*, 21 February 1921.

79. *Negro World*, 29 October 1921.

80. Rolinson, *Grassroots Garveyism*, 143–46; Stein, *World of Marcus Garvey*, 154–58; Grant, *Negro with a Hat*, 333–34.

81. Rolinson, *Grassroots Garveyism*, 145–46; Stein, *World of Marcus Garvey*, 159; Grant, *Negro with a Hat*, 333–34.

82. Rolinson, *Grassroots Garveyism*, 145–46; Stein, *World of Marcus Garvey*, 159; Grant, *Negro with a Hat*, 333–34.

83. *Negro World*, 1 July 1922.

84. *Negro World*, 1 July 1922, 15 July 1922, 22 July 1922, 29 July 1922, 5 August 1922.

85. *Negro World*, 1 July 1922.

86. *Negro World*, 15 July 1922.

87. Stein, *World of Marcus Garvey*, 153–54.

88. Stein, *World of Marcus Garvey*, 154–58.

89. Rolinson, *Grassroots Garveyism*, 143–44.

90. Rolinson, *Grassroots Garveyism*, 143–46, 173.

91. *Negro World*, 1 July 1922, 8 July 1922, 15 July 1922, 22 July 1922, 29 July 1922, 5 August 1922; Grant, *Negro with a Hat*, 338–48.

92. Grant, *Negro with a Hat*, 320.

93. Rolinson, *Grassroots Garveyism*, 146–47; Stein, *World of Marcus Garvey*, 158–70; Grant, *Negro with a Hat*, 334–38.

94. Rolinson, *Grassroots Garveyism*, 146–47; Stein, *World of Marcus Garvey*, 163–66; Grant, *Negro with a Hat*, 334–38.

95. *St. Louis Argus*, 28 July 1922.

Notes to Chapter Three

96. *St. Louis Argus*, 28 July 1922.

97. *St. Louis Post-Dispatch*, 2 August 1922; *St. Louis Star*, 1 August 1922, 7 August 1922.

98. *St. Louis Argus*, 28 July 1922.

99. For information on UNIA activity in Missouri, see Roll, *Spirit of Rebellion*, 52–75; *Negro World*, 26 March 1921, 16 April 1921, 5 November 1921, 10 December 1921, 11 March 1922, 25 March 1922; *St. Louis Post-Dispatch*, 27 May 1921, 6 June 1921, 21 October 1922, 9 February 1925, 18 August 1925, 2 May 1926, 31 March 1929; *St. Louis Star*, 2 March 1922, 18 December 1922, 6 October 1922; *St. Louis Argus*, 18 February 1921, 11 March 1921, 8 April 1921, 15 April 1921, 3 March 1922, 19 May 1922, 28 July 1922; and *Kansas City Call*, 4 March 1922, 11 March 1922, 13 May 1922, 10 June 1922.

100. *Negro World*, 10 March 1923.

101. Grant, *Negro with a Hat*, 388–412.

102. Grant, *Negro with a Hat*, 413–50.

103. Deborah Dash Moore, *B'nai B'rith and the Challenge of Ethnic Leadership*, 1–13.

104. D. Moore, *B'nai B'rith and the Challenge of Ethnic Leadership*, 102–6.

105. D. Moore, *B'nai B'rith and the Challenge of Ethnic Leadership*, 102–19; MacLean, *Behind the Mask of Chivalry*, 12.

106. D. Moore, *B'nai B'rith and the Challenge of Ethnic Leadership*, 106–9.

107. *Modern View*, 26 September 1913.

108. D. Moore, *B'nai B'rith and the Challenge of Ethnic Leadership*, 115–17; Leo P. Ribuffo, "Henry Ford and the International Jew," in *The American Jewish Experience*, ed. Jonathan D. Sarna, 201–16; Steven Watts, *The People's Tycoon: Henry Ford and the American Century*, 376–97; Vincent Curcio, *Henry Ford*, 131–58.

109. D. Moore, *B'nai B'rith and the Challenge of Ethnic Leadership*, 115–17.

110. *Modern View*, 24 June 1921.

111. D. Moore, *B'nai B'rith and the Challenge of Ethnic Leadership*, 116–19.

112. Ehrlich, *Zion in the Valley*, 1:111–12.

113. Sachs, "Development of the Jewish Community of Kansas City," 350–60; Schultz, *Mid-America's Promise*; Weissbach, *Jewish Life in Small-Town America*, 2, 54; Hessler, *German Jews in Small Towns in Missouri*; S. Peterson, "'One Heart, Many Souls,'" 1–74.

114. *St. Louis Post-Dispatch*, 5 March 1921; *St. Louis Star*, 5 March 1921.

115. *St. Louis Post-Dispatch*, 18 March 1921, 19 March 1921, 28 March 1921, 29 March 1921, 8 April 1921, 29 April 1921, 20 May 1921, 21 May 1921, 26 May 1921, 4 June 1921, 5 June 1921, 7 June 1921; *St. Louis Star*, 18 March 1921, 19 March 1921, 28 March 1921, 29 March 1921; *Modern View*, 18 March 1921.

116. *Modern View*, 15 April 1921, 13 May 1921, 29 September 1922, 1 December 1922.

117. *Jewish Voice*, 24 March 1921.

118. *Jewish Voice*, 20 October 1922.

119. *Jewish Voice*, 3 November 1922.

120. *Kansas City Jewish Chronicle*, 6 April 1923.

121. *Modern View*, 24 November 1922.

122. *Modern View*, 16 February 1923, 6 April 1923.

123. *Modern View*, 2 November 1923.

Notes to Chapter Three 331

124. *St. Louis Argus*, 30 September 1921.

125. Kauffman, *Faith and Fraternalism*, 396; Luke E. Hart to Francis J. Heazel, 27 January 1941, File 24, Box 51, Record Group 0024, Sub-Group 4, SALEHR, KCSCA; R. P. Cummins to Luke E. Hart, 24 April 1947, File 25, Box 51, Record Group 0024, Sub-Group 4, SALEHR, KCSCA; Luke E. Hart to R. P. Cummins, 28 April 1947, File 25, Box 51, Record Group 0024, Sub-Group 4, SALEHR, KCSCA.

126. *Joplin Globe*, 5 April 1922.

127. *Joplin Globe*, 6 April 1926, 7 April 1926, 3 July 1926.

128. *Joplin Globe*, 5 August 1923.

129. *Joplin Globe*, 23 February 1923.

130. *Joplin Globe*, 6 April 1926.

131. P. W. Burden to Charles Becker, 14 December 1922, folder 366, AMH, SHS-MO; Charles Becker to P. W. Burden, 16 December 1922, folder 366, AMH, SHSMO.

132. Arthur Hyde to P. W. Burden, 27 December 1922, folder 366, AMH, SHSMO.

133. *Joplin Globe*, 12 January 1923.

134. *Joplin Globe*, 18 January 1923.

135. *Joplin Globe*, 18 November 1922.

136. *Joplin Globe*, 23 January 1923.

137. *Joplin Globe*, 25 January 1923.

138. *Joplin Globe*, 28 January 1923.

139. *Joplin Globe*, 15 March 1924, 18 March 1924.

140. *Joplin News-Herald*, 18 October 1921.

141. *Joplin Globe*, 25 March 1924.

142. *Joplin Globe*, 20 March 1924, 21 March 1924, 23 March 1924, 26 March 1924, 28 March 1924, 29 March 1924, 30 March 1924; *Joplin News-Herald*, 20 March 1924, 26 March 1924, 29 March 1924.

143. *Joplin Globe*, 15 March 1924.

144. *Joplin Globe*, 18 March 1924; *Joplin News-Herald*, 18 March 1924.

145. *Joplin Globe*, 19 March 1924.

146. *Joplin Globe*, 19 March 1924. A few days before the municipal election, M. B. Harutun issued a public statement in both the *Joplin Globe* and the *Joplin News-Herald* denying that he was a Klansman or that he had been solicited by the Klan. Harutun cited that even if he wanted to join the Klan, he could not because of his foreign birth. For Harutun's official statement, see *Joplin Globe*, 30 March 1924; and *Joplin News-Herald*, 31 March 1924. For a letter inquiring about Harutun's stance on the Klan, see George Grayston to M. B. Harutun, 25 March 1924, folder 15, Perl D. Decker Papers, SHSMO.

147. *Joplin Globe*, 19 March 1924.

148. *Joplin Globe*, 18 March 1924, 19 March 1924, 21 March 1924, 25 March 1924, 26 March 1924; *Joplin News-Herald*, 19 March 1924, 26 March 1924; *Carthage Evening Press*, 18 March 1924, 24 March 1924, 27 March 1924; *Jasper County Democrat*, 21 March 1924.

149. *Joplin Globe*, 20 March 1924, 21 March 1924, 23 March 1924, 25 March 1924, 26 March 1924, 28 March 1924, 29 March 1924, 30 March 1924; *Joplin News-Herald*, 20 March 1924, 26 March 1924, 29 March 1924; *Carthage Evening Press*, 28 March 1924, 29 March 1924, 31 March 1924.

332   Notes to Chapter Four

150. *Joplin Globe*, 28 March 1924.

151. *Joplin Globe*, 21 March 1924.

152. *Joplin Globe*, 27 March 1924.

153. *Joplin Globe*, 27 March 1924.

154. Decker's personal papers contain a folder consisting of undated and untitled drafts of anti-Klan speeches and JAKO advertisements submitted to local newspapers. For this information, see folder 15, Perl D. Decker Papers, SHSMO.

155. *Joplin Globe*, 27 March 1924.

156. *Joplin Globe*, 27 March 1924.

157. *Joplin Globe*, 27 March 1924.

158. *Joplin Globe*, 29 March 1924; *Joplin News-Herald*, 29 March 1924; *Carthage Evening Press*, 29 March 1924.

159. *Joplin Globe*, 29 March 1924; *Joplin News-Herald*, 29 March 1924; *Carthage Evening Press*, 29 March 1924.

160. *Joplin Globe*, 30 March 1924; *Joplin News-Herald*, 31 March 1924.

161. *Joplin Globe*, 30 March 1924; *Joplin News-Herald*, 31 March 1924.

162. *Carthage Evening Press*, 18 March 1924.

163. *Joplin Globe*, 30 March 1924.

164. *Joplin Globe*, 2 April 1924; *Joplin News-Herald*, 2 April 1924; *Carthage Evening Press*, 2 April 1924.

165. *Joplin Globe*, 1 April 1924; *Joplin News-Herald*, 1 April 1924.

166. *Jasper County Democrat*, 4 April 1924.

Chapter Four
"A Curious and Interested Spectator"
The "Klan Issue" in Missouri Politics

1. *St. Louis Post-Dispatch*, 9 November 1924; *Kansas City Journal-Post*, 9 November 1924; *St. Louis Globe Democrat*, 9 November 1924; *Versailles Statesman*, 13 November 1924; *Kansas City Star*, 22 October 1924; John Judson Large, "The 'Invisible Empire' and Missouri Politics: The Influence of the Revived Ku Klux Klan in the Election Campaign of 1924 as Reported in Missouri Newspapers," 108–9.

2. *Baltimore Sun*, 10 November 1924; *Memphis Commercial Appeal*, 10 November 1924; *Detroit Free Press*, 10 November 1924; *New York Daily News*, 10 November 1924.

3. *St. Louis Post-Dispatch*, 9 November 1924; *Kansas City Journal-Post*, 9 November 1924; *St. Louis Globe Democrat*, 9 November 1924; *Versailles Statesman*, 13 November 1924; *Kansas City Star*, 22 October 1924; Large, "'Invisible Empire' and Missouri Politics," 108–9.

4. *Kansas City Journal-Post*, 9 November 1924; *St. Louis Globe Democrat*, 9 November 1924; *Versailles Statesman*, 13 November 1924; *Kansas City Star*, 22 October 1924; Large, "'Invisible Empire' and Missouri Politics," 108–9.

5. *Jefferson City Daily Capital News*, 21 October 1924.

6. *Kansas City Post-Journal*, 22 October 1924; *Kansas City Star*, 22 October 1924; *St. Louis Post-Dispatch*, 21 October 1924; *St. Louis Globe Democrat*, 22 October 1924. In addition to being at the California Klan rally, Nelson also admitted that he had been at the 1923 Southwest Missouri Fair in Jasper County when "several automobiles

Notes to Chapter Four 333

containing persons in klan [*sic*] costumes drive [*sic*] around the racetrack and then drove on out."

7. Pegram, *One Hundred Percent American*, 185–216; McVeigh, *Rise of the Ku Klux Klan*, 180–93; Chalmers, *Hooded Americanism*, 291–99; MacLean, *Behind the Mask of Chivalry*, 177–88.

8. Christensen et al., *Dictionary of Missouri Biography*, 641–43.

9. Mitchell, *Embattled Democracy*, 55; Franklin D. Mitchell, "The Re-election of the Irreconcilable James A. Reed," 423–33; *St. Louis Post-Dispatch*, 1 June 1922, 11 June 1922, 18 June 1922, 3 August 1922; *St. Louis Argus*, 21 July 1922, 28 July 1922; *Kansas City Call*, 22 July 1922, 5 August 1922; *St. Louis Star*, 1 June 1922, 11 June 1922, 12 June 1922, 19 June 1922, 3 August 1922; *Kansas City Star*, 2 August 1922, 3 August 1922, 4 August 1924; *Kansas City Journal*, 3 August 1922, 4 August 1922.

10. Mitchell, *Embattled Democracy*, 16–19, 43–57; Mitchell, "Re-election of the Irreconcilable James A. Reed," 416–31.

11. *St. Louis Argus*, 28 April 1922.

12. *St. Louis Argus*, 7 July 1922, 11 August 1922.

13. *St. Louis Post-Dispatch*, 2 August 1922.

14. *Jewish Voice*, 4 August 1922.

15. *Kansas City Star*, 10 October 1922; *Kansas City Journal*, 10 October 1922.

16. *Kansas City Star*, 10 October 1922; *Kansas City Journal*, 10 October 1922.

17. *Kansas City Journal*, 11 October 1922.

18. *Kansas City Journal*, 11 October 1922.

19. *Kansas City Star*, 11 October 1922; *Kansas City Catholic Register*, 12 October 1922.

20. *Kansas City Star*, 11 October 1922.

21. *Kansas City Catholic Register*, 19 October 1922.

22. *Kansas City Journal*, 11 October 1922.

23. *Kansas City Catholic Register*, 2 November 1922.

24. *Kansas City Journal*, 29 October 1922.

25. *Kansas City Star*, 29 October 1922.

26. *St. Louis Post-Dispatch*, 2 November 1922.

27. *Kansas City Catholic Register*, 2 November 1922.

28. *Kansas City Jewish Chronicle*, 26 October 1923; *St. Louis Post-Dispatch*, 3 April 1924.

29. *Kansas City Catholic Register*, 22 June 1922.

30. *Kansas City Jewish Chronicle*, 12 August 1921.

31. *St. Louis Post-Dispatch*, 18 September 1922; *Jewish Voice*, 22 September 1922.

32. Mitchell, *Embattled Democracy*, 53; Mitchell, "Re-election of the Irreconcilable James A. Reed," 426–28; *Missouri Counselor*, June 1922, September 1922; *Union Signal*, 1 June 1922, 16 November 1922; *Kansas City Journal*, 3 June 1922, 14 June 1922.

33. *Kansas City Call*, 27 October 1922. Ben Tillman and James Vardaman were US senators from South Carolina and Mississippi, respectively.

34. *Kansas City Journal*, 13 October 1922; *St. Louis Argus*, 24 March 1922; *Kansas City Call*, 18 February 1922, 1 April 1922, 19 August 1922.

35. *Kansas City Call*, 18 February 1922, 27 October 1922; *St. Louis Argus*, 31 March 1922.

334 Notes to Chapter Four

36. *Kansas City Call*, 27 October 1922.

37. *Jefferson City Daily Capital News*, 2 November 1922, 3 November 1922; *Joplin Globe*, 3 November 1922; *St. Louis Post-Dispatch*, 3 November 1922.

38. *St. Louis Post-Dispatch*, 4 November 1922.

39. *Kansas City Journal*, 13 October 1922.

40. *Joplin Globe*, 14 October 1922.

41. *St. Louis Post-Dispatch*, 24 October 1922.

42. *St. Louis Post-Dispatch*, 8 November 1922; *New York Times*, 10 December 1922.

43. Mitchell, *Embattled Democracy*, 60–61.

44. *Kansas City Catholic Register*, 9 November 1922.

45. *Kansas City Catholic Register*, 9 November 1922, 16 November 1922. Though it declared the Klan dead and vowed not to fight "dead ones" and "cripples," the *Catholic Register* did continue to publish articles about Klan activity around the United States for the rest of 1922. *Kansas City Catholic Register*, 23 November 1922, 30 November 1922, 7 December 1922, 14 December 1922, 21 December 1922, 28 December 1922.

46. *Kansas City Catholic Register*, 9 November 1922.

47. Mitchell, *Embattled Democracy*, 69–75.

48. *St. Louis Post-Dispatch*, 14 April 1924; *Kansas City Star*, 15 April 1924, 16 April 1924.

49. *St. Louis Post-Dispatch*, 14 April 1924; *Kansas City Star*, 15 April 1924, 16 April 1924.

50. *St. Louis Post-Dispatch*, 14 April 1924; *Kansas City Star*, 15 April 1924, 16 April 1924.

51. *St. Louis Post-Dispatch*, 14 April 1924; *Kansas City Star*, 15 April 1924, 16 April 1924.

52. *St. Louis Post-Dispatch*, 15 April 1924.

53. *St. Louis Post-Dispatch*, 15 April 1924.

54. *Patriot*, 17 April 1924.

55. *St. Louis Post-Dispatch*, 16 April 1924; *Kansas City Star*, 16 April 1924.

56. *St. Louis Post-Dispatch*, 16 April 1924; *Kansas City Star*, 16 April 1924; *Joplin Globe*, 17 April 1924.

57. *St. Louis Post-Dispatch*, 16 April 1924; *Kansas City Star*, 16 April 1924; *Joplin Globe*, 17 April 1924.

58. *St. Louis Post-Dispatch*, 16 April 1924.

59. *St. Louis Post-Dispatch*, 16 April 1924; *Kansas City Star*, 16 April 1924.

60. *Kansas City Post*, 16 April 1924.

61. *St. Louis Argus*, 18 April 1924.

62. *St. Louis Post-Dispatch*, 18 April 1924, 27 April 1924; *Kansas City Star*, 28 April 1924, 29 April 1924.

63. *St. Louis Argus*, 16 May 1924; *St. Louis Post-Dispatch*, 29 April 1924, 11 May 1924.

64. *St. Louis Post-Dispatch*, 29 April 1924, 30 April 1924; *Kansas City Star*, 29 April 1924, 30 April 1924.

65. *St. Louis Post-Dispatch*, 30 April 1924; *Joplin Globe*, 30 April 1924; *Klan Kourier*, 1 May 1924.

Notes to Chapter Four

66. *St. Louis Post-Dispatch*, 30 April 1924.

67. *Modern View*, 30 May 1924, 20 March 1925.

68. *Modern View*, 30 May 1924. For Louis Marshall's views on the Ku Klux Klan, see M. M. Silver, *Louis Marshall and the Rise of Jewish Ethnicity in America: A Biography*, 462–66.

69. Bruce J. Schulman, "Farewell to the 'Smoke-Filled Room': Parties, Interests, Public Relations, and the Election of 1924," in *America at the Ballot Box: Elections and Political History*, ed. Gareth Davies and Julian E. Zelizer, 145; Chalmers, *Hooded Americanism*, 202–12; McVeigh, *Rise of the Ku Klux Klan*, 27–28, 184–87; Pegram, *One Hundred Percent American*, 212–16.

70. Schulman, "Farewell to the 'Smoke-Filled Room,'" in *America at the Ballot Box*, ed. Davies and Zelizer, 139–52; Chalmers, *Hooded Americanism*, 202–12; McVeigh, *Rise of the Ku Klux Klan*, 27–28, 184–87; Pegram, *One Hundred Percent American*, 212–16.

71. *St. Louis Post-Dispatch*, 26 June 1924.

72. Schulman, "Farewell to the 'Smoke-Filled Room,'" in *America at the Ballot Box*, ed. Davies and Zelizer, 139–52; Chalmers, *Hooded Americanism*, 202–12; McVeigh, *Rise of the Ku Klux Klan*, 27–28, 184–87; Pegram, *One Hundred Percent American*, 212–16.

73. Chalmers, *Hooded Americanism*, 202–12; McVeigh, *Rise of the Ku Klux Klan*, 27–28, 184–87; Pegram, *One Hundred Percent American*, 212–16.

74. *St. Louis Argus*, 4 July 1924.

75. *St. Louis Post-Dispatch*, 30 June 1924.

76. *Jefferson City Democrat-Tribune*, 12 July 1924, 14 July 1924, 15 July 1924; *Jefferson City Daily Capital News*, 13 July 1924, 15 July 1924; Butcher, *Ku Klux Klan*.

77. Schulman, "Farewell to the 'Smoke-Filled Room,'" in *America at the Ballot Box*, ed. Davies and Zelizer, 139–52; *St. Louis Star*, 19 August 1924.

78. Schulman, "Farewell to the 'Smoke-Filled Room,'" in *America at the Ballot Box*, ed. Davies and Zelizer, 139–52.

79. Douglass, *History of Southeast Missouri*, 571–72; *St. Louis Post-Dispatch*, 14 February 1950. Though the "Washington Dispatch," or some variation of a news report from Washington, DC, made regular appearances in both newspapers, for prime examples and commentaries of the series, see *Missouri Valley Independent*, 10 January 1924; and *Klan Kourier*, 15 May 1924.

80. *Missouri Valley Independent*, 10 January 1924.

81. *Missouri Valley Independent*, 15 May 1924, 29 May 1924; *Klan Kourier*, 15 May 1924.

82. *Missouri Valley Independent*, 15 May 1924, 29 May 1924; *St. Louis Post-Dispatch*, 17 June 1924.

83. *Joplin Globe*, 12 October 1924; *Sioux City Journal*, 16 October 1924.

84. *Missouri Valley Independent*, 12 June 1924, 26 June 1924.

85. *St. Louis Post-Dispatch*, 6 July 1924.

86. *Missouri Valley Independent*, 14 August 1924; *St. Louis Post-Dispatch*, 31 August 1924, 8 September 1924, 26 September 1924; *Joplin Globe*, 31 August 1924.

87. *St. Louis Post-Dispatch*, 26 September 1924.

88. *Washington Evening Star*, 31 August 1924.

Notes to Chapter Four

89. *St. Louis Post-Dispatch*, 10 September 1924.

90. *Missouri Valley Independent*, 26 June 1924.

91. Schulman, "Farewell to the 'Smoke-Filled Room,'" in *America at the Ballot Box*, ed. Davies and Zelizer, 139–52.

92. *Kansas City Jewish Chronicle*, 30 May 1924.

93. *St. Louis Post-Dispatch*, 8 May 1924.

94. *St. Louis Argus*, 27 June 1924, 31 October 1924; *Kansas City Call*, 25 July 1924, 31 October 1924. For examples of the NAACP questionnaire and other inquiries about a candidate's stance on the Klan, see NAACP Committee to Frank E. Atwood, July 1924, folder 97, Frank Ely Atwood Papers, State Historical Society of Missouri (hereafter cited as FEAP, SHSMO); Vincent M. Carroll to Frank E. Atwood, 22 July 1924, Western Union Telegram, folder 101, FEAP, SHSMO; St. Louis Post-Dispatch to Frank Atwood, 24 July 1924, Western Union Telegram, folder 101, FEAP, SHSMO; Frank Atwood to St. Louis Post-Dispatch, 24 July 1924, Western Union Telegram, folder 101, FEAP, SHSMO; George Grayston to Frank Atwood, 24 May 1924, folder 103, FEAP, SHSMO; A. E. Spencer to Frank Atwood, 29 July 1924, folder 103, FEAP, SHSMO; Frank Atwood to A. E. Spencer, 31 July 1924, folder 103, FEAP, SHSMO; Frank Atwood to George Grayston, 31 July 1924, folder 103, FEAP, SHSMO; Frank Atwood to W. N. Andrews, 31 July 1924, folder 103, FEAP, SHSMO; A. E. Spencer to Frank Atwood, 6 August 1924, folder 103, FEAP, SHSMO; and Frank Atwood to B. K. Blair, 2 September 1924, folder 106, FEAP, SHSMO.

95. Large, "'Invisible Empire' and Missouri Politics," 7–9.

96. *St. Louis Post-Dispatch*, 10 July 1924.

97. Large, "'Invisible Empire' and Missouri Politics," 9.

98. *St. Louis Post-Dispatch*, 9 June 1924.

99. Large, "'Invisible Empire' and Missouri Politics," 8; *St. Louis Post-Dispatch*, 21 June 1924.

100. Large, "'Invisible Empire' and Missouri Politics," 9–10.

101. *St. Louis Post-Dispatch*, 5 August 1924, 6 August 1924, 7 August 1924.

102. *St. Louis Argus*, 13 June 1924; *Kansas City Call*, 1 August 1924.

103. *St. Louis Post-Dispatch*, 7 August 1924.

104. *Jefferson City Daily Capital News*, 21 October 1924.

105. For a detailed overview of the 1924 gubernatorial election, see Large, "'Invisible Empire' and Missouri Politics."

106. *St. Louis Post-Dispatch*, 21 October 1924, 22 October 1924.

107. *St. Louis Globe Democrat*, 22 October 1924; *St. Louis Post-Dispatch*, 22 October 1924; *Jefferson City Daily Capital News*, 22 October 1924.

108. *Jefferson City Democrat-Tribune*, 22 October 1924; *Kansas City Post-Journal*, 23 October 1924; *St. Louis Post-Dispatch*, 22 October 1924; *Jefferson City Daily Capital News*, 23 October 1924.

109. *St. Louis Post-Dispatch*, 23 October 1924; *Jefferson City Daily Capital News*, 26 October 1924.

110. *Jefferson City Daily Capital News*, 29 October 1924; *Jefferson City Democrat-Tribune*, 29 October 1924.

Notes to Chapter Five

111. *St. Louis Post-Dispatch*, 24 October 1924; *Jefferson City Democrat-Tribune*, 24 October 1924; *Jefferson City Daily Capital News*, 25 October 1924.

112. *Jefferson City Democrat-Tribune*, 23 October 1924.

113. *Kansas City Journal*, 22 October 1924.

114. *Jefferson City Democrat-Tribune*, 27 October 1924.

115. *Kansas City Star*, 22 October 1924.

116. *Jefferson City Democrat-Tribune*, 25 October 1924.

117. *St. Louis Globe Democrat*, 4 November 1924; *Jefferson City Daily Capital News*, 29 October 1924, 30 October 1924; *Kansas City Journal-Post*, 26 October 1924, 27 October 1924, 31 October 1924; Large, "'Invisible Empire' and Missouri Politics," 86–128.

118. *Jefferson City Daily Capital News*, 26 October 1924.

119. *Kansas City Star*, 21 October 1924; *St. Louis Post-Dispatch*, 21 October 1924; *Jefferson City Daily Capital News*, 2 November 1924.

120. *Jefferson City Daily Capital News*, 30 October 1924.

121. *Jefferson City Daily Capital News*, 2 November 1924.

122. *Modern View*, 10 October 1924, 31 October 1924. Zuzak's comments in the *Modern View* were followed by a paid ad repeating Zuzak's defense of Nelson and cosigned by six other Jewish residents of Cooper County.

123. *Jefferson City Daily Capital News*, 2 November 1924.

124. *St. Louis Post-Dispatch*, 29 October 1924, 2 November 1924; *St. Louis Globe Democrat*, 2 November 1924, 4 November 1924; *Jefferson City Daily Capital News*, 2 November 1924.

125. *Jefferson City Daily Capital News*, 4 November 1924; *Jefferson City Democrat-Tribune*, 4 November 1924.

126. *St. Louis Globe Democrat*, 6 November 1924.

127. *Jefferson City Daily Capital News*, 7 November 1924.

128. *St. Louis Post-Dispatch*, 9 November 1924.

Chapter Five
"Behind the Mask"
Fraud, Bribery, and Scandal in Missouri's Invisible Empire

1. *Missouri Valley Independent*, 15 July 1926.

2. Pegram, *One Hundred Percent American*, 186–216; L. Moore, *Citizen Klansmen*, 151–81.

3. *Missouri Valley Independent*, 15 January 1925, 14 May 1925, 1 October 1925.

4. *Missouri Valley Independent*, 12 February 1925, 28 May 1925.

5. *Missouri Valley Independent*, 13 August 1925, 4 March 1926, 3 June 1926, 17 June 1926, 8 July 1926, 15 July 1926, 22 July 1926, 29 July 1926, 5 August 1926, 12 August 1926, 19 August 1926, 9 September 1926.

6. *St. Louis Post-Dispatch*, 8 January 1925; *Jefferson City Daily Capital News*, 3 February 1925; *Jefferson City Daily Post*, 3 February 1925; *Missouri Valley Independent*, 15 January 1925.

7. *St. Louis Post-Dispatch*, 19 September 1926; *St. Louis Argus*, 24 September 1926; *St. Louis Globe-Democrat*, 6 January 1927.

338 Notes to Chapter Five

8. *Missouri Valley Independent*, 3 June 1926, 17 June 1926, 8 July 1926, 15 July 1926, 22 July 1926, 29 July 1926, 5 August 1926, 12 August 1926, 9 September 1926, 5 May 1927, 12 May 1927, 21 July 1927, 4 August 1927, 11 August 1927, 18 August 1927, 13 October 1927.

9. *Missouri Valley Independent*, 15 July 1926.

10. *Missouri Valley Independent*, 15 July 1926.

11. *Missouri Valley Independent*, 3 June 1926, 17 June 1926, 8 July 1926, 15 July 1926, 22 July 1926, 29 July 1926, 5 August 1926, 12 August 1926, 9 September 1926, 5 May 1927, 12 May 1927, 21 July 1927, 4 August 1927, 11 August 1927, 18 August 1927, 13 October 1927.

12. *Missouri Valley Independent*, 9 September 1926.

13. *Missouri Valley Independent*, 3 June 1926.

14. *Missouri Valley Independent*, 3 June 1926, 17 June 1926, 8 July 1926, 15 July 1926, 22 July 1926, 29 July 1926, 5 August 1926, 12 August 1926, 9 September 1926, 5 May 1927, 12 May 1927, 21 July 1927, 4 August 1927, 11 August 1927, 18 August 1927, 13 October 1927.

15. *Missouri Valley Independent*, 3 June 1926, 17 June 1926, 8 July 1926, 15 July 1926, 22 July 1926, 29 July 1926, 5 August 1926, 12 August 1926, 9 September 1926, 5 May 1927, 12 May 1927, 21 July 1927, 4 August 1927, 11 August 1927, 18 August 1927, 13 October 1927.

16. *Fraternalist*, 1 December 1927.

17. Pegram, *One Hundred Percent American*, 189, 201–2, 205–7; Chalmers, *Hooded Americanism*, 127–34, 162–74; L. Moore, *Citizen Klansmen*, 14–19, 151–83; Baker, *Gospel according to the Klan*, 226–31.

18. *St. Louis Post-Dispatch*, 15 January 1924.

19. *Patriot*, 10 August 1923. For advertisements in the *Patriot* for the farm-slogan contest, see 10 August 1923, 17 August 1923, 24 August 1923, 6 September 1923, 21 September 1923, 28 September 1923, 5 October 1923, 11 October 1923, 17 October 1923, 25 October 1923, 1 November 1923, 8 November 1923, 15 November 1923, 6 December 1923, and 12 December 1923.

20. *St. Louis Post-Dispatch*, 15 January 1924.

21. *St. Louis Post-Dispatch*, 15 January 1924, 17 January 1924.

22. *St. Louis Post-Dispatch*, 15 January 1924, 17 January 1924.

23. *St. Louis Post-Dispatch*, 15 January 1924, 17 January 1924.

24. *St. Louis Post-Dispatch*, 15 January 1924, 17 January 1924, 7 March 1924; *St. Louis Star*, 7 March 1924; *St. Louis Globe-Democrat*, 7 March 1924.

25. *St. Louis Post-Dispatch*, 7 March 1924; *St. Louis Star*, 7 March 1924; *St. Louis Globe-Democrat*, 7 March 1924.

26. *St. Louis Post-Dispatch*, 7 March 1924; *St. Louis Star*, 7 March 1924; *St. Louis Globe-Democrat*, 7 March 1924.

27. *St. Louis Post-Dispatch*, 7 March 1924; *St. Louis Star*, 7 March 1924; *St. Louis Globe-Democrat*, 7 March 1924.

28. *Patriot*, 10 October 1923.

29. *St. Louis Post-Dispatch*, 7 March 1924.

Notes to Chapter Five 339

30. *Patriot*, 24 January 1924.

31. *St. Louis Post-Dispatch*, 7 March 1924.

32. *Poplar Bluff Republican*, 8 March 1924; *Church Progress*, 13 March 1924; *Vienna Home Advisor*, 13 March 1924; *Washington Citizen*, 14 March 1924, 11 April 1924, 9 May 1924.

33. *St. Louis Star*, 8 March 1924.

34. *Washington Citizen*, 14 March 1924.

35. *Jefferson County Republican*, 6 March 1924.

36. *Kansas City Catholic Register*, 13 March 1924.

37. *St. Louis Post-Dispatch*, 8 March 1924, 10 March 1924; *St. Louis Star*, 8 March 1924, 10 March 1924; *St. Louis Globe-Democrat*, 8 March 1924; *Missouri Fiery Cross*, 13 March 1924.

38. *St. Louis Post-Dispatch*, 8 March 1924.

39. *Missouri Fiery Cross*, 13 March 1924.

40. *St. Louis Post-Dispatch*, 8 March 1924.

41. *St. Louis Post-Dispatch*, 15 November 1926.

42. *St. Louis Post-Dispatch*, 7 March 1924.

43. *St. Louis Post-Dispatch*, 20 March 1924, 4 May 1924; *Patriot*, 27 March 1924; *Klan Kourier*, 1 May 1924. While trying to sell the newspaper to the Klan, Crawford temporarily changed the name from the *Patriot* to *Missouri Fiery Cross*. When the deal fell through, he changed it back to the *Patriot*. After the Klan sought to punish Crawford, the organization took control of the newspaper and changed its name to the *Klan Kourier*.

44. *St. Louis Post-Dispatch*, 26 April 1924; *St. Louis Star*, 26 April 1924.

45. *St. Louis Post-Dispatch*, 4 May 1924.

46. *Patriot*, 12 July 1923, 27 July 1923, 17 August 1923, 24 August 1923, 7 September 1923, 28 September 1923, 5 October 1923, 17 October 1923, 1 November 1923, 15 November 1923, 22 November 1923, 13 December 1923, 27 December 1923, 3 January 1924, 10 January 1924, 7 February 1924; *St. Louis Post-Dispatch*, 10 October 1922, 31 May 1923, 25 June 1923, 5 August 1923, 26 February 1924.

47. *St. Louis Post-Dispatch*, 5 August 1923.

48. *Missouri Valley Independent*, 24 April 1924.

49. For information on Nations's involvement with renting the House of Representatives chambers for a Klan event, see *St. Louis Post-Dispatch*, 14 February 1924, 15 February 1924.

50. Courtaway, *Wetter than the Mississippi*, 88–89; *St. Louis Post-Dispatch*, 9 March 1924.

51. Courtaway, *Wetter than the Mississippi*, 88–89; *St. Louis Post-Dispatch*, 9 March 1924, 11 March 1924.

52. Courtaway, *Wetter than the Mississippi*, 90; *St. Louis Post-Dispatch*, 10 March 1924, 11 March 1924; *Weekly Kansas City Star*, 12 March 1924.

53. *St. Louis Post-Dispatch*, 11 March 1924; *Weekly Kansas City Star*, 12 March 1924, 19 March 1924.

54. *St. Louis Post-Dispatch*, 12 March 1924; *Weekly Kansas City Star*, 12 March 1924, 19 March 1924.

340 Notes to Chapter Five

55. Courtaway, *Wetter than the Mississippi*, 91; *St. Louis Post-Dispatch*, 7 May 1924; *Weekly Kansas City Star*, 14 May 1924.

56. *St. Louis Post-Dispatch*, 19 April 1925.

57. Courtaway, *Wetter than the Mississippi*, 94; *St. Louis Post-Dispatch*, 17 May 1925, 20 May 1925, 22 May 1925.

58. *St. Louis Post-Dispatch*, 25 May 1925.

59. Courtaway, *Wetter than the Mississippi*, 94–101; *St. Louis Post-Dispatch*, 26 May 1925; *Kansas City Star*, 26 May 1925.

60. Courtaway, *Wetter than the Mississippi*, 94–101; *St. Louis Post-Dispatch*, 26 May 1925; *Kansas City Star*, 26 May 1925.

61. *St. Louis Post-Dispatch*, 26 May 1925.

62. Courtaway, *Wetter than the Mississippi*, 94–101; *St. Louis Post-Dispatch*, 27 May 1925; *Kansas City Star*, 27 May 1925.

63. *St. Louis Post-Dispatch*, 28 May 1925; *Kansas City Star*, 28 May 1925.

64. *St. Louis Post-Dispatch*, 12 March 1924, 13 March 1924, 21 April 1924, 6 May 1924, 7 May 1924, 27 May 1925, 28 May 1925.

65. *St. Louis Post-Dispatch*, 28 May 1925; *Kansas City Star*, 28 May 1925.

66. Courtaway, *Wetter than the Mississippi*, 100–101; *St. Louis Post-Dispatch*, 30 May 1925, 1 June 1925; *Kansas City Star*, 29 May 1925, 1 June 1925.

67. *St. Louis Post-Dispatch*, 30 May 1925.

68. *St. Louis Post-Dispatch*, 30 May 1925.

69. Courtaway, *Wetter than the Mississippi*, 88–105; *St. Louis Post-Dispatch*, 1 June 1925, 23 September 1925. In 1929, Gus Nations sued Mabel Willebrandt after a series of articles were published by her claiming that she fought the Anti-Saloon League to remove a popular St. Louis Prohibition agent. Nations interpreted the story as being about him. His libel suit was eventually thrown out in 1933.

70. *Jefferson City Tribune*, 22 May 1925.

71. Courtaway, *Wetter than the Mississippi*, 92, 101; *Jefferson City Daily Capital News*, 4 June 1925; *Cole County Weekly Rustler*, 5 June 1925; *Jefferson City Tribune*, 5 June 1925. For more information on Klan involvement in liquor raids, see McGirr, *War on Alcohol*, 132–53.

72. *Jefferson City Tribune*, 5 June 1925.

73. *Jefferson City Tribune*, 5 June 1925.

74. Courtaway, *Wetter than the Mississippi*, 92, 101; *Jefferson City Tribune*, 5 June 1925. In addition to a number of controversies surrounding his ties to the Klan and the qualifications of his deputies, Withaup was also found guilty in federal court of not properly maintaining the county jail, particularly his leniency when it came to special privileges he offered prisoners. He was sentenced to a $500 fine and probation. *Jefferson City Post-Tribune*, 22 November 1927, 23 November 1927, 22 December 1927.

75. *Jefferson City Post-Tribune*, 14 July 1927.

76. *Jefferson City Tribune*, 22 June 1925, 23 June 1925.

77. *Jefferson City Tribune*, 22 July 1925. Around the same time, the Jefferson City Klan also held a large outdoor memorial service for William Jennings Bryan who died in the summer of 1925. *Jefferson City Daily Capital News*, 7 August 1925, 8 August 1925.

Notes to Chapter Five

341

78. *Jefferson City Daily Capital News*, 25 November 1925; *Jefferson City Tribune*, 25 November 1925; *Cole County Weekly Rustler*, 27 November 1925.

79. *Jefferson City Daily Capital News*, 25 November 1925.

80. *St. Louis Post-Dispatch*, 17 July 1926, 18 July 1926; *Weekly Kansas City Star*, 21 July 1926.

81. *St. Louis Post-Dispatch*, 8 August 1926, 29 November 1926.

82. *St. Louis Post-Dispatch*, 24 January 1928, 25 January 1928, 26 January 1928, 27 January 1928, 28 January 1928, 20 February 1928.

83. *St. Louis Post-Dispatch*, 20 February 1928.

84. *St. Louis Post-Dispatch*, 22 April 1929, 6 August 1931.

85. *St. Louis Post-Dispatch*, 22 April 1929, 11 January 1930, 12 January 1930.

86. *St. Louis Post-Dispatch*, 8 January 1930, 9 January 1930, 11 January 1930, 12 January 1930, 13 January 1930. While Raymond Griesedieck died before his sentencing, the Griesedieck Brothers Brewery was fined $10,000 for its role in the beer-protection scandal. Federal prosecutors used Prather's guilty plea and possible sentence as leverage for his continued testimony. He was eventually fined $500. *St. Louis Post-Dispatch*, 1 July 1933, 2 July 1933, 16 October 1933.

87. *St. Louis Post-Dispatch*, 13 January 1930, 15 January 1930, 16 January 1930. At his third trial, Nations relied on Charles M. Hay, former chairman of the Democratic State Convention; Charles Becker, Missouri secretary of state; L. D. Thompson, state auditor; and William C. Irwin, former state senator, to defend his character.

88. *St. Louis Post-Dispatch*, 13 August 1931.

89. *St. Louis Post-Dispatch*, 16 October 1933.

90. *Poplar Bluff Republican*, 22 July 1926.

91. *Poplar Bluff Republican*, 22 July 1926.

92. *Poplar Bluff American*, 22 August 1921.

93. *Poplar Bluff Weekly Citizen-Democrat*, 25 January 1923; *Missouri Valley Independent*, 1 February 1923; *Wayne County Journal*, 22 February 1923; *Poplar Bluff Interstate-American*, 27 February 1923, 24 March 1923.

94. *Des Moines Evening Tribune*, 4 September 1921, 16 September 1921; *Des Moines Register*, 18 September 1921.

95. *Memphis Commercial Appeal*, 9 September 1923; *Missouri Valley Independent*, 27 September 1923.

96. *Poplar Bluff Interstate-American*, 22 October 1923; *Poplar Bluff Weekly Citizen-Democrat*, 15 November 1923.

97. *Poplar Bluff Republican*, 22 November 1923; *Poplar Bluff Interstate-American*, 14 March 1924, 5 June 1924, 6 June 1924, 7 June 1924, 20 June 1924, 24 June 1924, 14 July 1924, 17 July 1924; *Dexter Statesman*, 30 May 1924; *Dunklin County News*, 18 July 1924, 8 August 1924.

98. *Poplar Bluff Interstate-American*, 5 June 1924, 6 June 1924, 7 June 1924.

99. *Poplar Bluff Interstate-American*, 24 June 1924, 16 July 1924.

100. *Memphis Commercial Appeal*, 19 August 1924; *Poplar Bluff Republican*, 20 August 1924, 27 August 1924.

101. *Poplar Bluff Republican*, 27 August 1924.

Notes to Chapter Five

102. *Missouri Kourier*, 17 October 1924.

103. Blee, *Women of the Klan*, 23–28; Chalmers, *Hooded Americanism*, 100–108; L. Gordon, *Second Coming of the KKK*, 15–16, 109–38; Harcourt, *Ku Klux Kulture*, 4–5.

104. *Joplin Globe*, 20 June 1924; *Memphis Commercial Appeal*, 3 September 1924, 5 September 1924, 18 September 1924.

105. *Memphis Commercial Appeal*, 3 September 1924, 5 September 1924, 18 September 1924, 6 November 1924.

106. *Springfield Leader*, 14 December 1924; *Kansas City Star*, 26 April 1925.

107. *St. Louis Post-Dispatch*, 11 February 1925; *Missouri Valley Independent*, 12 February 1925.

108. *Missouri Valley Independent*, 28 May 1925.

109. *St. Louis Star*, 28 February 1926; *St. Louis Globe-Democrat*, 28 February 1926.

110. *Memphis Commercial Appeal*, 6 November 1924.

111. *Memphis Commercial Appeal*, 3 September 1924.

112. *St. Louis Star*, 19 February 1925.

113. *St. Louis Post-Dispatch*, 31 March 1926; *Memphis Commercial Appeal*, 6 April 1926.

114. *Word and Way*, 13 May 1926.

115. *Poplar Bluff Republican*, 2 February 1928, 17 January 1929.

116. *Joplin Globe*, 16 July 1929, 27 July 1929.

117. *Joplin Globe*, 30 October 1921, 7 February 1923, 8 February 1923, 20 January 1924, 5 October 1924, 23 November 1924.

118. *Joplin Globe*, 16 July 1929, 27 July 1929.

119. *Joplin Globe*, 18 April 1922, 17 September 1922, 22 September 1922, 5 October 1922, 12 November 1922, 3 March 1923, 12 May 1923, 12 September 1923, 13 March 1924, 15 March 1924, 4 May 1924, 15 March 1925, 13 December 1925, 21 November 1926.

120. *Joplin Globe*, 14 April 1926.

121. *Kansas City Times*, 17 July 1929.

122. *Joplin Globe*, 16 July 1929, 27 July 1929.

123. *Joplin Globe*, 4 November 1926.

124. *Joplin Globe*, 4 November 1926.

125. Joplin *Globe*, 4 November 1926, 7 February 1926.

126. *Joplin Globe*, 7 March 1926.

127. *Joplin Globe*, 2 April 1926, 4 April 1926.

128. *Joplin Globe*, 7 March 1926.

129. *Joplin Globe*, 4 April 1926.

130. *Joplin Globe*, 4 April 1926.

131. *Joplin Globe*, 6 April 1926. According to Skoggman, his firing related to leaving his beat to visit a local rooming house. In his defense, Skoggman claimed that fellow officers ordered him to stop at the rooming house. When he arrived, three other officers cornered him and told him to stop investigating alcohol-related offenses at local drugstores.

132. *Joplin Globe*, 6 April 1926.

133. *Joplin Globe*, 7 April 1926.

Notes to Chapter Five 343

134. *Joplin Globe*, 11 April 1926, 13 April 1926, 14 April 1926, 15 April 1926, 17 April 1926, 18 April 1926, 20 April 1926.

135. *Joplin Globe*, 10 April 1926, 11 April 1926, 3 July 1926.

136. *Joplin Globe*, 15 July 1926, 17 July 1926, 21 July 1926, 23 July 1926, 25 July 1926, 27 July 1926, 28 July 1926, 29 July 1926, 31 July 1926, 1 August 1926, 29 October 1926, 31 October 1926. Some of the candidates who spoke on the Klan were John H. Flanigan, P. E. Donnell, Henry C. Johns, Robert W. Moore, Waldo Hatler, Frank Birkhead, A. H. Garner, Frank B. Davis, A. J. Edwards, Thomas Thoutman, J. W. Page, Joseph E. Turner, Glenn Skoggman, A. M. Baird, Uriah Smith, Mrs. S. L. Bradley, Earnest A. Hart, and Grant Emerson.

137. *Joplin Globe*, 18 July 1926.

138. *Joplin Globe*, 4 August 1926, 29 October 1926, 31 October 1926, 3 November 1926, 4 November 1926. The Jasper County Anti-Klan Association mounted a particularly strong and successful challenge to the campaign of Roy Bond for circuit-court judge.

139. For information on the Joplin special election, see *Joplin Globe*, 7 November 1926, 9 November 1926, 11 November 1926, 16 November 1926, 23 November 1926, 3 December 1926, 5 December 1926, 8 December 1926, 9 December 1926, 11 December 1926, 12 December 1926, 14 December 1926, 16 December 1926, and 17 December 1926.

140. *Joplin Globe*, 27 July 1929.

141. *Joplin Globe*, 16 July 1929.

142. *Joplin Globe*, 27 July 1929.

143. *Joplin Globe*, 27 July 1929.

144. Pegram, *One Hundred Percent American*, 189, 201–2; Chalmers, *Hooded Americanism*, 162–71; L. Moore, *Citizen Klansmen*, 14–19, 151–79; Baker, *Gospel according to the Klan*, 226–27; Blee, *Women of the Klan*, 94–95.

145. Pegram, *One Hundred Percent American*, 206; Chalmers, *Hooded Americanism*, 162–72; L. Moore, *Citizen Klansmen*, 151–82; Baker, *Gospel according to the Klan*, 226–28; Blee, *Women of the Klan*, 94–96.

146. Pegram, *One Hundred Percent American*, 206; Chalmers, *Hooded Americanism*, 171–72; L. Moore, *Citizen Klansmen*, 181–82; Baker, *Gospel according to the Klan*, 226–29; Blee, *Women of the Klan*, 95–96.

147. Pegram, *One Hundred Percent American*, 206–7; Chalmers, *Hooded Americanism*, 171–72; L. Moore, *Citizen Klansmen*, 181–82; Baker, *Gospel according to the Klan*, 226–29; Blee, *Women of the Klan*, 95–96.

148. Pegram, *One Hundred Percent American*, 206–7; Chalmers, *Hooded Americanism*, 172–74; L. Moore, *Citizen Klansmen*, 181–83; *St. Louis Post-Dispatch*, 10 October 1926, 11 October 1926.

149. Pegram, *One Hundred Percent American*, 206–7; Chalmers, *Hooded Americanism*, 172–74; L. Moore, *Citizen Klansmen*, 181–83; *St. Louis Post-Dispatch*, 9 October 1926, 10 October 1926, 11 October 1926.

150. *St. Louis Post-Dispatch*, 9 October 1926.

151. *St. Louis Post-Dispatch*, 12 October 1926, 17 October 1926.

152. *St. Louis Post-Dispatch*, 15 October 1926, 17 October 1926.

344 Notes to Chapter Six

153.*St. Louis Post-Dispatch*, 12 October 1926, 17 October 1926, 19 October 1926; *Kansas City Star*, 14 October 1926, 19 October 1926.

154. *Kansas City Star*, 14 October 1926.

155. *St. Louis Post-Dispatch*, 19 October 1926, 20 October 1926, 21 October 1926, 22 October 1926; *Kansas City Star*, 19 October 1926, 20 October 1926, 21 October 1926, 22 October 1926.

156. Chalmers, *Hooded Americanism*, 169–73.

157. *St. Louis Post-Dispatch*, 19 October 1926, 20 October 1926, 21 October 1926, 22 October 1926, 23 October 1926, 24 October 1926; *Kansas City Star*, 19 October 1926, 20 October 1926, 21 October 1926, 22 October 1926, 23 October 1926.

158. *St. Louis Post-Dispatch*, 24 October 1926; *Kansas City Star*, 24 October 1926, 25 October 1926.

159. *St. Louis Post-Dispatch*, 23 October 1926, 24 October 1926.

160. *St. Louis Post-Dispatch*, 17 May 1925, 19 May 1925, 20 May 1925, 22 May 1925, 25 May 1925; *Kansas City Star*, 25 May 1925, 29 May 1925.

161. *Missouri Valley Independent*, 22 July 1926; *St. Louis Post-Dispatch*, 24 July 1926; *Kansas City Star*, 23 July 1926, 24 July 1926, 25 July 1926; *St. Louis Argus*, 30 July 1926.

162. *St. Louis Post-Dispatch*, 24 July 1926, 21 October 1926, 22 October 1926; *Kansas City Star*, 23 July 1926, 24 July 1926, 25 July 1926; *St. Louis Argus*, 30 July 1926; *Missouri Valley Independent*, 5 August 1926, 30 September 1926; *Joplin Globe*, 24 September 1926, 22 October 1926, 23 October 1926.

163. Blee, *Women of the* Klan, 113–16; *St. Louis Post-Dispatch*, 23 October 1926, 25 October 1926; *Kansas City Star*, 25 October 1926.

164. *St. Louis Post-Dispatch*, 23 October 1926, 25 October 1926.

165. *St. Louis Post-Dispatch*, 23 October 1926, 25 October 1926, 28 October 1926.

166. Chalmers, *Hooded Americanism*, 169–73; L. Moore, *Citizen Klansmen*, 151–81; *St. Louis Post-Dispatch*, 24 October 1926, 28 October 1926; *Kansas City Star*, 25 October 1926.

167. *St. Louis Post-Dispatch*, 28 October 1926, 1 November 1926; *Kansas City Star*, 25 October 1926.

168. *St. Louis Post-Dispatch*, 23 October 1926; *Springfield Republican*, 22 October 1926, 24 October 1926; *Joplin Globe*, 22 October 1926; *St. Louis Star*, 22 October 1926.

169. *St. Louis Post-Dispatch*, 29 October 1926.

170. *Kansas City Call*, 24 June 1927.

171. Chalmers, *Hooded Americanism*, 100–108, 171–74, 291–318; Blee, *Women of the Klan*, 21–28, 93–98, 175; Dumenil, *Modern Temper*, 235–45.

Chapter Six
"Kampaigning"
Activism, Lily-Whitism, and the
Political Realignment of Missouri's Black Voters

1. *St. Joseph Gazette*, 27 October 1952, 1 November 1952; *Springfield Daily News*, 27 October 1952.

2. *Kansas City Call*, 31 October 1952.

Notes to Chapter Six 345

3. *St. Louis Argus*, 31 October 1952.

4. *St. Louis Post-Dispatch*, 27 October 1944, 30 October 1944; *St. Louis Star-Times*, 26 October 1944, 27 October 1944, 28 October 1944, *St. Louis Globe-Democrat*, 27 October 1944, *Kansas City Star*, 26 October 1944; *Kansas City Times*, 27 October 1944, 28 October 1944; *St. Joseph News-Press*, 27 October 1944, 29 October 1944.

5. *St. Louis Post-Dispatch*, 27 October 1944, 30 October 1944; *St. Louis Star-Times*, 26 October 1944, 27 October 1944, 28 October 1944, *St. Louis Globe-Democrat*, 27 October 1944, *Kansas City Star*, 26 October 1944; *Kansas City Times*, 27 October 1944, 28 October 1944; *St. Joseph News-Press*, 27 October 1944, 29 October 1944.

6. Jeffrey L. Pasley, "Big Deal in Little Tammany: Kansas City, the Pendergast Machine, and the Liberal Transformation of the Democratic Party," in *Wide Open Town*, ed. Mutti Burke, Roe, and Herron, 32–55.

7. Larry Grothaus, "The Negro in Missouri Politics, 1890–1941," 97–112; Clarence Lang, *Grassroots at the Gateway: Class Politics and Black Freedom Struggle in St. Louis, 1936–75*, 22–24; John W. McKerley, "The Other Tom's Town: Thomas T. Crittenden Jr., Black Disfranchisement, and the Limits of Liberalism in Kansas City," in *Wide Open Town*, ed. Mutti Burke, Roe, and Herron, 11–31; John W. McKerley, "Citizens and Strangers: The Politics of Race in Missouri from Slavery to the Era of Jim Crow."

8. Kremer, "William J. Thompkins," 168–71; Pasley, "Big Deal in Little Tammany," in *Wide Open Town*, ed. Mutti Burke, Roe, and Herron, 32–55; Schirmer, *City Divided*, 162–63.

9. Pasley, "Big Deal in Little Tammany," in *Wide Open Town*, ed. Mutti Burke, Roe, and Herron, 32–55; *Kansas City Star*, 21 April 1922, 29 May 1922.

10. *St. Louis Post-Dispatch*, 16 September 1924; *St. Louis Argus*, 19 September 1924.

11. Kremer, "William J. Thompkins," 170–71; Wilson, "Chester A. Franklin and Harry S. Truman," 53–54; Schirmer, *City Divided*, 153, 160–61; Pasley, "Big Deal in Little Tammany," in *Wide Open Town*, ed. Mutti Burke, Roe, and Herron, 32–55.

12. Schirmer, *City Divided*, 162–63; Kremer, "William J. Thompkins," 172.

13. Kremer, "William J. Thompkins," 173; Pasley, "Big Deal in Little Tammany," in *Wide Open Town*, ed. Mutti Burke, Roe, and Herron, 32–55.

14. *Kansas City American*, 27 February 1930; Schirmer, *City Divided*, 156–64.

15. Pasley, "Big Deal in Little Tammany," in *Wide Open Town*, ed. Mutti Burke, Roe, and Herron, 32–55.

16. *Kansas City Star*, 16 March 1924, 30 March 1924, 31 March 1924, 1 April 1924, 2 April 1924.

17. *Kansas City Star*, 5 April 1924.

18. *Kansas City Call*, 4 April 1924.

19. *Kansas City Star*, 3 April 1924.

20. *Kansas City Call*, 4 April 1924.

21. *Kansas City Star*, 29 March 1924, 30 March 1924, 31 March 1924, 1 April 1924, 4 April 1924, 5 April 1924, 7 April 1924.

22. *Kansas City Star*, 9 April 1924; Larsen and Hulston, *Pendergast!*, 64.

23. *Kansas City Call*, 25 April 1924.

Notes to Chapter Six

24. *Kansas City American*, 27 February 1930; *Kansas City Star*, 16 March 1930; Schirmer, *City Divided*, 156.

25. *Kansas City American*, 27 February 1930; Schirmer, *City Divided*, 156–64.

26. *Kansas City American*, 13 February 1930, 20 February 1930, 20 March 1930.

27. Schirmer, *City Divided*, 112–16; *Kansas City Call*, 21 March 1930.

28. *Kansas City Star*, 10 March 1930, 26 March 1930; *Kansas City American*, 27 March 1930; *Kansas City Call*, 28 March 1930; Schirmer, *City Divided*, 165–66; Grothaus, "Negro in Missouri Politics," 122–24; Larsen and Hulston, *Pendergast!*, 87–88.

29. Larsen and Hulston, *Pendergast!*, 88–89.

30. *St. Joseph Gazette*, 4 November 1924.

31. *St. Louis Post-Dispatch*, 30 September 1928; *St. Louis Globe-Democrat*, 9 October 1928; *Kansas City American*, 27 September 1928, 25 October 1928.

32. Primm, *Lion of the Valley*, 327–450.

33. Mitchell, *Embattled Democracy*, 86; *St. Louis Post-Dispatch*, 20 April 1953.

34. *St. Louis Post-Dispatch*, 21 March 1925, 24 March 1925, 26 March 1925, 27 March 1925, 4 April 1925, 5 April 1925; *St. Louis Argus*, 3 April 1925.

35. *St. Louis Argus*, 20 March 1925, 3 April 1925.

36. *St. Louis Argus*, 27 March 1925.

37. *St. Louis Globe-Democrat*, 26 July 1926; *St. Louis Post-Dispatch*, 28 July 1938.

38. *St. Louis Argus*, 27 March 1925.

39. *St. Louis Argus*, 27 March 1925; *St. Louis Post-Dispatch*, 4 April 1925; Mitchell, *Embattled Democracy*, 86–88.

40. *St. Louis Argus*, 27 March 1925.

41. Mitchell, *Embattled Democracy*, 86–88.

42. *St. Louis Argus*, 27 March 1925; Mitchell, *Embattled Democracy*, 86–88; Lang, *Grassroots at the Gateway*, 24–25.

43. Mary Welek, "Jordan Chambers: Black Politician and Boss," 353; Grothaus, "Negro in Missouri Politics," 113–14.

44. *St. Louis Argus*, 3 April 1925.

45. *St. Louis Argus*, 10 April 1925.

46. *St. Louis Post-Dispatch*, 20 March 1925, 6 April 1925.

47. *St. Louis Post-Dispatch*, 20 March 1925, 22 March 1925, 6 April 1925.

48. *St. Louis Post-Dispatch*, 8 April 1925; *St. Louis Argus*, 10 April 1925; Mitchell, *Embattled Democracy*, 86–88.

49. Mitchell, *Embattled Democracy*, 86–88; Larry Grothaus, "Kansas City Blacks, Harry Truman, and the Pendergast Machine," 73.

50. *St. Louis Argus*, 10 April 1925.

51. *St. Louis Argus*, 10 April 1925.

52. Welek, "Jordan Chambers," 353–54; *St. Louis Argus*, 2 March 1928, 15 February 1929, 1 March 1929.

53. *St. Louis Globe-Democrat*, 21 July 1926; *St. Louis Argus*, 30 July 1926.

54. *St. Louis Globe-Democrat*, 21 July 1926, 26 July 1926; *St. Louis Post-Dispatch*, 4 August 1926, 1 November 1926.

55. *St. Louis Globe-Democrat*, 21 July 1926.

Notes to Chapter Six

56. *St. Louis Post-Dispatch*, 4 November 1926.

57. *St. Louis Post-Dispatch*, 4 August 1927, 29 November 1971.

58. *St. Louis Argus*, 10 August 1928.

59. *St. Louis Argus*, 2 November 1928.

60. *St. Louis Post-Dispatch*, 4 November 1926, 8 November 1928.

61. Welek, "Jordan Chambers," 353–54; *St. Louis Argus*, 29 March 1929, 5 April 1929.

62. Welek, "Jordan Chambers," 353–58; Lang, *Grassroots at the Gateway*, 23–24; Grothaus, "Negro in Missouri Politics," 136–37.

63. Welek, "Jordan Chambers," 354; *St. Louis Post-Dispatch*, 8 August 1922, 23 March 1933, 24 March 1933, 12 October 1956; *St. Louis Argus*, 3 March 1933.

64. *St. Louis Argus*, 17 February 1933, 24 February 1933.

65. Welek, "Jordan Chambers," 353–58; Grothaus, "Negro in Missouri Politics," 136–37; *St. Louis Argus*, 10 March 1933, 17 March 1933.

66. *St. Louis Argus*, 10 March 1933.

67. Welek, "Jordan Chambers," 353–58; Grothaus, "Negro in Missouri Politics," 136–37; *St. Louis Argus*, 10 March 1933, 17 March 1933, 24 March 1933.

68. *St. Louis Argus*, 31 March 1933.

69. *St. Louis Argus*, 7 April 1933.

70. *St. Louis Argus*, 7 April 1933, 21 April 1933.

71. Mitchell, *Embattled Democracy*, 101–3.

72. Mitchell, *Embattled Democracy*, 84–85.

73. Mitchell, *Embattled Democracy*, 85–86.

74. *St. Louis Argus*, 5 November 1926; *St. Louis Post-Dispatch*, 16 October 1926.

75. Mitchell, *Embattled Democracy*, 84–86, 96–100.

76. Mitchell, *Embattled Democracy*, 101; *Kansas City Call*, 29 October 1926.

77. Mitchell, *Embattled Democracy*, 99–101, 96–98, 104–8.

78. Mitchell, *Embattled Democracy*, 107–8.

79. Mitchell, *Embattled Democracy*, 104–5.

80. *St. Louis Post-Dispatch*, 30 September 1928.

81. Grothaus, "Negro in Missouri Politics," 119–21; Kremer, "William J. Thompkins," 168–73; Pasley, "Big Deal in Little Tammany," in *Wide Open Town*, ed. Mutti Burke, Roe, and Herron, 32–55; *St. Louis Post-Dispatch*, 30 September 1928.

82. Wilson, "Chester A. Franklin and Harry S. Truman," 54.

83. Wilson, "Chester A. Franklin and Harry S. Truman," 54; Schirmer, *City Divided*, 157–58.

84. Wilson, "Chester A. Franklin and Harry S. Truman," 55; Schirmer, *City Divided*, 156; Pasley, "Big Deal in Little Tammany," in *Wide Open Town*, ed. Mutti Burke, Roe, and Herron, 32–55.

85. Wilson, "Chester A. Franklin and Harry S. Truman," 56.

86. Wilson, "Chester A. Franklin and Harry S. Truman," 56.

87. Wilson, "Chester A. Franklin and Harry S. Truman," 57–75.

88. *Kansas City Call*, 7 September 1928.

89. *Kansas City Call*, 12 October 1928.

90. Wilson, "Chester A. Franklin and Harry S. Truman," 57–75.

348 Notes to Chapter Six

91. *Kansas City Call*, 12 October 1928, 19 October 1928, 26 October 1928, 2 November 1928.

92. *Kansas City American*, 1 November 1928.

93. *Kansas City Call*, 26 October 1928, 2 November 1928.

94. Pasley, "Big Deal in Little Tammany," in *Wide Open Town*, ed. Mutti Burke, Roe, and Herron, 32–55.

95. *Kansas City American*, 23 August 1928, 27 September 1928, 25 October 1928.

96. Kansas City American, 1 November 1928.

97. Kansas City American, 18 October 1928.

98. *Kansas City Call*, 26 October 1928.

99. *St. Louis Post-Dispatch*, 30 September 1928.

100. *Kansas City American*, 1 November 1928; *St. Louis Argus*, 2 November 1928.

101. *Kansas City Call*, 2 November 1928.

102. Mitchell, *Embattled Democracy*, 119, 124–25, 119.

103. *Kansas City Call*, 9 November 1928.

104. *St. Louis Argus*, 26 October 1928.

105. Mitchell, *Embattled Democracy*, 126–35; Grothaus, "Negro in Missouri Politics," 126–29.

106. Mitchell, *Embattled Democracy*, 127–28; Grothaus, "Negro in Missouri Politics," 130.

107. *Kansas City American*, 27 March 1930.

108. Mitchell, *Embattled Democracy*, 139–59.

109. *St. Louis Post-Dispatch*, 3 May 1932; *St. Louis Globe-Democrat*, 3 May 1932, 7 May 1932.

110. *St. Louis Globe-Democrat*, 1 May 1932. For letters discussing the Klan's ties to Dearmont, see John B. Crum to Francis M. Wilson, 11 July 1932, letter, folder 310, Francis M. Wilson Papers, State Historical Society of Missouri (hereafter cited as FMWP, SHSMO); H. L. Stanley to Francis M. Wilson, 18 July 1932, letter, folder 376, FMWP, SHSMO; Francis M. Wilson to W. G. Dillon, 7 June 1932, letter, folder 432, FMWP, SHSMO; William C. Reynolds to Francis M. Wilson, 15 July 1932, letter, folder 577, FMWP, SHSMO; W. B. Fahy to Francis M. Wilson, 16 February 1932, letter, folder 688, FMWP, SHSMO; S. E. Juden to Francis M. Wilson, 8 November 1931, letter, folder 729, FMWP, SHSMO; S. E. Juden to Francis M. Wilson, 10 November 1931, letter, folder 729, FMWP, SHSMO; and Francis M. Wilson to Sterling McCarty, 12 June 1932, letter, folder 732, FMWP, SHSMO.

111. Christensen et al., *Dictionary of Missouri Biography*, 595–96; Mitchell, *Embattled Democracy*, 153–59.

112. Grothaus, "Negro in Missouri Politics," 135–36.

113. Grothaus, "Negro in Missouri Politics," 137–38, 143–68; Welek, "Jordan Chambers," 362–63; Thomas F. Soapes, "The Fragility of the Roosevelt Coalition in Missouri," 39–42.

114. Grothaus, "Negro in Missouri Politics," 139–43; Kremer, "William J. Thompkins," 173–78; Schirmer, *City Divided*, 165–66; Soapes, "Fragility of the Roosevelt Coalition in Missouri," 38–42.

Notes to Chapter Seven 349

115. Grothaus, "Negro in Missouri Politics," 146–50; Soapes, "Fragility of the Roosevelt Coalition in Missouri," 38–42.

116. Grothaus, "Negro in Missouri Politics," 150–52; Soapes, "Fragility of the Roosevelt Coalition in Missouri," 38–42.

117. Grothaus, "Negro in Missouri Politics," 154–68; Soapes, "Fragility of the Roosevelt Coalition in Missouri," 38–43.

118. Grothaus, "Negro in Missouri Politics," 157–61; Soapes, "Fragility of the Roosevelt Coalition in Missouri," 38–43.

119. Grothaus, "Negro in Missouri Politics," 154–68; Soapes, "Fragility of the Roosevelt Coalition in Missouri," 38–58.

120. Soapes, "Fragility of the Roosevelt Coalition in Missouri," 38–58.

121. L. Greene, Kremer, and Holland, *Missouri's Black Heritage*, 241–44.

Chapter Seven
"The Spirit of the Klan"
The Fracturing of the Anti-Klan Coalition

1. William G. Pinsley to Myron Schwartz, letter, 19 September 1946, "Ku Klux Klan," box 34, Jewish Community Relations Council Collection, Kaplan Feldman Holocaust Museum (hereafter cited as JCRC, KFHM).

2. Myron Schwartz to William G. Pinsley, letter, 25 September 1946, "Ku Klux Klan," box 34, JCRC, KFHM.

3. *St. Louis Argus*, 14 June 1946; *St. Louis Post-Dispatch*, 17 June 1946, 18 June 1946; *St. Louis Globe-Democrat*, 18 June 1946; *St. Louis Star-Times*, 18 June 1946.

4. *St. Louis Post-Dispatch*, 19 June 1946; *St. Louis Star-Times*, 19 June 1946, 20 June 1946; *St. Louis Argus*, 21 June 1946.

5. *St. Louis Star-Times*, 19 June 1946, 20 June 1946.

6. *St. Louis Argus*, 21 June 1946, 28 June 1946, 5 July 1946; *St. Louis Post-Dispatch*, 24 June 1946, 19 July 1946; *St. Louis Star-Times*, 28 June 1946, 6 July 1946, 15 July 1946, 25 July 1946; *St. Louis Globe-Democrat*, 13 July 1946, 19 July 1946.

7. *St. Louis Post-Dispatch*, 9 July 1946; *St. Louis Star-Times*, 9 July 1946.

8. *St. Louis Post-Dispatch*, 14 October 1946; *St. Louis Argus*, 18 October 1946.

9. *St. Louis Argus*, 28 June 1946.

10. *St. Louis Argus*, 12 October 1945.

11. *St. Louis Argus*, 31 May 1946.

12. MacLean, *Behind the Mask of Chivalry*, 177–88.

13. Leo P. Ribuffo, *The Old Christian Right: The Protestant Far Right from the Great Depression to the Cold War*, xi–xix, 178–224. For more information on the overlaps between various right-wing groups in the interwar period, see Bennett, *Party of Fear*; Ribuffo, *Old Christian Right*; Chalmers, *Hooded Americanism*; and Bradley W. Hart, *Hitler's American Friends: The Third Reich's Supporters in the United States*.

14. Donald J. Kemper, "Catholic Integration in St. Louis, 1935–1947."

15. Chalmers, *Hooded Americanism*, 304–8.

16. *St. Joseph News-Press*, 4 July 1930; *St. Joseph Gazette*, 12 March 1933.

17. *Kansas City Star*, 8 November 1922; *St. Joseph News-Press*, 5 September 1925, 1 May 1928, 4 July 1930; *St. Joseph Observer*, 2 May 1929.

350 Notes to Chapter Seven

18. *St. Louis Post-Dispatch*, 11 July 1930; *St. Joseph Gazette*, 13 July 1930; *St. Joseph News-Press*, 14 July 1930.

19. *Bloomfield Vindicator*, 5 June 1931.

20. *St. Joseph News-Press*, 24 January 1931, 15 November 1939; *St. Louis Globe-Democrat*, 25 November 1931; *St. Louis Star-Times*, 30 April 1935; *St. Joseph Union Observer*, 18 November 1936.

21. Gilbert O. Nations, *The Political Career of Alfred E. Smith*, 84.

22. *New Menace*, 2 July 1927.

23. *Missouri Valley Independent*, 10 January 1924.

24. *New Menace*, 28 April 1928; *Monitor*, 20 July 1935.

25. *Brooklyn Torch*, 22 July 1933.

26. Chalmers, *Hooded Americanism*, 307–8, 313–16.

27. Bennett, *Party of Fear*, 247–48; Chalmers, *Hooded Americanism*, 308–10.

28. Chalmers, *Hooded Americanism*, 310–24.

29. David M. Kennedy, *Freedom from Fear: The American People in Depression and War, 1929–1945*; Ira Katznelson, *Fear Itself: The New Deal and the Origins of Our Time*; Alan Brinkley, *Voices of Protest: Huey Long, Father Coughlin, and the Great Depression*; William Leuchtenburg, *Franklin D. Roosevelt and the New Deal, 1932–1940*; Studs Terkel, *Hard Times: An Oral History of the Great Depression*; Ribuffo, *Old Christian Right*; John A. Garrity, "The New Deal, National Socialism, and the Great Depression."

30. *Kansas City Journal-Post*, 3 March 1933.

31. *Kansas City Jewish Chronicle*, 3 March 1933.

32. *Kansas City Star*, 3 April 1933.

33. *Kansas City Star*, 18 July 1933.

34. *St. Louis Globe-Democrat*, 23 March 1933; *Modern View*, 25 May 1933; *St. Louis Argus*, 2 June 1933.

35. *Kansas City Call*, 7 April 1933.

36. *Kansas City Times*, 28 March 1933.

37. *Jefferson City Post-Tribune*, 28 March 1933, 9 April 1934; *Weekly Kansas City Star*, 29 March 1933; *Los Angeles Times*, 9 April 1934; *St. Louis Star-Times*, 9 April 1934; *Kansas City Journal-Post*, 9 April 1934.

38. The transcript of James A. Reed's speech can be found in box 42 of the James Alexander Reed Papers, State Historical Society of Missouri–Kansas City (hereafter cited as JARP, SHSMO). The direct quote used here come from pages 6–8. For correspondence between Reed and the Committee for the Defense of Human Rights against Nazism, see Jacob Billikopf to James A. Reed, 8 November 1933, folder 11, box 41, JARP, SHSMO; James M. Yard to James A. Reed, 23 March 1934, folder 11, box 41, JARP, SHSMO; James M. Yard to James A. Reed, 27 March 1934, folder 11, box 41, JARP, SHSMO; James M. Yard to James A. Reed, 27 March 1934, Western Union Telegram, folder 11, box 41, JARP, SHSMO; and Salmon O. Levinson to James A. Reed, 9 March 1934, folder 11, box 41, JARP, SHSMO.

39. Petra DeWitt, *Degrees of Allegiance: Harassment and Loyalty in Missouri's German-American Community during World War I*.

40. Sander A. Diamond, *The Nazi Movement in the United States, 1924–1941*, 85–86.

Notes to Chapter Seven

41. Arnie Bernstein, *Swastika Nation: Fritz Kuhn and the Rise and Fall of the German-American Bund*, 22–49; Diamond, *Nazi Movement in the United States*, 85–102; Hart, *Hitler's American Friends*, 23–48; Petra DeWitt, "Hitler's American Friends: The German American Bund in Missouri."

42. Bernstein, *Swastika Nation*, 22–49; Diamond, *Nazi Movement in the United States*, 106–27; Hart, *Hitler's American Friends*, 23–48; DeWitt, "Hitler's American Friends."

43. Burton Alan Boxerman, "Reaction of the St. Louis Jewish Community to Anti-Semitism: 1933–1945," 63–73; DeWitt, "Hitler's American Friends"; Diane Everman, "Right in Our Own Backyard: A Nazi Bund Camp on the Meramec River." For information on efforts to track the Friends of New Germany activity in St. Louis by the Jewish Community Relations Council, see "Friends of New Germany," box 24–25, JCRC, KFHM.

44. Bernstein, *Swastika Nation*, 22–49; Diamond, *Nazi Movement in the United States*, 106–201; Hart, *Hitler's American Friends*, 23–48; DeWitt, "Hitler's American Friends."

45. Bernstein, *Swastika Nation*, 1–56; Diamond, *Nazi Movement in the United States*, 157–222; Hart, *Hitler's American Friends*, 23–48; DeWitt, "Hitler's American Friends."

46. Bernstein, *Swastika Nation*, 1–56; Diamond, *Nazi Movement in the United States*, 202–69; Hart, *Hitler's American Friends*, 23–48.

47. Boxerman, "Reaction of the St. Louis Jewish Community to Anti-Semitism," 71–74; DeWitt, "Hitler's American Friends"; Everman, "Right in Our Own Backyard."

48. Boxerman, *Reaction of the St. Louis Jewish Community to Anti-Semitism*, 74–84; DeWitt, "Hitler's American Friends"; Everman, "Right in Our Own Backyard." Though still largely known as a stop on the Frisco Railroad line connecting St. Louis to Springfield at the time, Stanton and the surrounding Ozarks communities were in the process of becoming recreation hot spots in Missouri with the development of Route 66. In addition to the German-American Commercial League's camp, there were several other youth camps in the area, including Camp River Cliff, a segregated facility operated by the Pine Street YMCA and geared toward African Americans from St. Louis, as well as Meramec State Park and Meramec Caverns.

49. Bernstein, *Swastika Nation*, 229–35; Diamond, *Nazi Movement in the United States*, 273–337; Hart, *Hitler's American Friends*, 23–48; DeWitt, "Hitler's American Friends."

50. Diamond, *Nazi Movement in the United States*, 318–20; Bennett, *Party of Fear*, 247; Bernstein, *Swastika Nation*, 3, 68, 97, 146, 273–75; Brinkley, *Voices of Protest*, 266–67. For a detailed study of the Christian Front, see Charles Gallagher, *Nazis of Copley Square: The Forgotten Story of the Christian Front*.

51. Diamond, *Nazi Movement in the United States*, 223–50; Bennett, *Party of Fear*, 245–47; Bernstein, *Swastika Nation*, 3, 68, 97, 146; Hart, *Hitler's American Friends*, 49–67.

52. Bennett, *Party of Fear*, 245–47; Hart, *Hitler's American Friends*, 49–67.

53. Bernstein, *Swastika Nation*, 177–302; Diamond, *Nazi Movement in the United States*, 325–28; Hart, *Hitler's American Friends*, 23–48; DeWitt, "Hitler's American Friends."

Notes to Chapter Seven

54. Boxerman, "Reaction of the St. Louis Jewish Community to Anti-Semitism," 74–89; DeWitt, "Hitler's American Friends"; Everman, "Right in Our Own Backyard." For information on efforts to track Nazi activity in St. Louis by the Jewish Community Relations Council, see "Nazis and Fascists (Local), ca. 1933–1954," boxes 46–47, JCRC, KFHM.

55. Brinkley, *Voices of Protest*, 82–92; Bennett, *Party of Fear*, 253–66; Hart, *Hitler's American Friends*, 68–95; *Kansas City Times*, 12 July 1930; *St. Louis Star-Times*, 16 December 1930; *Kansas City Star*, 5 May 1933.

56. Brinkley, *Voices of Protest*, 93–123; Bennett, *Party of Fear*, 253–66; Hart, *Hitler's American Friends*, 68–95; *St. Louis Post-Dispatch*, 14 January 1934; *Kansas City Star*, 8 February 1932.

57. *St. Louis Globe-Democrat*, 22 March 1931, 29 March 1931; *St. Louis Post-Dispatch*, 6 September 1931, 25 October 1931, 19 April 1932, 21 August 1932, 20 August 1933, 12 August 1934, 19 August 1934; *Jefferson City Daily Capitol News*, 28 April 1933; *St. Louis Star-Times*, 23 November 1933; *Kansas City Catholic Register*, 25 October 1934.

58. *St. Louis Post-Dispatch*, 4 January 1932.

59. *Western Watchman*, 6 April 1933.

60. *Tri-City Independent*, 16 November 1934.

61. *Kansas City Catholic Register*, 17 September 1936.

62. Brinkley, *Voices of Protest*, 269–73; Bennett, *Party of Fear*, 253–66; Hart, *Hitler's American Friends*, 68–95.

63. *Kansas City Jewish Chronicle*, 16 November 1934.

64. Boxerman, "Reaction of the St. Louis Jewish Community to Anti-Semitism," 138–58; *St. Louis Jewish Light*, 15 March 1972; Debra Griffith, "Rabbi Ferdinand Isserman Sounds a Warning—Missourians and the Holocaust."

65. *Modern View*, 3 January 1935.

66. Boxerman, "Reaction of the St. Louis Jewish Community to Anti-Semitism," 155–58; *Modern View*, 25 April 1935; "The Necessity for Establishing Social Justice," folder 26, box 1, Ferdinand Isserman Collection, KFHM (hereafter cited as FIC, KFHM).

67. Charles Coughlin to Ferdinand Isserman, 12 April 1935, Western Union Telegram, folder 13, box 1, FIC, KFHM; Ferdinand Isserman to Charles Coughlin, 15 April 1935, folder 13, box 1, FIC, KFHM; Charles Coughlin to Ferdinand Isserman, 16 April 1935, Western Union Telegram, folder 13, box 1, FIC, KFHM; Ferdinand Isserman to Charles Coughlin, 26 April 1935, folder 13, box 1, FIC, KFHM; Charles Coughlin to Ferdinand Isserman, 13 May 1935, folder 13, box 1, FIC, KFHM.

68. *Modern View*, 13 June 1935.

69. Brinkley, *Voices of Protest*, 124–27, 178–79, 269–73; Bennett, *Party of Fear*, 253–66.

70. *Modern View*, 22 November 1934, 3 January 1935, 7 February 1935, 21 March 1935.

71. *Kansas City Jewish Chronicle*, 21 August 1936.

72. Brinkley, *Voices of Protest*, 242–62; Bennett, *Party of Fear*, 253–66; Ribuffo, *Old Christian Right*, 140–47; Glen Jeansonne, *Gerald L. K. Smith: Minister of Hate*, 51–62; Hart, *Hitler's American Friends*, 68–95.

Notes to Chapter Seven

73. Brinkley, *Voices of Protest*, 266–73; Bennett, *Party of Fear*, 253–66; Hart, *Hitler's American Friends*, 68–95; Gallagher, *Nazis of Copley Square*.

74. *Kansas City Jewish Chronicle*, 9 December 1938.

75. Brinkley, *Voices of Protest*, 128–33, 265–68; Bennett, *Party of Fear*, 253–66; Hart, *Hitler's American Friends*, 68–95.

76. *Modern View*, 5 October 1939

77. Kauffman, *Faith and Fraternalism*, 334.

78. *Modern View*, 5 October 1939.

79. *Modern View*, 23 February 1939.

80. *Modern View*, 22 June 1939, 6 July 1939, 20 July 1939.

81. *Modern View*, 2 March 1939.

82. Boxerman, "Reaction of the St. Louis Jewish Community to Anti-Semitism," 105–59; Griffith, "Rabbi Ferdinand Isserman Sounds a Warning."

83. *Modern View*, 26 October 1939.

84. Boxerman, "Reaction of the St. Louis Jewish Community to Anti-Semitism," 138–54; Griffith, "Rabbi Ferdinand Isserman Sounds a Warning."

85. Boxerman, "Reaction of the St. Louis Jewish Community to Anti-Semitism," 160–223.

86. Boxerman, "Reaction of the St. Louis Jewish Community to Anti-Semitism," 224–49.

87. *St. Louis Post-Dispatch*, 14 October 1945.

88. Boxerman, "Reaction of the St. Louis Jewish Community to Anti-Semitism," 196–203; *St. Louis Post-Dispatch*, 13 October 1937, 19 October 1937.

89. *St. Louis Globe-Democrat*, 20 October 1937.

90. *St. Louis Star-Times*, 27 October 1937.

91. *St. Louis Star-Times*, 1 November 1937.

92. *St. Louis Star-Times*, 13 August 1938.

93. *St. Louis Post-Dispatch*, 21 August 1938; *St. Louis Globe-Democrat*, 21 August 1938.

94. *St. Louis Post-Dispatch*, 22 November 1937.

95. *St. Louis Star-Times*, 22 November 1937.

96. *St. Louis Post-Dispatch*, 18 August 1938, 19 August 1938, 5 April 1939, 23 July 1939, 6 September 1939; *St. Louis Star-Times*, 14 March 1938; *St. Louis Globe-Democrat*, 4 March 1939.

97. Thomas Howell, "Kansas City Crusader: Leon Birkhead and the Fight against Fascism," 237–38; Ribuffo, *Old Christian Right*, 85–86; *St. Louis Post-Dispatch*, 3 September 1944.

98. *St. Louis Post-Dispatch*, 3 September 1944.

99. *St. Louis Post-Dispatch*, 3 September 1944.

100. *Moberly Evening Democrat*, 16 October 1922; *Kansas City Times*, 30 October 1922, 3 November 1924.

101. *Kansas City Times*, 23 March 1923.

102. Howell, "Kansas City Crusader," 239–40; Ribuffo, *Old Christian Right*, 123–24.

354 Notes to Chapter Seven

103. Howell, "Kansas City Crusader," 239–41; *Kansas City Jewish Chronicle*, 4 September 1936, 11 September 1936, 25 September 1936, 2 October 1936, 23 October 1936, 30 October 1936.

104. Howell, "Kansas City Crusader," 239–41; Ribuffo, *Old Christian Right*, 123–24; *Columbia Missourian*, 16 March 1939.

105. Howell, "Kansas City Crusader," 239–44; Ribuffo, *Old Christian Right*, 179–92.

106. Howell, "Kansas City Crusader," 242–51; Ribuffo, *Old Christian Right*, 179–92.

107. *St. Louis Star-Times*, 24 July 1946.

108. *St. Louis Star-Times*, 24 July 1946.

109. *St. Louis Argus*, 14 June 1946.

110. Jeansonne, *Gerald L. K. Smith*, 11–42; Ribuffo, *Old Christian Right*, 128–40; Bennett, *Party of Fear*, 252–53; *St. Louis Globe-Democrat*, 7 November 1935; *St. Louis Star-Times*, 27 November 1935.

111. Jeansonne, *Gerald L. K. Smith*, 28–31, 48–62; Ribuffo, *Old Christian Right*, 140–77; Bennett, *Party of Fear*, 252–53. For materials related to the Christian Nationalist Crusade, including copies of the *Cross and the Flag*, see Christian Nationalist Crusade Collection, State Historical Society of Missouri, St. Louis (hereafter cited as CNCC, SHSMO).

112. *St. Louis Star-Times*, 12 September 1936; *St. Louis Globe-Democrat*, 26 November 1939.

113. *St. Louis Post-Dispatch*, 17 August 1940, 19 September 1941, 6 October 1941, 3 April 1942, 3 May 1942; *St. Louis Star-Times*, 14 February 1944.

114. Jeansonne, *Gerald L. K. Smith*, 84–85; *St. Louis Star-Times*, 14 February 1944, 17 February 1944; *St. Louis Post-Dispatch*, 17 February 1944.

115. Jeansonne, *Gerald L. K. Smith*, 138–41.

116. *Cross and the Flag*, February 1950, folder 3, CNCC, SHSMO. For additional issues of the *Cross and the Flag* that feature Don Lohbeck, see folders 3–4, CNCC, SHSMO.

117. Jeansonne, *Gerald L. K. Smith*, 139–41; Ribuffo, *Old Christian Right*, 159–71.

118. *Cross and the Flag*, March 1949, folder 3, CNCC, SHSMO.

119. *Cross and the Flag*, February 1950, folder 3, CNCC, SHSMO.

120. *Cross and the Flag*, April 1949, December 1949, February 1950, May 1950, folder 3, CNCC, SHSMO; *Attack!*, 1 May 1950, folder 3, CNCC, SHSMO.

121. *St. Louis Star-Times*, 18 February 1944, 24 February 1944; *St. Louis Post-Dispatch*, 18 February 1944.

122. Jeansonne, *Gerald L. K. Smith*, 84–85; *St. Louis Star-Times*, 17 November 1944.

123. *St. Louis Star-Times*, 2 April 1946; *St. Louis Globe-Democrat*, 2 April 1946; *St. Louis Post-Dispatch*, 3 April 1946, 7 April 1946; *St. Louis Argus*, 6 April 1946.

124. *St. Louis Post-Dispatch*, 31 May 1946.

125. *St. Louis Post-Dispatch*, 29 June 1946; *St. Louis Argus*, 14 June 1946, 21 June 1946, 28 June 1946, 5 July 1946.

126. *St. Louis Star-Times*, 24 July 1946.

127. Ribuffo, *Old Christian Right*, 173–75; *St. Louis Post-Dispatch*, 4 June 1944; *St. Louis Star-Times*, 8 June 1944.

128. Jeansonne, *Gerald L. K. Smith*, 158–63.

Notes to Chapter Seven

129. Jeansonne, *Gerald L. K. Smith*, 158–59; *St. Louis Post-Dispatch*, 19 August 1948, 20 August 1948, 21 August 1948, 22 August 1948.

130. Jeansonne, *Gerald L. K. Smith*, 160–63; Ribuffo, *Old Christian Right*, 233; St. *Louis Post-Dispatch*, 24 March 1952, 25 March 1952; *St. Louis Globe-Democrat*, 27 March 1952.

131. *St. Louis Post-Dispatch*, 25 April 1944, 2 August 1944.

132. *St. Louis Post-Dispatch*, 10 January 1949, 23 February 1949, 23 March 1949, 26 March 1949.

133. *Kansas City Times*, 19 January 1950; *St. Louis Post-Dispatch*, 17 July 1950; 1 March 1951, 4 March 1951, 10 March 1951; *Attack!*, 1 November 1950; *St. Louis Globe-Democrat*, 1 March 1951.

134. *St. Louis Post-Dispatch*, 2 April 1952; *Kansas City Times*, 30 April 1952; *State of Missouri Official Manual for the Years 1953–1954*, 904.

135. *St. Louis Post-Dispatch*, 23 February 1949.

136. *Kansas City Times*, 19 January 1950.

137. *Kansas City Times*, 20 May 1950; *St. Louis Post-Dispatch*, 21 May 1950, 17 July 1950; *Attack!*, 1 November 1950.

138. *St. Louis Post-Dispatch*, 16 September 1951, 23 September 1951, 4 October 1951, 20 October 1951, 21 November 1951, 26 November 1951; *Kansas City Times*, 21 November 1951; *St. Louis Globe-Democrat*, 21 November 1951.

139. *Kansas City Times*, 30 April 1952; *St. Louis Post-Dispatch*, 14 July 1952.

140. Jeansonne, *Gerald L. K. Smith*, 98–100.

141. *St. Louis Post-Dispatch*, 13 December 1949; *St. Louis Globe-Democrat*, 13 December 1949.

142. *St. Louis Post-Dispatch*, 24 March 1952, 2 April 1952, 19 May 1952, 15 April 1953, 23 August 1954, 25 August 1954; *St. Louis Globe-Democrat*, 12 April 1952, 10 October 1952, 15 April 1953.

143. Jeansonne, *Gerald L. K. Smith*, 124–25; *St. Louis Post-Dispatch*, 30 December 1948, 13 December 1949; *St. Louis Globe-Democrat*, 13 December 1949; *Columbia Missourian*, 21 April 1950.

144. *St. Louis Post-Dispatch*, 11 October 1947; *St. Louis Argus*, 16 January 1948.

145. *Attack!*, 1 November 1950.

146. *St. Louis Post-Dispatch*, 2 November 1950, 5 November 1950, 8 November 1950, 14 November 1950, 4 March 1951; *St. Louis American*, 2 November 1950.

147. *St. Louis Post-Dispatch*, 5 March 1951, 7 March 1951, 8 March 1951, 11 March 1951, 17 March 1951, 25 March 1951, 28 March 1951, 30 March 1951; *St. Louis American*, 8 March 1951, 29 March 1951; *St. Louis Globe-Democrat*, 25 March 1951.

148. *Columbia Missourian*, 3 May 1950.

149. *St. Louis Post-Dispatch*, 7 March 1951.

150. Jeansonne, *Gerald L. K. Smith*, 98–100; *St. Louis Post-Dispatch*, 6 May 1953.

151. *St. Louis Post-Dispatch*, 23 August 1954, 25 August 1954, 16 October 1956, 21 February 1957.

152. For copies of the *White Sentinel*, see folder 5, CNCC, SHSMO.

153. *St. Louis Post-Dispatch*, 25 September 1960.

154. Ribuffo, *Old Christian Right*, 231–36; Jeansonne, *Gerald L. K. Smith*, 171–213.

Notes to Epilogue

155. Ribuffo, *Old Christian Right*, 165; Jeansonne, *Gerald L. K. Smith*, 23; Chalmers, *Hooded Americanism*, 328, 352–53.

156. Jeansonne, *Gerald L. K. Smith*, 103, 179; Michael Barkun, *Religion and the Racist Right: The Origins of the Christian Identity Movement*, 60–69.

157. Barkun, *Religion and the Racist Right*, 55–67; *Cross and the Flag*, June 1950, folder 3, CNCC, SHSMO; *Cross and the Flag*, March 1954, folder 7, CNCC, SHSMO.

158. Bennett, *Party of Fear*, 349–52; Barkun, *Religion and the Racist Right*, 66–69.

159. Ribuffo, *Old Christian Right*, xi–xix, 178–224.

160. Kauffman, *Faith and Fraternalism*, 368–73, 396–97. For larger works that survey Catholicism and white supremacy, see John T. McGreevy, *Parish Boundaries: The Catholic Encounter with Race in the Twentieth-Century Urban North*; and Shannen Dee Williams, *Subversive Habits: Black Catholic Nuns in the Long African American Freedom Struggle*.

161. Brinkley, *Voices of Protest*, 266–73; Bennett, *Party of Fear*, 253–66; Gallagher, *Nazis of Copley Square*.

162. *Cross and the Flag*, June 1950, folder 3, CNCC, SHSMO.

163. Williams, *Subversive Habits*, 229.

Epilogue

1. *St. Louis Post-Dispatch*, 24 April 1982.

2. *St. Louis Post-Dispatch*, 24 April 1982.

3. *St. Louis Post-Dispatch*, 18 April 1982, 24 April 1982.

4. For a detailed review of the Greensboro incident, see Kathleen Belew, *Bring the War Home: The White Power Movement and Paramilitary America*, 55–76.

5. *Kansas City Times*, 25 March 1982; *Kansas City Star*, 18 April 1982, 19 April 1982; *St. Louis Post-Dispatch*, 25 April 1982; *St. Louis Jewish Light*, 5 May 1982; Sergeant E. W. Schroeder to Captain E. E. Kelsey, 16 April 1982, Inter-Office Communication, box 130630, Patrol Records Division, Missouri State Highway Patrol, Jefferson City, Missouri (hereafter cited as PRD, MSHP); Sergeant L. D. Belshe to Captain E. E. Kelsey, 19 April 1982, Inter-Office Communication, box 130630, PRD, MSHP; Sergeant D. D. LePage to Commanding Officer, 21 April 1982, Inter-Office Communication, box 130630, PRD, MSHP.

6. *St. Louis Post-Dispatch*, 25 April 1982; *St. Louis Jewish Light*, 5 May 1982.

7. *St. Louis Post-Dispatch*, 25 April 1982.

8. *Kansas City Times*, 25 March 1982. According to the *St. Louis Jewish Light*, Don McLeod allegedly resigned from the Klan following the rally and publicly apologized for the events that took place. *St. Louis Jewish Light*, 5 May 1982.

9. *St. Louis Post-Dispatch*, 25 April 1982; *Kansas City Star*, 25 April 1982; *Springfield News-Leader*, 25 April 1982; *Tennessean*, 25 April 1982; *Chicago Tribune*, 25 April 1982; *Miami Herald*, 25 April 1982; *St. Louis Jewish Light*, 5 May 1982. As a national organization, IN-CAR had several confrontations with the Klan nationwide. For more information on these clashes, see Belew, *Bring the War Home*, 59–60. For articles on earlier IN-CAR protests in Missouri, see *St. Louis Post-Dispatch*, 4 April 1976, 29 March 1978, 14 August 1978; *St. Louis Jewish Light*, 7 April 1976, 22 April 1981; *Kansas City Times*, 30 October 1978; and *Kansas City Star*, 22 January 1978, 14 August 1978, 7 December 1980.

10. *St. Louis Post-Dispatch*, 25 April 1982.

Notes to Epilogue

11. Chalmers, *Hooded Americanism*, 325–26; Cunningham, *Klansville, U.S.A.*, 26–27.

12. Chalmers, *Hooded Americanism*, 325–26; Cunningham, *Klansville, U.S.A.*, 26–27.

13. Chalmers, *Hooded Americanism*, 329–30; Cunningham, *Klansville, U.S.A.*, 26–27.

14. Chalmers, *Hooded Americanism*, 326–34; Cunningham, *Klansville, U.S.A.*, 26–27.

15. Chalmers, *Hooded Americanism*, 335–74; Cunningham, *Klansville, U.S.A.*, 26–42.

16. Chalmers, *Hooded Americanism*, 348–49.

17. *St. Louis Post-Dispatch*, 1 May 1966, 4 May 1966, 28 May 1967; *Sikeston Daily Standard*, 2 May 1966, 17 October 1966.

18. *St. Louis Post-Dispatch*, 28 May 1967.

19. *St. Louis Post-Dispatch*, 11 March 1948, 14 June 1953; *St. Joseph News-Press*, 13 June 1953.

20. Bennett, *Party of Fear*, 273–31; Chalmers, *Hooded Americanism*, 343–65; *St. Louis Post-Dispatch*, 24 March 1968.

21. *St. Louis Post-Dispatch*, 24 March 1968.

22. *St. Louis Post-Dispatch*, 24 March 1968.

23. *St. Louis Post-Dispatch*, 4 May 1966.

24. Christensen et al., *Dictionary of Missouri Biography*, 385–86, 418–19, 641–43, 769–70; *St. Louis Argus*, 13 August 1926, 26 December 1952; Howell, "Kansas City Crusader," 253.

25. Christensen et al., *Dictionary of Missouri Biography*, 542–43.

26. *St. Louis Jewish Light*, 31 March 1965, 15 March 1972.

27. Kauffman, *Faith and Fraternalism*, 374–97.

28. Sullivan, *Lift Every Voice*, 152–53, 373–75; Christensen et al., *Dictionary of Missouri Biography*, 798–800.

29. *St. Louis Post-Dispatch*, 30 July 1978.

30. *St. Louis Post-Dispatch*, 30 July 1978, 7 March 1979; *Kansas City Times*, 24 March 1979.

31. Belew, *Bring the War Home*, 20.

32. *St. Louis Post-Dispatch*, 30 July 1978, 7 March 1979; *Kansas City Times*, 24 March 1979.

33. *St. Louis Post-Dispatch*, 4 November 1979.

34. *Columbia Daily Tribune*, 22 April 1977; *Kansas City Star*, 13 November 1977; *St. Louis Post-Dispatch*, 30 July 1978, 7 March 1979, 28 October 1979, 4 November 1979, 26 January 1981; *Kansas City Times*, 24 March 1979.

35. "Known Missouri Members of the Ku Klux Klan," Inter-Office Communication, box 130630, PRD, MSHP.

36. Sergeant E. J. Dayringer to Commanding Officer, 1 September 1983, Inter-Office Communication, box 130630, PRD, MSHP; Sergeant E. J. Dayringer to Commanding Officer, 6 September 1983, Inter-Office Communication, box 130630, PRD, MSHP; Sergeant R. G. Plymell to Commanding Officer, 8 September 1983, Inter-Office Communication, box 130630, PRD, MSHP; Sergeant E. J. Dayringer to Commanding Officer, 9 September 1983, Inter-Office Communication, box 130630, PRD, MSHP; Sergeant J. S. Gordon to Commanding Officer, 10 September 1983, Inter-Office Communication, box 130630, PRD, MSHP. Additional documents related to the National Conservative Party can be found in box 130630, PRD, MSHP. For an example of the

358 Notes to Epilogue

National Conservative Party's call to "make America great again," see *Kansas City Star*, 22 May 1983.

37. "Posse Comitatus," July 1983, Special Report, Crime Analysis Unit, Kansas Bureau of Investigation, box 130630, PRD, MSHP. For an extensive look at some of these Missouri groups and their ties to the Christian Identity movement, see Larry G. Brown, "The Mind of White Nationalism: The Worldview of Christian Identity."

38. Sergeant L. D. Belshe to Captain E. E. Kelsey, 19 April 1982, Inter-Office Communication, box 130630, PRD, MSHP.

39. *St. Louis Post-Dispatch*, 24 April 1982.

40. David Chalmers, *Backfire: How the Ku Klux Klan Helped the Civil Rights Movement*, 137–44, 187–89.

41. Sergeant L. D. Belshe to Captain E. E. Kelsey, 19 April 1982, Inter-Office Communication, box 130630, PRD, MSHP.

42. *Columbia Daily Tribune*, 1 November 1979, 9 November 1979, 20 November 1979, 22 April 1980, 25 April 1980.

43. *St. Louis Post-Dispatch*, 10 January 1988, 6 March 2001, 16 April 2002.

44. Belew, *Bring the War Home*, 103–34.

45. *St. Louis Post-Dispatch*, 16 April 1985, 7 January 1986.

46. *St. Louis Post-Dispatch*, 12 December 1988, 9 February 1989.

47. *Kansas City Star*, 9 October 1988.

48. *Kansas City Star*, 9 October 1988, 14 April 1989, 27 September 1992.

49. *Kansas City Star*, 27 September 1992.

50. *St. Louis Post-Dispatch*, 30 July 1978.

51. *St. Louis Post-Dispatch*, 3 August 1987, 12 December 1988, 25 January 1990, 23 February 1990.

52. *St. Louis Post-Dispatch*, 20 May 1992.

53. *Kansas City Star*, 14 April 1989.

54. Belew, *Bring the War Home*, 209–34.

55. Blee, *Women of the Klan*, 1.

BIBLIOGRAPHY

ARCHIVAL SOURCES

Ball State University Archives & Special Collections, Muncie, IN
Ku Klux Klan Collection

Black Archives of Mid-America, Kansas City, MO
Williams Photo Studio Collection (AC27)

Duke University Archives, Durham, NC
Charles A. Ellwood Papers
Ku Klux Klan Collection

First Christian Church, Jefferson City, MO
Minutes of Board, 1921–1930.

Harry S. Truman Library & Museum, Independence, MO
Aylward, James P. Interview by James R. Fuchs, 27 June 1968. Tape recording.
Babcock, Gaylon. Interview by James R. Fuchs, 12 February 1964. Tape recording.
Connelly, Matthew J. Interview by Jerry N. Hess, 28 November 1967. Tape recording.
Daniels, Jonathan. Interview by James R. Fuchs, 4 October 1963. Tape recording.
Democratic National Committee. Records.
Donnelly, Eugene, and Edward Meisburger. Interview by William D. Stilley and Jerald L. Hill, 27 December 1975. Tape recording.
Evans, Tom L. Interview by James R. Fuchs, 8 August, 28 November 1962. Tape recording.
Hinde, Edgar G. Interview by James R. Fuchs, 15 March 1962. Tape recording.
Holeman, Frank. Interview by Niel M. Johnson, 9 June 1987. Tape recording.
Howard, May C. Interview by Niel M. Johnson, 19 August 1985. Tape recording.
McKim, Edward D. Interview by James R. Fuchs, 17 February 1964. Tape recording.
Nash, Philleo. Interview by Jerry N. Hess, 18 October 1966. Tape recording.
Noland, Mary Ethel. Interview by James R. Fuchs, 9 September 1965. Tape recording.
Peters, Mize. Interview by James R. Fuchs, 21 August 1963. Tape recording.
Rice, Stuart A. Papers.
Sanders, Ted J. Interview by Niel M. Johnson, 23 July 1982. Tape recording.

360 Bibliography

Sweeney, Robert L. Interview by Carol A. Briley, 12 December 1977. Tape recording.
Trohan, Walter. Interview by Jerry N. Hess, 7 October 1970. Tape recording.

Jackson County Historical Society, Independence, MO
Wilborn Collection

Kaplan Feldman Holocaust Museum, St. Louis
Ferdinand Isserman Collection
Jewish Community Relations Council Collection

Knights of Columbus Supreme Council Archives, New Haven, CT
Bogus Oath Collection
Reconstruction Collection
Supreme Advocate Luke E. Hart Records

Library of Congress, Washington, DC
National Association for the Advancement of Colored People Records

Missouri State Archives, Jefferson City
First Presbyterian Church, Jefferson City, MO, Cole County, Minutes of Session
Missouri Governors Collection
   Benjamin Gratz Brown
   Thomas Clement Fletcher
   Joseph Washington McClurg
   William Joel Stone
   Silas Woodson
Saint Louis Urban League, Files
Dr. Joseph Summers Collection
Van Gundy Photograph Collection

Missouri State Highway Patrol, Jefferson City
Patrol Records Division

State Historical Society of Missouri, Columbia, Kansas City, and St. Louis
Frank Ely Atwood Papers (C3131)
Charles Merlin Barnes Papers (C2802)
Leon Milton Birkhead Papers (K0280)
Edwin Bayer Branson Papers (C2404)
Christian Nationalist Crusade Collection (S0467)
Perl D. Decker Papers (C0092)
Bernard Dickmann Photograph Collection (S0555)
Gentry Family Papers (C4026)
David M. Grant Papers (S0552)
Arthur Mastick Hyde Papers (C0007)

Bibliography 361

Kansas City Convention Hall Records (K0269)
Marion County, Missouri, Photograph Collection (P1147)
William Fletcher McMurry Papers (C3487)
Metropolitan Church Federation Records (S0618)
Missouri Legislators Portraits (P1084)
Guy Brasfield Park Papers (C0008)
Matthew K. Partin Collection (K1254)
James Alexander Reed Papers (K0443)
Benny G. Rodgers Photograph Collection (S0629)
Ruth Rust Studio Photographs (P0860)
Llloyd Crow Stark Papers (C0004)
St. Louis Post-Dispatch Editorial Cartoon Collection (P0077)
Frank Fletcher Stephens Papers (C3599)
Strauss Studio Photographs (P0879)
University of Missouri, St. Louis Black History Project Collection (S0201)
University of Missouri President's Office Papers (C2582)
Francis M. Wilson Papers (C1039)
Women of the Mansion Photograph Collection (P0536)

University of Chicago Special Collections Research Center
Luther Lee Bernard Papers

University of Notre Dame Archives, Notre Dame, IN
Anti-Catholic Printed Material Collection
Catholic Central Verein of America Records
Catholic Press Collection

PERIODICALS

American Mercury [NY]
APA Magazine
Arkansas Gazette [AR]
Atlanta Constitution
Attack!
Baltimore Sun
Blackwell (OK) Daily News
Blackwell (OK) Morning Tribune
Bloomfield (MO) Vindicator
Brooklyn Torch
Canton Press
Cape Girardeau Southeast Missourian
Carthage (MO) Evening Press
Caruthersville (MO) Democrat-Argus
Central-Blatt and Social Justice
Centralia (MO) Courier

362 Bibliography

Chariton (MO) Courier
Charleston (MO Enterprise-Courier
Chicago Daily Tribune
Chicago Defender
Chillicothe (MO) Constitution
Church Progress
Cole County (MO) Weekly Rustler
Columbia (MO) Daily Tribune
Columbia Missourian
Crisis (New York)
Daily Oklahoman
Des Moines Evening Tribune
Des Moines Register
Detroit Free Press
Dexter (MO) Statesman
East Prairie (MO) Eagle
Ellington (MO) Press
Farmington (MO) Times
Fayette (MO) Advertiser
Fayette (MO) Democrat-Leader
Fellowship Forum (Washington, DC)
Fraternalist
Fredericktown (MO) Democrat-News
Fulton (MO) Daily Sun
Fulton (MO) Gazette
Fulton (MO) Sun-Gazette
Fulton (MO) Telegraph
Grandin (MO) Herald
Greenfield (MO) Vedette
Greenville (MO) Sun
Hannibal (MO) Courier-Post
Hayti Missouri Herald
Imperial Night-Hawk (Georgia)
Independence (MO) Examiner
Iron County (MO) Register
Jackson (MO) Herald
Jasper County Democrat
Jefferson City Daily Capital News
Jefferson City Daily Post
Jefferson City Democrat-Tribune
Jefferson City Missouri State Times
Jefferson City People's Tribune
Jefferson City Tribune
Jefferson County Republican

Bibliography 363

Jefferson Democrat
Joplin Globe
Joplin News-Herald
Kansas City American
Kansas City Call
Kansas City Catholic Register
Kansas City Jewish Chronicle
Kansas City Journal
Kansas City Journal-Post
Kansas City Kansan
Kansas City Post
Kansas City Star
Kansas City Times
Kourier Magazine
Lexington (MO) Intelligencer
Lexington (MO) Weekly Caucasian
Lincoln Journal
Los Angeles Times
Macon (MO) Daily Chronicle Herald
Malden (MO) Merit
Mariner
Marion County (MO) Herald
Memphis Commercial Appeal
Menace
Mexico (MO) Daily Ledger
Mexico (MO) Missouri Message
Miami Herald
Missouri Cash-Book
Missouri Counselor
Missouri Fiery Cross
Missouri Klan Kourier
Missouri Kourier
Missouri Valley Independent
Moberly (MO) Evening Democrat
Moberly (MO) Monitor-Index
Modern View
Mokane (MO) Missourian
Monitor
Negro World (New York)
Nevada (MO) Southwest Mail
New Madrid (MO) Weekly Record
New Menace
New York Age
New York Daily News

New York Herald
New York Times
New York Tribune
New York World
Opportunity (New York)
Palmyra (MO) Spectator
Patriot
Perry County (MO) Sun
Piedmont (MO) Weekly Banner
Pittsburgh Courier
Poplar Bluff (MO) American
Poplar Bluff (MO) Daily American Republic
Poplar Bluff (MO) Interstate-American
Poplar Bluff (MO) Republican
Poplar Bluff (MO) Weekly Citizen-Democrat
Protestant
Shreveport (LA) Journal
Sikeston (MO) Standard
Springfield (MO) Daily News
Springfield (MO) Leader
Springfield Missouri Republican
Springfield (MO) News & Leader
Ste. Genevieve (MO) Fair Play
St. Joseph (MO) Catholic Tribune
St. Joseph (MO) Gazette
St. Joseph (MO) News-Press
St. Joseph (MO) Observer
St. Louis American
St. Louis Argus
St. Louis Globe-Democrat
St. Louis Jewish Light
St. Louis Jewish Voice
St. Louis Post-Dispatch
St. Louis Star
St. Louis Star-Times
Stoddard (MO) Tribune
Tennessean
Tolerance (Illinois)
Tri-City Independent
Union Signal (Illinois)
Versailles (MO) Statesman
Vienna (MO) Home-Advisor
Warrensburg (MO) Star-Journal
Washington (MO) Citizen

Washington (DC) Evening Star
Wayne County (MO) Journal
Western Watchman (St. Louis)
Word and Way (Kansas City, MO)

OTHER SOURCES

Alexander, Charles C. *The Ku Klux Klan in the Southwest*. Lexington: University Press of Kentucky, 1965.

Allen, Frederick L. *Only Yesterday: An Informal History of the 1920s*. New York: HarperCollins, 2000.

Anbinder, Tyler. *Nativism and Slavery: The Northern Known Nothings and the Politics of the 1850s*. Oxford: Oxford University Press, 1992.

Anderson, Carol. *White Rage: The Unspoken Truth of Our Racial Divide*. New York: Bloomsbury, 2016.

Angle, Paul M. *Bloody Williamson: A Chapter in American Lawlessness*. New York: Knopf, 1952.

Annual Report, Woman's Christian Temperance Union of the State of Missouri. Vols. 1–53. St. Louis: n.p., 1883–1935.

Arenson, Adam. *The Great Heart of the Republic: St. Louis and the Cultural Civil War*. Cambridge, MA: Harvard University Press, 2011.

Aron, Stephen. *American Confluence: The Missouri Frontier from Borderland to Border State*. Bloomington: Indiana University Press, 2009.

Astor, Aaron. *Rebels on the Border: Civil War, Emancipation, and the Reconstruction of Kentucky and Missouri*. Baton Rouge: Louisiana State University Press, 2012.

Ayabe, Masatomo. "Ku Kluxers in a Coal Mining Community: A Study of the Ku Klux Klan Movement in Williamson County, Illinois, 1923–1926." *Journal of the Illinois State Historical Society* 102, no. 1 (2009): 73–100.

Baker, Kelly J. *Gospel according to the Klan: The KKK's Appeal to Protestant America, 1915–1930*. Lawrence: University Press of Kansas, 2011.

Barkun, Michael. *Religion and the Racist Right: The Origins of the Christian Identity Movement*. Chapel Hill: University of North Carolina Press, 1997.

Barnes, Harper. *Never Been a Time: The 1917 Race Riot That Sparked the Civil Rights Movement*. New York: Walker, 2008.

Barnes, Kenneth. *Anti-Catholicism in Arkansas: How Politicians, the Press, the Klan, and Religious Leaders Imagined an Enemy, 1910–1960*. Fayetteville: University of Arkansas Press, 2016.

——— *The Ku Klux Klan in 1920s Arkansas: How Protestant White Nationalism Came to Rule a State*. Fayetteville: University of Arkansas Press, 2021.

Beilein, Joseph M., Jr. *Bushwhackers: Guerilla Warfare, Manhood, and the Household in Civil War Missouri*. Kent, OH: Kent State University Press, 2016.

Belew, Kathleen. *Bring the War Home: The White Power Movement and Paramilitary America*. Cambridge, MA: Harvard University Press, 2018.

Bennett, David H. *The Party of Fear: The American Far Right from Nativism to the Militia Movement*. New York: Vintage, 1995.

Bernstein, Arnie. *Swastika Nation: Fritz Kuhn and the Rise and Fall of the German-American Bund*. New York: St. Martin's Press, 2013.

Billington, Ray Allen. *The Protestant Crusade, 1800–1860: A Study of the Origins of American Nativism*. Chicago: Quadrangle Books, 1968.

Blee, Kathleen M. *Inside Organized Racism: Women in the Hate Movement*. Berkeley: University of California Press, 2002.

———. *Women of the Klan: Racism and Gender in the 1920s*. Berkeley: University of California Press, 1991.

Blevins, Brooks. *A History of the Ozarks*. Vol. 1, *The Old Ozarks*. Urbana: University of Illinois Press, 2018.

———. *A History of the Ozarks*. Vol. 2, *The Conflicted Ozarks*. Urbana: University of Illinois Press, 2019.

———. *A History of the Ozarks*. Vol. 3, *The Ozarkers*. Urbana: University of Illinois Press, 2021.

———. "The Strike and the Still: Anti-radical Violence and the Ku Klux Klan in the Ozarks." *Arkansas Historical Quarterly* 52, no. 4 (1993): 405–25.

Blumer, Herbert. "Race Prejudice as a Sense of Group Position." *Pacific Sociological Review* 1, no. 1 (1958): 3–7.

Bordin, Ruth. *Frances Willard: A Biography*. Chapel Hill: University of North Carolina Press, 1986.

———. *Woman and Temperance: The Quest for Power and Liberty, 1873–1900*. Philadelphia: Temple University Press, 1981.

Boxerman, Burton Alan. "Reaction of the St. Louis Jewish Community to Anti-Semitism: 1933–1945." PhD diss., Saint Louis University, 1967.

Brinkley, Alan. *Voices of Protest: Huey Long, Father Coughlin, and the Great Depression*. New York: Alfred A. Knopf, 1982.

Brock, Frederick E. "The American Party in Missouri, 1854–1860." Master's thesis, University of Missouri–Columbia, 1949.

Brown, Larry G. "The Mind of White Nationalism: The Worldview of Christian Identity." PhD diss., University of Missouri–Columbia, 2003.

Butcher, Jerry. *Ku Klux Klan: The "Invisible Empire" in the Missouri Capital, Governor Arthur M. Hyde versus the Ku Klux Klan*. N.p.: n.p., 1966.

Butts-Runion, B. Blanche. *"Through the Years": A History of the First Seventy-Five Years of the Woman's Christian Temperance Union of Missouri, 1882–1957*. N.p.: n.p., 1957.

Campney, Brent M. S. "'The Drift of Things in Southeast Missouri': Demographic Transformation and Anti-Black Violence, 1900–1930." *Missouri Historical Review* 113, no. 3 (2019): 185–205.

———. *Hostile Heartland: Racism, Repression, and Resistance in the Midwest*. Urbana: University of Illinois Press, 2019.

Chalmers, David. *Backfire: How the Ku Klux Klan Helped the Civil Rights Movement*. New York: Rowman & Littlefield, 2005.

———. *Hooded Americanism: The History of the Ku Klux Klan*. New York: F. Watts, 1981.

Bibliography

Christensen, Lawrence O. "Race Relations in St. Louis, 1865–1916." *Missouri Historical Review* 78, no. 2 (1984): 123–36.

Christensen, Lawrence O., William E. Foley, Gary R. Kremer, and Kenneth H. Winn, eds. *Dictionary of Missouri Biography*. Columbia: University of Missouri Press, 1999.

Christensen, Lawrence O., and Gary Kremer. *A History of Missouri*. Vol. 4, *1875 to 1919*. Columbia: University of Missouri Press, 1997.

Churchwell, Sarah. *Behold, America: The Entangled History of "America First" and "the American Dream."* New York: Basic Books, 2018.

Courtaway, Robbi. *Wetter than the Mississippi: Prohibition in St. Louis and Beyond*. St. Louis: Reedy Press, 2008.

Cunningham, David. *Klansville, U.S.A.: The Rise and Fall of the Civil Rights–Era Ku Klux Klan*. Oxford: Oxford University Press, 2013.

Curcio, Vincent. *Henry Ford*. Oxford: Oxford University Press, 2013.

Davies, Gareth, and Julian E. Zelizer, eds. *America at the Ballot Box: Elections and Political History*. Philadelphia: University of Pennsylvania Press, 2015.

DeArmond, Fred. "Reconstruction in Missouri." *Missouri Historical Review* 61, no. 3 (1967): 364–77.

DeWitt, Petra. *Degrees of Allegiance: Harassment and Loyalty in Missouri's German-American Community during World War I*. Columbia: University of Missouri Press, 2012.

——— "Hitler's American Friends: The German American Bund in Missouri." 20 October 2022. https://www.youtube.com/watch?v=UogRKdxako8&t=1408s.

Diamond, Sander A. *The Nazi Movement in the United States, 1924–1941*. Ithaca, NY: Cornell University Press, 1974.

Dinnerstein, Leonard. *Antisemitism in America*. Oxford: Oxford University Press, 1994.

Dorr, Jeffrey R. "Race in St. Louis' Catholic Church: Discourse, Structures, and Segregation, 1873–1941." Master's thesis, St. Louis University, 2015.

Dorsett, Lyle W. *The Pendergast Machine*. New York: Oxford University Press, 1968.

Douglass, Robert Sidney. *History of Southeast Missouri: A Narrative Account of Its Historical Progress, Its People and Its Principal Interests*. Chicago: Lewis, 1912.

Dowden-White, Priscilla A. *Groping toward Democracy: African American Social Welfare Reform in St. Louis, 1910–1949*. Columbia: University of Missouri Press, 2011.

Dumenil, Lynn. *The Modern Temper: American Culture and Society in the 1920s*. New York: Hill & Wang, 1995.

——— "The Tribal Twenties: 'Assimilated' Catholics' Response to Anti-Catholicism in the 1920s." *Journal of Ethnic History* 11, no. 1 (1991): 21–49.

Earle, Jonathan, and Diane Mutti Burke, eds. *Bleeding Kansas, Bleeding Missouri: The Long Civil War on the Border*. Lawrence: University Press of Kansas, 2013.

Efford, Alison. *German Immigrants, Race, and Citizenship in the Civil War Era*. Cambridge: Cambridge University Press, 2013.

Ehrlich, Walter. *Zion in the Valley: The Jewish Community in St. Louis*. Vol. 1, *1807–1907*. Columbia: University of Missouri Press, 1997.

368 Bibliography

———— *Zion in the Valley: The Jewish Community of St. Louis.* Vol. 2, *The Twentieth Century.* Columbia: University of Missouri Press, 2002.

Epps, Kristen. *Slavery on the Periphery: The Kansas-Missouri Border in the Antebellum and Civil War Eras.* Athens: University of Georgia Press, 2016.

Ervin, Keona K. *Gateway to Equality: Black Women and the Struggle for Economic Justice in St. Louis.* Lexington: University Press of Kentucky, 2017.

Everman, Diane. "Right in Our Own Backyard: A Nazi Bund Camp on the Meramec River." Sixty-first Missouri Conference on History, Kansas City, 8 March 2019.

Faherty, William Barnaby. *Dream by the River: Two Centuries of Saint Louis Catholicism, 1766–1980.* St. Louis: River City, 1981.

———— "Nativism and Midwestern Education: The Experience of St. Louis University, 1832–1856." *History of Education Quarterly* 8, no. 4 (1968): 447–58.

Fellman, Michael. *Inside War: The Guerilla Conflict in Missouri during the Civil War.* New York: Oxford University Press, 1989).

Ferrell, Robert H. *Harry S. Truman: A Life.* Columbia: University of Missouri Press, 1994.

———— *Truman and Pendergast.* Columbia: University of Missouri Press, 1999.

Fluker, Amy Laurel. *Commonwealth of Compromise: Civil War Commemoration in Missouri.* Columbia: University of Missouri Press, 2020.

Foner, Eric. *Reconstruction: America's Unfinished Revolution, 1863–1877.* New York: Harper & Row, 1988.

Ford, James E. *A History of Jefferson City: Missouri's State Capital, and of Cole County.* Jefferson City, MO: New Day Press, 1938.

Fox, Craig. *Everyday Klansfolk: White Protestant Life and the KKK in 1920s Michigan.* East Lansing: Michigan State University Press, 2011.

Francis, Megan Ming. *Civil Rights and the Making of the Modern American State.* Cambridge: Cambridge University Press, 2014.

Frazier, Harriet C. *Lynchings in Missouri, 1803–1981.* Jefferson, NC: McFarland, 2009.

Frost, Stanley. *The Challenge of the Klan.* Indianapolis: Bobbs-Merrill, 1924.

Fry, Henry P. *The Modern Ku Klux Klan.* Boston: Small and Maynard, 1922.

Gallagher, Charles. *Nazis of Copley Square: The Forgotten Story of the Christian Front.* Cambridge, MA: Harvard University Press, 2021.

Garrity, John A. "The New Deal, National Socialism, and the Great Depression." *American Historical Review* 78, no. 4 (1973): 907–44.

Gellman, Erik S., and Jarod Roll. *The Gospel of the Working Class: Labor's Southern Prophets in New Deal America.* Urbana: University of Illinois Press, 2011.

Gerber, David A., ed. *Anti-Semitism in American History.* Urbana: University of Illinois Press, 1986.

Gerlach, Larry R. *Blazing Crosses in Zion: The Ku Klux Klan in Utah.* Logan: Utah State University Press, 1982.

Gilmore, Glenda Elizabeth. *Defying Dixie: The Radical Roots of Civil Rights, 1919–1950.* New York: W. W. Norton, 2008.

———— *Gender and Jim Crow: Women and the Politics of White Supremacy in North Carolina, 1896–1920.* Chapel Hill: University of North Carolina Press, 1996.

Bibliography

Gleason, Philip. *The Conservative Reformers: German-American Catholics and the Social Order*. Notre Dame, IN: University of Notre Dame Press, 1968.

Goldberg, David. *Discontented America: The United States in the 1920s*. Baltimore: Johns Hopkins University Press, 1999.

——— "Unmasking of the Ku Klux Klan: The Northern Movement against the KKK, 1920–1925." *Journal of American Ethnic History* 15, no. 4 (1996): 32–48.

Goldberg, Robert A. *Hooded Empire: The Ku Klux Klan in Colorado*. Urbana: University of Illinois Press, 1981.

Gonda, Jeffrey D. *Unjust Deeds: The Restrictive Covenant Cases and the Making of the Civil Rights Movement*. Chapel Hill: University of North Carolina Press, 2015.

Gordon, Colin. *Mapping Decline: St. Louis and the Fate of the American City*. Philadelphia: University of Pennsylvania Press, 2008.

Gordon, Linda. *The Second Coming of the KKK: The Ku Klux Klan of the 1920s and the American Political Tradition*. New York: Liveright, 2017.

Grant, Colin. *Negro with a Hat: The Rise and Fall of Marcus Garvey*. Oxford: Oxford University Press, 2008.

Greene, Debra Foster. "Published in the Interest of Colored People: The *St. Louis Argus* Newspaper in the Twentieth Century." PhD diss., University of Missouri–Columbia, 2003.

Greene, Lorenzo J., Gary R. Kremer, and Antonio F. Holland. *Missouri's Black Heritage*. Rev. ed. Columbia: University of Missouri Press, 1993.

Griffith, Debra. "Rabbi Ferdinand Isserman Sounds a Warning—Missourians and the Holocaust." Missouri S&T Library and Learning Resources. Accessed December 4, 2023. https://libguides.mst.edu/Missourians_and_the_Holocaust.

Grothaus, Larry. "Kansas City Blacks, Harry Truman, and the Pendergast Machine." *Missouri Historical Review* 69, no. 1 (1974): 65–82.

——— "The Negro in Missouri Politics, 1890–1941." PhD diss., University of Missouri–Columbia, 1971.

Hahn, Steven. *A Nation under Our Feet: Black Political Struggles in the Rural South from Slavery to the Great Migration*. Cambridge, MA: Belknap Press of Harvard University Press, 2003.

Hall, Jacquelyn Dowd. "The Long Civil Rights Movement and the Political Uses of the Past." *Journal of American History* 91, no. 4 (2005): 1233–63.

Hamby, Alonzo. *Man of the People: A Life of Harry S. Truman*. New York: Oxford University Press, 1995.

Harcourt, Felix. *Ku Klux Kulture: America and the Klan in the 1920s*. Chicago: University of Chicago Press, 2017.

Harper, Kimberly. *White Man's Heaven: The Lynching and Expulsion of Blacks in the Southern Ozarks, 1894–1909*. Fayetteville: University of Arkansas Press, 2010.

Hart, Bradley W. *Hitler's American Friends: The Third Reich's Supporters in the United States*. New York: Thomas Dunne Books, 2018.

Hernandez, Miguel. *The Ku Klux Klan and Freemasonry in 1920s America: Fighting Fraternities*. London: Routledge, 2019.

Bibliography

Hernando, Matthew J. *Faces Like Devils: The Bald Knobber Vigilantes in the Ozarks*. Columbia: University of Missouri Press, 2015.

Hessler, Anne. "German Jews in Small Towns in Missouri, 1850–1920." Master's thesis, University of Missouri–Columbia, 1991.

Higham, John. *Strangers in the Land: Patterns of American Nativism, 1860–1925*. 2nd ed. New Brunswick, NJ: Rutgers University Press, 1988.

Holland, Antonio F. *Nathan B. Young and the Struggle over Black Higher Education*. Columbia: University of Missouri Press, 2006.

Hornbeck, Thomas. "Historical Geography of the Catholic Church in Kansas City, Missouri: 1822–1930." Master's thesis, University of Kansas, 2009.

House Committee on Rules. *The Ku-Klux Klan: Hearing before the Committee on Rules*. 67th Cong., 1st sess., 1921.

Howell, Thomas. "Kansas City Crusader: Leon Birkhead and the Fight against Fascism." *Missouri Historical Review* 110, no. 4 (2016): 237–59.

Huber, Patrick. "The Lynching of James T. Scott: The Underside of a College Town." *Gateway Heritage* 12, no. 1 (1991): 1–20.

—— "Town versus Gown: The James T. Scott Lynching and the Social Fracture between the University of Missouri and the Larger Columbia Community." Bachelor's thesis, University of Missouri–Columbia, 1990.

Hughes, John Starrett. "Lafayette County and the Aftermath of Slavery, 1861–1870." *Missouri Historical Review* 75, no. 1 (1980): 51–63.

Hunt, Doug. "A Course in Applied Lynching." *Missouri Review* 27, no. 2 (2004): 122–70.

—— *Summary Justice: The Lynching of James Scott and the Trial of George Barkwell in Columbia, Missouri, 1923*. Charleston: n.p., 2010.

Hunter, Lloyd A. "Missouri's Confederate Leaders after the War." *Missouri Historical Review* 67, no. 3 (April 1973): 371–96.

Hurt, R. Douglas. *Agriculture and Slavery in Missouri's Little Dixie*. Columbia: University of Missouri Press, 1992.

Ioannides, Mara Cohen. *Creating Community: The Jews of Springfield, Missouri*. Springfield, MO: Greene County Historical Society Press, 2021.

Ioannides, Mara Cohen, and Rachel Gholson. *Jews of Springfield in the Ozarks*. Charleston: Arcadia, 2013.

Jackson, Kenneth T. *The Ku Klux Klan in the City, 1915–1930*. New York: Oxford University Press, 1967.

Jeansonne, Glen. *Gerald L. K. Smith: Minister of Hate*. Baton Rouge: Louisiana State University Press, 1997.

Jenkins, Roy. *Truman*. New York: Harper & Row, 1986.

Jenkins, William D. *Steel Valley Klan: The Ku Klux Klan in Ohio's Mahoning Valley*. Kent, OH: Kent State University Press, 1990.

Johnson, Walter. *The Broken Heart of America: St. Louis and the Violent History of the United States*. New York: Basic Books, 2020.

Katznelson, Ira. *Fear Itself: The New Deal and the Origins of Our Time*. New York: Liveright, 2013.

Bibliography

Kauffman, Christopher. *Columbianism and the Knights of Columbus: A Quincentenary History.* New York: Simon & Schuster, 1992.

—— *Faith and Fraternalism: The History of the Knights of Columbus.* New York: Simon & Schuster, 1992.

Kemper, Donald J. "Catholic Integration in St. Louis, 1935–1947." *Missouri Historical Review* 73, no. 1 (1978): 1–22.

Kennedy, David M. *Freedom from Fear: The American People in Depression and War, 1929–1945.* Oxford: Oxford University Press, 1999.

Kerr, K. Austin. *Organized for Prohibition: A New History of the Anti-Saloon League.* New Haven, CT: Yale University Press, 1985.

Kinney, Brandon G. *The Mormon War: Zion and the Missouri Extermination Order of 1838.* Yardley, PA: Westholme, 2011.

Kinzer, Donald L. *An Episode in Anti-Catholicism: The American Protective Association.* Seattle: University of Washington Press, 1964.

Kirkendall, Richard S. *A History of Missouri.* Vol. 5, *1919 to 1953.* Columbia: University of Missouri Press, 1986.

Kittel, Audrey Nell. "The Negro Community of Columbia, Missouri." Master's thesis, University of Missouri–Columbia, 1938.

Knights of the Ku Klux Klan, Inc. *Proceedings of the Second Imperial Klonvokation: Held in Kansas City, Missouri, Sept. 23, 24, 25 and 26, 1924.* N.p., n.d.

Kremer, Gary R. *Heartland History.* Vol. 3. Jefferson City, MO: City of Jefferson, 2004.

—— *Race and Meaning: The African American Experience in Missouri.* Columbia: University of Missouri Press, 2016.

—— *This Place of Promise: A Historian's Perspective on 200 Years of Missouri History.* Columbia: University of Missouri Press, 2021.

—— "William J. Thompkins: African American Physician, Politician, and Publisher." *Missouri Historical Review* 101, no. 3 (2007): 168–82.

Lang, Clarence. *Grassroots at the Gateway: Class Politics and Black Freedom Struggle in St. Louis, 1936–75.* Ann Arbor: University of Michigan Press, 2009.

Large, John Judson. "The 'Invisible Empire' and Missouri Politics: The Influence of the Revived Ku Klux Klan in the Election Campaign of 1924 as Reported in Missouri Newspapers." Master's thesis, University of Missouri–Columbia, 1957.

Larsen, Lawrence H., and Nancy J. Hulston. *Pendergast!* Columbia: University of Missouri Press, 1997.

Lay, Shawn. *Hooded Knights on the Niagara: The Ku Klux Klan in Buffalo, New York.* New York: New York University Press, 1995.

——, ed. *The Invisible Empire in the West: Toward a New Historical Appraisal of the Ku Klux Klan of the 1920s.* Urbana: University of Illinois Press, 1992.

The Lead Belt Jewish Oral History Project. Madison, WI: Life History Services, 2012.

LeSueur, Stephen C. *The 1838 Mormon War in Missouri.* Columbia: University of Missouri Press, 1987.

Leuchtenburg, William. *Franklin D. Roosevelt and the New Deal, 1932-1940.* New York: Harper & Row, 1963.

Bibliography

Lichtman, Allan J. *White Protestant Nation: The Rise of the American Conservative Movement*. New York: Atlantic Monthly Press, 2008.

Litwack, Leon F. *Trouble in Mind: Black Southerners in the Age of Jim Crow*. New York: Alfred A. Knopf, 1998.

Lucander, David. *Winning the War for Democracy: The March on Washington Movement, 1941–1946*. Urbana: University of Illinois Press, 2014.

Lumpkins, Charles. *American Pogrom: The East St. Louis Race Riot and Black Politics*. Athens: Ohio University Press, 2008.

MacLean, Nancy K. *Behind the Mask of Chivalry: The Making of the Second Ku Klux Klan*. Oxford: Oxford University Press, 1994.

Madison, James H. *The Ku Klux Klan in the Heartland*. Bloomington: Indiana University Press, 2020.

Manfra, Jo A. "Hometown Politics and the American Protective Association, 1887–1890." *Annals of Iowa* 55 (1996): 138–66.

McCandless, Perry. *A History of Missouri*. Vol. 2, *1820–1860*. Columbia: University of Missouri Press, 1972.

McCullough, David. *Truman*. New York: Simon & Schuster, 1992.

McDonald, Jason. "'Watch Adair County Klan Grow': The Second Ku Klux Klan in Kirksville, Missouri, 1923–1925." *Missouri Historical Review* 118, no. 1 (2023): 1–24.

McElroy, George A. "Roy Wilkins as a Journalist." Master's thesis, University of Missouri–Columbia, 1970.

McGirr, Lisa. *The War on Alcohol: Prohibition and the Rise of the American State*. New York: W. W. Norton, 2016.

McGreevy, John T. *Parish Boundaries: The Catholic Encounter with Race in the Twentieth-Century Urban North*. Chicago: University of Chicago Press, 1996.

McKerley, John W. "Citizens and Strangers: The Politics of Race in Missouri from Slavery to the Era of Jim Crow." PhD diss., University of Iowa, 2008.

McLaurin, Melton Alonza. *Celia, a Slave*. Athens: University of Georgia Press, 1991.

McVeigh, Rory. *The Rise of the Ku Klux Klan: Right-Wing Movements and National Politics*. Minneapolis: University of Minnesota Press, 2009.

Mecklin, John M. *The Ku Klux Klan: A Study of the American Mind*. New York: Harcourt, Brace, 1924.

Michaeli, Ethan. *The Defender: How the Legendary Black Newspaper Changed America*. Boston: Houghton Mifflin Harcourt, 2016.

Miller, Merle. *Plain Speaking: An Oral Biography of Harry S. Truman*. New York: Berkley, 1974

Miller, Richard Lawrence. *Truman: The Rise to Power*. New York: McGraw-Hill, 1986.

Mitchell, Franklin D. *Embattled Democracy: Missouri Democratic Politics, 1919–1932*. Columbia: University of Missouri Press, 1968.

———. "The Re-election of Irreconcilable James A. Reed." *Missouri Historical Review* 60, no. 4 (1966): 416–35.

Moore, Deborah Dash. *B'nai B'rith and the Challenge of Ethnic Leadership*. Albany: State University of New York Press, 1981.

Bibliography

Moore, Jesse Thomas, Jr. *A Search for Equality: The National Urban League, 1910–1961.* University Park: Pennsylvania State University Press, 1981.

Moore, Leonard J. *Citizen Klansmen: The Ku Klux Klan in Indiana, 1921–1928.* Chapel Hill: University of North Carolina Press, 1991.

Mutti Burke, Diane. *On Slavery's Border: Missouri's Small Slaveholding Households, 1815–1865.* Athens: University of Georgia Press, 2010.

Mutti Burke, Diane, Jason Roe, and John Herron, eds. *Wide-Open Town: Kansas City in the Pendergast Era.* Lawrence: University Press of Kansas, 2018.

Nations, Gilbert O. *The Blight of Mexico; or, Four Hundred Years of Papal Tyranny and Plunder.* Aurora, MO: Menace, n.d.

——— *Papal Guilt of the World War.* Washington, DC: Protestant, 1921.

——— *Papal Sovereignty: The Government within Our Government.* Cincinnati: Standard, 1917.

——— *The Political Career of Alfred E. Smith.* Washington, DC: Protestant, 1928.

Nelson, Lawrence J. *Rumors of Indiscretion: The University of Missouri's "Sex Questionnaire" Scandal in the Jazz Age.* Columbia: University of Missouri Press, 2003.

Nordstrom, Justin. *Danger on the Doorstep: Anti-Catholicism and American Print Culture in the Progressive Era.* Notre Dame, IN: University of Notre Dame, 2006.

Norton, Sydney J. ed. *Fighting for a Free Missouri: German Immigrants, African Americans, and the Issue of Slavery.* Columbia: University of Missouri Press, 2023.

Olson, Greg. *Indigenous Missourians: Ancient Societies to the Present.* Columbia: University of Missouri Press, 2023.

One Hundred Years of Medicine and Surgery in Missouri: Historical and Biographical Review of the Careers of the Physicians and Surgeons of the State of Missouri, and Sketches of Some of Its Notable Medical Institutions. St. Louis: Star, 1900.

Painter, Nell Irvin. *Exodusters: Black Migration to Kansas after Reconstruction.* New York: Alfred A. Knopf, 1977.

Park, Benjamine E. *Kingdom of Nauvoo: The Rise and Fall of a Religious Empire on the American Frontier.* New York: Liveright, 2020.

Parrish, William E. *A History of Missouri.* Vol. 3, *1860 to 1875.* Columbia: University of Missouri Press, 1973.

——— *Missouri under Radical Rule, 1865–1870.* Columbia: University of Missouri Press, 1965.

Parsons, Elaine Frantz. *Ku-Klux: The Birth of the Klan during Reconstruction.* Chapel Hill: University of North Carolina Press, 2016.

Pegram, Thomas R. *Battling Demon Rum: The Struggle for a Dry America.* Chicago: Ivan R. Dee, 1998.

——— *One Hundred Percent American: The Rebirth and Decline of the Ku Klux Klan in the 1920s.* Chicago: Ivan R. Dee, 2011.

Peterson, Norma L. "The Political Fluctuations of B. Gratz Brown: Politics in a Border State, 1850–1870." *Missouri Historical Review* 51, no. 1 (1956): 22–30.

Peterson, Sandra Rubinstein. "'One Heart, Many Souls': The National Council of Jewish Women and Identity Formation in St. Louis, 1919–1950." PhD diss., University of Missouri–Columbia, 2008.

Primm, James Neal. *Lion of the Valley: St. Louis, Missouri, 1764–1980.* 3rd ed. St. Louis: Missouri Historical Society Press, 1998.

Rabin, Shari. *Jews on the Frontier: Religion and Mobility in Nineteenth Century America.* New York: New York University Press, 2017.

Reddig, William M. *Tom's Town: Kansas City and the Pendergast Legend.* Philadelphia: J. B. Lippincott, 1947.

Reed, Toure. *Not Alms but Opportunity: The Urban League and the Politics of Racial Uplift, 1910–1950.* Chapel Hill: University of North Carolina Press, 2008.

Rhodes, Joel P. *A Missouri Railroad Pioneer: The Life of Louis Houck.* Columbia: University of Missouri Press, 2008.

Ribuffo, Leo P. *The Old Christian Right: The Protestant Far Right from the Great Depression to the Cold War.* Philadelphia: Temple University Press, 1983.

Ritter, Luke. *Inventing America's First Immigration Crisis: Political Nativism in the Antebellum West.* New York: Fordham University Press, 2021.

Rives, Timothy. "The Second Ku Klux Klan in Kansas City: Rise and Fall of a White Nationalist Movement." Kansas City Public Library, 15 March 2018. http://pendergastkc.org/article/second-ku-klux-klan-kansas-city-rise-and-fall-white-nationalist-movement.

Rolinson, Mary G. *Grassroots Garveyism: The Universal Negro Improvement Association in the Rural South, 1920–1927.* Chapel Hill: University of North Carolina Press, 2007.

Roll, Jarod. *Poor Man's Fortune: White Working-Class Conservatism in American Metal Mining, 1850–1950.* Chapel Hill: University of North Carolina Press, 2020.

——— *Spirit of Rebellion: Labor and Religion in the New Cotton South.* Urbana: University of Illinois Press, 2010.

Rush, Barbara J. "The Ku Klux Klan in Kansas City during the Twenties." Master's thesis, Marquette University, 1970.

Ryan, Yvonne. *Roy Wilkins: The Quiet Revolutionary and the NAACP.* Lexington: University Press of Kentucky, 2014.

Sable, Jacob M. "Some American Jewish Organizational Efforts to Combat Anti-Semitism, 1906–30." PhD diss., Yeshiva University, 1964.

Sachs, Howard F. "Development of the Jewish Community of Kansas City, 1864–1908." *Missouri Historical Review* 60, no. 3 (1966): 350–60.

Sandweiss, Eric. *St. Louis: The Evolution of an American Urban Landscape.* Philadelphia: Temple University Press, 2001.

Sarna, Jonathan D., ed. *The American Jewish Experience.* 2nd ed. New York: Holmes & Meier, 1997.

——— *American Judaism: A History.* New Haven, CT: Yale University Press, 2004.

Savage, W. Sherman. *The History of Lincoln University.* Jefferson City, MO: New Day Press, 1939.

Schirmer, Sherry Lamb. *A City Divided: The Racial Landscape of Kansas City, 1900–1960.* Columbia: University of Missouri Press, 2002.

Schmidt, Daniel A. *The Heritage of St. Thomas: Community-City-Parish; Showing the Early Development, Expanding Civilization, and Resources of a Progressive Community*

Bibliography

through Sketches of the People and Events Who Have Made Its Past and Whose Lives Are Moulding Its Future. N.p.: Bob Dew, 1974.

Schmidt, Joseph H. "Recollections of the First Catholic Missions in Central Missouri." *Missouri Historical Review* 5, no. 2 (1911): 83–93.

Schneider, John C. "Riot and Reaction in St. Louis, 1854–1856." *Missouri Historical Review* 68, no. 2 (1974): 171–85.

Schneiderman, Harry, ed. *The American Jewish Year Book 5681, September 13, 1920 to October 2, 1921.* Vol. 22. Philadelphia: Jewish Publication Society of America, 1920.

Schultz, Joseph P., ed. *Mid-America's Promise: A Profile of Kansas City Jewry.* Kansas City: Jewish Community Foundation of Greater Kansas City, 1982.

Schwalm, Leslie. *Emancipation's Diaspora: Race and Reconstruction in the Upper Midwest.* Chapel Hill: University of North Carolina Press, 2009.

Shelton, Vanessa. "Interpretative Community and the Black Press: Racial Equality and Politics in the *St. Louis American* and the *St. Louis Argus*, 1928–1956." PhD diss., University of Iowa, 2007.

Silver, M. M. *Louis Marshall and the Rise of Jewish Ethnicity in American: A Biography.* Syracuse, NY: Syracuse University Press, 2013.

Snow, Thad. *From Missouri: An American Farmer Looks Back.* Edited by Bonnie Stepenoff. Columbia: University of Missouri Press, 2012.

Soapes, Thomas F. "The Fragility of the Roosevelt Coalition in Missouri." *Missouri Historical Review* 72, no. 1 (1977): 38–58.

Stein, Judith. *The World of Marcus Garvey: Race and Class in Modern Society.* Baton Rouge: Louisiana State University Press, 1986.

Steinberg, Alfred. *The Man from Missouri: The Life and Times of Harry S. Truman.* New York: Putnam, 1962.

Stepenoff, Bonnie. *Thad Snow: A Life of Social Reform in the Missouri Bootheel.* Columbia: University of Missouri Press, 2003.

Sullivan, Patricia. *Lift Every Voice: The NAACP and the Making of the Civil Rights Movement.* New York: New Press, 2009.

Terkel, Studs. *Hard Times: An Oral History of the Great Depression.* New York: Pantheon Books, 1970.

Thelen, David. *Paths of Resistance: Tradition and Democracy in Industrializing Missouri.* Columbia: University of Missouri Press, 1991.

This Far by Faith: A Popular History of the Catholic People of West and Northwest Missouri. Kansas City: Diocese of Kansas City–St. Joseph, 1992.

Truman, Margaret. *Harry S. Truman.* New York: William Morrow, 1973.

Tyrrell, Ian. *Woman's World, Woman's Empire: The Woman's Christian Temperance Union in International Perspective, 1880–1930.* Chapel Hill: University of North Carolina Press, 1991.

Wade, Wyn C. *The Fiery Cross: The Ku Klux Klan in America.* New York: Oxford University Press, 1998.

Watts, Steven. *The People's Tycoon: Henry Ford and the American Century.* New York: Alfred A. Knopf, 2005.

Bibliography

Weiss, Nancy. *The National Urban League, 1910–1940*. Oxford: Oxford University Press, 1974.

Weissbach, Lee Shai. *Jewish Life in Small-Town America*. New Haven, CT: Yale University Press, 2005.

Welek, Mary. "Jordan Chambers: Black Politician and Boss." *Journal of Negro History* 57, no. 4 (1972): 352–69.

Wilkerson, Isabel. *The Warmth of Other Suns: The Epic Story of America's Great Migration*. New York: Random House, 2010.

Wilkins, Roy. *Standing Fast: The Autobiography of Roy Wilkins*. New York: Viking Press, 1982.

Williams, Shannen Dee. *Subversive Habits: Black Catholic Nuns in the Long African American Freedom Struggle*. Durham, NC: Duke University Press, 2022.

Wilson, Thomas D. "Chester A. Franklin and Harry S. Truman: An African-American Conservative and the 'Conversion' of the Future President." *Missouri Historical Review* 88, no. 1 (1993): 48–77.

Wood, Amy Louis. *Lynching and Spectacle: Witnessing Racial Violence in America, 1890–1940*. Chapel Hill: University of North Carolina Press, 2009.

Worley, William S. *J. C. Nichols and the Shaping of Kansas City: Innovation in Planned Residential Communities*. Columbia: University of Missouri Press, 1990.

Yacovazzi, Cassandra. *Escaped Nuns: True Womanhood and the Campaign against Convents in Antebellum America*. Oxford: Oxford University Press, 2018.

INDEX

African Americans: alleged Klan violence against, 76, 102–8; anti-Black violence against, 102–8; and the anti-Klan press, 11, 77–78, 83–84, 132, 281, 286; and Buder Park, 242–43; and enslavement in Missouri, 32–33; and Gerald L. K. Smith, 276–80; and the Independent Klan of America, 196; and lynchings in Missouri, 36, 98–99, 104, 108–9, 124–25, 234; Ku Klux Klan attitude towards, 3, 32, 35–37, 246, 288, 292; and the Missouri Democratic Party, 14, 35, 45, 107, 155, 211–40, 286–87; and the Missouri Republican Party, 14, 35, 78, 154–55, 160, 211–40; and the NAACP, 12, 105, 122–129, 132, 154, 166; opposition to James A. Reed, 149, 153–55; and the Reconstruction Ku Klux Klan, 32, 35–36, 122; and the UNIA, 12, 105, 122–29. See also *Kansas City Call*; *Kansas City American*; *St. Louis Argus*

Ahrens, H. S., 61, 103–4

Allen, Henry J., 4, 118

Aloe, Louis, 161, 220, 222

American Clan, 4–5, 15, 42

American Jewish Committee, 13, 161, 265

American Jewish Congress, 13, 265

American League against War and Fascism, 266

American Party: 1924 presidential election, 42, 163–65; in the 19th Century, 38

American Protective Association, 38–40, 113, 115–16, 140, 306n74

American Unity League, 8, 12, 108, 112, 120–22, 142–43

Anti-Catholicism: in the 19th Century, 38–39, 113, 116; and Al Smith, 245–47, 268;

and Allen McReynolds, 140; anti-Klan newspaper responses to, 11, 80, 90–91,112, 263; and Arthur Hyde, 103; and Billy Parker, 4, 40–42, 152–53; and the Catholic Central Verein, 13, 112–15; and Charles McGehee, 52; and Gilbert O. Nations, 40–42, 152–53, 247–48; and Henry P. Fry, 95; and John Fugel, 90–91; and the Knights of Columbus, 13, 80, 112–13, 116–20, 291; and the Ku Klux Klan, 23, 32, 42, 55, 65, 245; and Luke E. Hart, 13, 80, 117–20, 291; and *The Menace*, 9, 39–41, 62, 91, 114; and the *Missouri Valley Independent*, 65; and *The Monitor*, 9; and the NAACP, 110; and *The New Menace*, 9, 41, 65, 118–19, 130, 152–53, 247; and O. L. Spurgeon, 62; and *The Patriot*, 51, 91

Anti-Defamation League. *See* B'nai B'rith

Anti-Klan newspapers. *See* *Church Progress*; *Jewish Voice*; *Kansas City American*; *Kansas City Call*; *Kansas City Catholic Register*; *Kansas City Jewish Chronicle*; *Modern View*; *New York World*; *St. Joseph Catholic Tribune*; *St. Louis Argus*; *St. Louis Catholic Herald*; *St. Louis Post-Dispatch*; *St. Louis Star*; *Vienna Home-Advisor*; *Western Watchman*

Anti-Klan organizations. *See* American Unity League; B'nai B'rith; Carthage Anti-Klan Association; Catholic Central Verein; International Committee against Racism; Jasper County Anti-Klan Association; Jewish Community Relations Council; Joplin Anti-Klan Organization; Knights of Columbus; National Association for the Advancement of Colored People; Operation

377

378 Index

PUSH; United Front against the Klan; Universal Negro Improvement Association

Anti-Klan political figures. *See* Louis Aloe; Perl Decker; Harry Hawes; Arthur M. Hyde; Joseph L. McLemore; Allen McReynolds; J. F. Osborne; Henry Priest; James A. Reed; Al Smith; George B. Vashon, George L. Vaughn

Anti-Nazi League, 265

Anti-Saloon League, 22, 41–44, 168, 189–90

Antisemitism: activism against, 11, 13, 110, 112, 129–31, 250, 266, 270, 291; and the Anti-Defamation League, 129–31, 266; and the Catholic Church, 281; and Charles Coughlin, 244, 260–62, 264, 266, 270, 281; and the *Dearborn Independent*, 80, 262; directed at Jews, 9, 81–82, 161; and Gerald B. Winrod, 270; and Gerald L. K. Smith, 243, 262, 274, 277, 280; and the German-American Bund, 255; and the Ku Klux Klan, 11, 23, 95, 315n41; and William Pelley, 256

Aryan Nations, 280, 295–96

Association of Carolina Klans, 289

Association of Georgia Klans, 288–89

Aurora (MO): and the *Menace*, 9, 39–41, 247; Ku Klux Klan activity in 58

B

Baker, J. E., 66

Baker, Sam A.: 1924 gubernatorial campaign, 47–48, 94, 148, 167–74; as governor, 47–48, 178, 185, 205, 212, 216, 231; early life, 47–48

Baldknobbers, 36

Beach, Albert, 216–18

Bernie (MO): anti-Black violence in, 106; Ku Klux Klan activity in, 61

Betts, James L., 283–84, 291–97

Birkhead, Leon M.: critiques of fascism and antisemitism, 269–71; death, 291; early life, 268; and the Friends of Democracy, 270–72; and Gerald L. K. Smith, 271–72, 275–76; and the Ku Klux Klan, 269, 271, 275–76

Black, Hugo, 248

Black Legion, 16, 248–49, 262, 272

B'nai B'rith: and the 1982 Hannibal rally, 294–95; Anti-Defamation League, 12–13, 129, 241, 265–66, 283, 294–95; anti-Klan activity, 8, 12–13, 108, 110, 112, 130, 141–42, 241; anti-Nazism, 265–66; antisemitism, 129–30; origins, 129–30

Bogus Oath, 90, 116–19, 291

Bowling Green (MO): Ku Klux Klan activity in, 179; lynching of Roy Hammonds, 109, 124

Brewster, R. R., 14, 150–51, 155

Brown, B. Gratz, 34

Brown, Dwight H., 88–89

Brown Scare, 245, 281

Bruner, Glen, 55, 151–52, 155–56

Buder Park, 241–44, 275–76, 288

Burns, C. S., 145–47, 170–72, 174, 200

Butler, Richard, 280

C

Campbell, William M.: early life, 64; exalted cyclops of St. Joseph Klan No. 4, 64–66, 100–101; imperial kloncilium, 245–46; Missouri Grand Dragon, 25–26, 177–80, 205, 227, 290; political activism, 48, 162, 205, 227

Cape Girardeau: anti-Klan activism in, 86, 124, 197, 235; cotton prospects in the Bootheel, 104; Missouri State Normal School Third District, 47, 68, 86

Carr, Mary, 283–84, 291–97

Carter, Cora J., 109–11, 125, 291

Carthage Anti-Klan Association, 8, 112, 137, 140–43, 198

Caruthersville, anti-Black violence near, 106; Ku Klux Klan activity in, 61

Catholic Central Verein, 8, 12–13, 108, 112–16, 120, 142

Catholics: and the American Protective Association, 38–40, 113, 115–16, 140, 306n74; and the American Unity League, 8, 12, 108, 112, 120–22, 142–43; and the Bogus Oath, 13, 90, 116–19, 291; and the Catholic Central Verein, 8, 12–13, 108, 112–16, 120, 142; and Charles Coughlin,

Index

258–64; Ku Klux Klan attitude towards, 3, 23, 26, 30–32, 37, 41–42, 151–53; and the Knights of Columbus, 8, 12–13, 80, 90, 96, 108, 110, 112–13, 116–20, 132, 142, 170–71, 264, 281, 291; settlement in Missouri, 38; and Luke E. Hart, 13, 80, 117–18, 132, 281, 291; See also Anti-Catholicism; *Church Progress*; *Kansas City Catholic Register*; *St. Joseph Catholic Tribune*; *St. Louis Catholic Herald*; *Vienna Home-Advisor*; *Western Watchman*

Caulfield, Henry, 229–31, 234, 242

Cedar County, 73–74

Chambers, Jordan, 221–25, 229

Charleston (MO): Ku Klux Klan activity in, 61; lynching of Roosevelt Grigsby, 108

Christian Front, 256, 258, 262–63, 281–82

Church Progress, 76, 114, 183

Citizens Protective Association, 278–80

Clarke, E. Y.: and Marcus Garvey, 13, 126–27; and the Southern Publicity Association, 22–23; and William Joseph Simmons, 15–16, 22–23, 30

Colescott, James, 249, 256, 287

Collins, F. A., 146, 170

Columbia: anti-Klan activism in, 295; lynching of James T. Scott, 109; newspaper interpretations of the Klan, 76, 86, 279

Congress of Industrial Organizations, 266–67

Coolidge, Calvin, 20, 94, 148, 157, 161–63, 165–66, 173, 187, 219

Coughlin, Charles: charges of antisemitism, 244, 259–66, 270–71; Christian Front, 256, 258, 262–63, 281–82; early life, 258; radio broadcasts, 258–63; relationship with Ferdinand Isserman, 260–62, 264–65; Union Party, 262, 272

Council for American Democracy, 265–68, 275

Craig, J. F., 3–5, 10–11, 13–17, 285

Crawford, C. C.: early life, 49–50; and the Fourth Christian Church, 3–4, 11, 14, 16–17, 50, 52–53, 184–85; investigation for mail fraud, 16, 180–86, 197–98, 202–3, 207; as Ku Klux Klan lecturer, 50–51, 89,

183, 185; and the *Patriot*, 50–51, 180–86, 339n43

Cromwell, Frank, 215, 217

Crossley, Wallace, 86, 91–94

D

Davis, John W., 148, 162–63, 165–66, 215

Dearmont, Russell, 235

Decker, Perl, 138–39, 142

Democratic Party in Missouri: and the 1922 U.S. Senate campaign, 14, 147, 150–55; and the 1924 Democratic State Convention, 56, 157–59; and the 1924 gubernatorial campaign, 145–47, 167–75; and the 1926 U.S. Senate campaign, 8, 205–7, 212, 226–28; and African American voters, 14, 35, 45, 107, 155, 211–40, 286–87; and divided sentiments over James A. Reed, 148–50, 156, 211, 227; and the Ku Klux Klan, 46–48, 150–61, 167–75, 215–19, 231–33; and the Pendergast Machine, 45–47, 149, 152, 159, 210–12, 215–18, 227, 229, 231, 235, 237–38; and support for Jim Crow, 35. *See also* Arthur W. Nelson; James A. Reed; Guy B. Park; Harry Hawes; Harry S. Truman; Lloyd Stark

Dickmann, Bernard, 225–26, 238–39, 266

Dixie Klans, Inc., 289

Du Bois, W. E. B., 77, 83, 116, 123, 126

Duke, David, 280, 293, 296

Dyer, L. C.: 1925 St. Louis mayoral campaign, 221–22; 1926 congressional campaign, 223, 226; 1928 congressional campaign, 223–24, 229; anti-Klan activism, 8, 75, 96–97, 212; anti-lynching bill, 125, 154, 166, 328–29n70

E

Eisenhower, Dwight D., 209, 276–77

Evans, Hiram: 1925 parade in Washington D.C., 70, 94; antisemitism, 131; and the Junior Ku Klux Klan, 25, 54; and the WKKK, 23–24, 98; at Second Imperial Klonvokation, 26, 30, 297; coup against Simmons, 16, 23, 98, 202; in the 1930s, 16, 71, 245–46, 249; political activities,

380 Index

Evans, Hiram (*continued*)
161–62, 206; visits to Missouri, 36–37, 50,
57, 133, 171, 178–79, 246

F

Fair Employment Practices Committee, 274,
288
Fair Play (MO), 73–74, 76, 94
Fascism: 243–45, 250, 281, 287–88; and
Charles Coughlin, 244, 261, 264, 281;
and Gerald L. K. Smith, 243, 279; and the
German-American Bund, 254, 270–71;
opposition to, 251, 264–67, 270–71; and
William Dudley Pelley, 256, 270–71
Federated Ku Klux Klans of Alabama, 289
Fellowship Forum, 41, 65, 68, 247–48
Ford, Henry, 9, 80, 129–30, 262
Franklin, C. A.: and Black voter realignment,
83, 212–13, 215–18, 228, 230–31, 237;
early life, 82–83; and Harry S. Truman,
237; and the Pendergast Machine, 83, 230,
237; and Roy Wilkins, 83–84, 291
Fry, Henry P., 5, 95
Fugel, John: anti-Klan speeches, 91; early life,
89; and Luke E. Hart, 119; and the *Vienna
Home-Advisor*, 75, 86, 89–92, 94, 113–14,
183

G

Garvey, Marcus, 13, 83, 125–29
Gale, William Potter, 280
German-American Bund: activity in Missouri,
254–55, 258; and Anton Kessler, 254, 258,
266–68; and the Christian Front, 256, 262–
63, 281, 287; and Fritz Kuhn, 253–58; and
the Ku Klux Klan, 16, 256–57, 287, 289;
opposition to, 265–68, 270–71; origins,
253–54; and the Silver Legion, 256, 287
German Liberty Union, 266
Gibson, Benjamin Franklin, 290–91, 294
Gillespie, Gilbert S., 290–91
Glennon, John J., 22, 119–20, 244–45
Gomberg, Paul, 284–85, 295
Gordon, John P., 19, 21–22, 48, 67–68, 70–72
Grand League of Protestant Women of
America, 65

Gray, Howard, 137, 140, 142
Grayston, George, 135–37, 142
Green, Samuel, 287–89

H

Hale, Nellie, 65, 75, 99–103, 118, 319n138
Hamilton, John W., 277–79
Hamilton, Tom, 289
Harris, Zach, 54, 57–58, 67, 69
Hart, Luke E.: early life, 117; involvement with
the Missouri Knights of Columbus, 117–
18; and the St. Louis Board of Aldermen,
80, 117, 132; as Supreme Advocate, 13, 113,
117–20, 132, 281, 291, 300n25; as Supreme
Knight, 281, 291
Hawes, Harry: 1924 gubernatorial campaign,
8, 92, 172; 1926 US Senate campaign, 8,
205, 207, 212, 226–28; as a US senator, 234
Hay, Charles M., 229, 233
Herrin (IL), 103
Hitler, Adolf: as chancellor of Germany,
250–51, 253, 256–57, 259–60, 262–63,
265, 270, 275; comparisons to the Ku Klux
Klan, 243, 250; relationship with Nazi–
sympathetic groups in the United States,
252–57
Hoffman, Harvey "Harry," 55–56
Hoover, Herbert, 207, 213, 230–34, 247
Hueller, Fred, xi
Hyde, Arthur M.: and anti-Black violence in
the Bootheel, 105–6; anti-Klan sentiments
of, 8, 14, 47–48, 75, 102, 121, 133, 155,
162, 212; anti-Nazi statements, 250–51;
criticism of, 153, 155, 157, 160, 171–73;
and the death of Nellie Hale, 100–2; early
life, 47; and Heber Nations, 68, 94, 180,
186–87; and the Ku Klux Klan, 58, 61,
69–70, 93, 101, 103, 162; and the NAACP,
98–99, 109, 124–25, 212

I

Independent Klan of America, 180, 195–97
Independent Protestant Woman's Association,
65
International Committee against Racism (IN-
CAR), 284–85, 356n9

Index

381

Isserman, Ferdinand: early life, 260; opposition to Nazism and antisemitism, 265–66, 291; relationship with Charles Coughlin, 260–62, 264–65; and *The Cross and The Flag*, 274

J

Jasper County Anti-Klan Association, 8–9, 198–201, 291, 343n138

Jasper County Bar Association, 133–35, 137, 141

Jefferson City: anti-Klan sentiments in, xi–xii, 10, 22, 68, 70–71, 86; dedication of the new state capitol building, 19–22; Klan activity in, 20–22, 44, 67–70, 162, 190–91, 241, 289; Prohibition raids in, 190–91; WKKK activity in, 25

Jewish Community Relations Council: as Jewish Coordinating Council, 265–66, 268; and the Ku Klux Klan, 241; opposition to Charles Coughlin, 266; opposition to Gerald L. K. Smith, 275; opposition to the German-American Bund, 266, 268; work to combat antisemitism, 291, 351n43, 352n54

Jewish Federation, 13, 265

Jewish Voice, 76, 96, 131, 151

Jews: and Adolf Hitler, 244, 250–51, 255, 259–60; and the American Jewish Committee, 13, 161, 265; and the American Jewish Congress, 13, 265; and the anti-Klan press, 11, 76, 81–82, 84, 96, 131, 166; and the Anti-Nazi League, 265; and B'nai B'rith, 8, 12–13, 108, 110, 112, 130, 141–42, 241, 265; and campaigns against antisemitism, 7, 11–13, 79–82, 84, 116, 129–132, 265, 281; and Charles Coughlin, 244, 259–66, 270–71; and the Christian Front, 262; and Christian Identity theology, 280; and Don Lohbeck, 273–74, 276, 278; and Ferdinand Isserman, 260–62, 264–65, 274, 291; and the German-American Bund, 252, 257, 265–66, 268; and H. T. Zuzak, 172; and James A. Reed, 149, 153–54, 250–51; and the Jewish Community Relations Council, 241, 265–66, 268,

275, 291, 351n43, 352n54; and the Jewish Federation, 265; and Jewish War Veterans, 265; Ku Klux Klan attitude towards, 3, 5, 23, 32, 131–32, 165, 248, 288, 292; and Louis Aloe, 161, 220, 222; and *The Protocols of the Elders of Zion*, 116, 130, 262, 264; settlement in Missouri, 37–38; and William Dudley Pelley, 256; and Vaad Hoir, 265; and Zionist Organization, 265. *See also Jewish Voice*; *Kansas City Jewish Chronicle*; *Modern View*

John Birch Society, 290

Jones, John R., 55, 151, 156

Joplin: anti-Klan activity in, 8–9, 102, 112, 133–42, 148, 198–201, 291, 343n138; and the *Globe*, 31–32, 37, 58–59, 134–37, 140–41, 201; Klan activity in, 9, 31–32, 37, 57–60, 133, 148, 179, 198–99; and Pierre Wallace, 59, 198–201; and Sam Baker, 47–48; and Taylor Snapp, 132–33, 198–200; WKKK activity in, 25

Joplin Anti-Klan Organization, 8, 112, 135–43, 198–99

Junior Ku Klux Klan, 25–26, 54, 178

K

Kamelia, 24, 65, 178, 195

Kansas City: Ku Klux Klan activity in, 4, 26–31, 151–53, 209–10; politics in, 151–56, 213–19, 234–36; Second Imperial Klonvokation in, 26–31, 54, 108, 297. *See also Kansas City American*; *Kansas City Call*; *Kansas City Catholic Register*; *Kansas City Jewish Chronicle*; *Kansas City Post*; *Kansas City Star*

Kansas City American, 215–19, 231–32

Kansas City Call: anti-Klan coverage in, 75, 81–82, 84, 207, 250; and Black voter realignment, 212, 215–18, 228, 230–31, 237; and Harry S. Truman, 209; and James A. Reed, 154; and the Ku Klux Klan, 11–12, 81, 84, 209; and the NAACP, 13, 83–84, 166–67; origins, 82–83; and the Pendergast Machine, 83, 217, 230–31, 237; and Roy Wilkins, 83–84, 291; and the UNIA, 13, 83

382   Index

Kansas City Catholic Register: anti-Klan coverage, 75, 81, 84–85, 108, 113–14, 184; publication of 1922 business directory, 85; interpretation of the 1922 US Senate campaign, 151–56

Kansas City Jewish Chronicle: and Charles Coughlin, 260, 262–63; comparisons between Adolf Hitler and the Klan, 250; and James A. Reed, 154; and the Ku Klux Klan, 81–82, 84, 131, 166; and Leon M. Birkhead, 270

Kansas City Post, 31, 159

Kansas City Star: and Albert Beach, 217; anti-Klan coverage in, 76, 152; comparison between the Klan and Nazism, 250; coverage of Klan activity, 76, 123–24, 296–97

Kennedy, Stetson, 5–6, 288

Kimball, George E., 217–218

Knights of Columbus: and the Bogus Oath, 13, 90, 116; and Charles Coughlin, 264; and the Compulsory Education Act, 113; criticism of, 69, 141, 152–53; and Luke E. Hart, 13, 80, 117–18, 132, 281, 291; and the NAACP, 110; and the *New Menace*, 13, 118–19; opposition to the Ku Klux Klan, 8, 12, 96, 108, 112, 118–20, 142, 170–71; origins, 116

Ku Klux Klan: after World War II, 283–85, 287–97; attitudes about African Americans, 3, 32, 35–37, 246, 288, 292; attitudes about anti-Klan activism, 3, 26, 30, 74, 122, 134, 167, 179, 183, 185; attitudes about Catholicism, 3, 23, 26, 30–32, 37, 41–42, 151–53; attitudes about Jews, 23, 26, 31–32, 37, 131–32; early newspaper interpretations of, 10–12, 74–96, 108; and Gilbert O. Nations, 41–42, 148, 152, 164–66; and immigration, 3, 23, 31–32, 37, 41–42, 164, 245, 293; and the Independent Klan of America, 180, 195–97; and the Junior Ku Klux Klan, 25–26, 54, 178; and the "Klan issue," 14–15, 79–80, 143, 147–48, 157, 160, 165–70, 173–74, 199, 212–13, 286–87; and law enforcement, 23, 31–32, 35–36, 41–44, 78, 80, 98–102,

200–1; and morality, 23, 26, 31–32; origins of the second Klan, 22–23; and philanthropy, 9–10, 59–60, 65, 82, 84–85, 107, 133, 155, 198; political activity of, 44–48, 98, 132–143, 147–48, 151–53, 155–56, 160–66, 168, 174–75, 198–207, 227–28; and Prohibition enforcement, 23, 32, 41–44, 72, 164, 186–93; and public education, 112–13, 152; and the Reconstruction Era Klan, 22–23, 32–35, 76; recruitment of, 4, 10–11, 22–24, 31–32, 35–37, 42–70, 72, 74, 87, 89, 98–100, 104, 124, 166, 180,185, 245–46; responses to vigilantism, 10, 36, 74–75, 94–95, 97–98, 103–8; scholarly interpretations of, 5–7, 16–17; and the Second Imperial Klonvokation, 26–31, 54, 108, 297; and the Southern Publicity Association, 22–23; and the Tri-K Club, 26; violence allegedly committed by, 10, 72–76, 81, 95–97, 103–8, 135–36, 139; and white supremacy, 16, 23, 26, 31–32, 35–37; and William "Billy" Parker, 4–5, 15, 40–42, 151–53, 248; and the Women of the Ku Klux Klan, 23–26, 54, 63, 65, 93, 153, 178, 206. *See also* William J. Simmons; Hiram Evans

Ku Klux Klan activity in Missouri: Adrian, 58; Agency, 58; Aurora, 58; Bernie, 61; Bethany, 66; Bloomfield, 61; Bowling Green, 179; California, 145–47, 170, 172, 179; Callaway County, 69–70; Campbell, 61; Cape Girardeau, 124, 241, 289–90; Carthage, 60, 133–42, 148, 171, 179, 241; Cartersville, 133; Caruthersville, 61; Cass County, 56; Centralia, 70; Chaffee, 61, 246; Charleston, 61; Chillicothe, 66; Clay County, 56; Clinton, 56, 179; Columbia, 70, 179; Cooper County, 69–70; Desloge, 177; DeSoto, 183; Dexter, 61, 88, 289–90; Diamond, 58, 60; Doniphan, 61; Elvins, 177; Excelsior Springs, 179; Fairfax, 58, 66; Flat River, 177–79; Fornfelt, 61; Franklin County, 183; Gasconade County, 69–70; Gideon, 61; Gower, 58, 66; Granby, 58, 60; Greenfield, 60; Hannibal, 67, 167, 283–86, 293–95; Hardin, 66; Harviell,

61; Hayti, 61, 241; Higginsville, 58; Holden, 58; Holt, 66; Holt County, 58; Illmo, 61; Independence, 4, 10, 15, 56–58, 179; Jefferson City, 19–22, 44, 67–70, 162, 186, 190–92, 241, 289; Johnson County, 56, 93–94; Jonesburg, 70; Joplin, 9, 31–32, 37, 57–60, 133–142, 148, 179, 198–202; Kansas City, 4, 26–31, 151–53, 209–10; Kennett, 61; Kirksville, 66–67; Koshkonong, 58, 61; Lafayette County, 56; Lilbourn, 61, 63; Malden, 58, 61, 63; Maries County, 69–70; Marshfield, 58, 61; Marston, 61, 63; Maryville, 66; Maysville, 66; Monett, 60; Moniteau County, 69–70, 145–47, 170, 172, 179; Morehouse, 61; Morley, 61; Naylor, 58, 61; Neelyville, 61; Neosho, 58, 60; New Madrid, 61; Odessa, 58; Parma, 61; Pettis County, 56; Phelps County, 69–70; Piedmont, 61; Platte County, 56; Pleasant Hill, 58; Poplar Bluff, 61–63, 87–88, 179–80, 194, 197; Portageville, 61, 63–64; Puxico, 61, 88; Ray County, 56; Rochester, 66; Sarcoxie, 60; St. Joseph, 9, 25, 57–58, 64–66, 100–1, 103, 177–179, 245–46; St. Louis, 3–4, 48–53, 57, 178–79, 181–85, 241, 289–90; Senath, 61; Sikeston, 61; Springfield, 58, 60–61, 124, 179, 241, 289–90; Steele, 61; Sullivan, 290; Tipton, 146–47, 170; Trenton, 58, 66; Union Star, 66; Wallace, 58; Warrensburg, 93–94; Washburn, 58; Webb City, 60, 133, 241; West Plains, 61; Weston, 66; Williamsville, 61; Willow Springs, 58, 61

L

La Follette, Robert, 148, 163, 165–66
Lemke, William, 262, 272
Locke, John Galen, 16
Lohbeck, Don: early life, 273; and Gerald L. K. Smith, 273–82; political activism, 273–82; and *The Cross and The Flag*, 273–75; and the Racial Purity Committee, 278, 280
Lynching: Dyer Anti-Lynching Bill, 125, 154, 166, 211; of James T. Scott, 109; in Missouri, 36, 98–99, 104, 108–9, 124–25, 234; NAACP campaigns against, 109, 111,

123–24, 149, 166; of Raymond Gunn, 234; of Roosevelt Grigsby, 108; of Roy Hammonds, 109, 124–25, 328–329n70

M

McAdoo, William, 156–157
McCarron, George C.: early life, 53; as imperial representative, 53–55, 57–58, 160, 185–86, 290; and Missouri politics, 160; in Oklahoma, 53
McDonald, Clay, 99–100
McElroy, Henry, 216–18
McLemore, Joseph L., 212, 219, 224, 229, 231–32, 236
McMurry, W. F., 52
McReynolds, Allen, 137, 140, 142, 291
Mahon, Dennis, 296–97
Maryville (MO): Ku Klux Klan activity in, 66; lynching of Raymond Gunn, 234
Mayer, Harry H., 81–82, 84
Menace: and anti-Catholicism, 9, 39–42, 62, 91, 113–14, 247–48; and Billy Parker, 40–42, 247–48; and Gilbert O. Nations, 40–42, 68, 164, 247; origins, 39–40; rebranding as the *New Menace*, 41, 118, 247
Mer Rouge (LA), 103, 107, 183
Metzger, Tom, 280
Miller, Victor: and the 1924 gubernatorial primary, 167–68; 1925 St. Louis mayoral campaign, 220–23, 227; as mayor of St. Louis, 223–25; as St. Louis police commissioner, 78, 80
Missouri State Highway Patrol, 238, 293–96
Missouri Valley Independent: and the American Unity League, 122; and the Anti-Saloon League, 43; coverage of Klan events in Missouri, 54–55, 57–58, 65–66, 178–79, 185–86; and Gilbert O. Nations, 164–66; and the Independent Klan of America, 196; and the Junior Ku Klux Klan, 25–26; origins, 66; promotion of public schools, 113; and the Tri-K Club, 26; and the WKKK, 25, 65
Mitchell, Joseph E.: anti-Klan sentiments, 80, 220, 222–23; early life, 77–78; and Missouri politics, 212–13, 219–220,

Mitchell, Joseph (*continued*)
222–23, 225–28, 233; and the *St. Louis Argus*, 77–80, 220, 222–23, 233, 291
Modern View: and Abraham Rosenthal, 131; anti-Klan coverage, 76, 132, 161, 250; and Charles Coughlin, 260–65; coverage of antisemitism, 130, 250, 265; and Ferdinand Isserman, 260–62, 265; and Missouri politics, 172
Monitor, 9, 247
Moran, J. Allen, 296–97
Morris, B. L., 146, 170
Morris, William, 289

N

National Associated Klans, 55
National Association for the Advancement of Colored People (NAACP): anti-Klan activity, 8, 12, 108–12, 122–25, 132, 142–43, 283–85, 294; anti-lynching campaign, 98–99, 109–12, 123–25, 154; and Arthur Hyde, 98–99, 124–25, 212; in the Bootheel, 105, 108; in Cape Girardeau, 124; and Cora J. Carter, 109–11, 125; coverage in newspapers, 83, 132; and George L. Vaughn, 109–11, 212; and Gerald L. K. Smith, 275; and James Weldon Johnson, 98, 110–11; in Jefferson City, 125; in Kansas City, 123–24; origins, 122–23; questionnaires to political officials, 124, 154, 166; and Roy Wilkins, 83–84, 291; in Springfield, 124; in St. Louis, 79, 109–11, 123; and the Universal Negro Improvement Association, 13, 125–28; and Walter White, 110–11, 248; and W. E. B. Du Bois, 123; and William Pickens, 127–28
National Conservative Party, 294, 357–58n36
National Knights Federation, 289
National Knights of the Ku Klux Klan, 282, 289–91
National States Rights Party, 280, 290
Nations, Gilbert O.: 1924 presidential campaign, 14, 148, 163–66; early life, 40–41, 44; and the Free Press Defense League, 41; and the Ku Klux Klan, 41–42, 148, 152, 164–66; publications, 41, 164,

246–47; and *Fellowship Forum*, 41, 247–48; and the *Menace*, 9, 41, 164, 247; and the *New Menace*, 41, 247; and the *Protestant*, 41, 164, 247
Nations, Gus, 44, 168, 186–89, 192
Nations, Heber: early life, 68; as exalted cyclops of the Jefferson City Klan, 44, 67, 69, 160, 191–92; graft scandal, 16, 44, 94, 157, 180–81, 185–93, 197–98, 202–3, 207; and L. C. Withaup, 190–91; and Missouri politics, 48, 160, 187, 290
Nelson, Arthur W.: 1924 gubernatorial campaign, 48, 92–93, 146–48, 169–74, 210–11, 332–33n6; and C. S. Burns, 145–46, 200; Klan allegations in gubernatorial primary, 167–68
New Madrid County: anti-Black violence in, 105–6; Ku Klux Klan activity in, 61, 63
New Menace: and Billy Parker, 4–5, 41, 151–53; and the Ku Klux Klan, 9, 41, 65, 68; and the *Monitor*, 9, 247; opposition to, 118–19, 130; origins, 41
New York World, 95–96, 102, 126
Nixon, Richard, 209
Northern and Southern Knights of the Ku Klux Klan, 289
Nuen, Walter J. G., 225–26

O

Operation PUSH, 284
Original Southern Klans, Inc., 289
Osborne, J. F., 199–201
Ozark Klan (1960s), 291

P

Park, Guy B., 236–238
Parker, William "Billy," 4–5, 15, 40–42, 151–53, 248
Patriot: and anti-Catholicism, 51, 91, 120, 158; and C. C. Crawford, 50–51, 180–85, 339n43; coverage of Klan events, 25, 68; and the fake slogan scandal, 180–85; and Frederick Barkhurst, 50, 182, 309n114; and the WKKK, 24–25
Patterson, Roscoe, 124, 233–34
Pearson, Drew, 5–6, 288

Pelley, William Dudley: early life, 256; and Gerald L. K. Smith, 272, 274; opposition to, 270–71, 281, 287; and the Silver Legion, 16, 256, 258

Pendergast, Thomas: and C. A. Franklin, 83, 230–31, 237; and Casimir Welch, 47, 215; early life, 45; and Harry S. Truman, 210; and Henry McElroy, 218; and Joseph Shannon, 46–47; Klan efforts to defeat Pendergast allies, 46–47, 56, 152–53; and L. M. Birkhead, 268; and Missouri politics, 45–47, 149, 152, 159, 210–12, 215–18, 227, 229, 231, 235, 237–38; and William J. Thompkins, 47, 215–16

Petito, Oren, 280

Phares, W. F., 146, 169–73

Platte County: 56, 236, 296

Polk County, 73–74

Poplar Bluff: and J. H. Wolpers, 75, 86–88, 193–94, 196–97; Klan activity in, 61–63, 87–88, 179–80, 194, 197; and O. L. Spurgeon, 61–63, 88, 180, 193–94

Posse Comitatus, 280, 294, 296

Priest, Henry, 167, 172

Progressive Party, 47, 163

Protestant, 41, 65, 68, 164, 247

Protestant Women of Missouri, 24

Q

Queens of the Golden Mask, 24

R

Reed, James A.: 1922 US Senate campaign, 14, 147, 150–55; 1924 presidential campaign, 156–57; 1928 presidential campaign, 207, 228–29; anti-Klan statements, 8, 47, 92–93, 151, 153–55, 162, 172–73, 212; anti-Nazi statements, 250–51; criticism of, 8, 56, 149–50, 154; early life, 149–50; opposition from Missouri Democrats, 148–50, 156, 211, 227; and the Senate Campaign Fund Investigating Committee, 203–7

Republican Party in Missouri: and the 1922 U.S. Senate campaign, 14, 150–55; and the 1924 gubernatorial campaign, 145–47, 167–75; and the 1924 Republican State Convention, 56, 159–61, 205; and the 1926 U.S. Senate campaign, 205–7; and accusations of lily–whitism, 15, 215–19, 231–33; and African American voters, 14, 35, 77–78, 80–81, 83, 103, 154–55, 160, 211–40; and the Ku Klux Klan, 46–48, 68, 93–94, 141, 150–55, 159–61, 167–75, 205–6, 215–19, 231–33. See also Arthur M. Hyde; George H. Williams; Henry Caulfield; L. C. Dyer; R. R. Brewster; Sam A. Baker; W. F. Phares

Robb, Thomas, 294

Roosevelt, Franklin D., 209–11, 224–26, 236–39, 248–50, 256, 259–62, 272

Roper, Sam, 289

Rosenthal, Abraham, 130–32

S

Schurz, Carl, 35

Second Imperial Klonvokation, 26–31, 54, 108, 297

Senevey, Felix, xi–xii

Shelton, Robert M., 289–90

Sievers, Samuel, 266, 291

Sigel, Albert, 34

Sikeston (MO): anti-Klan sentiments in, 86, 197; Ku Klux Klan activity in, 61

Simmons, William J.: at 1921 congressional hearing, 97–98; comments on alleged Klan activity in Missouri, 74, 94–95; coup against, 16, 23, 26, 30, 98, 195, 202; early life, 22; as imperial wizard, 5, 15, 22–23, 37, 77, 123–24, 126, 131, 285; and the Kamelia, 24, 195; visits to Missouri, 49, 55

Smith, Al: 1928 presidential campaign, 207, 213, 228–33, 245–47, 268; comments on antisemitism, 250

Smith, Bryce B., 217–18, 234

Smith, Gerald L. K.: and the America First Party, 272–76; and Buder Park, 243, 276; and the Christian Nationalist Party/ Christian Nationalist Crusade, 272–80, 282, 289–90; early life, 243, 272; in Eureka Springs (AR), 279; and Huey Long, 262, 271–72; opposition to, 243, 271–72, 274–75, 278–79; *The Cross and the Flag*,

273–74; and the Union Party, 262, 272; and Wesley Swift, 280, 282

Snapp, Taylor, 132–33, 198–201

Southern Poverty Law Center, 294–95

Springfield: 1924 Democratic State Convention, 157–59; 1924 Republican State Convention, 159–61, 205; anti-Klan sentiments in, 86, 103, 134; Klan activity in, 58, 60–61, 124, 179, 241, 289–90; WKKK activity in, 25

Spurgeon, O. L.: banishment from the Klan, 16, 63, 180–81, 195–98, 202–3, 207; early life, 61–62; as exalted cyclops of Poplar Bluff No. 48, 62–63, 193–94; and the Independent Klan of America, 195–97; involvement with the Klan outside of Missouri, 62–63, 88, 194; legal suits against the Klan, 196; and the *Menace*, 62

Stark, Lloyd, 237–39

Stephenson, D. C.: and Indiana politics, 180, 202–4, 206–7; involvement with coup against Simmons, 23, 202; and the Ku Klux Klan, 23–24, 195, 202; and Madge Oberholtzer, 16, 180–81, 202–3

Stewart, C. A., 54

St. Joseph: and the American Unity League, 121–22; anti-Klan sentiments in, 64–65, 85–86, 113–14, 118, 121–22, 219; and the death of Nellie Hale, 75, 99–103, 118–19; Klan activity in, 9, 25, 57–58, 64–66, 100–1, 103, 178–79, 245–46; and the *Missouri Valley Independent*, 25, 57, 65–66, 178; and Thomas Pendergast, 45; and William Campbell, 64, 177–78, 205, 245–46; WKKK activity in, 25, 65

St. Joseph Catholic Tribune, 113–14, 119, 121, 264

St. Louis: Ku Klux Klan activity in, 3–4, 48–53, 57, 178–79, 181–85, 241, 289–90; and Gerald L. K. Smith, 242–243, 273–79; and the German-American Bund, 254–55, 258, 265–68, 270–71; politics in, 219–26, 234–36, 238–39. *See also St. Louis Argus; St. Louis Catholic Herald; St. Louis Globe-Democrat; St. Louis Post-Dispatch; St. Louis Star*

St. Louis Argus: anti-Klan coverage in, 11–12, 75, 77–81, 150–51, 159, 162, 250; and Black voter realignment, 212, 220–28, 230–31, 233; and Buder Park, 242–43; and Dedication Day, 21–22; and Gerald L. K. Smith, 243, 272, 275; and Harry S. Truman, 209; and J. F. Craig, 11–12; and Luke E. Hart, 80, 132; and the NAACP, 13, 128, 166; origins, 77–78; and the UNIA, 13, 128

St. Louis Catholic Herald, 114

St. Louis Globe-Democrat, 11, 76, 94, 119, 250

St. Louis Post-Dispatch: and anti-Black violence in the Bootheel, 106; anti-Klan coverage in, 75–76, 95–96, 151; on Black voter realignment, 229; and Charles Coughlin, 259; coverage of the 1924 election, 157–58, 160, 164–68, 174; coverage of the 1926 U. S. Senate campaign, 227–28; and the death of Nellie Hale, 101; and Dedication Day, 19; and Don Lohbeck, 273, 278–79; and German-American Bund, 255, 257; and Gilbert O. Nations, 164–65; and Heber Nations, 186, 189, 193; and J. F. Craig, 11; and James L. Betts and Mary Carr, 285, 291–93, 296; and Jordan Chambers, 224; and Leon M. Birkhead, 268–69; and Marcus Garvey, 128; and *The Patriot*, 181–83

St. Louis Star (and *Star-Times*): and the American Unity League, 120; anti-Klan coverage in, 11, 44, 69, 76, 92, 183; coverage of Klan activity, 49, 207; critiques of the newspaper by C. C. Crawford, 51; and Gerald L. K. Smith, 242; and J. F. Craig, 4, 11; and Marcus Garvey, 128; and *The Birth of a Nation*, 9; and Victor Miller, 221

Swift, Wesley, 280, 282

T

Talmadge, Eugene, 271–72, 288

Tate, David, 295–96

The Birth of a Nation, 9–10, 79, 122

The Columbians, 278–80, 289

The Protocols of the Elders of Zion, 116, 130, 262, 264

Index 387

Thompkins, William J.: accusations of lily-whitism in the Republican Party, 215–16, 219, 232; and the Democratic Party, 212–16, 219, 229–32, 236; early life, 213–14; and Joseph Shannon, 46–47, 213–15; and the *Kansas City American*, 215–16, 219; and the Smith-for-President Colored League, 229, 231–32; and Tom Pendergast, 46–47, 215
Townsend, Francis, 262, 272
Travis, Wesley Civert, 4, 15
Tri-K Club, 26
Truman, Harry S.: denouncements of the Klan, 210; as president, 210, 239; rumored involvement with the Klan, 56, 209–10, 212; as US Senator, 230–31, 237–39
Tyler, Elizabeth, 22–23

U
United Front against the Klan, 284
United Klans of America, 289–90
Universal Negro Improvement Association: activities in Missouri, 83, 105, 107–8, 112, 122, 128, 142, 330n99; and Marcus Garvey, 13, 125–29; and the NAACP, 13, 125, 127–29; and the *Negro World*, 125–26; origins, 125
Unsell, C. D., 61, 322n178
Urban League, 266

V
Vaad Hoir, 265
Vashon, George B., 212, 219–21, 223–24, 228–32
Vaughn, George L.: 1926 congressional campaign, 223; and the Co-operative Civic Association, 225; death, 291; early life, 109; involvement with NAACP, 109–11; political realignment, 212–13, 221

Venable, James R., 290–91
Veterans of Foreign Wars, 266–67
Vienna Home-Advisor, 75, 86, 89–92, 94, 113–14, 183

W
Wallace, Flora, 59, 198, 201–2
Wallace, Pierre: controversial ties to Taylor Snapp, 16, 133, 180–81, 198–203, 207; death, 201–2; early life, 59, 197–98; as exalted cyclops of Ozarks Klan No. 3, 59–60, 198
Welch, Casimir, 46–47, 214–15
Western Watchman, 39, 114, 259, 306n74
Wheatcraft, Vivian Tracy, 205–6, 227
White Citizens Councils, 290
Wilkins, Roy, 83–84, 291
Wilkinson, Bill, 293
Williams, George H., 205–7, 227–28
Wilson, Francis M., 229–30, 234
Wilson, Woodrow, 20, 147, 150, 156–57, 211, 226–28
Winchell, Walter, 5–6, 209–10, 288
Winrod, Gerald Burton, 270–71, 280–81, 294
Withaup, L. C., xi, 190–91, 340n74
Wolpers, John H., 86–89, 94, 193, 196–97
Woman's Christian Temperance Union (WCTU), 41–44, 154, 187–89
Women of the Ku Klux Klan: leadership of, 24, 54; in Missouri, 24–25, 54, 63, 65, 93, 178, 206; origins, 23–24; and the Tri-K Club, 26; and the WCTU, 43–44
Woog, Edmund S., 34

Z
Zionist Organization, 265